The Illustrated History of Magic

THE
Fatal Book Opened!

AN AUTHENTIC ACCOUNT OF
JOHN ALBERT, A YOUNG GENTLEMAN IN HAMBURGH,
WHO BY THE CONSTANT STUDY OF
The Works of Friar Bacon and Doctor Faustus,
AND OTHER BOOKS OF MAGIC AND ASTROLOGY,
HAD ACQUIRED AN AWFUL KNOWLEDGE OF CABALISTICS,
NECROMANCY, and the BLACK ART:

Shewing how he obtained access to the Study of Anthony Cornel, a noted Professor of the Black Art, and having locked himself in, began to read a most Horrible Book, which lay open upon the Table, the Letters of which were written in Human Blood, and the Leaves of Dead Men's Skins; when a dreadful clap of Thunder alarmed him, the door was broken open with great violence, and in came the TERRIBLE ONE, the Chief of the Powers of Darkness, attended by a host of Griffins and other Monsters of most hideous appearance, vomiting Sulphur and Fire! "What wouldst thou with me?" cried the Demon: and on his repeating it the third time, struck the affrighted Youth with his dreadful Claws, and killed him on the spot!

ONCE a famed necromancer, one Cornel of old,
Had long made the Black Art his study, we're told;
He the stars and the planets pretended to rule;
No doubt he was learned, at least was a fool.

He was gloomy, morose, and was ne'er known to smile;
Like his deeds, most misshapen, he bent as with toil;
Whomsoever approached him, were stricken with fear;
His wife only spoke to him once in the year,

And that was each year, on the eve of St. Mark,
Then he hied from his studio, at sun-set, when dark,
With pale haggard look! and the dew on his cheek
Spoke plainly,—the countenance plainly can speak.

His wife heard his usual terrible charge,
As he from his closet at night did emerge:
Observe well my words, but approach not the door;
Behold! here's the key—and of this be you sure:

'Twas wrought in a cavern, 'midst sulphurous flame!
'Tis spell-bound, by magical, mystical name!
Therefore, mark well my words, nor speak 'bove your breath;
To neglect them, were awful and horrible death!

Should man dare to ask you my chamber to see,
Their life's of no value, scarce worth a pin's fee!
Whomsoever may beg, or entreat, or implore,
Let no living creature e'er enter that door!

She faithfully swore his command to obey,
When forth to the church-yard he wended his way,

Saying, dare not look back, neither left nor the right,
And expect my return when the bell tolls midnight.

She follow'd in order the portal to close,
When she felt that resistance did strongly oppose;
For in rush'd a youth quite determined to see
The magical room, who wrench'd from her the key.

Then the magical key he applied to the lock,—
The door open'd wide with a terrible shock!
And such sights met the eye, (protect us from evil!)
Only known to the wretch who's enslaved to the devil!

'Mongst horrible relics of dead men's bleach'd bones,
'Midst terrible visions,'midst shrieks, and 'midst groans;
Gaping skulls, grinning skeletons, ghosts at their gambols,

Aye, this and much more,—'tis not my muse rambles.

There lay on a tombstone a magical book,
On which none but Cornel had e'er dared to look,
Inscribed full of blood-written symbols within,
And the leaves were all made of a murderer's skin;

Except those of magic inserted between,
On which strange hieroglyphics unnumber'd were seen
Which would horror-strike all who were doom'd to behold

Such sights so unearthly, not fit to be told.

Impell'd by his fate, the youth view'd it again;
He scarce could proceed, yet he could not refrain:

Once entangled in sin, 'tis most hard to retreat,
He'd have given all the world to have been in the street.

He opened the book, when the magical spell
Was broken, and heard was a horrible yell!
A fierce fiend-like form, quite enveloped in flame,
Rush'd into the chamber, and bellow'd his name!

Two hideous horns he beheld on his head,
Like two bars of iron when heated to red;
The breath of his nostrils was brimstone and fire,
And his serpent-like tail he lash'd round him with ire.

With hideous laugh, he cried out "Thou art mine!
I am come of thy call—thou art mine—I am thine!"
His hair like the porcupine's quills stood upright,
While the poor trembling youth shook with fear and affright.

"What wouldst thou with me?" cried the author of ill;
"What wouldst thou with me?" again the fiend cries,
And a flame of blue lightning flashed forth from his eyes.

"I come at thy will, from the pit of despair!"
He lifted his griffin-like claw in the air,
Then he tore out his heart, which he seiz'd for his prey,
And in thunder and lightning vanished away!

CERTAIN authors on Conjuration, account it next to death for an illiterate person to raise an Evil Spirit; for by reason of his ignorance he knoweth not how to dismiss it: and they give many cautions against attempts to force a Goblin to appear. If the incantation be imperfect, so much the better for him that useth it, for then he shall only have trouble for his pains; because such creatures obey not but upon compulsion of a real enchanter, or through his art stolen by a pretender, who may have pains for his trouble; as Eucrates had with the Goblin, (as hereafter,) which he could not have enchanted if he had not privily discovered so much of the enchantment as would make the Goblin appear, but which he could not lay again, because he knew not the form.

The learned in the Black Art say, if you raise an Evil Spirit, and do not dismiss him quickly, or fully employ him till you can lay him again, he will be your master instead of your servant, and do you bodily harm or slay you. Yet if my readers require information from my own knowledge, or experience herein, I have none to give them; except that passion hath sometimes become my master, and so I have been under the dominion of an Evil Spirit, and suffered accordingly; as must every one who submitteth to be ruled by that which he ought to control.

There is a wonderful narrative of a Goblin by a celebrated thor who lived some years ago. He saith that one Eucrates

became acquainted in Egypt with an enchanter named Pancrates, who had resided twenty years in the subterranean recesses, where he learned the Art Magic. And one day he persuaded Eucrates to leave all his servants at Memphis, and follow him alone, telling him that they should not be in want of attendants to wait upon them: and so it happened. For when they came to any inn, Pancrates would take a wooden pin, or latch, or a bolt, or any such like thing, and clothe it; and then he would repeat a verse over it, and so, by enchantment, it would walk, and appear a man to every one. And this creature would go about as a servant, and prepare their supper, and lay the cloth, and wait upon them right courteously, and always do as they desired. And when they had not occasion for such services, then Pancrates would repeat another verse, and it would become a pin, a latch, or a bolt, or whatever it was before it had been enchanted. Eucrates, seeing this, desired to perform the like wonder, but Pancrates would not acquaint him with the verses, nor again make enchantment in his presence. And so Eucrates remained ignorant until, one day, he hid himself in a dark place, while Pancrates, thinking himself alone, said the verse over a pin, which thereupon became a serving man. And the next day, when Pancrates had gone to the market-place, Eucrates remembered the words, and repeated them over a stick which he dressed up; and thereby he enchanted the stick into

a like creature, which, to keep it employed as the enchantment required, he was obliged to find in work, and therefore he ordered it to fetch some water, and when it had brought a full jar, he cried " Stop! draw no more water, but be a stick again;" but it heeded him not, and, instead of obeying him, it went in and out drawing and bringing in water till it almost filled the house. Then Eucrates feared the return of Pancrates, lest he should be displeased; and he was also alarmed at the coming in of so much water, and tried to prevail on the goblin to leave off, but to no end; for, as though he had been deaf, he kept swiftly going from the house to the well, drawing jars full of water and bringing them, so that Eucrates felt great fear; and being suddenly angered by the disobedience of this mere walking-stick which he had made, he suddenly seized a hatchet, and split it; but instead of its being destroyed, the two pieces forthwith became two goblins, and each taking a jar ran and drew water, so that Eucrates had two servants in the place of one; and he was ready to swoon with terror, when Pancrates happily returned, and, understanding the matter, he presently slayed the goblins, by repeating a verse that dismissed them both into one piece of wood again, as they were before the incantation. This is the narration of a Latin writer called Lucian, whose works you may lawfully read; and if you understand them, and be of a right mind, the perusal shall stand you in good stead.

THE ILLUSTRATED HISTORY OF
MAGIC

MILBOURNE CHRISTOPHER

THOMAS Y. CROWELL COMPANY
New York   Established 1834

Books by Milbourne Christopher

The Illustrated History of Magic
ESP, Seers & Psychics
Houdini: The Untold Story
Panorama of Magic

The illustrations are from the Christopher Collection.

TITLE PAGE: Woodcut used by Antonio Grassi of
Reggio, an Italian magician of the same period.

FRONTISPIECE: Broadside printed by William Walker
in Otley, England, about 1850.

DESIGNED BY ABIGAIL MOSELEY

Manufactured in the United States of America

ISBN 0–690–43165–1

2 3 4 5 6 7 8 9 10

LIBRARY OF CONGRESS CATALOGING IN PUBLICATION DATA

Christopher, Milbourne.
    The illustrated history of magic.

    Bibliography: p.
    1. Conjuring—History. I. Title.
GV1543.C45   793.8   73–10390
ISBN 0–690–43165–1

For Phil Thomas

who as a boy was my first partner in magic,
and in memory of Hen Fetsch, Dr. Henry Ridgely Evans,
Jean Hugard, and John Mulholland.

Contents

COLOR PLATES   *Following page 6*

Herrmann

Kellar

Houdini

Chung Ling Soo

Thurston

Le Roi, Talma, and Bosco

Carter

Blackstone

The Illustrated History of Magic

1
Myth or Magic

A fourteenth-century Chinese conjurer, entertaining banquet guests in the courtyard of the Khan's summer palace in Hangchau, hurled a wooden ball into the air. Fastened to the ball was a seemingly endless strip of leather, composed of many thongs tied end to end. The ball rose higher and higher, finally disappearing into the clouds. The magician's assistant, a boy, proceeded to climb the leather strip dangling from the sky. Hand over hand, ever higher, he climbed, until he also was lost to sight. The magician called for him to return—once, twice, three times—but received no reply. Angry now, the magician picked up a knife and climbed after his assistant. Soon a hand, a foot, and other parts of the boy's anatomy rained to the ground. Then the magician slid down the long leather strip, kissed the ground at the Khan's feet, and carefully began fitting together the pieces of the boy. When he was finished, he gave the body a kick, and—wonder of wonders —the boy "stood up, complete and erect."

Overcome by this performance, Abu-Abdullah Mohmed, a visiting sheikh from far-off Tangier, suffered palpitations of the heart. Restored to normal when given a drink, Mohmed was greatly embarrassed; all the other diners had watched the exhibition calmly. A judge, who sat by the Arab's side, helpfully explained that what seemed so miraculous was merely a trick.

A miraculous trick indeed, but apparently reported by an eyewitness, for the preceding account is drawn from *Travels in Asia and Africa,* the book that Mohmed dictated in 1355, following his return to North Africa. The Marco Polo of the Muhammadan world, he is usually remembered today by his pen name, Ibn Batuta (The Traveler). The amazing feat he described is, of course, the same that later became known as "The Indian Rope Trick"—undoubtedly the most famous of all feats of Oriental magic. But did Mohmed, whose observations are thought to be generally reliable, actually see what he said he saw in this instance?

Many widely held beliefs about magic and magicians are erroneous: The hand is not quicker than the eye; skill and misdirection—getting the audience to focus its attention on the wrong place at the right time—is responsible for the mystery. Master manipulators deal themselves royal flushes and change deuces to aces, but they are seldom expert card players. "It's done with mirrors" applies to only a tiny fraction of modern deceptions. "It's up his sleeve" rarely explains the feats that provoke this comment.

The history of magic abounds with similar examples. Even if one is familiar with the techniques of conjuring, it is often difficult to separate myth from fact. The great Indian rope mystery is a case in point.

Mohmed's account of the trick is the first by an eyewitness, but many other persons have also described it. In a thousand-year-old commentary on the *Vedanta Sutra,* the theologian, Shankaracharya, explained the meaning of an obscure word by saying that its true meaning differed from the accepted definition as much as the conjurer who performed on the ground differed from the magician who climbed the rope with sword and shield.

Two centuries after Mohmed, Johann Weir mentioned a European variation of the rope trick in *De Prestigiis Daemonum,* a book about devils and sorcerers. In this work, published in Basle in 1566, Weir told of a magician who, irked by the smallness of his profit from a performance in Magdeburg, Germany, announced he was going to heaven, where he would be better rewarded. He threw a cord in the air. His small horse ran up the cord, towing the magician, who grasped the animal's tail; the magician's wife, who clutched him, and a maid, clasping her mistress's hand. Seeing a crowd gaping at the sky, a passerby asked what had happened. When the spectators told him, he replied that they had been deceived. He himself had seen the conjurer enter a tavern just down the road!

The memoirs of Jahangir, Emperor of Hindustan from 1605 to 1627, include a story of a similar feat in the courtyard of his Delhi palace. Seven Bengalese magicians tossed a chain toward the clouds.

Belgian illusionist Servais Le Roy featured a stage version of
"The Indian Rope Trick," as did Carl Hertz, Howard Thurston,
Horace Goldin, and Kalanag.

A dog, hog, panther, lion, and tiger scampered up the chain until they were swallowed in space.

In his 1650 collection of folklore, Pú Sing Ling, a noted Chinese writer, wrote of a man, a woman, and a boy who disappeared after ascending a tall ladder that rested against a tree. The author reported hearing that magicians of the White Lily Society had performed a marvelous rope trick in the fourteenth century, and he said that he had seen such a feat about 1630 when, as a small boy, he went to the annual Ch'ing Ming spring festival. On this occasion, according to Pú, a conjurer urged his young assistant to climb a suspended rope to fetch fruit from heaven. After the assistant complied, a huge peach dropped from the sky, the rope fell, and parts of the boy's body plummeted to the ground. The magician put the pieces in a box, and the boy stepped out intact.

In the late nineteenth century, stories of "The Indian Rope Trick," rivaling the tale of "Jack and the Beanstalk," were printed as fact throughout the world. Yet the trick proved mysteriously elusive. Harry Kellar, Charles Bertram, Howard Thurston, and other Western illusionists were eager to add the widely discussed feat to their shows. While on tour in India, they searched for performances of it—but always in vain.

The Occult Committee of The Magic Circle considered the legendary marvel at a meeting in London in April 1934. Letters were read from Lord Halifax, former Viceroy of India, from the Bishop of Calcutta, and from other eminent men who had lived in India for many years. All had heard of the feat; none had seen it. Lieutenant Colonel R. H. Elliott summed up the committee's findings: no substantial evidence had been presented to prove the trick had ever been exhibited. Elliott himself doubted that anyone would ever perform it outdoors in the manner described in the fables. The Magic Circle offered five hundred guineas for a single open-air performance. Later, the *Times of India* added ten thousand rupees to this amount. No one came forward to win the reward.

Perhaps the final, most logical refutation of the myth of "The Indian Rope Trick" came in 1942 from H. L. Varma, a member—appropriately enough—of the Society of Indian Magicians in Bombay. He pointed out that the fantastic feat could not possibly have been performed in the way that Mohmed and others related for a very simple reason: "If a ball of rope was thrown up [so high that an end disappeared], this hank must have exceeded in bulk the size of an elephant . . . so it would have been beyond the prowess of a man to manipulate it."

On another level, but with much the same effect, the history of magic has been warped by the publicity of the performers themselves

The open-air rope trick? No, an early nineteenth-century juggler balanced at the top of a pole.

Stage setting for Thurston's presentation of "The Indian Rope Trick." The boy vanished in a cloud of smoke.

as well as by popular myth. For example, a historian who has not seen Kellar's letter calling himself a "jackass" for permitting John Paul Bocock to ghost an article under his name for the *North American Review* would be unlikely to know that "Kellar's" account of an American Indian medicine man who shot six arrows straight up into the air and made them disappear is a fabrication.

Traveling as a professional magician myself in sixty-eight countries, meeting the outstanding conjurers of our time, collecting the letters of Robert-Houdin, Harry Kellar, John Nevil Maskelyne, and Harry Houdini, as well as notebooks and scrapbooks of Servais Le Roy, Horace Goldin, and Howard Thurston, I have had unusual opportunities to study the background and development of magic.

Magicians have been called the scientists of show business. Robert-Houdin designed the world's first electrically controlled protection system and installed it on his estate at St. Gervais, near Blois in France. When the master clock struck midnight, burglar alarms were activated. Should a prowler attempt to force open a window or door, a warning bell immediately sounded.

Another automatic timing device set off three wakeup signals at different times in different areas. This also tripped the suspended container in the barn which delivered morning oats to his mare.

When a visitor rapped the knocker on the post by the gates of the winding road that led to the magician's house, a bell sounded in the hallway. Fifteen years before Thomas A. Edison perfected his incandescent lamp, Robert-Houdin installed a battery-powered circuit to illuminate the chateau on the occasion of his daughter Eglantine's first communion.

Earlier performers—Garnerin, Pinetti, and Oehler—made balloon ascensions. Garnerin is credited with inventing the first practical parachute. John Nevil Maskelyne, founder of the British conjuring dynasty, devised a ribbonless typewriter with ninety-six characters, and patented and sold coin-operated locks for public doors and coin-activated vending machines.

Houdini designed the multidrawer theatrical trunk, was a pioneer aviator and made the first successful flight in Australia. Georges Méliès introduced many movie camera techniques still in use today.

All magic is illusion, but illusion among conjurers is a term applied to feats with human beings, large animals, or sizable pieces of apparatus. Mentalism encompasses simulated telepathy, clairvoyance, and other marvels in which the mind, rather than skill or equipment, seems to produce mystifying results. Secret devices the audience

HERRMANN

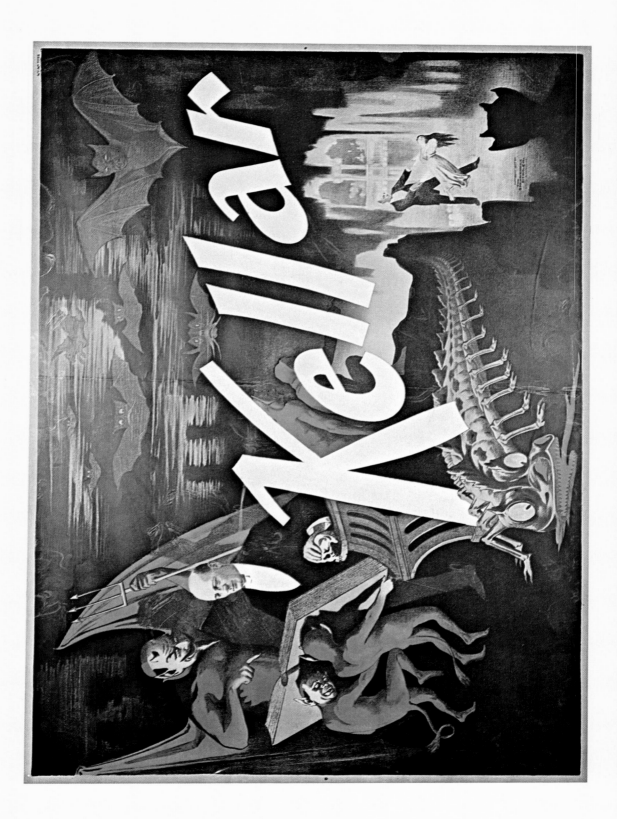

HARRY HOUDINI THE JAIL BREAKER

INTRODUCING HIS LATEST & GREATEST

PRISON CELL & BARREL MYSTERY

HOUDINI is strapped & locked in a barrel placed in a police cell which is also locked and in less than 2 seconds changes places,

£100. WILL BE PAID TO ANYONE FINDING TRAPS, PANELS OR FALSE DOORS IN THE CELL

CHUNG LING SOO
MARVELLOUS CHINESE
CONJURER
JAMES UPTON LTD
ART COLOUR PRINTERS
BIRMINGHAM

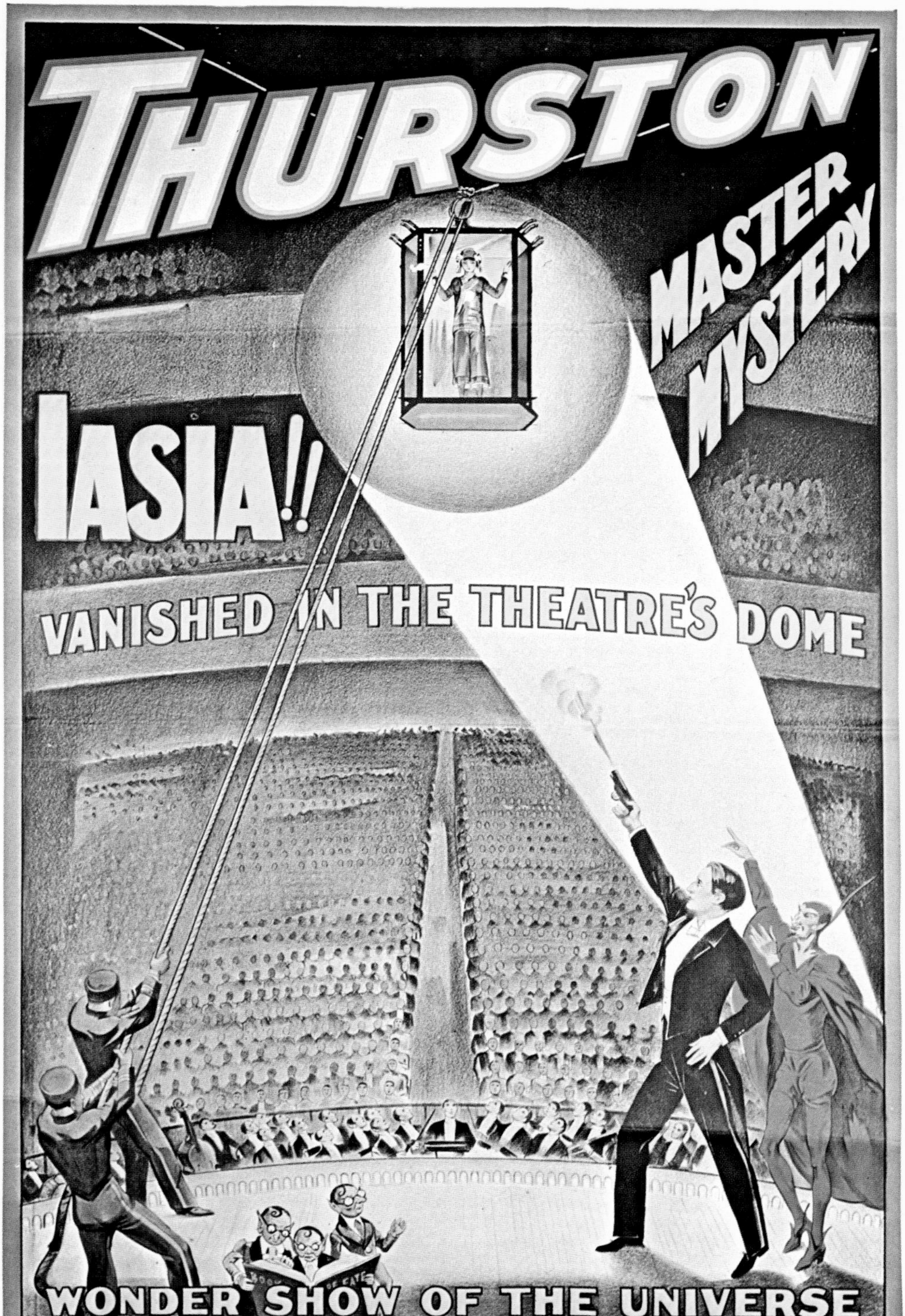
THURSTON
MASTER MYSTERY
IASIA!!
VANISHED IN THE THEATRE'S DOME
WONDER SHOW OF THE UNIVERSE

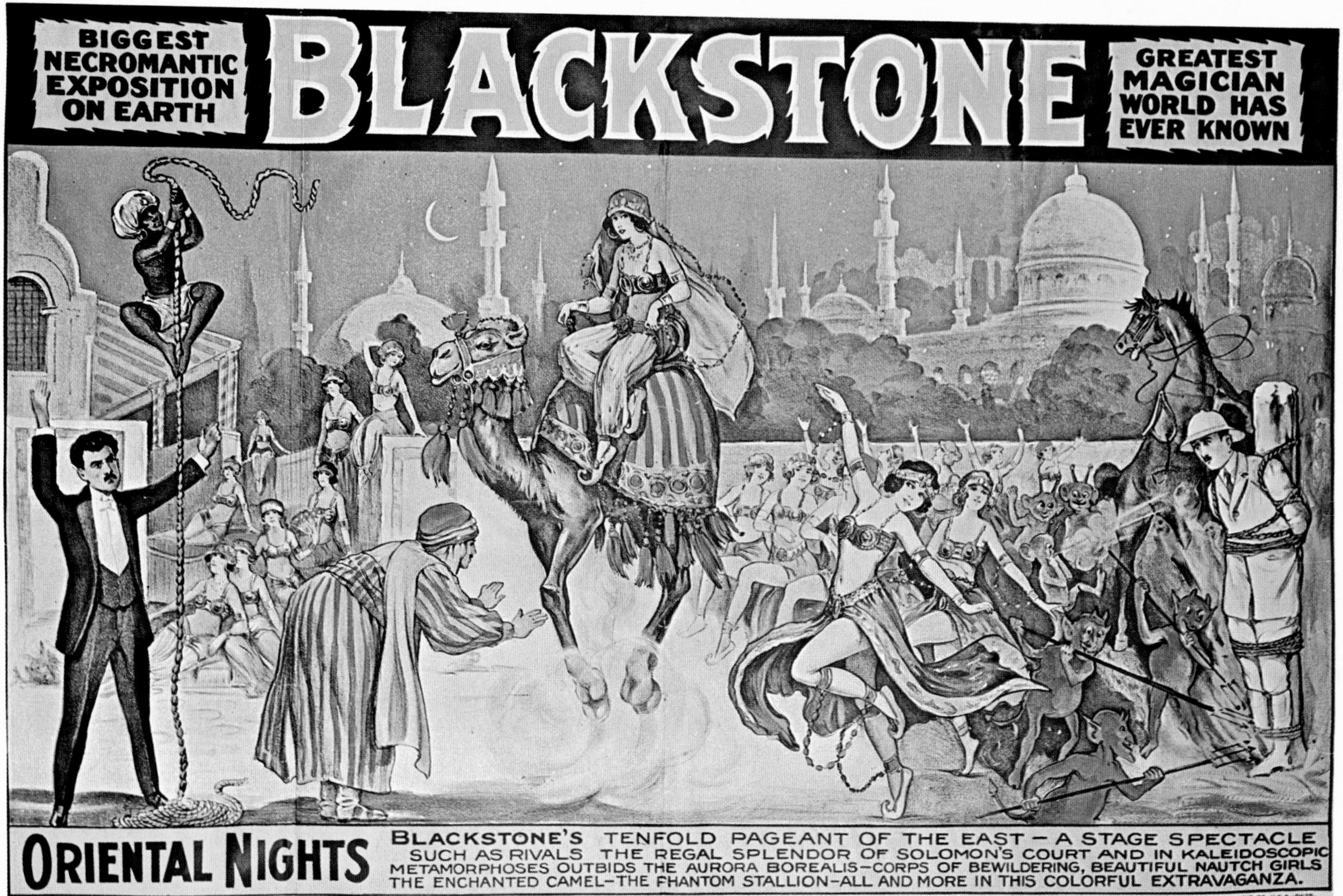

BLACKSTONE

GREATEST MAGICIAN WORLD HAS EVER KNOWN

BIGGEST NECROMANTIC EXPOSITION ON EARTH

ORIENTAL NIGHTS

BLACKSTONE'S TENFOLD PAGEANT OF THE EAST — A STAGE SPECTACLE SUCH AS RIVALS THE REGAL SPLENDOR OF SOLOMON'S COURT AND IN KALEIDOSCOPIC METAMORPHOSES OUTBIDS THE AURORA BOREALIS—CORPS OF BEWILDERING, BEAUTIFUL NAUTCH GIRLS THE ENCHANTED CAMEL—THE PHANTOM STALLION—ALL AND MORE IN THIS COLORFUL EXTRAVAGANZA.

ERIE LITHO. & PTG CO. ERIE, PA, U.S.A. 6453

does not see are called gimmicks. The advertising business later borrowed this word to describe something that attracts attention by giving an unusual twist or a new approach to specific advertisements.

Johann Beckmann, an eighteenth-century professor of economy at the University of Göttingen, said in his *History of Inventions, Discoveries and Origins* that if conjuring had "no other end than to amuse the most ignorant of our citizens," it "should be encouraged for the sake of those who cannot enjoy the more expensive deceptions of the opera." Magic served other purposes, he continued. It conveyed "instruction in the most acceptable manner" and was "a most agreeable antidote to superstition."

This is the history of the ancient art of honest deception, of magicians, who, unlike mystics, soothsayers, and diviners, did not pretend to have supernatural powers. Robert-Houdin defined a magician as an actor playing the role of a man who could work miracles. The whole secret of the art, Kellar added, was that the magician knows more about what he is doing than his audience does.

The more sophisticated people become, the more naively they react to the ageless appeal of magic. They take moon shots and atomic-powered submarines for granted, but are puzzled and delighted when an adroit close-up conjurer causes the card they selected to rise from a shuffled pack, when a manipulator produces a dove from nowhere, when an illusionist changes a lady into a lion, or when a mentalist reveals their secret thoughts.

Magic is the most universal of the performing arts. Italian opera holds little interest for the people of Thailand; Japanese music sounds discordant to many Western ears. A magician, whose visual feats seem to violate the laws of nature and reason, finds no language or cultural barriers as he travels around the world. Magic challenges the imagination, stimulates audiences to think—gives them an opportunity to relax and escape from the problems of reality.

2
The First
Wonder-Workers

AN account of the first-known royal command conjuring performance may still be seen in the Westcar papyrus at the State Museum in East Berlin. The hieroglyphics were inscribed about 1700 B.C., but the king for whom the show was given, and who is best remembered as the builder of the Great Pyramid, reigned almost five thousand years ago. Egyptologists say it is probable that the words were copied from an earlier source.

According to the text, the sons of Cheops were amusing him with tales of fabulous magic. Dedefhār, the youngest prince, was skeptical when his turn came to speak. No one alive could verify the tales told by the others: that Weba-āner, Ptah temple ritualist in the time of King Nebka, had changed a wax model into a live crocodile more than twelve feet long, that the creature had seized the lover of the priest's wife and drowned him, or that Weba-āner had picked up the ferocious animal and converted it back into wax. Nor could anyone testify that Jajamānekh, Ptah priest under King Snefru, had parted a lake with magic words, then stacked one half of the lake on top of the other, all in order to recover a turquoise hair ornament accidentally dropped out of a boat by a lady of the court.

However, the young prince Dedefhār said, he did know of one man, then living in his father's own kingdom, who could restore decapitated heads and make a lion follow him. The name of this magician was Dedi. He lived in Ded-Snefru, and he was 110 years old. Every day this old man ate a shoulder of beef, five hundred loaves of bread, and drank a hundred jugs of beer. It was said he knew the number of secret rooms in the sanctuary of Thōth, the god who invented magic.

Cheops was intrigued. He hoped to learn more about the concealed chambers, so the design could be used for his own tomb. He was eager to talk with Dedi and see him perform. He sent the youngest prince south on the Nile with two royal ships. The vessels anchored near Ded-Snefru, and Dedefhār was carried inland on an ebony litter with gold inlaid handles.

The magician had not been expecting visitors. He was reclining on a mat; slaves stroked his head and massaged his feet. After salutations had been exchanged, the prince assured the venerable performer that if he came to Memphis he could live in luxury as a member of the court, eat the finest delicacies, and look forward to a royal funeral. Dedi agreed at once to make the journey, since, like every other Egyptian, he wished to enter the afterlife under the most auspicious circumstances possible. He sailed on one of the royal vessels; the second carried his children and his library.

Cheops, when he greeted Dedi, asked why they had never met. The magician replied that he had never before been invited to the palace; once summoned, he had come.

Dedi proceeded to stage a magic show for Cheops. The king volunteered to supply a prisoner who had been condemned to be executed. Dedi politely declined this offer. It was forbidden, he said, to conjure with men, the "Noble Herd." Instead, a goose was decapitated, and its head placed to the east of the great hall and its still-quivering body to the west. Dedi pronounced a magic spell; the two parts of the bird melded together, and the restored goose cackled. The feat was repeated with a pelican and an ox.

Dedi apparently made a lion obey him, too, but this portion of the papyrus is incomplete, and the only words that remain are "follow him, its leash dropped to the floor."

While Dedi's name is the only one that has survived from this period, it is probable that contemporary conjurers were performing in Babylonia, India, and China. A long Chinese scroll painting, made about two thousand years ago, shows a magician working behind a table on a raised platform; he is one of the many outdoor entertainers at the annual Ch'ing Ming spring festival.

The earliest-known representation of a conjuring feat, however, was found on the wall of a burial chamber in Beni Hasan, Egypt. The original drawing, made about 2500 B.C., is now underwater; the tomb area was flooded in 1966 during the Nile Reclamation Project.

The Beni Hasan picture of the cups and balls depicts only one

The First Wonder- Workers

phase of a series of sleight-of-hand passes that were later popular in every part of the world.

A spectator, resting on one knee to the right of four inverted bowls, has been led to believe that a ball is under the bowl he indicates. The magician, in a similar posture to the left, seems to be about to produce the illusive sphere from the top of another. This action is suggested by the heiroglyphics: "Up from under."

In Egypt and India cup-and-ball performers knelt on the ground; in Turkey they conjured on a carpet in the open air; in Greece and Rome they preferred to work standing behind a table.

Seneca the Younger, who was born in Spain in 3 B.C., said the bewildering sleights were similar to the tricks of speech used by orators. Both were "pleasing deceptions, harmless to those who do not know them, and without interest to those who do."

Sextus Empiricus made a like analogy two hundred years later; he admitted he was as deceived by sleight of hand as he was by fallacious arguments "which only have a show of being sound, although we cannot say exactly where the catch is."

Alciphron, an Athenian of the same period, was "almost speechless" with amazement as he watched a performer invert three bowls on a table with three legs and display several white pebbles. He described the trick in these words:

> These he placed one by one under the dishes, and then, I do not know how, made them appear all together under one.
> At one time he made them disappear from beneath the dishes and showed them in his mouth. Next, when he swallowed them, he brought those who stood nearest him into the middle, and then pulled one stone from the nose, another from the ear, and another from the head of the man standing near him. Finally he caused the stones to vanish from the sight of everyone.

Alciphron proclaimed this unknown conjurer more dexterous than Eurybates of Oechalia, of whom everyone had heard. If he took this man to his farm, he continued, "We should never be able to catch him in his tricks, and he would steal everything I had, and strip my farm of all it contains." The modern equivalent is, "Here comes the magician; keep your hands on your wallet."

Weba-āner and Jajamānekh were identified in the Westcar papyrus as priests or sacred magicians, but Dedi and all the other conjurers mentioned so far were entertainers.

From the days when mankind first began to search for explanations of life and nature, the two types of magic were closely related. The peoples of the ancient world believed that unseen forces called gods controlled the heavens, the earth, and the destinies of mankind. If the gods were pleased, crops flourished, hunters found

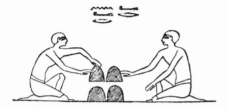

Cup-and-ball conjuring in ancient
Egypt: a wall painting in a Beni
Hasan tomb, made about 2500 B.C.

Seventeenth-century European performer,
working behind a table and using a wand
to divert his audience's attention.

Sixteenth-century magician shows
his empty left hand, while his right
hand dips into the bag tied to a
cord fastened around his waist.

game, and men lived in harmony. When the gods were angered, there was famine, pestilence, and war.

Rites were devised to honor the invisible deities and to appease their wrath in times of trouble. Ancient religious wonder-workers played on the superstitions of their followers by performing impressive feats. The temple ritualists, medicine men, soothsayers, and oracles employed the same basic principle—misdirection to divert attention from the method to the effect—as the conjuring entertainers, who candidly admitted they were only human. Of course, those who claimed to be the intermediaries of the gods, and those who could "prove" their claims with their feats, often attained positions of great power and influence. Rulers knelt before them and offered bountiful sacrifices to the deities they represented.

Cyrus the Great, the Persian king who captured Babylonia in 539 B.C., sent a daily offering of six vessels of wine, forty sheep, and twelve measures of wheat to placate the deity Bel. According to an Apocryphal account, Daniel, the Hebrew prophet, suspected that the priests and their families feasted on these gifts. Cyrus took him to the sanctuary when the food and drink were placed before the altar. The temple doors were sealed in Daniel's presence. The next day when the sanctuary was opened, the wine, meat, and wheat were gone. This was proof to Cyrus that Bel had consumed them; Daniel thought otherwise. He had taken the precaution of sprinkling a light coating of ashes on the floor the previous day. Now there were footprints that led to what appeared to be a solid wall. Closer examination revealed a cleverly concealed door. This was forced open onto a secret passageway leading to the priests' living quarters. The outraged Cyrus ordered the conniving priests slain and the temple leveled.

Gods and goddesses appeared in the sanctuaries dedicated to them, according to Cicero, Pliny, Livy, and other early writers. Aesculapius was seen in his temple in Tarsus; Hercules materialized from a sacred stone in the building where he was worshipped in Tyre; Enguinium made frequent visits to her temple in Sicily.

Eusèbe Salverte, a skeptical French scholar, attempted to explain these apparitions in *The Occult Sciences,* published by Harper and Brothers in New York in 1847. He reasoned that reflections from mirrors, or some primitive form of magic lantern, could have been used. It seems more logical to suppose that, in the days before those devices were invented, temple attendants garbed as deities came from concealed panels in the walls under the cover of smoke from altar fires.

Graven images sometimes spoke to the early believers. Theophrastus, an early Christian bishop of Alexandria, delighted in taking new friends to the ruins of a temple and showing them the hollow statue in which a pagan priest once stood and spoke through the opening in the figure's marble lips. In the temple of Isis at Pompeii the speaker was in a passageway behind an image. The well-preserved ruins of a temple in Alba, Italy, contained a hidden master sound-control chamber. From this, a network of sound pipes extended; when the structure was still standing, the voices of the gods could be heard coming from several places.

Lucian, the second-century Greek satirist, wrote a most engaging saga of skullduggery in sanctified robes. He said the man who became famous as Alexander the Paphlagonian had been apprenticed to a rogue who dealt in potions and spells. Once aware of the tricks of the trade and the money to be made as a mystic, the young man, who was "tall, handsome, godlike, with fair skin and long locks, partly natural," persuaded an older woman of Macedonia to supply the capital for the business Alexander and a partner set up.

After his friend died, Alexander returned to his hometown, Abonouteichos. Realizing that a dramatic incident was essential if he were to be recognized as a favorite of the gods, Alexander staged one. He sealed a baby snake in a goose egg and buried it in the mud of a pool on the site where a temple was being built.

In the marketplace the next day he announced that a god would appear. A curious throng followed him to the pool. He scooped up some mud, and with it the egg. He cracked the shell to disclose the snake. Gods show up in curious guises! News spread that in three days the tiny reptile had grown to mammoth size. When patrons entered Alexander's dimly lit room, they saw a serpent with an almost human head. When they asked the snake-god questions, it answered.

Lucian explained that the big snake was tame; it coiled at Alexander's feet with its head tucked under his arm. A cleverly constructed human mask was attached to the upper part of the snake; tugs on concealed lengths of horsehair opened and closed the mouth of the mask. A hidden assistant provided the voice through a long, thin tube made from the windpipes of several cranes.

This was only one of Alexander's tricks. He returned answers to questions sent to him on sealed scrolls, apparently without opening them. Applying a long red-hot needle to the part of the seal closest to the parchment, he melted the wax and lifted the seal with the upper surface intact. After reading the scroll, he heated the bottom of the seal and carefully replaced it.

The intimate queries of some followers gave Alexander the data he used to blackmail other clients. Occasionally in the rush of business he did not bother to open every scroll. A few discreetly worded questions to the slaves who brought them usually revealed their contents. When Alexander was in Rome, Lucian told the man who carried his scroll that he had inquired about medicine for a pain in his side. The messenger returned with a magic potion. The written question obviously had not been read; it said, "How old is Homer?"

13

The First
Wonder-
Workers

The day Lucian visited the oracle, he was expected to kneel, along with the others, and kiss the great man's feet. Instead Lucian bit Alexander's toe.

Alexander the Paphlagonian's tricks were picayune compared to the elaborate mystifications staged in the ornate temples. The priests, the best educated men of their time, put their knowledge to practical use when they demonstrated the wonders of the gods they represented. Altar fires lighted mysteriously, blazed high. Servius, a fourth-century Roman writer, said the priests drew the sacred flames from heaven, but pans of burning coals concealed under the slotted tops of altars, would have produced the same result. When oil or wine libations were poured on sacrificial heaps surrounded by dry wood, the flammable liquid would have reached the coals through the openings in the surface, causing tongues of fire to leap up immediately, igniting the saturated material. Several early writers said that naphtha, a mineral that bursts into brilliant flames, heightened the spectacle.

Hero of Alexandria, the Greek scientist who lived some sixteen hundred years ago, explained two systems for another awe-inspiring temple trick in his treatise on pneumatics; he revealed the secret of doors that opened as though the invisible gods had moved them. One arrangement was based on an airtight metal box concealed at the top of an altar. Heat from the fire expanded the air in the container, forced it through a tube into a large globe filled with water. As pressure mounted, the liquid was siphoned off into a bucket suspended in an underground chamber. Two chains went from the handle of the bucket to a pair of posts extending down from the hinged sides of the doors. The increasing weight of the water caused the bucket to descend, pulling the far ends of the chains that had been wound around the posts. As the posts turned, the doors opened.

Hero also described devices that produced the sound of trumpets as the temple doors opened wide, illustrated how statues could be activated to pour libations on fires, and gave clear instructions on how to make partitioned vessels from which any one of several concealed liquids could be poured. Hero did not say he invented these deceptions; some may have been centuries old.

In his *Descriptive and Historical Account of Hydraulic and Other Machines for Raising Water,* published in New York in 1842, Thomas Ewbank told how a water trick possibly saved the life of Tutia, a Roman vestal virgin who was charged with violating her oath of chastity and faced a sentence of living burial. Tutia called on the goddess Vesta to establish her innocence by helping her perform a miracle. Then she filled a sieve at the Tiber River, held it high, and carried it through the streets to the temple without a drop of water leaking out on the way. Pliny and Valerius Maximus said this

The First
Wonder-
Workers

Banks and Morocco, his famous
"talking horse." The white steed
stomped out the numbers on a pair of
rolled dice. Other educated animals
also indicated the values of coins and the
total of the spots on various playing cards.

Chinese showman thrusts a sword through a basket without injuring
the assistant inside, while an equilibrist stands on one foot atop a
long pole, and an animal trainer exhibits his pets on an outdoor stage.

seemingly impossible feat silenced her slanderers and proved to the onlookers that she was indeed a virgin. Whatever the fact of that matter, Ewbank suggested that Tutia might have used a trick sieve. Roman sieves were essentially pans with tapering sides and holes at the bottom. Such a sieve could be gimmicked by fitting a shallower, solid pan into it, joining the two around their rims, and making a small control hole just below the rim of the sieve. On being dipped into the river, water would be caught and contained in the upper pan. Water also would flow through the perforations in the bottom of the sieve, filling the space between the two parts, providing the control hole was kept open so air could escape. Then, if Tutia placed her finger over the control hole as she raised the sieve, the water between the sections would be retained by atmospheric pressure. To allay any suspicions, Tutia might have dipped such a sieve in the river once or twice, allowing the water to escape each time as she raised it, before closing the control hole and performing her "miracle." After Tutia reached the temple, the original sieve may have been switched for another that the faithful could examine, even venerate.

As Christianity spread throughout Europe, pious churchmen censured all forms of magic, including theatrical amusements. Sleight-of-hand men, jugglers, and acrobats were still in disfavor in the twelfth century. They could not live or work in some cities in France. An exception was Paris where so many entertainers resided that a street was named for them—the Rue des Jongleurs (later Rue de St. Julien des Ménétriers). St. Bernard of Clairvaux spoke for the majority of the clergy when he told the people that the tricks of mountebanks "never pleased God." A century later, Louis IX of France echoed his sentiments; he said sleight-of-hand performers and jugglers engendered "many evil habits and tastes." He hoped to drive them from his country. In England, Roger Bacon, the thirteenth-century Franciscan friar, reported more dispassionately:

> there are men who create illusions by the rapidity of the movements of their hands, or by the assumption of various voices, or by ingenious apparatus, or by performing in the dark, or by means of confederacy show to men many wonderful things which do not exist.

Higher church authorities were not so understanding when they launched their long, ruthless campaign against witchcraft, devil worship, and sorcery. Conjurers, who claimed no demonic powers, suffered along with other innocent victims. A girl who ripped a handkerchief apart and restored it before a large audience was tried for witchcraft in Cologne in the fifteenth century. After performing in Padua and Mantua, Italy, a man named Reatius was seized and tortured until he admitted he produced his deceptions with sleight of hand and the help of confederates. A performer of allegedly Satan-inspired card tricks was jailed in Paris in 1571.

There was no suggestion that Boccal, a contemporary Italian magician was in league with the devil. As his story is told in a satirical poem by Teofilo Folengo, published in Venice in 1517, the mounte-bank from Bergamo enjoyed his greatest success during a shipboard show on the Adriatric Sea.

On that occasion Boccal improvised a table on deck by placing a plank across two trestles. Strapped to his waist was a bag in which he carried his paraphernalia. He took out three copper cups and put them side by side on the plank. Then he pulled up his sleeves and performed so adroitly that the three balls "seemed fifty."

Calling for a bottle of Malmsey, he popped the cork, drained the wine, and threw the cork overboard. Opening his mouth wide to show that it was empty, Boccal gnashed his teeth, then blew a stream of dry flour through his lips, spraying the passengers.

The cork that had been tossed into the sea reappeared tied to a string around the neck of a spectator. Boccal stuffed a piece of bread into the man's gaping mouth; when the man spit it out, the bread had changed to manure.

A lace was yanked without breaking from another man's clothes; then it vanished. Boccal said the lace had passed into a third spectator's jacket and asked the man standing by him to take it out. The obliging volunteer assistant reached in, but instead of the lace, he found a bottle, a mirror, a pen, a bell, the sole of a shoe, a curry-comb, a fragment of glass, and several church candles.

The dazzled crowd was still gasping as Boccal approached an-other entertainer, who earlier had sung to the accompaniment of a harp. He was told to blow lustily through his nose. The singer sneezed, then "a horsefly, a cricket, and thirty fleas" emerged from his nostrils with a terrifying bang.

In another account of this era, the stir that Damautus, a Spanish magician, created when he traveled to Milan in the retinue of Em-peror Charles V in 1543 was recalled seven years later by Girolamo Cardano, the noted mathematician, physician, astrologer, and gam-bler, when he came to write his *De Subtilitate Rerum* (On the Subtlety of Things). Cardano said he doubted that anyone could match the Spanish knight's "unheard-of and incredible" feats.

Another, or possibly the same, conjurer is mentioned in Car-dano's *Liber de Luda Aleae* (A Book on Games of Chance). This "condemned Spaniard" was prohibited from participating in card games on "pain of death" because he could produce four cards of a kind whenever he wished. Cardano was critical of showmen who performed in public places. Fire-eating, he said, was more a feat of

Temple doors swung open
mysteriously, as if the
gods pulled them, when
fires were lighted on
ancient altars. Hero of
Alexandria described two
systems in his treatise
on pneumatics.

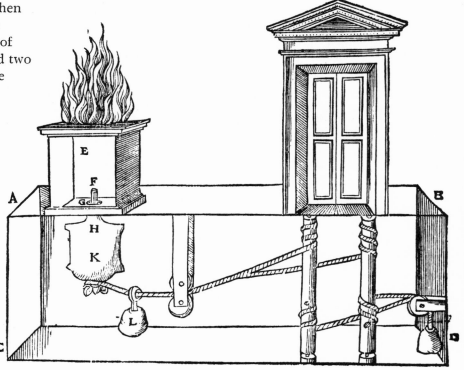

daring than of intellect. He had seen men swallow liquids and produce them from their eyes and their foreheads (probably with a trick funnel). Others pulled "nails and a string from their mouth" (possibly an early version of the needle-threading mystery), changed pictures in a book by flicking the pages, and linked single rings by tossing them into the air.

By the mid-sixteenth century some conjurers were presenting the illusion of human decapitation. Cardano reported seeing a live head with no body and a living body with no head; this, he noted, was accomplished without injury to the participants. The showmen were "of low station," and "not as much admired for their skill as a good cook."

Yet Francisco Soma, a young aristocrat from Naples, who performed privately in Milan, clearly enthralled Cardano, judging from the 1582 edition of his *Piazza Universale* (Universal Place). Soma spread a pack of cards face down, invited an onlooker to select one, remember it, and put it back in the deck. Then Soma named the chosen card. Possibly, Cardano admitted, this could have been done by sleight of hand, but digital skill, he insisted, could not explain what followed. Once a spectator had taken a card, the same card was chosen by him again and again. Had every spectator selected the same card, Cardano said, he would have assumed that the pack was made up of fifty-two identical cards. Different people, however, selected different cards. Cardano insisted that skill could not account for this feat: "It was too wonderful to be understood by human cognition."

Despite Cardano's bafflement, any skillful card conjurer can duplicate the feat with the technique called "forcing." This was one of the specialties of another of Cardano's countrymen, Girolamo Scotto. This knight from Placentia, who carried out diplomatic missions for Holy Roman Emperor Rudolf II and several lesser heads of state, was the most celebrated court conjurer of the late sixteenth century. Slender, regal in bearing, with a neatly trimmed beard and moustache, he wore a puffed hat with an ostrich plume, the wide-ruffed collar favored during this period, and clothes as fine as any prince's.

He was never known to perform for the public, but his feats must have smoothed the way for successful negotiations with officials who were charmed and perplexed by his magic. A Dr. Handsch, who saw Scotto entertain Archduke Ferdinand, the Regent of the Tyrol, and his friends in 1572, wrote a careful description of the tricks that utterly puzzled him.

Scotto asked the court physician to think of any card, then take one from the face-down pack. Handsch thought of the eight of hearts —and to his surprise, this was the card Scotto pulled from the deck.

It was not a coincidence, the doctor stressed; ten other people present had the same experience.

Then someone was given four face-down cards to hold, and invited to make a choice—kings, queens, or knaves. "Kings." Scotto spread the cards; each was a king. A less cooperative subject, perhaps hoping to ruffle the conjurer, said, "Nothing." Scotto took the cards, fanned them, and displayed four blanks.

Handsch was even more startled when the conjurer casually suggested that he mentally select one of the ingredients that made up the dish he was about to eat. He concentrated as instructed; Scotto reached across and touched a crayfish claw with his knife. "Truly, this is no small matter," the physician commented in his account.

Later in the evening the Italian knight presented the first full mental-magic routine on record. A heap of coins was brought to the table and placed before Philippine, Ferdinand's wife. She was instructed, Handsch said, to think of any coin; Scotto found it.

Next came the court chamberlain's turn to try to stump the magician-mentalist. Scotto asked the chamberlain to select any syllable in any word in a book; he then told him the syllable. He also revealed "the actual weight that the court apothecary made note of." The magician left the room while Ferdinand himself wrote whatever he chose on a piece of paper; when Scotto returned, carrying a second sheet of paper, it seemed that he had predicted exactly what the Archduke would write.

Handsch's notations show he did his best to describe what he had seen—which is not a simple matter. Audiences usually remember what a skilled performer wishes them to. They recall the general effect, not the important details. For example, there is a coin stunt in which a spectator is told to concentrate upon one coin among many. The conjurer turns his back, tells the spectator to pick up the coin he has mentally chosen, to hold it in his closed hand, visualize first one side, then the other, and then to replace it with the rest. The performer finds it, not by thought-reading, but by the sense of touch. The chosen coin will be warmer than the others, retaining some of the body heat from the spectator's hand. Later, in describing this, most people will say only, "I thought of a coin; he found it."

Scotto performed for Archbishop Gebhard Truchess von Walburg in Cologne in 1579, and was a popular figure at the court in Coburg a year later. While he was in Coburg, Antonio Abondio, the Milanese sculptor, made him a medallion that bore his likeness, and the magician had impressions struck in gold and silver; on at least one occasion, Scotto used the medal in a trick. When entertaining the Duke of Prussia in Königsberg, he tore the soft center from a piece of bread, squeezed it in his hand, then opened his fingers

Superstitious spectators believed devils and supernatural forces aided medieval magicians perform their seemingly inexplicable feats.

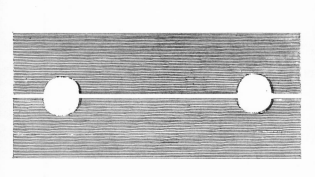

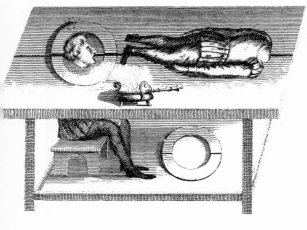

Body-without-a-head and head-without-a-body illusion was explained by Reginald Scot and other early writers.

Tutia, the Roman vestal virgin, and a trick sieve of the sort she may have used for a "miracle."

to show that it had changed into a gold medallion, which he gave to Chancellor Christoph von Kappen as a souvenir.

Only once in Europe was Scotto publicly branded as a sorcerer. Anna of Saxony, the wife of Count Palatine John Casimir, was charged with committing adultery in Coburg in 1592. She testified that the magician, who by then was in another country, had entered her boudoir one night, holding a cross, bound with heavy wire. She said he commanded the wire to untwist and wrap around her body so tightly that she could not resist as he made love to her. Later, she charged, Scotto tired of her, brought Ulrich von Lichtenstein, a handsome Coburg knight, to console her, and he himself fled with her most precious jewels.

Anna delivered this testimony after having been found in Ulrich's arms. Even in an age when many people believed in witchcraft, it was unconvincing. Not a shred of evidence was introduced to prove that Scotto had performed the fantastic feat, seduced her, or purloined her gems. Anna and her lover were imprisoned for life.

Though he had been born in Italy, Scotto said his ancestors were members of the Irish Douglas clan. Certainly he made himself as welcome in Britain as on the Continent. There is a reference to a performance he gave for Queen Elizabeth in Thomas Nash's *The Unfortunate Traveller, or The Life of Jack Wilton* (1594). King James of Scotland, a firm believer in witchcraft, said in his 1601 *Daemonology* that Satan taught man tricks with cards and dice, and cited Scotto as one who, with diabolical assistance, could "deceive man's senses thereby." Considerably more space is allotted to Scotto and his foibles in the court journal a year later:

> There is an Italian at Court that doth wonderful strange things upon the cards, as telling any card that is thought of, or changing one card from another, though it be held by any man ever so hard under his hand. The Queen gave him 200 crowns for showing his tricks, and divers gentlemen make meetings with him where he getteth sometimes 20, sometimes 40 crowns, and yet they say he spends it so strangely as he cannot keep a penny in his purse.

Where, when, or how this colorful conjurer died is not known.

Another Italian of this period presented a feat that was to become a conjuring classic. Abram Colorni, court engineer in 1574 to Don Alfonso III, Duke of Ferrara, invented and constructed such useful things as a collapsible boat, an extension ladder, and a rapid-firing gun. For relaxation he gave magic shows for his friends. He performed with cards in the manner of Soma and Scotto, and he devised at least two unusual mysteries: in the first, words thought of by a spectator appeared on the face of a playing card where the pips had been; and in the second, selected cards were placed in the pack and rose of their own accord at his command. The latter feat has since been shown by thousands of magicians, and more than four hundred different methods have been devised to do it.

Tomoso Garzoni, a clergyman, begged Colorni for a clue to his methods. The magician, said Garzoni, "was polite and had impeccable manners." He freely admitted he had no aid from demons; he admitted he made use of natural secrets disguised in such a way that even educated people wouldn't recognize them, and—like any wise conjurer—he absolutely refused to tell how even his simplest trick was done.

In sixteenth-century France, Gonin, the first French magician whose name is still remembered, achieved such renown that "a trick of Master Gonin's" became a synonym for a clever deception. No one knows the feats that made up his program. This Gonin was the first of a family of mystifiers; a Gonin, believed to be his grandson, performed for King Charles IX, and another later conjured with cups and balls on the Pont Neuf in Paris.

There were no manuals of instruction for these early magicians. Secrets were passed from one generation to the next. The first French book on practical magic appeared in Lyons early in 1584. The title of Jean Prévost's *La Première Partie des Subtiles et Plaisantes Inventions* (The First Part of Subtle and Pleasant Tricks) implies that a second volume was planned, but no record of it exists. Prévost gave pithy explanations of how to balance a knife on the point of a needle, how to construct trick knives that seem to penetrate the tongue or arm, and how to take three threaded beads from two cords while someone holds the ends; occasional illustrations helped make the descriptions clear. Cup-and-ball manipulations are not explained, nor are the popular card tricks of the time.

Later that year Reginald Scot, a former justice of the peace in Kent, England, published a treatise that was to have a worldwide impact. *The Discoverie of Witchcraft* (he used the word *discovery* in the sense of "explanation" or "exposure") was intended to combat the witchhunting craze, then almost as prevalent in England as on the Continent. Many people thought sleight-of-hand men needed the devil's help with their tricks; Scot decided to set them straight. Though only thirty-one pages of the bulky text and four illustrative plates are devoted to conjuring, these pages became the source for countless smaller books in many lands—and Scot's own book is still in print after nearly four hundred years! Scot received his information from John Cautaures, a Frenchman then living in London, who, Scot said, was the ablest sleight-of-hand performer he had ever seen.

In addition to a sound rebuttal of the Church's allegations about the people it branded as witches, Scot's treatise included a thorough exposition of the cups and balls; tricks with coins, cards, handkerchiefs, and paper; and the explanation of "the decollation of John Baptist," a head without a body, and a body without a head, similar to the illusion Cardano had seen earlier in Italy. A showman named Kingsfield presented this attraction in England in a booth at Bartholomew Fair. Scot said the body of the apparently decapitated head was concealed in a long boxlike table, on which rested the body of another man, whose head was hidden in the table too. A woodcut illustrated the arrangement.

The first English-language volume devoted to conjuring, *The Art of Jugling,* was published in 1612. The preface was signed Sa. Rid. This may have been an abbreviated form of the author's name or a pseudonym; no one knows for sure. Most of the tricks were copied from Scot; the most interesting addition is an eyewitness account of Morocco, "the dancing horse" alluded to by Shakespeare and Ben Jonson, of whose exhibitor Sir Walter Raleigh wrote: "If Banks had lived in olden times, he would have shamed all the enchanters of the world." Morocco, a white steed, stamped out with his hoof the total number of spots on a pair of rolled dice, the number of shillings in a person's pocket, or the age of anyone who whispered it to his trainer.

Not one person in a thousand, the author of *The Art of Jugling* claimed, knew how the "pretty tricks" were done. And he then proceeded to enlighten his readers. He said the method was the same for any question asked: "Marke the eye of the horse is always upon his master. . . . the horse paws with his foote while the master stands stone still." When the horse reached the correct number for the answer, Banks "lifts up his shoulder and stirres a little." Without that visual cue, Rid went on, "the horse will pawe an hundred times." It was useless for anyone to question the horse without telling the trainer: "the master must know . . . the horse is ruled by him by signes."

Later, when Banks took Morocco to the Continent, many fanciful tales were related of their adventures. According to one, the clever horse saved Banks, when he was being tried in Orléans on a charge of having practiced witchcraft in France, by approaching a high official and kneeling. According to another equally unsubstantiated account, after this narrow escape in France, Banks and his horse were both burned by less tolerant—or less gullible—officials in Rome.

People who enjoyed wondrous animals and sleight of hand were also amused by "the human fountains"—men who swallowed large amounts of water and spouted streams of wine. Blaise Manfre of Malta was the strongest attraction among the early seventeenth-century water magicians, though Jean Royer of Lyons was credited

Wall rubbing from a Chinese temple. It was not unusual for a conjurer to present balancing and juggling feats as well as sleight of hand.

with spewing out liquids for a greater length of time. One writer said the stream continued for as long as it would take to recite the Fifty-first Psalm (approximately two minutes and fifteen seconds); another said the time involved was precisely that required to walk two hundred paces. Royer and Manfre were tried by the Church for using supernatural methods; both were acquitted when they privately explained their techniques to the inquisitors.

Another famous water conjurer, Floram Marchand, a native of Tours, was brought to London by Thomas Peedle and Thomas Cozbie, two enterprising promoters. After Marchand and his sponsors parted company, the men, who until then had advertised him as a marvel, called him a "moist cheat." In June 1650 they produced and sold *The Falacie of the Great Water-Drinker Discovered*, an eight-page pamphlet with a woodcut of the Frenchman in action, and a clear, clinical, and complete explanation of his secrets.

Many noble ladies and gentlemen had "offered vast sums of money" for the secret; now, proclaimed Peedle and Cozbie, the public at large could read for a pittance the inside facts: Marchand, they said, prepared for his work each morning by swallowing a pill about the size of a hazelnut "confected with the gall of a Heifer & wheat flower baked." This, washed down with four or five pints of water, cleansed his stomach. Next he boiled a mixture of two ounces of thinly sliced "Brazile" and three pints of water until the liquid was saturated with the dark red color. Before each appearance he swallowed half a pint of this brew and washed the glasses he was to drink from in fine white vinegar.

Numerous glasses in a basket, a large bucket of lukewarm water, and a table were the only visible props when Marchand made his entrance. Using a glass that had been rinsed to wash away any trace of the vinegar, the performer filled it twenty-three times and drank. This liquid, plus that which he had downed earlier, forced his stomach to reject some of its contents. The strong red dye and the lukewarm water blended to produce a stream of "claret" from his lips.

After drinking more water, he regurgitated again, directing streams of "claret" and "beer" through pursed lips into individual glasses. The "claret" went into well-rinsed glasses; the "beer" into those still damp with vinegar. The vinegar turned this liquid a light brown. Fifteen more glasses of warm water were swallowed to dilute the solution in his stomach; the next fountain that sprayed from his mouth was the color of burgundy. The intake of more water further lightened the shade. The stream, caught in the glasses that had been washed with vinegar, now appeared to be sherry.

By this time spectators were accustomed to the performer's tak-

Girolamo Scotto, Placentian knight,
performed for Holy Roman Emperor
Rudolf II, and later entertained
Queen Elizabeth in England.

Floram Marchand sent three
streams of wine from his
mouth after drinking water
in London in 1650.

ing fresh glasses from the basket and discarding used ones. No one noticed when he put a glass of water behind the basket and took one filled with rose water in its place. His closed fingers masked the color. He drank this and fourteen glasses of the now tepid water from the pail.

The rose water blended with the liquid in his stomach; the long stream he then spurted in the air was fragrant, and drew fresh bursts of applause. While the audience was still discussing this new marvel, he drank from a glass filled with another aromatic solution. This and the usual quota of plain water produced a fountain of an entirely different aroma—and aroused even greater astonishment.

Marchand's closing feat was his most spectacular. He drank as much water as he could hold, then gripped a mouthpiece fitted with three short tubes between his teeth. He tilted back his head and sent up three massive streams in as many directions.

The Frenchman, according to Peedle and Cozbie, had learned the trick from "Bloise an Italian" (Blaise Manfre). It required not only the ability to hold and regurgitate a large quantity of liquid, but also an empty stomach. On days that he was to perform, Marchand skipped breakfast, lunch, and dinner. When he finally sat down to supper after the show, he ate as much as two or three normal men.

Some water-spouters also performed sleight of hand. Hocus pocus was common parlance in England to describe both a magician and his tricks. Some writers thought the phrase came into the language after it became customary for Italian performers to appeal to "Ochus Bochus," a long-dead wizard, to assist them in their conjuring. A German author transcribed what he heard the magicians say as "Hogges and Bogges."

Some members of the clergy later accused the magicians of profaning *"Hoc est enim Corpus meum,"* the Latin words spoken by priests at the most solemn moment of the sacramental ritual of the Mass. This is unlikely considering the difficulties conjurers had had with the Church in the past.

Thomas Ady, a British writer, says in *A Candle in the Dark* (1655) that the best performer in King James's day (James was King of Scotland from 1567 to 1625 and King of Great Britain from 1603 to 1625) "called himself the King's Majesty's most excellent Hocus Pocus" and used the words in his patter. Ben Jonson wrote in his *Staple of the News* in 1624 that "Iniquity came in like Hocus Pokus, in a juggler's jerkin, with false skirts, like the Knave of Clubs."

Hocus Pocus Junior. The Anatomy of Legerdemain, the first illustrated book on conjuring in English, was published in 1634. There was even a facetious epitaph in *The Witt's Recreations* six years later.

Here Hocas lyes with his tricks and his knocks
Whose death has made sure as a jugler's box;
Who many hath cozen'd by his leiger-demain,
Is presto convey'd and here underlain.
Thus Hocas he's here, and here he is not,
While death plaid the Hocas, and brought him to th' pot.

Unlike Hocas, conjuring was flourishing. Earlier conjurers had been limited to ingenious but simple trick knives, boxes, cans, and funnels; new mechanical devices were to add another fascinating dimension to the art of magic.

3

The Automaton
Chess Player

No automaton has ever excited as much admiration and controversy as did the chess-playing Turk in the late eighteenth and early nineteenth centuries; Edgar Allan Poe was just one of the many who tried to puzzle out the secrets of its mechanism. However, long before the Turk's creation by an ingenious Hungarian baron, magicians and other showmen were exhibiting curious machines that were marvels of precision clockwork.

Jacques Besson explained how a keg dispensed wine, water, and oil through a single spigot in a Latin treatise on mathematical and mechanical instruments in 1578; eighteen years later the text appeared in French.

Henry Winstanley, who, like Besson, was an engineer, may have been inspired by his predecessor's book. A "Wonderful Barrel" drew curious Londoners to his Water Theatre on Piccadilly, near Hyde Park, in 1606. This was the first permanent building in the city to house a magical attraction. Conjurers had sometimes worked in booths at fairs, but their shows in the city were given in the streets, in taverns, or in the homes of the wealthy.

Winstanley's perpetual fountains and other hydraulic displays delighted his patrons. Advertised to produce "several sorts of liquids, hot and cold, suitable to the season, and without mixture," the barrel had a stronger appeal; it slaked their thirst.

One of Winstanley's competitors, Charles Butcher, enjoyed a brief vogue in 1708 with a "New Mechanical Fountain" in a room at the Black Horse Inn. This glass contrivance was about eight feet high. Advertisements said that it "at command runs at one cock hot and cold liquor"; sherry, white wine, and claret; teas, coffee, and chocolate; raspberry and cherry brandy and punch; were among the drinks offered.

Winstanley's Water Theatre celebrated the Peace of Utrecht with a gala performance in 1713. Six streams of various wines and brandies and jets of claret, stout, and ale spouted simultaneously from the head of "The Wonderful Barrel."

Later a miniature "Dairy House" was added to the show. From this, theatregoers could select "curds, several sorts of creams, Milk, Wheye, Cakes, Cheese-cakes, Syllabubs [mixtures of wine and milk], New Butter, Butter Milk." A milkmaid added to the excitement as she worked a churn preparing the dairy delicacies that were served to the spectators in the boxes and pit. The old showplace was renamed the Mechanical Theatre in 1715.

Isaac Fawkes, the most famous of the early eighteenth-century British sleight-of-hand men, followed the trend toward automated attractions. He still produced gold and silver coins as well as eggs and a live chicken from a small cloth bag; changed the pips on the faces of playing cards; and converted a card into a pigeon; but in 1722 he was also advertising a musical clock "that plays variety of Tunes, on the Organ, Flute, and Flageolet, with Birds Whistling and Singing." Later, at his booth at Bartholomew Fair, he gave top billing to a machine called "The Temple of the Arts." As small automated musicians played, spectators saw a mechanized view of Gibraltar with tiny warships crossing the painted bay, and a duck swimming close to shore. On the island a platoon of toy Spanish soldiers marched in unison. The Gibraltar scene was replaced in 1728 with a representation of King George II's coronation procession. Three years later when the ambassador from Algeria paid a visit to Fawkes's London theatre, the "moving picture" was an Algerian scene, and the principal trick was an apple tree that blossomed and bore fruit in less than a minute. The master machinist who constructed these marvels, Christopher Pinchbeck, a London clockmaker, sometimes worked with the magician at fairs.

Fawkes died in May 1731, leaving an estate of fifty thousand pounds; his son took his place in the theatre and appeared seasonally in a booth at Bartholomew Fair. He was assisted by a younger member of the Pinchbeck family.

An apothecary shop exhibited by Balducci, an Italian showman, at the Red Lion Tavern, Pall Mall, in 1738 was reminiscent of

Baron von Kempelen's
Chess Player as seen
from the front.

Rear view of
the famous
"clockwork" Turk.

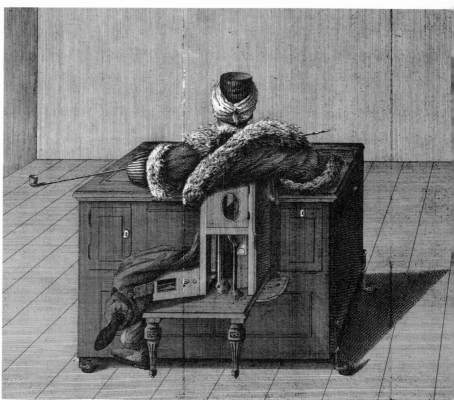

Winstanley's Dairy. A mechanical druggist opened the door of the small establishment, took orders from the audience, went inside, and returned with the requested cinnamon, cloves, nutmegs, and teas.

There also was, the advertisement said, "A Blackmoore, which by striking with a hammer on a bell does all that is commanded." If someone took a playing card with seven spots, the little figure struck seven times on the bell hanging beside it. Neither this nor the drugstore was purely mechanical. A concealed live assistant operated the first; offstage strings attached to levers in a table motivated the second.

The automata creations of Jacques de Vaucanson, displayed in Paris in 1738, were an immediate success. The lifelike movements enthralled audiences there, and in other European cities. Vaucanson's flute player, a figure five and a half feet tall, performed so realistically that many learned men thought the mechanical man was human. Earlier an organist in Troyes had constructed an automaton harpsichord player. When this was exhibited at the French court, the King, eager to see the complicated machinery, opened a panel despite the efforts of the inventor to dissuade him. He found not the expected conglomeration of wheels and springs but a five-year-old child.

The marvelous Vaucanson mechanical pieces all functioned without the help of human hands. His masterpiece, a duck, performed almost convincingly enough to fool a live duck. It quacked, seemed to breathe, ate, and drank. Sir David Brewster, the Scotch physicist, said in his *Letters on Natural Magic* (1832), "When corn was thrown down before it, the duck stretched out its neck to pick it up, it swallowed it, digested it, and discharged it in a digested condition." Brewster thought this man-made bird was "perhaps the most wonderful piece of mechanism ever made."

As ingenious as Vaucanson's figures were, they created far less public excitement than the clockwork chess player constructed by a Hungarian nobleman; this near-human machine was to be a center of controversy for more than fifty years. The inventor, Baron Wolfgang von Kempelen, served as counselor on mechanics to Empress Maria Theresa. In 1769, while watching a Frenchman entertain a palace party with magnetic toys, he offhandedly remarked that he could easily devise a more thought-provoking entertainment. When the Empress said she would like to see the product of his imagination, he worked six months to perfect the automaton chess player; then he presented his invention to great acclaim before her court.

Newspaper articles and word of mouth sent news of the sensational "Thinking Machine" across Europe. The Baron was besieged by people who wished to see it in operation. Regularly as many as thirty guests assembled at his home in Pressburg. According to the account of Von Kempelen's friend and neighbor, Karl Gottlieb von Windisch, member of the Imperial Academy of Vienna, they were led

The Automaton Chess Player

up the stairs, through an area cluttered with carpenter's, blacksmith's and clockmaker's tools, and into the baron's old workshop, which now served as an exhibition room. Cases of books, antiques, and natural curiosities distracted the visitor's attention only momentarily from the automaton at the far end of the room.

Seated cross-legged behind a polished wooden chest, was the slightly larger than life-size figure of a moustached Turk, wearing a turban and a flowing robe. The wooden chest, measuring about three and a half feet in length, two feet in depth, and two and a half feet in height, was mounted on casters, as was the Turk's attached chair; both could be rolled forward or spun around with a minimum of effort.

The Turk's right hand rested to one side of the chessboard, which was fastened to the top of the chest. His left hand held a long-stemmed Oriental pipe. It must have amused the Baron to watch his spectators' eyes look first at the Turk and then at the chest, which was obviously large enough to hold a person. Von Kempelen began his demonstration by opening one of the three doors in the front of the chest—the one to the onlookers' left. This compartment was filled with wheels, cylinders, and levers. To prove that machinery alone occupied this space, he opened a smaller door at the back and let the rays of a candle illuminate the interior. He shut these doors and opened the other two in the front. They disclosed a space twice the width of the first compartment, holding fewer pieces of mechanism—two horizontally suspended quadrants, a few spring barrels and rods. Another small door at the rear was unlatched, and the light from the candle played on this area. After all the doors were closed, the Baron revolved the chest to display the back of the Turk. He lifted the robes and opened panels to reveal clockwork inside. The panels were shut; the costume was adjusted; and the chest was again spun so that the Turk faced the audience.

From a long drawer at the bottom of the chest, Von Kempelen took a set of red and white ivory chessmen and arranged them on the board; then he removed the pipe from the Turk's left hand, resting the Turk's elbow on a cushion.

Von Kempelen picked up from the floor a black box, which he said controlled the actions of the Turk. He put the box on a nearby table, drew a key from his pocket, inserted it in the left side of the chest, and wound the machinery. The first game was about to begin.

The challenger, a spectator who had volunteered to match wits with the Turk, moved his chair forward and sat opposite the automaton. The Turk played first, raising his left hand, grasping a white pawn between his fingers, lifting it, and depositing it on another square. The automaton's head turned stiffly as he followed the moves of his opponent, and his eyes rolled to scan the board. He himself

34

*The Automaton
Chess Player*

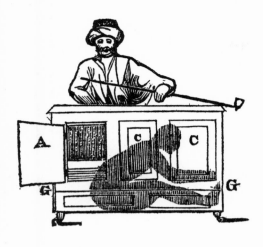

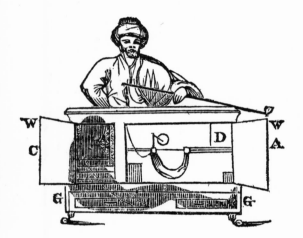

Robert Willis thought a man climbed up inside the Turk to move the pieces on the chess board.

Gamaliel Bradford, Sir David Brewster, and Edgar Allan Poe shared Willis' opinion.

Despite their "logical reasoning," many years later this solution was found to be wrong.

removed whatever pieces he captured from play. When the Turk attacked his opponent's queen, he nodded twice; when he checkmated the king, he nodded thrice. His challengers played as well as they could, but rarely won.

The first thorough account of the Chess Player's performance appeared in 1783 when Von Windisch's letters to a friend in Switzerland were published. He had heard that there was a person concealed somewhere in the machinery, but insisted there was not space enough between the parts to hide even a hat.

Von Kempelen eventually tired of playing host to the crowds that came to his house. He dismantled the Turk, stored the chest, and told people who pressed for invitations to his soirées that the mechanism was broken.

The Turk was not reassembled until Emperor Joseph II, Maria Theresa's son, commanded Von Kempelen to perform at the palace in Vienna for the Russian Grand Duke Paul and his wife. This time the response was so overwhelming that the Baron was offered a two-year leave of absence from the court to exhibit his amazing creation in the principal European cities. He hired two men: one, a Herr Anthon, to present the attraction; the other, whose name has not been recorded, to take tickets and make himself generally useful.

The Baron, his wife, four children, and two assistants went on tour in 1783. In Dresden the program opened with another of Von Kempelen's inventions—a talking doll with a vocabulary of a few dozen words. This novelty amused the audience, but the Chess Player remained the great attraction. The most enraptured spectator there, Freiherr Joseph Friedrich von Racknitz, resolved to build a mechanical Turk himself.

Von Kempelen's popular automaton was trounced occasionally at the Café de la Régence in Paris by French masters of the game; these defeats increased the Turk's drawing power. Who would win—an acknowledged expert or a wooden figure with a clockwork brain?

Von Kempelen's letter of introduction to Benjamin Franklin, who was then the American Ambassador to France, said that the Baron was more interested in finding buyers for his useful inventions than in giving shows, but that he was not averse to the Chess Player's paying his traveling expenses. A note from the Baron to the famous American scientist and inventor is still preserved. Written on May 28, 1783, after Von Kempelen had returned from an exhibition for the French court at Versailles, it invited the Philadelphian to play a game with the Turk and to see a new Von Kempelen invention. Franklin came from Passy, where he had been on holiday, participated in a performance, and was outmaneuvered by the Turk. Franklin gave the Baron a letter of introduction to another chess buff, Hans, Count von Brühl, Saxony's envoy to the British court.

Philip Thicknesse, who saw the exhibition at No. 8 Saville Row in London, complained in his pamphlet, *The speaking figure, and the automaton chess-player exposed and detected* (1784) that five shillings was too much to pay to see a deception. He believed a boy, concealed in the chest, could see the chessboard reflected by a mirror in the ceiling of the room. Actually, there was no mirror, but Thicknesse scored a point when he stressed that the youngster probably could not stand being shut up for more than sixty minutes; otherwise the attraction would have been open for four hours each afternoon.

Thicknesse claimed to be an old hand at exposing fraud. Forty years before three hundred gullible spectators had paid a shilling each to see a coach that moved without horses. He suspected at once that a man was concealed in the huge wheel at the rear of the carriage. The Duke of Atholl and others had not accepted his theory until Thicknesse dusted the wheel with snuff and proved it "could not only move, but sneeze too, like a Christian."

Another attempt to solve the mystery of Von Kempelen's Turk was published that year in Paris. Henri Decremps in *La Magie Blanche Devoilée* (Natural Magic Disclosed) conjectured that a dwarf was in the chest, his legs in two cylinders that were a part of the clockwork in the smaller compartment, his head and shoulders extending through a secret panel and hidden by the automaton's robes. Decremps said the dwarf could enter the larger compartment after the doors were closed, and then follow the movements of the chessmen in any one of three ways: compass needles under the squares of the board could indicate when pieces with magnetized-iron bases were lifted, or he could be cued by the words spoken by the presenter, or the chessboard could be made of some partially transparent material. In the latter case, the shadows of the chessmen could be seen. As the hypothetical dwarf was never glimpsed in or around the exhibition rooms, Decremps' suppositions were discounted. Further, there were no leg-size cylinders in the clockwork compartment.

In 1789, Freiherr von Racknitz, who had been so intrigued by Von Kempelen's first performance in Dresden, published a book, illustrated with color plates, describing his own chess player. A short, slender young man was hidden behind the long drawer in the bottom of the chest. Once the doors to the compartments had been shut, he sat up, fastened the panel that covered him to an inner wall, lit a candle, opened a section that dropped a chessboard to his lap, put pieces in position, and looked up. Indicators on springs were beneath each square of the chessboard on the top of the chest. When the magnetized pieces were touching the upper board, the indicators were motionless. Each time a play was made a dangling indicator stopped vibrating and clung to the square where the piece had been placed. Using a special pantograph which copied the actions of his own hand, the operator moved the Turk's hand, and opened and closed its fingers to grasp the chessmen. Von Racknitz's method was similar to that actually used by Von Kempelen, but fortunately for the safety of the secret at the time, his volume had a limited sale and was not translated from the German.

Despite the rumor that Frederick the Great, King of Prussia, purchased the Turk from Von Kempelen in 1785, Herr Anthon probably continued to exhibit it when Von Kempelen returned to Pressburg to resume his experiments, now with firefighting equipment and hydraulic systems; the automaton was a part of the Baron's estate when he died on March 26, 1804.

Johann Nepomuk Maelzel, a thirty-four-year-old Bavarian master craftsman who had already constructed several ingenious mechanical figures and musical devices himself, bought the Turk from the Baron's son. Best remembered today for patenting the metronome that beats time for aspiring pianists, Maelzel toured Europe with the famous Chess Player as his feature attraction. His presentation was the same as Von Kempelen's with two major exceptions. The mysterious black box that supposedly controlled the automaton was no longer used. Also, the challengers now made their moves on a second chessboard some distance away from the chest, and Maelzel duplicated their plays on the Turk's board, and the Turk's on the opponent's board.

In France, Napoleon Bonaparte reportedly tried to test the figure's reaction to unfair plays by deliberately making several false moves; each time the Turk corrected him. Napoleon's stepson, Eugène de Beauharnais, Viceroy of Italy, offered Maelzel thirty thousand francs for the machine. The showman accepted, while warning young Beauharnais that he might be disappointed since the Turk required a "secret director." Once the prince knew exactly how the automaton operated, he lost interest in his expensive toy and stored it away in his mansion in Milan.

Without the Chess Player, Maelzel's show receipts dwindled. For five years the Turk was idle; then Maelzel completed a deal to buy him back in 1817, promising to pay the price in installments over a period of several years.

An Oxford graduate undertook to explain how the Turk operated while Maelzel was in England; his *Observations on the Automaton Chess-Player* was published in 1819. Two years later, Robert Willis of Cambridge published *An Attempt to Analyze the Automaton Chess-Player* in a book with five plates showing various views of the machine. He reasoned that the man inside sat behind the drawer, which was shallower than it appeared, with his feet touching the right wall. When the small compartment was shown, he bent forward toward his toes. Then, before the double doors to the larger area were opened, he sat up straight in a space behind the machinery in

*The Automaton
Chess Player*

Baron Wolfgang von Kempelen, inventor of the first really great cabinet illusion.

An Italian engraving of the chess-playing Turk used with the 1788 translation of Henri Decremps' "exposure" published in Padua.

Edgar Allan Poe saw the Chess Player when Maelzel brought it to Richmond.

the small compartment. Finally he crawled up into the hollow body of the Turk, put his left arm in the Turk's hollow left arm, and followed the action on the chessboard by peering through the gauzelike fabric covering the Turk's front.

Willis' explanation, though not correct, was widely accepted. It was quoted, and his illustrations were copied by Gamaliel Bradford in *The History and Analysis of the Supposed Automaton Chess Player of M. De Kempelen*, published in Boston in 1826, and by Sir David Brewster in his book on natural magic in 1832.

A William Lewis and a man named Williams hid in the chest in England; later Mouret, a French chess expert, took over. Mouret told a Parisian journalist that the true secret of the Turk had almost been revealed in Germany. When the public ignored a sleight-of-hand show and flocked to patronize the Maelzel attraction, the irate conjurer, suspecting there was a human being in the chest, attended his rival's performance and yelled "Fire!" The audience rushed from the room, and the Turk, apparently just as eager to escape the flames, lurched and toppled over. Later, Maelzel promised Mouret that if a fire did break out, he would see to his safety.

Maelzel nearly missed a lucrative royal command performance in Holland, because Mouret had a will of his own. Business had been bad, and Maelzel was behind in paying his assistant. The king was to give three thousand florins for a private showing at thirty minutes past noon. At twelve the usually prompt Mouret had not arrived at the exhibition hall. A frantic Maelzel ran to the chess expert's lodging house and found him still in bed. He ordered Mouret to get dressed immediately. The Frenchman refused. "Tell the king that the automaton is sick," he said. Maelzel realized only one remedy would cure his assistant—the prompt payment of his back salary. Once this transaction had been completed the Turk appeared on schedule.

Mouret was not with Maelzel on April 13, 1826, when the Turk made his first appearance in the United States. Twice daily, at noon and at eight P.M., the Automaton Chess Player took on challengers from the members of the audience who had paid fifty cents to enter the assembly rooms of the newest hotel in New York City—the National, at 112 Broadway. The reviews were as extravagant as those in Europe and Great Britain. Maelzel, however, was worried. For the first time his secret operator was not a top-flight chess player. Hidden in the chest was a woman, the wife of a Frenchman who exhibited Maelzel's mechanical rope dancers earlier in the program. Maelzel was disturbed when his vaunted attraction was beaten, and he was embarrassed when people noticed that the French woman was never present while the automaton played. Maelzel explained his dilemma to William Coleman, the editor of the *Evening Post*. Coleman, a chess player himself, arranged for his son to fill in as the secret operator from time to time. When the woman was seen in the audience watching the Turk, the rumor that she was its brains faded.

Maelzel opened at Julien Hall in Boston in September. There, the *Centinel* reported, the Turk was defeated "for the first time in America." Not so, the *New-York American* pointed out; two players had won games in Manhattan. Soon news spread that three Bostonians had triumphed over the automaton. Meanwhile, William Schlumberger, an Alsatian chess master who was well known from his brilliant play at the Café de la Régence in Paris, had received a distress signal from Maelzel. He arrived in Boston just in time to bolster the Turk's sagging reputation.

In the United States, Maelzel was asked why he never used the mysterious black box that had been mentioned in early accounts of Von Kempelen's presentation. "The people are now intelligent," he replied, "then they were superstitious." Though the box was gone, Maelzel had added a dramatic sound effect. When the Turk checkmated an opponent, a mechanically produced voice shouted the French word *"Echec!"* With Schlumberger in residence, the victorious cry was heard at the end of nearly every game.

Americans continued to try to figure out the secret of the chess-playing automaton. Robert Gilmor, a Baltimore merchant, who saw the Turk on May 8, 1827 at the Fountain Inn on Light Street, noted in his diary: "I cannot conceive the possibility of a man being concealed within the desk at which the figure sits and plays. It would be a contemptible trick, and unworthy of the ingenuity of the inventor."

Later that month two inquisitive small boys climbed to the roof of a shed and looked down through a window into the adjacent Fountain Inn exhibition room. They could not see the show, only what was on the side of the curtain away from the audience. It was a hot, humid day, but they patiently waited until Maelzel rolled the Turk out at the end of the performance. They saw him open the chest and a tall, thin man in shirt sleeves, who was perspiring profusely, step out from admidst the machinery.

"The Chess-Player Discovered" was the heading on the story the *Baltimore Gazette* ran June 1. The Washington *National Intelligencer* discounted the exposure, calling it "a clever device of the proprietor to keep alive the interest of the public in his exhibition." Maelzel knew that the story had killed his attraction in Baltimore, at least for the moment. He ended his run. In the fall he advertised a new feature, "The Conflagration of Moscow," an imported mechanical scene that vividly portrayed the destruction of the Russian city. His "Austrian Trumpeter" and "Rope-Dancers" were billed above the Turk, who for more than forty years had piqued and puzzled audiences on both sides of the Atlantic.

MAELZEL'S EXHIBITION,
No. 29, St. James's Street.

The

Automaton

Chess

Player

Being returned from *Edinburgh* and *Liverpool*, where (giving the Pawn and Move) it baffled all Competition, in upwards of 200 Games, although opposed by ALL THE BEST PLAYERS.

Has opened its Second Campaign,
WITH THE ADDITION OF THE

AUTOMATON TRUMPETER,
AND THE

Conflagration of Moscow,

In which Mr. M. has endeavoured to combine the ARTS of DESIGN, MECHANISM, and MUSIC, so as produce, by a novel Imitation of Nature, a perfect Fac Simile of the real Scene. The View is from an elevated Station on the Fortress of the *Kremlin*, at the Moment when the Inhabitants are evacuating the Capital of the Czars, and the Head of the French Columns commences it Entry. The gradual Progress of the Fire, the hurrying Bustle of the Fugitives, the Eagerness of the Invaders, and the Din of warlike Sounds, will tend to impress the Spectator with a true Idea of a Scene which baffles all Powers of Description.

The MORNING EXHIBITIONS begin at 1 and 3 o'Clock, and the EVENING EXHIBITION at 8 precisely, when GAMES will be played AGAINST ANY OPPONENT, to whom the double Advantage of A PAWN AND THE MOVE WILL BE GIVEN.

Admission 2s.6d. Children 1s.6d. each.

☞ Each Exhibition lasts One Hour. Should a Game not be finished in that Time, the Party will be at Liberty to take it down with a View to its being resumed at another Opportunity.

Mr. M. begs leave to announce that the ORCHESTRION, the AUTOMATON TRUMPETER, the CONFLAGRATION OF Moscow, and the Patent for the METRONOMES, are to be disposed of.

Handbill advertising the Automaton Chess Player's second appearance in London as the feature of Johann Nepomuk Maelzel's exhibition in 1820.

Trouble also appeared from another direction—a competing automaton. Two brothers named Walker had offered their imitation of the Turk to Maelzel for five hundred dollars. After he refused to buy it, "The American Chess Player" opened at the American Museum in New York and received enthusiastic reviews. When Maelzel tried to buy it for a thousand dollars, and promised to give the Walkers jobs taking tickets for his exhibition, they were no longer interested in selling.

The Walker machine had one flaw—an operator who was no match for the best American players. Schlumberger, who directed Maelzel's automaton, rarely lost a game unless he had been drinking heavily. Too much alcohol made him sleepy, and sometimes Maelzel had to bang on the top of the chest to rouse him from a brandy-induced slumber. When this tactic failed, Maelzel informed the spectators that the machine was out of order and angrily pushed the Chess Player behind a curtain.

Maelzel, said Signor Antonio Blitz, a famous magician-ventriloquist who worked on the same show with him in Philadelphia, was "extremely irritable, yet very kind . . . he displayed great taste and refinement in his arrangements, without regard to cost." He was often annoyed by the volleys of laughter provoked by Blitz's funny tricks. "It is not schenteel to make them ha! ha! They laugh too loud; that's not schenteel," Maelzel complained after one show.

In his autobiography, *Fifty Years in the Magic Circle*, Blitz noted that Maelzel always kept the doors to the chest locked offstage, and that during the performance he locked each door immediately after the compartment behind it had been shown. This implied that if a spectator rushed up and threw the doors open while the Turk was playing, the secret would be revealed.

Despite occasional newspaper features which attempted to explain the enigma of the Turk, Maelzel's Chess Player continued to intrigue audiences. Edgar Allan Poe, whose poems and short stories were not yet widely read, was living in Richmond, Virginia, when he saw the Turk. The automaton inspired him to write an essay in the April 1836 issue of the *Southern Literary Messenger*. His biographer, Hervey Allen, called it "the first of Poe's work in which he emerged as the unerring, abstract reasoner."

In point of fact, Poe's reasoning was not entirely abstract, and his conclusion was wrong! Poe admitted he had studied Sir David Brewster's *Letters on Natural Magic* and a long, illustrated article in a Baltimore paper. Both presented the Willis theory that the man in the chest shifted positions to avoid being seen when the doors were opened, then entered the body of the Turk where he played the game with his arm in the figure's, as he looked through the thin material at the front of the costume to follow the play.

Poe said that while six lighted candles of different lengths were on the top of the chest during the game—three on each side of the chessboard—only one illuminated the duplicate board on which the challenger played. The six candles of varying heights were there, Poe explained, for two purposes: "to enable the man within to see through the transparent material (probably fine gauze) of which the breast of the Turk is composed," and to make it difficult for a viewer to see "the *material* of the breast of the figure."

Poe decided that the figure used its left arm "because under no circumstances could the man within play with his right." His last sentence stated: "We do not believe any reasonable objections can be urged against this solution of the Automaton Chess-Player."

Poe's argument that the man directing the play was concealed in the body of the automaton seems logical, but as was later revealed, the hidden player actually remained in the wooden chest during the entire procedure, never entering the upright portion of the figure.

Maelzel had limited his appearances to cities in the Eastern states. When receipts began to drop sharply, he traveled to western Pennsylvania and Ohio. Then he went down the Mississippi to New Orleans, and after a run there embarked for Cuba. Spanish was one of his several languages; the season was a great success. When he returned to the States and business slumped, he decided to show in Cuba again, en route to South America. His exhibition opened in Havana in late December 1837. Crowds were not as large during the holiday season as they had been on his first visit. In February Schlumberger began playing erratically; he died a few weeks later of yellow fever. The sixty-eight-year-old Maelzel despaired of finding another equally skillful or compatible operator. The aging Bavarian's principal recreation had been a game of chess and a bottle of wine with the Alsatian. Even with the Turk inactive, Maelzel thought his Cuban patrons would be satisfied with "The Conflagration of Moscow," his automaton trumpeter, and the mechanical rope dancers. He was wrong. Months went by, and fewer spectators came. The man and wife who took tickets and helped exhibit the figures left. Alone and dispirited, Maelzel boarded the brig *Otis,* bound for Philadelphia. His crated equipment was stored in the hold; he was seldom seen on deck. Seven days out of Havana, as the ship approached Charleston, South Carolina, on July 21, 1838, the great showman died in his cabin. There was no one to mourn when he was buried at sea.

Maelzel's apparatus was auctioned in Philadelphia in September. John F. Ohl, who had backed the last tour, bought the Chess Player for four hundred dollars, then sold it to Dr. John Kearsley Mitchell, who sponsored a chess club that later assembled the parts and put the Turk in good working order.

The machine proved more complicated than anyone had imag-

As-Rah, a later mechanical chess player, though not as ingeniously constructed as the celebrated Turk, also drew large crowds.

Robert-Houdin built a chess player for *La Czarine,* a French play about the Turk, which was presented in Paris in 1867.

ined. The operator slid from one part of the chest to another on a seat with a grooved base that rode along two parallel greased bars. These tracks were hidden by the back of the long drawer from which the chessmen were taken. The drawer was as cleverly constructed as a Chinese puzzle box. When it was pushed in, the sides and bottom went to the rear of the chest, but the back remained far enough forward for the director to ride along on the tracks behind it.

While the small compartment was being shown, he was hidden in the larger one, his back against a movable panel, his raised knees close to the right wall, and the sham pieces of mechanism folded back to give him room.

When he heard the key turn to lock the door of the small compartment, the director straightened his legs and pushed past the swinging wall panel into a space behind the machinery. Then he reached back, covered his legs by lowering two flaps to form a floor just above the drawer, rearranged the folded metal instruments, and pulled another secret panel in place to hide the upper part of his body.

As the interior of the chest was lined with dark cloth, the walls and floor appeared solid when seen by candlelight. The sound of the doors to the larger compartment being locked was the operator's cue to remove the paneling that concealed him from view.

He lit a small lamp, and pulled down a section of the right wall which became a table. This had a small chessboard fastened to the top. He opened a hidden door in the rear of the chest; through it he had direct access to the ingenious mechanism that governed the automaton's movements. He took out an extension rod and fitted it securely into a metal upright, which was attached to a rod in the Turk's left arm.

Near the end of the extension rod, which came into the cabinet above the operator's chessboard, was a lever that opened and closed the Turk's fingers. At the very end was a peglike metal tip.

The operator's chessboard was similar to those travelers use, except that it had two holes in each square. Miniature red and white chessmen were pegged in the positions of the larger ones on the Turk's board.

Whenever the operator played, he moved his own chessman from one hole to another. The automaton then carried out this action as the director raised the end of the extension rod to lift the Turk's arm, then brought the tip of the rod above the second hole in the square that was formerly occupied by the piece he had played. Before the tip entered the hole, the control lever on the rod was turned to make the Turk open his fingers. When the tip was in the hole, the lever was reversed, causing the Turk to grasp the matching piece. Again the extension rod was raised to make the Turk lift the piece, and take it to the proper square. Then, when he had deposited the piece, his fingers were opened to release it.

The operator followed the challenger's play by looking up through an open trapdoor in the top of the chest and watching dangling metal disks under each hollowed square of the chessboard above. Von Racknitz, who had made his own Turk in Dresden, guessed that the pieces were magnetized; his system was similar to Von Kempelen's.

A second metal upright in the body of the Turk—similar to the stick in a ventriloquist's dummy—made the automaton's head turn; strings brought about the nodding and the rolling of his eyes.

Wolfgang von Kempelen once said his Chess Player "was a mere *bagatelle*, which was not without merit in point of mechanism, but that the effects of it appeared so marvelous only from the boldness of conception and the fortunate choice of methods adopted for promoting the illusion."

The Hungarian baron never claimed to be a conjurer, yet he invented the first great cabinet illusion; introduced revolutionary techniques of concealment and misdirection. Mystery was the Turk's strongest appeal. After the members of the Philadelphia chess club found out how the mechanism worked, they lost interest. In 1850 they gave the automaton to the Chinese Museum.

Hidden away in a remote corner, the motionless Turk gathered dust; his exotic costume lost its luster. The day after the Fourth of July, 1854, the National Theatre at Ninth and Chestnut streets caught fire; the flames spread to the museum. Some of the curios were saved by firemen who fought for hours to bring the blaze under control. Though the newspapers didn't mention it in their lengthy accounts of the holocaust, the greatest illusionary device of its time was among the precious objects destroyed.

4

Magic in the Colonies

Aᴌʟ forms of amusement were forbidden in the British colonies in North America. Conjurers, actors, and other "idle persons" were barred from Jamestown, Virginia, in 1612. Anyone rash enough to practice "crafty science" or participate in an exhibition in Connecticut risked having his shirt stripped off and being lashed fifteen times.

There was work to be done. Every able-bodied person was needed to clear the wilderness, build cabins, plant crops, and protect the settlements from marauding Indians. Dedicated to the church, self-denial, and honest labor, the New England Puritans abhorred frivolous diversions. When a Massachusetts tavern owner announced that a man would "shew tricks" on his premises in 1691, outraged townspeople assembled to protest. Judge Samuel Sewall, the Boston diarist, noted that the innkeeper "saith seeing 'tis offensive, he will remedy it." After the performance was canceled, the crowd recited the Ninetieth Psalm, and went home. Miles Burroughs demonstrated his "Art of Legerdemain and Subtle Craft" briefly in nearby Newton in 1712—until the town council learned about the show and made him leave.

New York City, founded by the Dutch, gave a warmer reception to traveling showmen. The first known advertisement for a magician in an American newspaper appeared in the March 18, 1734, *Weekly Journal*. Beginning that evening at seven, Joseph Broome, "the famous German Artist," displayed his "Wonders of the World by

Dexterity of Hand" at the house of Charles Sleigh on Duke Street. Broome performed nightly well into April.

Though public magic performances were still forbidden in Virginia, William Byrd II—a member of the state council—and his family looked on as their friend Captain Thomas Bulling, master of the ship *Dunkirk*, entertained them informally with tricks at the Byrd home in June 1740.

Legerdemain was legal in New Jersey by 1763, but John Woolman, the Quaker, wrote in his *Journal* that he was troubled when handbills heralded the arrival of a conjurer in Mt. Holly. He was even more disturbed after being told that "strange" feats had been demonstrated. Woolman went to the tavern where the show was to be repeated and sat by the door. As patrons entered and took seats near him, Woolman "labored to convince them" that sleight-of-hand performers "were of no use to the world," and that spectators who paid to see them were acting "contrary to the nature of Christian religion."

One man tried to debate the issue; Woolman silenced him with quotations from the Bible. Then, before the show began, "feeling my mind at ease," the Quaker left.

While Woolman was being aroused by a simple display of digital dexterity in New Jersey, a conjurer from a neighboring state was evoking images of the dead in Europe—specters so terrifying to sensitive spectators in Vienna that this portion of his performance was forbidden.

Billed as Philadelphia—an exotic name on the far side of the Atlantic—the magician gave his first command performance for Catherine the Great in Russia four years prior to the American Revolution. Jacob Meyer had been born in Philadelphia, Pennsylvania, on April 14, 1734. His parents were Jewish immigrants from Polish Galicia. In his teens, Meyer became a protégé of William Augustus, Duke of Cumberland. After his patron's death in 1765, the twenty-one-year-old American, who had diverted the court with his amusing experiments in mathematics and physics, went on tour as a professional conjurer. He had taken the name of his birthplace following his conversion to Christianity; as a magician, he advertised himself as Meyer or, more frequently, Jacob Philadelphia.

From England he traveled to Ireland, Portugal, Spain, and Central Europe, performing a blend of tricks with apparatus and sleight of hand. A mechanical Bacchus held a small barrel filled with water, which changed to wine when the figure turned the tap. A small "Egyptian magician" gave answers to arithmetical problems, and indicated the suits and numbers of playing cards. An ordinary pen dipped into an inkwell wrote in several colors. Chosen cards were located, changed, or transported from one place to another. Philadel-

Jacob Philadelphia, the first American magician to win fame in Europe. His surname was Meyer; he was a Philadelphian.

Title page of a book on conjuring issued by Philadelphia during his engagement in Vienna in 1774.

Kleines
Traktätlein
seltsamer und approbirter
Kunststücke,
welche
der berühmte Amerikaner
Jacob Philadelphia,
zum
Vergnügen und Zeitvertreib
gewidmet.

Wien,
gedruckt im Jahr 1774.

phia's masterpiece, the production of ghostly figures, was clearly labeled as his impression of an ancient necromancer. He was not, did not claim to be, a sorcerer; the luminous figures that appeared in smoke on his darkened stage were projected by a magic lantern.

The plump, short-necked American conjured for Catherine II a second time in Focşani, Romania, in 1772. Then he went to Turkey to entertain Sultan Mustafa III in Constantinople.

During an engagement in Vienna in 1774, Philadelphia published *Kleines Tractalein seltsamer und approbirter Kunststücke* (Little Treatise on Strange and Suitable Feats), a seventy-two page collection of tricks and diversions. Readers were told how to make an egg jump from hat to hat (with a string); how to change an egg into a chicken (by switching one bag for another); and how to make a wooden fox answer questions (by pulling cords attached to the head and paws). Only a single copy—in this author's collection—is known today of this book, the first on conjuring issued by an American-born magician. Two years later, Gottlieb Rodiger, a German rival of Philadelphia's, lifted the title of the book and pirated part of the contents word for word in a sixteen-page pamphlet which is equally rare.

Philadelphia made lavish use of advertisements to attract audiences for his appearances. An undated handbill heralding his arrival in Lüneburg, Germany, said the magician, who had performed for the rulers of Sweden and Prussia, would present fifty new examples of his mathematical and mechanical art. The size of the hall would not allow him to present the hundreds more he knew. He was not to be compared to the tricksters who tried to imitate him; he had no doubt the citizens of the city would appreciate his performance.

The show did not always live up to the advance ballyhoo. As a result, Philadelphia was greeted on his arrival in the Germany university city of Göttingen in January 1777 by satirical broadsides, posted by a witty professor, Georg Christoph Lichtenberg:

> The admirers of supernatural physics are hereby informed that Philadelphus Philadelphia, the famous sorcerer, already mentioned by Cardanus [Cardano] in his book *De natura supernali*, where he is styled "the envy of heaven and hell," has arrived by ordinary coach some days ago, although it would have been just as simple for him to come through the air, as he is the same person, whom, in the year 1482 at the public market at Venice, threw a ball of cord into the clouds and climbed upon it into the air until he disappeared.

Philadelphia, the broadside continued, was to perform at the Merchant's Hall. He would begin with inexpensive tricks, then progress to those more than five hundred times costlier; some which "excel even the greatest marvels and are, so to speak, absolutely impossible." The show was to be presented daily with the exception of certain hours on Monday and Thursday, when the mystifier would be in his native city, Philadelphia, amusing American congressmen, doing business in Constantinople, or having his lunch.

The great magician, the handbill proclaimed, would:

> Spin ladies from the audience on their heads like tops "without breach either of their head-dress by the pressure, or of the decorum by the falling of their petticoats."
>
> Kill a man with one blow of a hatchet, revive him with another, so he would ask, "What music was that?"
>
> Extract teeth from several women, load the molars in a cannon, and fire at the victims. When the echoes of the explosion had died away, the ladies would find "their teeth, white and sound," back in their mouths.
>
> Gather watches, jewels and, if the audience requested it, cash, and put the valuables in a trunk, which would be dispatched to the city of Kassel. A week later, if each person tore up the receipt the magician had given him, the missing items would reappear.

"He has made a great deal of money with this trick," the handbill added.

Philadelphia came to a quick decision when he saw this libel on his legerdemain. He cancelled the Göttingen appearance and took the first coach to Gandersheim.

Goethe, who saw the show in Weimar that same year, later wrote *Faust,* based on legends about a sixteenth-century German conjurer; memories of Philadelphia's feats may have suggested elements of the plot. Other contemporary German authors mentioned Philadelphia and his fabulous feats. Schiller, the poet, suggested that the magician conjured with souls.

Philadelphia lived with his wife and two children in Koethen, Germany, when not on tour. As a sideline, he arranged for European products to be shipped to American merchants.

It is not known when or where the first American magician to perform in Europe died. While Philadelphia never made a return voyage across the Atlantic, other showmen from the Continent and England brought the ingenious creations of European mystifiers to the colonies in the New World.

Forty-seven years after Isaac Fawkes had intrigued the Algerian ambassador in London with the feat, Mr. Bayly, a British conjurer, produced "An Apple-Tree by Fire, which would bud, blossom and bear Fruit" at the Sign of the Orange Tree, a tavern on Golden Hill in New York City. Bayly promised to perform "without the use of Pockets, Bags or Sleeves" in his April 1767 advertisements. Like Isaac Fawkes, he exhibited a mechanical "view of the sea, with ships sailing, fish &c. &c. swimming," and for good measure, he offered a puppet show with twenty-eight "artificial comedians." Later Bayly made his home in

Alexandria, Virginia. (The state no longer banned entertainers.) It is likely, however, that George Washington was writing about another European showman when he noted in his diary on September 19, 1769, that he had attended court at Alexandria, spent the night, "and went to see slight of hand performed." Peter Gardiner was exhibiting in this area. He had played at the theatre in Williamsburg, Virginia, in April 1769, and in May of the following year, he appeared at the New Theatre in Annapolis, Maryland. Washington was in the audience on November 17, 1772, when the magician-puppeteer again gave his show in Williamsburg.

Gardiner featured puppet plays, "Babes in the Wood," "Dick Whittington and His Cat," and "Bateman and His Ghost"; mechanical displays "with sea monsters sporting on the waves," marching soldiers, the capture of Havana, and fireworks. The "fireworks" may have been flashes of light, produced when a slotted dial was spun on the front of an opaque box containing a lamp. A windmill changed into a woman "by clock-work"; a house became an orange tree, and the oranges were transformed into singing birds. Then, according to a newspaper advertisement, after several card tricks,

> the performer will allow any of the company to cut off the head of a fowl, which he will bring to life again in the most surprising manner. He will eat fire, which will appear as if his mouth was burnt to a coal. He will fry several eggs in a hat over a candle, as well as if in a frying pan on the fire, without doing the least damage to the hat.

One of Gardiner's feats is still seen in carnival sideshows. Stripped to the waist, the magician stretched his body between two chairs, his head on one, his feet on the other. A heavy rock was placed on his arched midsection, then he invited an onlooker to break the stone with a sledge hammer.

Gardiner is believed to have returned to Europe after his second season in Williamsburg; Bayly, who remained in America, lost most of his equipment and clothes during the Revolutionary War, and his wife, who had been his assistant, also left him.

A handbill printed in Alexandria in 1782 reveals more of his story. The magician had recovered from "illness and Lunacy," and, with the mayor's permission, would perform at William Ward's house. Money must have been scarce in the community. If brought to the door before show time, flax, wool, beeswax, or cotton would be accepted in lieu of cash.

In another leaflet, Bayly expressed his gratitude to the officials and the people of the city for their kindness. Due, however, to "the various disadvantages and expenses attending his performance, for want of proper assistance and his late state of health," he was not sure when he could pay his many creditors. As a start, he proposed to give another show; meanwhile, he would "extract teeth with a TOUCH as usual." Earlier European performers sometimes pulled teeth at marketplaces and in inns; the combination was rare in America.

By November, Bayly had enough money to go to Baltimore. It was snowing when he arrived. He sent a note to an old friend, Thomas Wall, the actor who was in town with his company, asking to use his theatre on the play's nights off. Bayly said he was "very Lame and Infirm," and "not able to walk in Such weather." He also needed aid "in some Trifling Matters, Relative to the Proper appearance of a Performer."

Wall may have helped Bayly. A playbill announced a December 2, 1782, opening at Henry Speck's Sign of the Indian King on Gay Street for the conjurer who had performed for three months for "polite audiences" in Alexandria, and who for thirty years had exhibited in Europe and America.

Each Monday and Thursday night he would offer "amazing Table Tricks and Sleight of Hand," and perform with fifty puppets "near four Feet high." As a prologue, he would recite "The Impossibility of Pleasing Everyone"; as an epilogue, he would give "A Defense for Lying." Bayly also advertised for an assistant: an affable young man who must stay sober, and "whose pride would not conquer his reason."

Early in January 1783, Bayly moved to a new location—the Sign of St. Patrick at Fell's Point. His oft-repeated calls for an assistant had been dropped. Now he featured a new stunt: "With his Arms extended, he, by Scent alone, carries every Gentleman's Hat in the Room with his Nose—or anything proposed, of equal weight." It must have been a curious sight as he inhaled through his nostrils to lift the objects.

Bayly's name was missing from the advertisements heralding the show later that month. Jacob Henninger replaced him with the table tricks and puppets "At the Next Door to the New England Coffee-House in Fell's Point." Instead of fifty puppets, there were a hundred, and a "newly imported Globe" had been added to the scenery.

Another British magician who worked in North America during this period was Hyman Saunders, who performed at Mr. Hyet's house on Hunter's Quay in New York City in October 1770. He boasted that his hands were so deft that his feats seemed supernatural. He fried German pancakes in a borrowed hat, passed a borrowed ring onto the thin blade of a sword while spectators held the tip and hilt, and pulled a man's shirt off without disturbing his jacket or waistcoat. For more than a decade Saunders traveled in the eastern colonies, and made periodic visits to the West Indies. He advertised that the governors of Pennsylvania, Maryland, and Virginia were among his patrons.

Unlike his predecessors, Signor Falconi, an Italian magician,

Woodcut of Isaac Fawkes from one of his 1726 advertisements.

Announcement of Signor Falconi's first performance in Baltimore in 1787. Rain delayed the opening.

OLD THEATRE.

THIS EVENING, *November* 20th, 1787,
SIGNIOR FALCONI,
Will have the honor to perform his first REPRESENTATION
of *Natural Philosophical*
EXPERIMENTS.

IT would be tedious to describe the many objects which this Performance will consist of, but he can, without vanity, assure the Public, that they will not find themselves disappointed in their expectations.—From the following list of some few of his Experiments, it will give the Public a small idea how far he will be deserving of engaging their attention. Having always met in *Europe* with general approbation, he is in hopes of having the same success in *America*.

1. A sympathetic WIND-MILL, that will work or stop at the command of any of the company.

2. Some Experiments of the CATOPTRIC, or appearances produced by the reflection of Mirrors.

3. A number of Sentiments will be handed to the Company, which any person retaining in their mind, a little artificial Butterfly will reply to them.

4. A small FIGURE, in a Turkish dress, will answer all Questions by signs, and will guess the number any Lady or Gentleman may throw with two dice.

5. Likewise, any Lady or Gentleman, may throw the dice under a hat, unseen by any person, the above-mentioned Figure will tell the number.

6. The EXPULSION, by Electricity, an entire new discovery.

7. To oblige, by sympathy, the will of three persons.

8. To tell before-hand, the Combinations or Arrangements of four different Numbers, given by any one of the Company.

There are several other Experiments too tedious to enumerate, which the Performer omits mentioning, not wishing to anticipate the pleasure and surprise the Company may receive from them.

Every Night of Performing entirely New.

The last Experiment of this first Representation, and with which he will conclude, will be striking and new. The following very surprising Experiment, which has been allowed by Connoisseurs to be the most astonishing ever exhibited. Signior FALCONI, will desire any person to write any Question they may please on paper, to be signed by as many of the Company as chuse; any person will be at liberty to put it into a loaded pistol, and discharge it out of the Theatre; the Performer will neither see or touch the paper, and to the astonishment of the Spectators, a DOVE will instantly appear with the answer in his bill.

⁎⁎ TICKETS to be had of Mrs. *Montgomery*, next Door to the Theatre, and at Mr. *Hayes*'s Printing-Office.

BOXES, *Three Quarters of a Dollar.*—PIT, *Half a Dollar.*

☞ The Doors to be opened at Five, and to begin precisely at Six o'Clock.

came to the states by way of Mexico. The advertisements for his debut at the Colisco theatre in Mexico City in June 1786 said he had appeared before the kings of Naples, France, Portugal, and Spain, and that he knew Dr. Mesmer's secrets of magnetism. Falconi's initial performance must have been a fiasco. The next day a jester, in a blue and gold costume, turned up in the lobby to harangue the magician for a display of "nonsense and stupidity" and for a shadow show "devoid of either warmth or humor." Whether this clown had been hired by the disappointed theatre management, or volunteered to appear on his own, the Mexican papers did not report.

By November 1787, Falconi had reached Baltimore. His first night at the Old Theatre was postponed. An advertisement said, "The moisture of Atmosphere was unfavorable" for his "Experiment of Expulsion by Electricity." When the rain stopped and the show went on, he received a rave review. Falconi performed "in so singular and masterly a manner" that the audience declared "they had never seen before in this part of the world anything equal to it," the *Maryland Gazette* stated.

A Turkish figure struck a bell on command, a gold head danced in a glass, a written question was fired from a window, then a bird was produced from a box with the answer on a piece of paper in its beak. A concealed magnet was used to stop watches, and attract a toy swan as it moved on the surface of the water in a bowl.

His principal mechanical piece, "Thunderstorm at Sea," offered the "Swelling of the sea and waves rolling with incredible impetuosity; the sky wonderfully covered with Clouds, the natural appearance of the Hail, with its concommitant noise, and a Brig in Distress, which after a long struggle is dismasted and goes down."

Years later, Falconi advertised an even more exciting sea scene, the battle between the *Ambuscade* and a Boston frigate, based on the reports of the encounter in a New York newspaper.

He played long engagements, varying his program weekly. One of his mechanical novelties was an Indian archer that shot arrows at a board to hit numbers called out by spectators, or to predict the total of the spots on the upper sides of three dice that had been rolled under the cover of a hat.

Falconi dazzled New York in 1816 with a luminous image of Jean Jacques Rousseau, the French philosopher, which rose majestically and mysteriously from a tomb on stage. Then, after more than thirty years in the Western Hemisphere, the aging Italian evidently entered a less arduous profession. In Bermuda in 1819 a man named Falconi advertised a "Phisiotrace," a new device for "taking likenesses." Four profiles for half a dollar—either life-size or small enough to fit into a locket, "No resemblance, no payment."

Most of the conjurers who toured in North America during

Falconi's time presented less elaborate shows. For example, Isaac Levy, who opened in New York in November 1782, made a living performing legerdemain. Five years later, John Brenon of Dublin balanced himself on a slack wire to catch a bullet fired from a pistol in his silk handkerchief. Mrs. Brenon, the first of her sex to perform magic professionally on this side of the Atlantic, showed less dangerous feats with "dexterity of hand."

Mr. Maginnis, "from the Sadler's Wells Theatre, London," was a more formidable rival. After an engagement in Halifax, he traveled to the Union Theatre in Newburyport, Massachusetts, in October 1795 to show his "Innocent Deceptions" with puppets, a shadow show, mechanical pieces, and legerdemain. He passed a marked coin invisibly from a pepper box to a cup, swallowed eggs "as quick as thought," made one card change into another under his foot, and cracked open a freely selected hickory nut to remove from it a piece of paper bearing the name of a previously chosen card. And there was Gabriel Salenka, the first magician on record to give a performance in Wall Street. He featured a "Learned Dog" at 78 Wall Street on the evening of March 16, 1799.

A more potent animal attraction was William Frederick Pinchbeck's "Learned Pig," which this scion of a British family of clockmakers, automata constructers, and showmen said was imported from England. He claimed to have paid a thousand dollars for his star. President John Adams gave the pig pundit "unbounded applause" in Washington, according to Pinchbeck's advertisements, and crowds flocked to see the show "in every major city of the Union."

The pig picked up numbered cards in its teeth to provide the answers to arithmetical problems, and letters of the alphabet to spell out words. As a climax, after a shuffled deck of playing cards had been spread in a circle, it lifted the cards that had been previously selected by the spectators.

Pinchbeck eventually tired of traveling with a porcine companion and turned to building and exhibiting mechanical marvels and singing comic songs. His book, *The Expositor; or Many Mysteries Unravelled*, published in Boston in 1805, explained how anyone with patience could teach a pig to do card tricks. Start when the pig is two months old, Pinchbeck suggested. Use slices of apple as a reward to teach the animal to hold a card in his mouth. Then train him to pick up from the floor a card with a bent corner when you sniff through your nose.

Pinchbeck believed it was easier to train a pig than to be a good magician. A really expert performer, he said,

> must be nimble with his hands and fingers, possess an extraordinary share of volubility, aided by a prepossessing carriage. . . . He must have acquired the faculty of dividing his thoughts, so as to ac-

*Magic in
the Colonies*

The PIG of KNOWLEDGE ! !

To be wise, observe ; for observation is the source of knowledge.

THE

EXPOSITOR;

OR

MANY MYSTERIES UNRAVELLED

DELINEATED

In a Series of Letters, between a Friend and his Correspondent.

COMPRISING

THE LEARNED PIG,—INVISIBLE LADY AND ACOUSTIC TEMPLE,—PHILOSOPHICAL SWAN,—PENETRATING SPY GLASSES OPTICAL AND MAGNETIC,

AND

Various other Curiosities on similar Principles :

ALSO,

A few of the most wonderful Feats as performed by the Art of Legerdemain :

WITH

Some Reflections on Ventriloquism.

By WILLIAM FREDERICK PINCHBECK.

Boston :
PRINTED FOR THE AUTHOR.
1805.

Frontispiece and title page of the first original conjuring book published in the United States. Author Pinchbeck was an Englishman.

complish several objects at the same moment, and that with certainty and ease; The flashes of his wit must attract the eyes of the spectator from the feat he is performing, as occasion may require, although he must not have this appear as his intention.

Aside from Breslaw in England, Pinchbeck said he had met only one other man who was "competent to the business"—Mr. Rannie.

John Rannie, a Scot, arrived in Boston early in December 1801, accompanied by his brother and a young, dark-skinned assistant. The voyage had been rough. Rannie was still feeling unsteady when he gave his first performance in a hall near the Boston Haymarket, but the audience was receptive. A juggler, "posture maker" (acrobatic contortionist), and ventriloquist as well as a conjurer, he was especially proud of his ventriloquial achievements. He claimed to be "the only *real* master of ventriloquism in Europe and America," and he offered a hundred guineas to anyone who could equal him.

Ventriloquism then was as mysterious as magic. Even today many people think performers "throw their voices." Actually a ventriloquist employs the same misdirective technique as a conjurer; he speaks without moving his lips, acts as if the sound is coming from another source. The ear is easier to deceive than the eye. A talented showman, by changing the tone of his voice and looking in another direction, can convince audiences an old woman is calling from backstage, a boy is shouting from a closet, or a baby is crying underneath the stage.

Early in the nineteenth century, ventriloquists usually carried on their conversations with bonnets, hats, or imaginary offstage characters. Dummies with rolling eyes, shaking heads, and moving lips had not been invented.

Rannie's offstage demonstrations publicized his show. Fishmongers fled from their stalls in Scotland when their merchandise began to talk. He chatted with horses about the weather, and with dogs about politics. He made it appear that a stranger's trunks were filled with squealing pigs, and stood by as an indignant American hosteler refused to assign the nonplussed man a room until his baggage was inspected.

When Rannie held a baby in his arms in Portland, Maine, the infant, who was less than a month old, said quite clearly that in three days the city would be destroyed by an earthquake. As word of this phenomenal prediction spread, frightened families packed their belongings and headed for safer areas.

The Scot's conjuring was as perfect as his acoustical deceptions. He sipped wine from a glass, threw the glass in the air, and it vanished. He pounded borrowed watches into bits, then made them whole again. He snipped a piece from a woman's satin gown and replaced it without any sign of the cut showing.

While John Rannie worked in Boston in 1801, his brother went to New York City and, billed as Mr. Rannie, performed there until early January 1802. Then he returned to Boston to appear briefly with John before sailing for England to buy more equipment.

After a run of forty-six nights in Boston, John Rannie went to New York himself, billed as Mr. Rannie, Senior; later he toured in the West Indies. In 1804 he featured a new "Philosophical Fish" in Boston. It pulled selected cards from a pack with its mouth, gripped a pen, and wrote numbers and words suggested by the audience. The fish was, of course, an ingenious mechanical device.

In a newspaper interview, Rannie said he should be proficient since he had studied his art for eighteen years. In earlier times people might have accused him of practicing witchcraft, but now Rannie claimed he exerted a strong moral influence on the community by alerting the public to the dangers of playing with sharpers who cheated at cards.

The *Political Calender* of Newburyport, Massachusetts, agreed. Many of his feats served "as a lesson to youth against the fatal and pernicious consequences of gambling," the paper stated. "This Scotchman is certainly one of the knowing ones," another paper commented in December 1810, "What he lacks in ventrilo—he makes up in quiz 'em. For, as he himself says, his greatest deception consists in fingering their cash."

A few months later, John Rannie announced his farewell tour of the United States, and gave his own assessment of his career in an eight-page pamphlet which detailed his major feats, and some of his achievements. Rannie, according to Rannie, stood alone in his chosen profession "having no competitor in any country, the vain attempts of pretenders to the contrary, notwithstanding."

Even before Rannie retired, one of his rivals, Mr. Martin, decided to leave the field. The Frenchman had been the center of a controversy in New York in 1808. A critical New Yorker had written a letter to the *Commercial Advertiser* protesting that Mr. Barney's Assembly Room, where Martin was exhibiting his "Phantasmagoria" and sleight of hand, had once been a church; now it was "a place of amusement for vulgar minds." Not only were tricks shown, but "the devil dances on stilts to the tune of a hand organ." Martin snapped back that since this letter had been printed, more people than ever were coming to see his show; though he had planned to move on to another city, he would now stay and show New Yorkers all the devils they wished to see. Apparently Martin made the devil dance for the last time in Baltimore; he offered his equipment for sale there in January 1811.

That year another conjurer published *The Life, Adventures and Unparalleled Sufferings of Andrew Oehler* in Trenton, New Jersey. Oehler said he had been born in Alstadt, Germany, on March 16, 1781. He had been a tailor in Germany, a hussar in the French army, and unjustly jailed for murder in Hanover, and for seduction in Paris. He had been shipwrecked in the Pacific, and he had commanded a black regiment during the Haitian revolution.

Oehler learned aeronautics and conjuring in Louisiana. His subsequent public exhibitions in Havana and Vera Cruz included balloon ascensions and fireworks displays. He made his biggest impact in Mexico City. Spectators there were astonished when a balloon took him "three miles" from his starting point, and they were awed as he stood on the top of a tower and, with a brass-tipped iron rod embedded in a barrel of resin, drew lightning and electricity from the sky.

When the profits from Oehler's magic show reached the equivalent of seven thousand American dollars, he staged a special séance for the governor of Mexico, and other high-ranking officials. More than forty distinguished guests attended. He led them through two dark rooms with a candle; only an occasional skeleton relieved the blackness. The fun began in a third chamber. Brilliant flares of intense light blazed momentarily in various parts of the room as the sounds of rain and thunder were heard overhead. Several candles were mysteriously snuffed out; then just as mysteriously they flamed up again. A ghostly apparition materialized in the smoke from a pan of burning coals. The ghost spoke—and vanished.

Oehler's guests left without a word. The next morning he was arrested for performing sorcery, taken to a subterranean dungeon, and locked in. Months went by. One evening a Spanish marquis dined with the Mexican governor, and heard about the imprisoned sorcerer. The Spaniard insisted the accused man was innocent, that he had used perfectly natural scientific principles for his demonstration. The dungeon door was unlocked. The ragged, heavily bearded magician was led up the steps, and out into blinding, bright sunshine.

Oehler went to his rooms, and learned that the innkeeper had gone to Peru with Oehler's money, clothes, and equipment. The apologetic governor offered the magician a thousand dollars, and said he would give him two thousand acres of land if he became a Mexican citizen. Oehler took the money, refused the land, and booked passage to New Orleans. There he bought new apparatus, then worked his way north through hostile Indian territory with a partner-assistant. In Trenton, Oehler's expenses exceeded his profits. He gave his conjuring paraphernalia to his co-worker, and early in September 1809, swore he would never perform again.

In the supplement to his autobiography, Oehler tells how he staged the séance that led to his incarceration. The brilliant flares of light that blazed in the darkness were produced when he touched the smoldering wick of his candle to powder-impregnated strings dangling

Mr. Bayly performed in Baltimore "without the use of Pockets, Bags or Sleeves" in December 1782.

A month later another magician, Jacob Henninger, took over the Bayly show, and added to it.

from the ceiling. Three pounds of shot shaken in a can with a ribbed lining simulated the sound of rain; cannonballs, rolled on the floor above, produced the thunder. The ghost was projected by a hidden magic lantern, then reflected by a slanting mirror on the rising smoke from the pan of coals. An assistant gave voice to the specter, speaking in a tube that extended through the wall. Blasts of air, fed through concealed pipes, extinguished the candles. Then, under the cover of darkness, those tapers were switched for others with bits of phosphorus in their wicks. Oehler heated the end of a sword in the burning coals and touched the hot tip to the phosphorus to light the candles. But, the magician believed, the trick that led the religious Mexicans to press charges against him, was the simple chemical feat of changing water into wine.

Oehler and his forerunners in the United States had been born abroad. The first American to establish himself as a successful conjurer in his own country was Richard Potter, son of Sir Charles Frankland, British tax collector for the port of Boston prior to the Revolution, and Dinah, one of Sir Charles's black slaves. Born in the Frankland town house in Boston in 1783, Potter grew up at his father's manor in Hopkinton, Massachusetts, and attended school there before signing on as a cabin boy to a Captain Skinner, one of Sir Charles's friends, and working his way to England. He traveled with a British circus, visited France, then joined John Rannie, the magician, and returned to Boston as his assistant.

Potter was twenty-eight when Rannie retired. The young man, who was slight in stature, with brown skin, dark hair, and a personable manner, appeared in November 1811 at the Columbian Museum in Boston. Some people thought he was a Hindu; others took him to be an American Indian. No matter, Potter's "upward of 100 Curious but Mysterious Experiments with Cards, Eggs, Money &c," and his ventriloquism and bird-call imitations were an immediate success. For more than twenty years his "Evening's Brush to Sweep away Care; or, a Medley to Please" drew crowds in the United States and eastern Canada. He traveled north as far as Quebec, as far south as Mobile, Alabama. Only in Mobile did color prejudice cause him discomfort. Despite this, he said he made forty-eight hundred dollars there during a twelve-day engagement.

Potter's magic included the cups and balls, "The Wonderful Sheet of Paper" (pleated and folded to form various designs), passing a chosen card into an egg "without breaking its yolk or losing its white," frying pancakes in a borrowed hat, and changing a woman's glove into a dove. A collection of objects, which couldn't possibly have fitted into it, were produced from "The Wonderful Factory"; a fascinating variety of refreshments came from "The Dutch House, or Obliging Landlady."

Occasionally Potter played the role of the "anti-combustible Man Salamander," extending his tongue, stroking it with a red-hot poker, then bending the rod into various shapes with his "bare feet." To finish this segment of his show, he heated a pot of lead, and boldly dipped his hands and feet into the molten metal.

Potter's more imaginative fans circulated wild stories about his prowess. They said he rode on stage in a fancy cart pulled by a pair of ganders. Some claimed to have seen him crawl through a solid log, or take a rooster from his pocket, hitch it to a wagon, and make it pull a load that would have strained a team of horses.

Many foreign magicians were working in the United States during Potter's time. The most successful were Day Francis, self-proclaimed "Emperor of all the Conjurors"; two troupes of "East Indian Jugglers"; Ramo Samee, an outstanding East Indian magician-juggler; Charles Mathews, a British specialist in vocal delusions; two Frenchmen—Mr. Brunel and Mr. Charles; and Robertson, the Belgian with his famous "Fantasmagoria." Some toured a few months, others a few years, but Potter continued to hold his own.

In Boston on March 25, 1808, Potter married Sally Harris, a talented, copper-complexioned girl from Roxbury, Massachusetts. His wife, who he said was a Penobscot Indian, sang in his show, presented a pantomimic specialty, "The Wonderful Little Giant," and sometimes danced with him in the finale.

Shortly after their marriage, Potter bought "about two hundred acres of nearly wild land in New Hampshire, and laid out a plan of improvement." He told a reporter many years later that he had hoped to give his family the advantages of country life, and to have property that would provide him with an income when he was too old to perform. "My purchases and improvements have cost me more than ten thousand dollars. . . . I found it necessary to build a house, and I thought I might as well have a genteel one, as a mean one."

Potter's home with its landscaped grounds was a showplace—a mansion among cabins. Each year when he returned from his seasonal tour, he observed that more settlers had moved nearby. Eventually, a bank was opened.

Potter's large tract of land was farmed, according to local historians. He bred horses and raised cattle and pigs. Visitors were impressed by his elegant furniture, his wife's stunning gowns, and the munificence of his meals. Some churchmen, however, were scandalized when he served wines and brandy; they made for the door when he began performing his tricks.

A favorite ventriloquial stunt was reserved for the dinner table. A roast suckling pig was placed before him. Potter sharpened his knife, and began to carve. As he cut the first slice, the pig let out a loud squeal; the pig continued to protest after each stroke of the blade, the squeals gradually becoming weaker.

As late as January 1833, Potter was playing in Roxbury, Massachusetts. He died in New Hampshire at the age of fifty-two on September 20, 1835; his wife, who was four years younger, died the following year. They were buried on his property. When a government post office was opened in the community in 1871, the village perpetuated the famous mystifier's name by postmarking the mail Potter Place. Motorists who drive along U.S. Route 4, from Concord to Connecticut Highway 11, can see the town where America's first successful native-born magician once lived. The gravestones, though moved a short distance from their original position, are still on the old Potter property.

The Potters had three children, two boys and a girl. Richard, Jr., was a magician, ventriloquist, dancer, and singer. For a few years he toured with a show patterned after his father's, using playbills with the same words. Later "Little Potter" worked as an act in variety theatres.

The elder Potter never played as far west as Missouri, nor did his competitors. Middle America's pioneer conjurer was Colonel Eugene Leitensdorfer, a soldier of fortune. Leitensdorfer was born as Gerrasio Probasie Santuri in a village near Brent in the Tyrol on October 21, 1772. At his parent's insistence, he studied theology for a time, but then left the seminary to work as a surveyor. Soon after Emperor Joseph II declared war on Turkey, he joined the army and marched on Belgrade. As hot tempered behind the lines as in battle, he killed a fellow soldier in a duel, then deserted to avoid being hanged.

Using the alias Carlos Hassanda, he enlisted in the French army; suspected of being a spy, he was jailed. He managed to poison his guards, and to escape to Switzerland, where he took the name Leitensdorfer. Letters to his family brought him enough money to buy a supply of watches and cheap jewelry. With a pack on his back, he peddled his way through Spain and France, finally booking a passage to Egypt from Toulon.

Leitensdorfer was hired by the French in Cairo for "agricultural and economical" projects. When the British army invaded Egypt, he made friends with several officers. With their help he opened a coffeehouse, earned enough money to buy a home and to start a theatre where military men presented shows during off-duty hours.

Life by the Nile appealed to Leitensdorfer. He married a Coptic woman and began to raise a family, yet when the British officers who had befriended him left Cairo, he abandoned his wife and his property and went with them.

Overcome with remorse in Messina, Sicily, he entered a Capuchin monastery under the name Padre Anselmo. The penitent mood passed. He ran off to Smyrna, and from there traveled to Constantinople, where he went hungry for three days. Somewhere during his roaming, he had learned several feats of conjuring. A Capuchin friar staked him to a pack of cards and a pistol so that he could earn a living as a magician. Then he turned religious again, became a dervish, and, as Murat Aga, traveled to the edge of the Black Sea. Eventually he returned to Cairo, and by mutual agreement formally separated from his wife.

In 1805 Leitensdorfer became an adjutant to William Eaton, former American officer and consul at Tunis, who had received orders from the United States to raise an army to restore the exiled Pasha Hamet to his throne in Tripoli. When peace returned to the Barbary coast, Leitensdorfer became restless again. He sailed as a seaman on a vessel bound for the United States, arriving in December 1809.

His old commanding officer, William Eaton, persuaded the American Congress to pass a bill giving Leitensdorfer a grant of 320 acres west of the Mississippi and captain's pay for the time he had served in North Africa. So it was that Eugene Leitensdorfer came to Missouri. He married a girl "of a fine European family" and settled twelve miles west of St. Louis. Murders by raiding Indians in the vicinity made his wife "timid"; they moved to suburban Carondelet near her parents.

When his money ran out, Leitensdorfer worked as an assistant storekeeper, cabinetmaker, watercolor painter, and vine cultivator. After his grape crop failed, he turned to magic as he had years earlier in Europe when out of funds. His advertisement in the January 15, 1814, *Missouri Gazette* announced he would present his "spectacle of Recreative Sports of Mathematics and Phisicks" the following Saturday, weather permitting, at the house of Joseph Robidoux.

The program of the first magic show in St. Louis featured "The Magic Picture," "Moses' Rod," "Dancing Eggs," and "The Egyptian Prophet, Habdala Rakmany," a figure three feet tall that predicted the cards selected from a pack. Leitensdorfer's most unusual mystery was "The Enchanted Pistol." After a corner was ripped from a chosen card, the magician's hands were bound behind his back, and the card was burned. The ashes were loaded in a pistol and fired at him. At the sound of the shot the card appeared, restored, on his chest. The corner, kept by a spectator, was fitted to the torn card for identification. Finally, Leitensdorfer tossed a burning coal that was balanced on top of his shoe into his mouth, and ate it "as young gentlemen and ladies would sugar plums."

The following October 22, the *Gazette* devoted almost three columns to the magician's background. Most of the material, Leitens-

The Potter show in the early
1800's offered many novelties.

Sometimes he featured a "Man
Salamander" routine.

Woodcut used by Richard Potter,
first American-born conjurer to
achieve success in his own land.

dorfer said, had appeared earlier in a publication called *Portfolio,* but that writer made him more ferocious and versatile than he was. In December, financial misfortunes again drove Leitensdorfer back to the stage. He opened on Christmas Eve, and appeared Saturdays thereafter with "New Wonders." He cut a handkerchief into bits and restored it. He beheaded a chick, then put it back together again. He demonstrated a test for diluted spirits. A knife was put into a glass of whiskey. If the whiskey was watered, the knife moved but slightly; if full strength, the knife leapt high in the air.

Leitensdorfer, who had planned to write his memoirs, died at the age of seventy-two at his home in Carondelet on March 11, 1849, before completing the autobiography.

Leitensdorfer's performances in Missouri met with no opposition from churchmen or pious citizens, but as late as 1834 the anonymous author of *Ventriloquism Explained: and Jugglers' Tricks or Legerdemain Exposed,* published in Amherst, Massachusetts, echoed the sentiments of the early New England Puritans: "His hope and prayer [was] that these pages may exert some feeble influence, in compelling wandering jugglers to live by honest labor, rather than by infamous deception." Despite his opposition to "penny-seeking idlers who impose on the public," it is clear that the writer had attended conjuring shows, read every book he could find on the subject, and practiced ventriloquism himself.

The mood of the times was more accurately reflected in *The Humorous Magician Unmasked,* which A. B. Engstrom, an art teacher, wrote two years later in Philadelphia. He said the tricks he described would enable his readers to provide "innocent amusement" at "social parties." The volume, he promised, "would not be out of place in a lady's parlor among the interesting objects on her center table."

Once generally regarded as "worthless idlers" or dangerous sorcerers, magicians could by then live and work wherever they chose in the United States. In rural areas sleight-of-hand men still entertained at inns, but in the larger cities Richard Potter and his contemporaries opened the way for conjurers with big shows to play in the same theatres and halls as touring Shakespearean troupes and opera companies.

*Magic in
the Colonies*

5
American Indian
Conjuring

THOUGH American Indians for centuries had matched and often surpassed the far more widely known fakirs of Calcutta and Bombay, few stories about their skill appeared in either the national or the international press, and this for a very sound reason: The Asian conjurers, lauded by travelers, performed in public for the money they could collect from their roadside shows. The American Indians' magic was reserved for their tribe; few white men had an opportunity to study it. If a rare outsider tumbled on to a secret, he was swiftly inducted as blood brother and sworn to secrecy.

The Navaho, like their counterparts in India, made snakes appear under inverted baskets. Pawnee, Hopi, and Zuñi performers made corn and beanstalks grow—mango trees were not available—during harvest rites. The feat in which a Hindu conjurer's assistant vanished and reappeared in a large basket was also done by the Apaches. Swords were jabbed through the sides to prove that no one was inside in Asia; the Apaches had a more effective argument; they shot arrows through the fibers.

American conjurers were at their best in the open air under the night sky. When tom-toms beat and campfires cast flickering shadows, their strange feats were as awe-inspiring to fellow tribesmen as the occasional flashes of lightning that streaked across the sky.

The earliest-known reference to magic in the Americas appeared in the chronicles Bernal Díaz del Castillo sent to Spain describing Hernando Cortez's gold-seeking expedition to Honduras in October 1524. Cortez was traveling southeast after conquering Mexico. Diáz mentioned that the Indians the Spanish explorers met along the way were familiar with *"jugaba de manos"*—sleight of hand. Cortez's retinue included a European conjurer, but Diáz did not record his name.

A generation later, Fray Bernardino de Sahagún, in his *Historia de las cosas de la Nueva España* (History of the Affairs of the New Spain) published in Mexico in 1600, but written at least ten years earlier, described a trick he had seen a medicine man perform while seated on the ground in the Tianquiztli marketplace. As a tiny figure in the Indian's hand rose and danced, the other Toltecs left their fruits and vegetables to cluster around him. The performer, who said his name was Tlacavepan, challenged: "What manner of trick is this? Ha, why do you not understand it?" No one, including the Spanish missionary, offered a solution.

Much of what we know about the magic practiced by the first Americans comes from missionaries who worked among the Indians in the years when the New World was being colonized by Europeans. French priests reported from Canada in 1613 that the medicine men of the Algonquin tribes were the most formidable opponents they faced in trying to convert the Indians. Twenty years later Gabriel Sagard-Theodat, a Recollect missionary, weary of the daily conflict with people whose customs he did not understand, called the Nipissing redmen "a nation of sorcerers."

Shamans of the tribes who lived along the St. Lawrence River boasted they could summon the rains or stop storms. They claimed their rites could render fields barren or produce bountiful crops. Louis Hennepin, a Franciscan friar, whose book on his trials and tribulations in North America was published in London in 1689, said: "It is impossible to imagine the horrible Howlings and strange Contortions that these Jugglers make of their bodies, when they are deposing themselves to Conjure, or raise their enchantments."

A 1723 French account of Indian life was more informative. The medicine men of the Canadian tribes performed "a thousand tricks of magic," among them a feat which made it appear that they could cure wounds: "With an arrow they pretend to stab the naked body of a man. To show the blood flowing, they lay on the supposed wound, very adroitly, the juice of a red beet. The arrow has its stem so made that when it strikes the body, instead of entering it, it slides within itself."

Algonquin wonder-workers claimed that they were invulnerable to the white man's bullets. The demonstration was breathtaking, but impractical in battle: "The ball is made of earth, rubbed over

70

American
Indian
Conjuring

with lead, which they break in pieces in the barrel of the piece as it is driven down [with a ramrod]."

A century and a half later, a variation of this thrilling feat was witnessed by a representative of the United States Bureau of Ethnology who attended a Ponca ceremony. As the scene was described in the report to Washington, Cramped Hand danced in a circle, flourishing a pistol. He loaded the weapon and passed it to Chief Antoine Primeau. The chief aimed at the conjurer's mouth and fired. Cramped Hand fell in a heap. His partner, Bent Horn, ran to his side, massaged his body. Soon Cramped Hand revived. He moaned, grimaced, and groaned as he crawled to a metal basin. Once there, with a tremendous effort, he spat out the lead, which landed with a thud.

Now Bent Horn danced, displaying a stone as big as a man's fist. Cramped Hand stood, tall and erect, fifteen feet away. With a sudden sweep of his arm, he hurled the missile at his partner's face. Bent Horn's head snapped back; he sagged to the ground. He gave a magnificent portrayal of a man in agony. He shrieked, saliva dribbled from his mouth, and he twitched. Cramped Hand brought him the basin. Bent Horn coughed; four smaller stones issued from between his lips and pinged in the pan.

While these feats were presented in the open, impressive examples of Indian skill at escapology took place in tents. One of the first sources is a book by Jonathan Carver, who studied the customs of the Crees in Canada from 1766 to 1768. Carver sat with members of the tribe on animal skins in a large lodge as a medicine man, stripped to his loincloth, stretched out full length on an elk hide, and folded it around his body so that only his head extended. Two assistants wound the Indian with forty yards of leather thongs and knotted the ends. He was lifted and deposited in the center of a fenced-in area, a topless cage made of stakes firmly driven in the earth. The Indian seemed to enter a trance, unintelligible words poured from his mouth in a mixture of various Indian tongues and gibberish. His voice grew louder as time passed. At one moment he was raving, the next he seemed to be praying. Eventually he "foamed at the mouth." After forty-five minutes had elapsed, the sounds ceased. Carver thought the Cree was exhausted. To Carver's complete surprise, the man sprang to his feet, free of his bonds.

Duncan Cameron, a nineteenth-century trader, who had heard that Canadian medicine men were masters at feats of escape, bet he could tie an Indian, who claimed he had the power to free himself from bonds of any sort, so securely that he would beg to be released. The challenge was accepted. The man was rolled in a net, then bound and placed alone in a tent. After he finished the trussing, Cameron waited patiently outside. "In sixteen minutes he began to shake his

71

American Indian Conjuring

Menomini medicine men in Wisconsin danced as
one produced two snakes from a red flannel bag.
A few moments later the snakes disappeared.

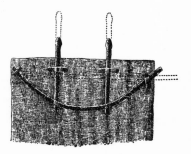

Construction of the special
bag used in the snake trick.

Ojibwa magic—objects move
mysteriously on command.

A tusk balanced on a mirror
adhered when the mirror was
turned toward the ground.
A secret daub of wax held
the tusk in place.

rattle, which made me think his hands were free, and six minutes after, he threw out the net and desired me to examine it and say whether it was cut; finding the net all right I paid the wager," Cameron said.

Paul Beaulieu, an interpreter for the Ojibwa at White Earth Agency, Minnesota, was also skeptical of the tales of Indian escape artists. In the 1850's he offered a hundred dollars to a medicine man at Leech Lake, Minnesota, for a successful demonstration. The Indian, clad in a breechcloth, was tied; a committee of twelve men, which included an Episcopal minister, observed the procedure. The shaman's ankles, wrists, and hands were bound; his tied hands were forced down so that his knees extended up above them. A heavy pole was thrust over his arms and under his knees; then his neck was tied to the knees. At the medicine man's request, a black stone amulet was placed on his thighs. He was carried into his tent. This structure was built on poles, interlaced with twigs, and covered with strips of birch and canvas.

The flap had scarcely been closed when strange words and thumping sounds came from within. The tent swayed violently as the sounds increased in volume. When the disturbance ceased, the Indian shouted that the rope could now be found in a nearby house. Cautioning the committee to keep a sharp watch on the tent, Beaulieu sprinted to the house. The rope was there, still knotted. He hurried back, let the other men examine the knots, then called to ask if he could enter the tent. Permission was granted. He found the Indian seated comfortably, puffing on a pipe. The committee—now eleven men, the clergyman having fled, crying that this was the work of the devil—agreed unanimously that the hundred dollars should be paid at once.

A contemporary eyewitness, Prince zu Weid, Alexander Philip Maximillian, who traveled in the American West about 1840, told of the curious feats performed by Mandan and Hidatsa conjurers:

> The medicine of one man consists in making a snowball, which he rolls a long time between his hands, so that at length it becomes hard and is changed into a white stone, which when struck emits sparks. Many persons, even whites, pretend that they have seen this and cannot be convinced to the contrary. The same man pretends that during a dance he plucked white feathers from a certain small bird, which he rolled between his hands, and formed of them in a short time a similar white stone.

American stage magicians of that era used sleight of hand to change the color of balls or cards. How much more effective to conjure with feathers and snow!

Escapology was one of their greatest accomplishments, but Indian conjurers also excelled at making images come to life, decapitating real people, and transporting themselves mysteriously from one place to another.

Ojibwa performers caused stopper-like heads of wooden images, buried to the hips in the ground, to bob up and down. For variety they commanded strands of beads far from their reach to twist and roll. The motivating force in both cases was a long strand of hair. An unsuspected assistant jiggled the string, or the medicine man sat on the ground with his blanket-covered legs extended and yanked the string with his big toe.

Even now, big city strollers are fascinated when they see a paper doll hopping on the sidewalk while a pitchman hawks envelopes containing the folded figure and the secret. They are modern counterparts of Tlacavepan, who dazzled the Spanish missionaries with his dancing doll in the sixteenth century. Sometimes smaller straw or wooden dolls dance on a street performer's palm. A bent wire in the base of the doll is hooked through the calloused skin near the base of the manipulator's second and third fingers. With the hand slightly cupped, the doll lies flat; stiffening and relaxing the fingers causes the doll to rise and "dance."

Legends say that the early medicine men could bring miniature images of buffalo and of warriors on horseback to life. They worked by the flickering light of a fire at the far side of the tent with observers grouped in a semicircle. At the command of the magician, the clay figures were supposed to have changed to flesh and blood. Then the miniature Indians corralled the buffalo and hurled their spears and shot their arrows with deadly accuracy until the last animal fell with an arrow through its heart. When the drama ended, the figures reverted to clay and were tossed into the fire.

Seldom has a puppet show received such praise. Whoever started the story must have imbibed too freely before attending the performance.

More reliable testimony came from Lewis Cass, who was Governor of Michigan Territory from 1813 to 1830. During those years he took a five-thousand-mile canoe trip and saw a woman conjurer perform at an Ottawa tribal ceremony. The spectators were seated in a circle around the magician. She began in low-key fashion, just shaking her snakeskin medicine bag. When Cass said there didn't seem to be much happening, the elderly squaw threw her bag in his direction. Upon hitting the ground some distance away from him, the bag changed into a serpent.

The reptile slithered his way; Cass quickly got up and moved out of the circle. Standing at a safe distance, he watched the woman pick up the snake and change it back into a bag. Another observer who had seen a similar trick surmised that a small animal hidden inside the bag produced the snakelike movement.

Trickery with snakes was also witnessed by Dr. Walter James

Hoffman, of the United States Bureau of Ethnology, at Keshena, Wisconsin, in 1890. One of two dancing conjurers moved backward, facing his partner, while gesturing toward a red flannel bag that the other medicine man kneaded and pummeled between his hands. The second man, after he was sure the onlookers were convinced the bag was empty, held it by the upper ends. The gesticulations of the first Indian became more pronounced as he repeatedly pointed to the bag. Slowly, almost in time with the accompanying tom-toms, the heads of two snakes reared up from the bag, then dropped out of sight. Once more they rose, even higher this time. Again they returned to the bag, which was folded and put away, ending the dance.

At one point during the dance the bag had been held with the strong rays of the afternoon sun behind it. The resulting shadows gave Hoffman enough clues to solve the mystery. The snakes, he said, were eight-inch-long sticks made of stuffed snakeskins and weighted at their lower ends. Loops inside the bag held them in place. A piece of tape, sewn to one inside corner of the bag, ran down through slots in the lower sections of the snakeskin sticks, then up to the far corner. As the free end was pulled by the dancer, who held the bag between his hands, the snakeskin sticks were raised until their tops extended a few inches above the upper edge of the bag. When the pull was relaxed, the weights made the "snakes" drop out of sight.

Medicine men who staged a spectacular decapitation took no chances of an accidental gleam of sunshine revealing their trickery. The ceremony was staged at night by the light of a campfire. The conjurers of the Kwakiutl tribe on Vancouver Island placed their victim face-down flat on the ground. When the executioner slowly raised his knife for the cutting stroke, assistants scurried forward to kneel and shield the horrible sight from sensitive eyes. Down flashed the blade. The men moved aside; the head was several inches from the body. It was lifted by the swordsman and held high to be seen by all who dared to look. After the head was put on the ground close to the neck, the assistants converged again and joined in the chant that would make the victim whole.

How was it done? Trapdoors are suspected on the stage but not in the earth—and thus are all the more effective in the open air. A realistic carved head with human hair was concealed in a hole under a trapdoor camouflaged to blend with the terrain. During the ceremony when the assistants knelt shoulder to shoulder before the knife came down, their eyes followed the raising of the blade, but their hands were busy opening the trapdoor, taking out the false head, putting the living head in the hole and closing the door to hide it. A cutout section folded back so the trap would fit around the victim's neck. Later, the human screen concealed the reverse procedure that brought about the restoration.

Another after-dark mystery performed by a Menomini medicine man at White Earth, Minnesota, was still being discussed in 1892, years after it had been seen. Two tepees had been built, fifty paces apart. The conjurer entered one; the other was empty. Rings of brushwood surrounding each wigwam, but a safe distance from them, were ignited. When the fires were raging, a shout came from the conjurer. He said he had transported himself to the empty tepee. To prove it, he crawled through its flap and stood up.

Some people, even today, believe a human being can send his body through space by the power of concentration alone. In this instance, skeptics who glanced in the first wigwam, suspecting that the Indian was still there and that a man similar in appearance had appeared in the second, were disappointed.

No explanation was offered for the astonishing feat. There is, however, a way it could have been performed, a method so obvious that most people would overlook it: a secret tunnel with cleverly concealed trapdoors at each end.

Think back to the Indian escape artist whose ropes vanished and appeared in a nearby house. A tunnel could have been used there too. An assistant concealed in a passage under the tent could have untied the medicine man, squirmed through the tunnel with the ropes, then dashed to the house where the conjurer had decided they should be found.

Far more advance preparation was required for a burning-alive illusion staged in northwest Canada. A young Indian girl was nailed inside a large wooden box that was burned in the center of a spacious medicine hut. As the smell of burning flesh permeated the structure, she could be heard singing. Eventually box and girl were consumed, only bones remaining among the ashes of the fire.

The keys to this mystery, said Dr. Franz Boas, the Columbia University anthropologist who saw it performed, were a secret tunnel, a long speaking tube, and a dead seal. The girl slipped through a panel that could be lifted in the bottom of the box, crawled through the tunnel to the outside of the lodge, and began her song, which filtered back inside via the tube. Meanwhile, a helper pushed the carcass of a seal through the tunnel and into the box. The charred bones, of course, were those of the seal.

Complicated advance arrangements and trained assistants were not needed for the oldest and most frequently performed American Indian mystery—the Shaking Tent. Gabriel Sagard-Theodat, the Recollect missionary, mentioned it in his 1623 report from Canada to his superiors in France. He told of the Nipissing medicine men "who profess to converse with the devil in little round towers isolated and apart in the woods or in the midst of their lodges." Sometimes the conjurers were bound before they were placed in their enclosures.

Artist's concept
of a street show
in India.

"The Basket Trick,"
presented by Abdul
in Thurston's show.

Chinese magicians sometimes carried their small props in a bag
tied around their necks, rather than around their waists.

Tied or not, they caused the "towers" (barrel-shaped tents with smaller tops than bottoms) to vibrate soon after the flaps were dropped. Some shamans, it was claimed, were so powerful that their beads, shirts, and moccasins alone were enough to agitate a structure. One man was credited with shaking four tents at once. There is a legend that a mighty conjurer was tied to one end of the forty-foot pole that was to be the principal support of a new tent. Then a pair of wings from a newly killed eagle was lashed to his shoulders. While his fellow shamans braced the other end of the pole, he commanded the eagle wings to flap and raised the pole until it was upright.

When a tent began to shake, weird voices—allegedly those of animal spirits—came from behind the birchbark or canvas. Turtles and beavers were particularly good conversationalists. The sly, personal jibes of the turtles caused the seated tribesmen to howl with laughter. If valuable objects were lost, the voices of animals told where they could be found; advice was also given to the ill, and to hunters who wished to know where wild game was plentiful. Many shamans produced the voice of only one animal; others boasted a wider repertoire. The more animals a conjurer had at his command, the more he was honored.

A stained-glass window in the Presbyterian church on Mackinac Island, Michigan, honors Was-chus-co, who was a renowned Shaking Tent conjurer until he became a Christian in 1830. William H. Johnson contributed an interesting feature story to the Detroit *Daily Tribune*, telling of the interview he had with the shaman before his death in 1840.

Was-chus-co said he prepared himself by fasting ten days before he entered what his tribe called a Ches-a-kee tent. This tent was quite different from those in which the Indians lived. Flexible poles, eight feet or so in length, were forced two feet into the ground at an angle, then they were bent inward at the top. Hoops of sturdy branches were tied at the top, in the middle, and at intervals in between. The framework was covered with birchbark, skins, blankets, or canvas. Tradition specified that the tents should never be built before sundown. (Some descriptions say that all the poles were stripped, except for one that had a cluster of green leaves at the end. These leaves vibrated as the lodge shook. The Ojibwas in Manitoba fastened rattles to the top of their conjuring structures for extra sound effects.)

Fasting, Was-chus-co explained, sharpened his senses and developed his mental powers. As a young man he was often tied before his sessions, *but* the ropes would fall off once he was in the enclosure. "Frequently I have seen a bright light at the opening at the top of the lodge, and strange faces were visible to me," Was-chus-co told the interviewer. The words could be heard by those outside, but were not understandable until he translated them.

Johnson asked what shook the tent. Was-chus-co answered: "I possessed a power which I cannot explain or describe to you. I never attempted to move the lodge. I held communication with supernatural beings, or thinking minds or spirits, which acted on my mind, or soul."

As it happens, the enclosures used by the tent-shakers were not actually as rigid as they seemed. Dr. A. Irving Hallowell emphasized in *The Role of Conjuring in Saulteaux Society* that "Bering River conjuring lodges built in this fashion were extremely easy to set in motion. They responded to the slightest pressure . . . as I can testify." Like Was-chus-co, other medicine men insisted they did nothing physically themselves to shake the tents. They believed the spirits entered their bodies and were in control when their hands gripped the poles and agitated the structures.

Other American Indian conjurers are supposed to have specialized in teleportation. One is reputed to have materialized fresh blueberries in his lodge in the midst of winter when snow covered the ground. Another is said to have whisked a heap of skins to a trader sixty miles away in exchange for several cases of whiskey, which appeared in the tent where the hides had been shortly before. A beneficent shaman, on one of the Parry Islands in Canada, reportedly conjured four marten skins a hundred miles away to a store, when food was scarce, and produced fifty pounds of flour for his tribe.

The American Indian conjurers, who reputedly transported objects great distances, were never willing to travel themselves and exhibit this feat for theatre audiences. However, the proprietors of medicine shows, who sold tribal cure-alls to small-town audiences in the late nineteenth century, always claimed that the man in the war bonnet who displayed the bottles was a celebrated Indian medicine man, Shungopavi, an Indian who, billed as a Moki medicine man, performed magic at the Cliff Dwellers' exhibit at the Louisiana Purchase Exposition in St. Louis, Missouri, in 1904 and later played in vaudeville. He wore beaded buckskins, moccasins, and a feathered headdress, but the tricks he performed were not of Indian origin. A bottle and a glass changed places when covered by two tubes; a silk handkerchief vanished, only to reappear tied between two others. He waved an eagle-feather fan instead of a wand when he pronounced his magic words.

Occasionally one still hears of a traditional feat being shown at an Indian tribal ritual in the Southwest or a Shaking Tent in northern Michigan or Canada, but the day of a snakeskin bag turning into a live reptile or one medicine man shaking three tents simultaneously has long past.

6
Professor Pinetti

Giovanni Giuseppe Pinetti, the leading magician of the late eighteenth century, conjured in the finest theatres of Europe, while sleight-of-hand men, who were more skillful with their fingers, manipulated cork balls, cups, and cards for throw money on the streets outside. The "Roman Professor of Mathematics and Natural Philosophy" claimed his stage marvels were based on strange scientific principles discovered in his laboratory; actually they were elegantly staged versions of earlier feats.

Half a century before the brilliant Italian showman amazed audiences by sprinkling a mysterious liquid on an orange tree to make it produce fruit in midwinter, Isaac Fawkes had featured a similar apple tree in London. Pinetti's bell-ringing "Grand Sultan" was a better-dressed descendant of Balducci's "Blackmoor." Pinetti's golden head that danced and struck the sides of a crystal goblet to answer questions was an elaboration of the fortune-telling finger ring that jigged in a common drinking glass for "The Famous North Holland Peasant," who exhibited at the St.-Germain Fair in Paris three years before Pinetti was born. (This versatile Dutch performer who wore a short-brimmed potlike hat, a handkerchief tied in a knot at the collar of his blouse, and baggy knee pants, drew large crowds in Western Europe; at least six of his tricks were included in Pinetti's repertoire.)

Pinetti's immediate predecessors were proud of their digital dexterity. Mr. Lane, a British magician who baffled spectators even before they saw him by advertising such feats as "His Enchanted Sciatorium" and "Operation Palingenesia"; Philip Jonas, a German who was especially adept with cards; and Highman Palatine, who conjured "à-la-mode Italiano," challenged competitors to surpass their skill. M. Boulevard, a Frenchman, accepted Palatine's dare. They met for a battle royal of magic at Bush Tavern in Bristol, England. Palatine was defeated; the victor gave his prize—the night's receipts—to the local marine society.

Another great magical event of the pre-Pinetti era was heralded by posters that appeared in London in 1749, announcing the marvelous feats to be performed by a magician whose name was not given:

> He takes a common Walking Cane from any of the Spectators, and thereon plays the Musick of every Instrument now in use. . . . He presents you with a Common Wine Bottle, which any of the Spectators may first examine; this bottle is placed on a Table in the middle of the Stage, and he (without any equivocation) goes into it, in the Sight of all the Spectators, and sings in it; during his stay in the Bottle any person may handle it, and see plainly that it does not exceed a common Tavern Bottle.

After the regular performance, anyone who paid an additional fee could see a "Representation of any deceased Person, such as Husband or Wife, or Sister or Brother, or any intimate Friend of either Sex." Then they would be told intimate secrets about their past, and the culprits who had wronged them would be named.

By six thirty on January 16, 1749, the theatre in the Haymarket was jammed with people eager to see a man insert himself into a bottle, to talk with dead loved ones, and to learn the names of their enemies. As time dragged by, the crowd became impatient. They stamped on the floor, beat tattoos with their canes, hooted and shouted. It was after seven when a man appeared on the stage and pleaded with the spectators to be patient. If the performer didn't arrive, everyone would get his money back. This announcement was greeted with a shout from someone who said he would give double what he paid to get in, if the conjurer would squeeze himself into a pint bottle instead of a quart one.

The commotion mounted. A burning candle was thrown from a box to the stage; the flame ignited the curtain. As the fire spread, people pushed and shoved their way to the exits. Men still in the theatre smashed seats, yanked down scenery, and passed the debris out to the street where a bonfire was lighted. No magician ever appeared.

The perpetrator of this hoax was never exposed, though Samuel Foote, an actor-writer, and the prankish John Montagu,

Earl of Sandwich, were suspected. "The Bottle Conjurer" became the topic of the day. Other ridiculous ads were printed; broadsides and cartoons satirizing the non-event were sold; and the subject provided hilarious scenes for contemporary theatrical productions.

Pinetti, by his own account, was born in 1750, the year after the Haymarket incident, in Orbitello, Tuscany. While he was a professor in Rome, before he became a showman, his pupils were so complimentary about his unusual classroom demonstrations of physics that he repeated the experiments for his friends and was encouraged to exhibit publicly. The professor knew there was money to be made with an entertainment that was both novel and mystifying. For example, Comus (Nicholas Philippe Ledru), the French conjurer, had gone to London in December 1765 to play a few weeks in a room on Panton Street. Five months later the *Gentleman's Magazine* reported that Comus "with his dexterity acquired no less than £5,000, most of which he will carry off with him." Later he returned to England for other profitable seasons before opening his own theatre on the Rue du Temple in Paris; Comus also appeared several times for King Louis XVI and performed in Austria for Emperor Francis II.

By the early 1780's Pinetti was playing in Germany, billed as "Joseph Pinetti, Roman Professor of Mathematics." His featured mystery was "Theophrastus Paracelsus," a feat that "The Famous North Holland Peasant" had shown earlier under a less imposing name. A pigeon was suspended from a small scaffold by a ribbon that was tied around its neck. The magician slashed with his knife across the shadow cast by the bird. At that instant the pigeon was decapitated.

While Pinetti was performing in Germany, Gustavus Katterfelto, a Prussian, was presenting a curious program in London from 10 A.M. to 5 P.M. "in a very warm room" at No. 24 Piccadilly. Using a large screen projection with his "Solar Microscope," he showed more than "500 insects" in a single drop of water, a pinhead in size. Later magnified organisms in water, milk, vinegar, wine, and beer moved around on the screen to astound his patrons.

At 7 P.M., Katterfelto lectured on natural philosophy and entertained by performing tricks with dice, cards, money, boxes, medals, and glasses. Part scientist, he made and sold the first phosphorus matches. Part charlatan, he advertised "Occult Secrets" to draw large crowds to the theatre. The Archbishop of Canterbury came to hear his "moral and divine" lecture; Samuel Johnson and other literary lights were among his fans. The poet William Cowper mentioned Katterfelto in "The Task":

with his hair on end at his own wonders,
Wondering for his bread.

Pinetti as he appeared in 1796
while touring in Germany.

Portrait of the great Italian
magician from the third
French edition of his book.

Pinetti's principal adversary, Henri
Decremps, attempted to explain all of
his tricks in 1784.

When a flu epidemic swept the city, Katterfelto treated the ill who came to him for help. Doctors and pharmacists sent letters to the newspapers calling the magician a mountebank for practicing medicine; he answered that he had turned down vast sums from various men who wanted him to turn loose his "dangerous insects" on the public, so they could profit on the money to be made from rampant illnesses.

Katterfelto kept himself in the news by hinting that his cat had supernatural powers, "appearing at one instant with a tail, and the next without any." Then he proclaimed "the celebrated Black Cat, which has nine times more excellent qualities than any other nine cats among those nine-lived animals, was safely delivered of NINE kittens."

Katterfelto wore an academic robe and a square black hat for his performance; Pinetti dressed in court costume, with silk stockings, silver-buckled shoes, close-fitting satin kneebreeches, brocaded coat, and a powdered wig. He had received a German knighthood, the Order of Merit of St. Philip, a pension from the Prussian court, and honors from the Royal Academy of Sciences and Belles Lettres in Bordeaux before his first appearance at the Théâtre des Menus-Plaisirs du Roi in Paris on the Rue Bergère in December 1783.

Pinetti's stage setting was magnificent though simple: silk curtains, gilded tables, and two crystal chandeliers. Short and pudgy, he carried himself as if he, not Louis XVI, was the reigning monarch. His bright eyes, expressive features, and bold gestures gave evidence of a strength of character that his overly polite manner could not dispel.

Augier, Fornet, Esprit, Mignot, and an Italian, Octave Giriodi, the most adept Parisian cup-and-ball manipulators, transported their cups, cork balls, and other equipment in bags tied around their waists and carried folding tables under their arms. It was a far cry from their brass and tin gadgets to Pinetti's gleaming gold and silver apparatus.

Critics wrote that a large and distinguished audience attended Pinetti's opening night. Outstanding among his many "inventions" was the gold head that became animated though shut inside a crystal goblet with a silver lid; the "Philosophical Bouquet" that was covered with a glass dome yet produced oranges when a mysterious fluid was applied; the selected cards that jumped from a silver box fastened to the top of a transparent bottle; "The Grand Sultan" automaton; and the severing of a pigeon's head "by electricity." Pinetti knew only a few words of French, but he had no difficulty bewildering and pleasing his audience.

The King commanded a private showing and complimented Pinetti on his scientific achievements. The twenty-three tricks featured nightly in his program became the talk of Paris; seats were booked weeks in advance. Then in early March 1784, a new book entitled "*La Magic Blanche Dévoilée* (Natural Magic Disclosed) became a best seller. In it the author, Henri Decremps, a lawyer and student of physics, music, and conjuring, attempted to lay bare the secrets of the Italian, who, he said, deliberately led the public to believe he had knowledge and skills he did not possess. Though this foreign entertainer had not yet claimed to predict the future, Decremps implied that any day he might. Pinetti's name was not mentioned in the text; the engraved frontispiece showed a slenderer performer on an obvious copy of Pinetti's handsome stage set.

Had Pinetti professed occult powers, had he swindled the rich or robbed the poor, Decremps' book would have been justified, but in actuality the magician's only offense was to claim greater knowledge and more originality than he possessed.

Decremps charged that "The Grand Sultan" was an old trick. Three pistons in the table on which the ornately dressed figure stood were controlled by offstage wires, operated by an assistant. One made the figure move its head from side to side to signify no. The second caused it to nod yes. The third pulled the arm holding a hammer, making it strike the bell. The conjurer cued his assistant with his remarks—either by words, syllables, or vowels; Decremps was not sure which.

A warbling imitation bird, which perched on the top of a bottle, blew out a candle, then made it light again, was not the marvelous piece of mechanism it appeared to be, Decremps wrote. When the bird's beak opened and closed, the sound came from behind the curtain, where a man stood near two amplifying horns; he had an onion skin in his mouth, like Rossignol, a great bird imitator of the time. Two trumpets were required; Pinetti moved the display table from one place to another during his presentation. When the magician held the bird in his hand, one of his fingers pulled a lever that closed a tiny bellows in the bird's body: the puff of air from the bellows extinguished the candle's flame. The charred wick ignited again as phosphorus in the bird's beak touched it.

The exposé continued: When the magician lowered a little bucket into a well, into which a quantity of mixed, colored seeds had been poured, he could bring up the bucket filled with whatever color he wanted because there were "four valves similiar to the keys of a German flute" near the bottom, hidden by the tapering sides of the well. Pressure on the proper lever, Decremps explained, released the requested color.

Threads, Decremps said, made the gold head enclosed in the crystal glass dance, cards leap from the pack, penknives jump from a silver goblet, eggs hop from one hat to another. A thread also pulled a concealed blade in the ribbon to cut the pigeon's throat.

Decremps offered solutions for every trick in Pinetti's reper-

Two cherubs pay homage to Pinetti in the frontispiece to the first edition of his book, published in Paris in 1784.

A third cherub crowns him with a laurel wreath in the British edition, published in London several months later.

toire. Even if they were not correctly explained—and several were not —the damage was done. Attendance at the theatre began to drop. Why pay to see a show when all the mysteries have been explained? Gone was the suspense and the fun of trying to figure out what was going on for oneself.

Pinetti reportedly fought back by hiring a tramp in shabby clothes to pose as Decremps. The magician told his audience that the book they had been hearing about had been written by a jealous would-be showman, who was not intelligent enough to appreciate the merits of an artistic performance. At that point the disreputable character stood up, identified himself as the author, and vilified the performer. Pinetti calmly accepted the abuse, and gave the "author" a few coins before he was thrown out of the theatre. The story is hard to believe. Pinetti was not the sort to parade his skill, and normally he went to great lengths to avoid confrontations with other conjurers.

What Pinetti did was more subtle. He published his own book of *Amusemens Physiques* (Physical Amusements) in June. He wrote the work not as a manual of conjuring, but as "a few easy means of amusing a company." He included thanks to the French King for his patronage. Without mentioning Decremps or his book, Pinetti corrected some of the mistakes the other had made.

Decremps had written that a coin fastened to a thread was the secret of the jumping penknife trick. He said that the magician put three penknives into the goblet with the chosen one resting on the coin, that a thread ran up to the ceiling of the stage and off to an assistant. A yank on the string, Decremps claimed, would send the knife out of the glass. This was not true. A strong tug would cause the knife to slip off the coin. If by some miracle the knife stayed in place, the coin would leave the glass with the knife.

Pinetti revealed the simple but practical device he had used— an inch-wide strip of flexible metal bent to form a rectangle. The ends met at the top, a quarter inch away from one edge. The longer end was forced down, and held in place, by a small lump of sugar wedged between it and the ledge formed by the short end. There was a hole in the long piece for the bottom of the knife. The device was hidden in a silver goblet. Pinetti poured in water which eventually dissolved the sugar, thus releasing the spring arm which propelled the knife into the air. Decremps hadn't mentioned that the goblet was opaque! If anyone wanted one of these devices, they were on sale at the stage door of the theatre.

Decremps had written that Pinetti used confederates; many people thought when the magician took off a volunteer's shirt without removing his coat that the man was a member of his staff. The feat seemed impossible otherwise. Pinetti explained the technique. First he made sure that the shirt was a loose-fitting one; then he opened the

89

Professor
Pinetti

A nineteenth-century Parisian cup-and-ball manipulator relaxes between performances.

Cup-and-ball conjurer of Pinetti's time, exhibiting on a folding table.

buttons at the cuffs and tied a long string to the right buttonhole. Next he unfastened the shirt front and pulled the back portion over the man's head, so the shirt, except for the sleeves, was free of the volunteer's body. He accomplished this while standing on a chair and gripping a cloth in his teeth to screen the upper portion of the man from the audience. After the shirt was over the volunteer's head, Pinetti reached up the left sleeve, grasped the cuff of the shirt, and tugged until this sleeve was off the man's arm and most of the shirt was bunched up in the left coat sleeve. Then he took up the dangling end of the cord that was tied to the right cuff. It had been pulled by the previous maneuver almost to the armpit; now by tugging on the cord, the whole shirt came down the right coat sleeve and away.

Pinetti's principal strategy for coping with the Decremps exposure was simple. He ended his run in Paris, went to the provinces, and rehearsed a change of program; then he crossed the channel to England. He opened in London at the New Theatre—the playhouse in the Haymarket that had suffered so much when the "Bottle Conjurer" failed to appear. Pinetti's ads were less specific than those of the hoaxer but equally magnetic. He announced, "The most wonderful, stupendous, and absolutely inimitable mechanical, physical and philosophical pieces, which his recent deep scrutiny in these sciences and assiduous exertions have enabled him to invent and construct." The advertisements were so good that prospective patrons were turned away nightly at the doors.

Soon after the Italian's arrival, Philip Breslaw, a dexterous German magician, whose show included a whistler and a "foreign young lady" who played the violin, decided it was time to make another tour of the provinces. He was an established favorite with British audiences, but his tricks with cards, watches, silver medals, small chests, gold boxes and caskets were not on the same scale as Pinetti's.

In late November 1784, Pinetti closed his theatre briefly to journey to Windsor Castle, where he entertained King George III and the royal family. The King himself wrote a letter praising the magician's skill, and on December 2, Pinetti resumed his London run. Featured in his playbills was a new mystery. His wife "with a handkerchief over her eyes" would sit in a front box "and guess at everything imagined and proposed to her, by any person in the company." It is clear she did more than guess; she accurately described snuffboxes, coins, and other objects.

Not speaking English, Pinetti relied on an "excellent and humorous interpreter," whose abilities must have been stretched to the limit the evening two tricks failed. The second and most obvious was Pinetti's attempt to fire a nail from a pistol so that a selected card would be pinned to a piece of scenery. A reviewer said the magi-

*Professor
Pinetti*

cian tried twice, failed twice, then "had the temerity to run up and fix the card to the back scene, but the imposition was too palpable."

The rarely ruffled Pinetti asked the interpreter to express his regrets at the end of the evening, while he himself stayed behind the curtain instead of coming forward as he usually did to accept the applause. The translator said the magician was not feeling well; he did not know when Pinetti would perform again.

Pinetti's embarrassment was short lived; the next night his show went on as usual. Before Christmas he advertised that an English edition of his book on diverting physical amusements had been published; either it or the French original could be purchased at the theatre. He played his last night in London on February 4, 1785. Copies of Decremps' exposure, written in French, had been circulating in London, and there were rumors that Thomas Denton, a showman who exhibited mechanical curiosities, was preparing a translation. This was soon on the market, and it had a brisk sale. Worse still, Philip Astley, the riding master at Westminster Bridge who was also a conjurer, issued a pirated version, *Natural Magic or Physical Amusements Revealed,* listing himself as the author.

On Pinetti's return to Paris, he found Decremps had written a supplement to his first attack, adding explanations of several of the new feats that had been shown in London. Again he did not mention Pinetti's name, but referred to him obliquely as "pilferer," "Bohemian," and "Three-Fingered Jack." Pinetti performed to acclaim in Paris, but his run was probably shortened by Decremps' abusive volumes. Decremps, pleased that his books were doing so well, made several attempts to perform before the public himself: he was not as skillful at prestidigitation as he was with words.

Billed as "Cavalheiro," the Portuguese equivalent of the title that had been given him in Germany many years before, Pinetti went to Lisbon in 1791. As usual, he listed in his advertisements the honors and decorations he had received in other countries. His success at the Theatro do Salitre was enormous.

A man, who had a copy of Decremps' book in French, spread the rumor that this conjurer who called himself a distinguished physicist was only an imitator of a great French magician—Henri Decremps! Obviously, though he used the same stage setting, the plump Pinetti was not the handsome young man shown in the book's frontispiece. An anonymous pamphleteer refuted the rumor by pointing out that Pinetti had been famous long before the book was printed. However, this writer was upset because so many people thought Pinetti's automata were masterpieces; he considered them trivial and proceeded to explain how they worked: The rifle that fired on command, for instance, was triggered by an assistant under the stage. The figure of a woman with two drawers built into her body was amusing, nothing more. The upper drawer was pulled out and shown empty. A spectator was then invited to shout "Viva" and the name of someone in the royal family. After this was done, a slip of paper with that person's name appeared in this drawer. Simple, the writer said. Springs inside the body held slips of paper with the names of all members of the royal household. When one was called, a concealed assistant pulled a string that released it. A borrowed ring traveled from the upper drawer to the lower; the upper drawer in which the ring was placed had a sliding bottom; the offstage attendant pulled a cord that opened the bottom, and the ring fell into the lower drawer.

A pen wrote any color after being dipped into a single inkwell. The inkwell was hollow. In the base of the stand was a revolving wheel with many smaller wells containing various inks. The offstage aide controlled this, too; the wheel turned until the selected color was under the hollow well. The pen would write any words, except those critical of the performer. The writer's explanation: another turn of the wheel brought a small pot of sand under the inkwell.

The pamphleteer was annoyed when less rational critics said Pinetti's marvelous scientific feats would prove to future generations how enlightened men had been in his day. To the contrary, the author asserted that these "futile amusements" were so admired would indicate how backward Europeans had been at the end of the eighteenth century.

As Pinetti continued to draw crowds, the battle of the books intensified. A Portuguese translation of Thomas Denton's English translation of Decremps' first French book was published. Then the anonymous pamphleteer issued another booklet. He commented on the magician's long run, lamented that more people were buying the Decremps volume than his own previous effort. The principal reason was, he said, because the translated volume was several times larger.

Pinetti's popularity on a return visit to Berlin in 1796 led J. W. A. Kosmann, a German professor of mathematics, to write a series of newspaper articles in which he, too, had a try at solving the magician's mysteries—with the aid of Decremps' book as a guide. The articles were published in book form in Germany and in Holland.

Pinetti went on to Russia, where he died in 1800. The chief source for his later years is Etienne Gaspard Robertson's *Mémoires Récréatifs Scientifiques et Anecdotiques* (Memoirs, Amusing, Scientific and Anecdotal).

Robertson himself was a showman of note. At the time Pinetti was in Germany, Robertson performed nightly a weird ritual in the chapel of what once was a Capuchin monastery in Paris. Attired in

Some street magicians were better dressed than their audiences.

Others wore strange costumes to attract attention.

a long cloak, he poured blood, vitriol, and an inflammable fluid on a fire. As a bell tolled, thunder rolled, and lightning flashed, clouds of smoke rose from the fire, and terrifying images of the dead and demons appeared in the air.

Robertson was presenting something new in entertainment—a "Fantasmagoria," or ghost show—and it filled the chapel with shrieking spectators. He had devised a special magic lantern in Liège, worked ten years to perfect the staging, then traveled to France, where he performed for six years before going on to other cities on the Continent.

Robertson never met Pinetti and never saw his show, but he heard many stories about the Italian when he arrived in Russia in 1806 to exhibit his phantoms and perform balloon ascents.

He was told that Pinetti had been very successful, and that he had changed his gold-embroidered clothes three or four times during each performance. A legend had circulated that while the magician was in Berlin, he had worn his royal decorations offstage as well as on and had been driven about town in an ornate carriage drawn by four white horses. The King of Prussia in a much plainer coach pulled by two horses was astonished when members of his guard saluted a man he had never seen before. After he asked a soldier the name of this important person and was told he was Pinetti the magician, the King ordered the conjurer to leave the city within twenty-four hours.

Pinetti worked hard to publicize his show in St. Petersburg, Robertson said. He bought cakes in a summer garden, broke them open, and extracted gold pieces from their centers. Supposedly, he even played tricks in a barbershop. A barber turned away from the conjurer's chair to get some lather, swung around to apply it, and almost fainted; Pinetti's head was gone, but his body was still there. The barber ran into the street and wouldn't come back until the conjurer put his head out the window to call him. *If* this happened, Pinetti would have slumped in the chair, quickly pulled the long cloth that had been around his neck higher, and folded his arms over his head under it to simulate shoulders.

Though Pinetti made a fortune in Russia, Robertson went on, he lost most of it trying to make balloon ascensions in partnership with an Italian sculptor named Petchi. The French ghostmaker met Pinetti's widow in Bialytok, and she offered to sell him the magician's equipment. He bought two unusual pieces of jewelry the Czar had given Pinetti: a large ring and a diamond-studded medallion.

While Robertson was astonished to hear that the Russian ruler had been the godfather of one of the Italian's two children, magic historian Henry Ridgely Evans thought it fitting that "the greatest autocrat" should honor "the greatest magician of the age." Pinetti's influence on the conjuring of his time was widespread. Performers in many countries tried to emulate him, and they were aided by the translations of Decremps' books. Professor Pinetti demonstrated that artistically presented magic is a theatre art as stimulating to the mind as drama or ballet.

*Professor
Pinetti*

7

Signor Blitz

SIGNOR Antonio Blitz, his Scottish wife, two sons, and two servants sailed from Liverpool in August 1835, aboard the packet *Columbus*, bound for the United States. The short, chin-whiskered "Professor of Mechanism and Metamorphosis" carried testimonials from the Duke of St. Albans and the Marquis of Stafford, as well as credentials from theatre owners in Britain, Scotland, and Ireland attesting to his skill and drawing power.

Blitz was a trailblazer—a magician who was as funny as he was baffling. He considered a show only partially successful if the spectators were merely mystified. When they roared with laughter, he knew they had been entertained.

His ship arrived at Staten Island; he opened in October at the Masonic Hall on Broadway in New York City. His program began with rice passing from one covered container to another. A bouquet, a bird, and a loaf of bread were produced from an onlooker's hat; two coins in two glasses clanged answers to questions.

Then the diminutive deceptionist presented his most perplexing feat. A spectator charged a pistol with gunpowder and a bullet. Blitz positioned himself on the stage, pointed to his heart, and instructed the man to fire. There was some hesitation, but Blitz assured the volunteer marksman that he had often been shot at—but had never been hit. A ripple of laughter eased the tension. The spectator took aim and pulled the trigger. Blitz's hand swept forward.

He opened his fingers, displaying the bullet, apparently caught in midair. The onlookers gasped, then gave Blitz tremendous applause.

The audience had been amused by Blitz's witty remarks and baffled by his magic; now he moved toward a hilarious finish. He set five dinner plates spinning on the top of a long table. One wobbled, began to fall off the edge; he rushed to it, set it twirling again. He paused, smiled, then darted to the opposite end of the table to revive another plate that was slowing down. His antics in keeping the five dishes simultaneously in motion had the audience weak from laughter before the curtain fell.

Blitz was advertised as a Moravian. Like other British showmen, he had found he could get more work in England as a foreigner. A European magician was a greater attraction than a conjurer from Kent, where he had been born in Deal on June 21, 1810. Blitz perpetuated the Moravian legend in his autobiography, *Fifty Years in the Magic Circle,* claiming he learned his first feats from gypsies in his Slavic homeland. He became, he said, so skillful as a boy of thirteen that he was taken from school and sent with a companion to Hamburg to give his first professional show. Following appearances in Lübeck, Copenhagen, Potsdam, and "all the principal cities of northern Europe," he went to England, and after engagements in the provinces, entertained at the Coburg Theatre in London "during the Lent season of 1828."

A Signor Blitz "from Moravia" did have a pre-Easter engagement at the Coburg Theatre in London—not in 1828, but two years earlier. Advertised as a former assistant and pupil of the famous Philadelphia, he conjured, caught bullets, and made five plates dance. His son, Signor Blitz, Jr., performed on his own at the Rotunda on Blackfriars Road in London in 1827.

In 1827 Antonio Blitz was seventeen. Was he the Blitz who worked at the Rotunda that year? Possibly. This performer was billed as "the young English necromancer." Yet Antonio never advertised himself in the United States as Signor Blitz, *Jr.,* never said his father had been a conjurer. In his memoirs he identified his parent as a merchant.

When Antonio Blitz moved from the Masonic Hall to Niblo's Gardens in New York, his fans followed him. Then, after forty-two nights in Manhattan, he took a steamer north to Boston for an engagement at the Artist's Gallery on Summer Street. The *Boston Advertiser* said Blitz "threw completely in the shade most of the professors of the black art who formerly exhibited here. He manages to make his exhibitions interesting and amusing as well as surprising. Some of his feats astonish by their boldness and apparent impossibility."

High praise this, for a year earlier, Mr. Saubert, a French

magician-ventriloquist, who advertised that his art had merited decorations from the rulers of Russia, Prussia, and Turkey, had baffled Bostonians at Julien Hall by a realistic decapitation illusion and by the disappearance of a heap of borrowed shawls, jewels, shoes, coats, and cravats piled high on his table. And, during the same year, Rahab Marcheal, "the famed Chaldean Magician," had drawn full houses at Boylston Hall. This was William Marshall, who later used other exotic names, including "The Fakir of Ava." He claimed to have been born in Persia, the son of a Scottish army officer and a Persian woman. In Boston he commemorated the Fourth of July by changing an eagle's egg into "the Guardian Spirit of America."

Blitz, too, capitalized on current events. The Governor of Massachusetts was a temperance advocate. The magician made news when he visited the State House, and pulled a bottle of whiskey out of the Governor's hat. "Bad for my reputation," the Executive commented, "but brilliant for yours."

Twice during his stay in Boston, Blitz performed at the "Court House" in Cambridge. He remembered most vividly the evening a Harvard student passed up a note: "Mr. Blitz is requested to swallow himself." In late December and early January he exhibited in the surrounding towns: Roxbury, Charleston, and Cambridgeport.

Money was tight in Marblehead, Massachusetts, Blitz noted in his autobiography, but fish were plentiful. Hundreds of citizens milled around in front of the hall, but only a few bought tickets. The doorman had a suggestion. Accept fish instead of cash as payment for admission. Blitz readily agreed. For one or two fish, patrons got seats of equal worth. The hall was soon full. The following night they packed the house again. A local merchant purchased the "box office receipts" before Blitz left town.

The Blitz show expanded in the United States. At first he had only a few trained canaries; later he advertised more than five hundred. Ventriloquism had not been one of his early features; after he mastered the technique, it became as great a source of comedy as the spinning plates. His dummy, Bobby, was smart and sassy; to heighten the fun, Blitz would put Bobby aside and ask a spectator to move his mouth without speaking. Equally amusing, impertinent remarks would come from the amazed man's lips. In Washington, Senator Henry Clay of Kentucky suggested that the ventriloquist sit in the visitors' gallery in the Senate. When Clay introduced a controversial bill, Blitz could make it appear that the opposition endorsed the measure.

Many children thought—as they do whenever they see an expert conjurer—that Blitz really had magic powers. One youngster was so overwhelmed by Blitz's skill at voice control that he asked the magician to come to his house and make his voiceless uncle speak. A small girl, who had seen him restore an apparently dead bird to life, came backstage with her pet canary wrapped in a piece of paper and pleaded with him to revive it. Admitting there was a limit to his capabilities, he gave her one of his own trained birds to console her.

On another occasion—a stormy night in Philadelphia—Blitz peered through the curtains at the Chinese Museum only to see that the large hall was empty, except for a woman and a boy. The magician stepped out to apologize for not being able to give a show for only two people. The distressed woman said she had traveled six miles so that her ten-year-old son could see the magic show before he went to boarding school the next day.

Blitz looked at the sad-faced youngster, than at the depressing expanse of empty seats. He instructed the ticket-taker and the pianist to sit in the first row. Then the two-hour performance started. It was the smallest house he ever had; he earned exactly thirty-seven and a half cents—and he made two people happy.

Blitz traveled up and down the East Coast, made a trip west to Illinois and Ohio, toured the Southern States, and went to Canada. Eventually he, like other magicians before him, sailed for the Caribbean, where new entertainment attractions were always welcome.

A writer in the *Jamaica Gazette* had noted in 1808:

> The want of public amusements and of amusing exhibitions in this island creates an eager and lively curiosity in the bulk of the people of all descriptions to see whatever has the appearance or promise of novelty. . . .
>
> Conjurers, sleight of hand men, dancers on the slack wire, exhibitors of waxwork figures, sometimes make their appearances here, and never fail to attract crowds of inquisitive people, to their great emolument, as they take care that the price of admission should be consonant to the supposed wealth and munificence of the West Indies.

Hyman Saunders had cooked pancakes in hats, and performed with money, rings, and swords in Kingston, Jamaica, as early as 1775. "The Incomparable Young Hollander" was in Montego Bay with his cups, cards, snuffboxes, and watches in 1784. Blindfolded, he swirled a sword above scattered facedown cards on the floor and stabbed the previously selected one.

An unnamed conjurer was censured in the Savanna-la-Mar *Gazette* in 1788. He had been pulling bandannas from the heads of blacks as he passed them on the street. "Though no Beadle happens to be in the Parish, he might still find there are not hands wanting to apply the whip, should he fall into the hands of justice," the paper warned.

Success on one island led to appearances on another. J. Castelli

Signor Antonio Blitz came to the United States from England in 1835.

Later his show included feats invented by Robert-Houdin in addition to the less complicated magic that had made him famous.

came to Trinidad from Europe, by way of Martinique, in April 1823. Mr. Handel, who had been in Demerara and Barbados, arrived in May. They were followed by Master Henderson, "the young Caledonian"; Mr. Harcourt from France; Mr. Field, with his puppets, automata, and optical devices; Mr. Hart, the fire-eater; and W. F. Lake, "from the Theatre Royal, Adelphia, Strand," who boasted of having performed before King William IV at the Royal Pavilion in Brighton.

A local resident, Mr. T. Bilby, had given a "Magic Lantern and Phantasmagoria" show in the Port-of-Spain Wesleyan Chapel in August 1837, raising funds to repair the windows, to build a fence, and aid in "Pewing the Gallery."

When Signor Blitz arrived in Port-of-Spain, Trinidad, in February 1842, following successes in Barbados and Grenada, he caused quite a stir with the package he carried. The package contained several thousand dollars in bills and notes; he had been asked by a Grenada bank manager to deliver it to Port-of-Spain. Though Blitz performed the mission faithfully, rumors soon spread around the island that the magician had spirited the money away, causing it to fly into his own strongbox. The Governor of Trinidad, at least, gave no credence to the report. He attended the theatre, and Blitz, in turn, went to a fancy-dress ball at Government House, attired in the robe and conical hat of an ancient wizard. A board, suspended by straps from his shoulders, served as a table on which he did tricks, as he circulated among the party-goers and produced flowers for the ladies.

Blitz gave half the receipts of one of his last shows in Port-of-Spain to the "Leper Establishment." Being charitable was difficult in some parts of the West Indies. The pastor of a church in St. John, Antigua, turned down the two hundred dollars Blitz sent him after a benefit performance for the needy. His response was, "What! receive alms from a wizard—a bewitched hand?" More levelheaded members of the community, however, accepted the contribution with thanks, and appointed a committee to distribute it.

The profitable tour also included British Guiana, Nevis, St. Thomas, St. Kitts, and Jamaica. On his return to New York, Blitz bought some property in Brooklyn. A later visit to Cuba was another bonanza; afterward, he purchased a home in Philadelphia, where he was living with his family when the Civil War started.

During the war, Philadelphia became a hospital center for Union troops. Blitz later said that he gave 123 shows at the various medical installations for an estimated 63,000 men.

Blitz is also reported to have made an impromptu appearance before President Abraham Lincoln in the beginning of July 1863. The President, who was staying at the time at the summer White House, then on the outskirts of Washington, left his desk to watch the rehearsal of a Fourth of July pageant. Little girls, with red, white, and blue sashes around their waists, paraded on the lawn; each carried a shield bearing the name of a state. Among the onlookers was Blitz, who suddenly reached out and plucked a canary from the curls of one of the marchers. The others broke ranks to watch. After several more tricks— including the production of an egg from the gaping mouth of Tad Lincoln, the President's young son—the magician asked the President if he had received any recent news of the great battle then raging at Gettysburg. Lincoln, who did not know who the magician was, shook his head. Asking permission, Blitz took the President's hat, waved his hand over it, and a white pigeon flew out. Under the bird's wing was a scrap of paper. The magician passed the slip to the President. On it were the words, "Victory. General Grant."

George Moran, a financier, then formally introduced the entertainer to the President; Moran had met the magician on the train from New York. As Moran told the story years later, Lincoln recognized the magician's name immediately. "Why, of course, it's Signor Blitz, one of the most famous men in America. How many children have you made happy, Signor Blitz?"

"Thousand and tens of thousands."

"While I fear that I have made thousands and tens of thousands unhappy," the President said. "But it is for each of us to do his duty in this world and I am trying to do mine."

There is no mention of Lincoln in Blitz's memoirs. Probably the magician Moran referred to was one of Blitz's imitators. Blitz himself admitted he wrote from memory and not from notes made during his travels. This may explain why he said he arrived in New York in 1834, a year before he actually landed, or why he gave the name of the Governor of Trinidad at the time he was there as Sir John McCloud, rather than Sir Henry McCloud.

Close calls with death during the performance of the dangerous bullet-catching feat were more readily recalled. In New York City a man slipped tacks, as well as a bullet, into the barrel as he loaded the gun. When he fired, some of the tacks tore into the flesh of the magician's hand; the rest were driven into the stage wall behind Blitz. Another volunteer tried to put a brass button into the gun along with the bullet; Blitz caught him in the act. The most terrifying moment came in Savannah when a spectator stood with a six-shooter in his hand, and shouted that if Blitz could catch one bullet, six should be just as easy. Keeping calm, talking quietly, Blitz dissuaded the man from pulling the trigger. Soon after this, Blitz dropped the bullet-catch from his repertoire; the strain had become too great.

Later, in New York, Blitz met Martin Van Buren, whom reporters had dubbed "the Little Magician" because of his political manipulations. The former President expressed his pleasure at see-

Many of Blitz' funniest tricks were performed with volunteer assistants.

Blitz dropped bullet-catching from his routine; it was too dangerous.

He attended a fancy-dress ball in Trinidad attired as a wizard.

At another party, Blitz pulled fruit and vegetables from a man's coat.

ing "so distinguished a brother professor." Blitz replied that no other conjurer had reached such lofty heights as the former President—"or so successfully deceived the public." Van Buren took the sally in good humor, saying he would concede the title to Blitz, as he himself was retired and no longer practicing magic.

Blitz completed his memoirs in time for publication to celebrate his sixtieth birthday in 1871. Six years later he died at his home in Philadelphia. A special train took his body to New York for burial in Cypress Hills Cemetery in Brooklyn.

Blitz married twice. One of his sons, Theodore, performed professionally as Haba Haba, the magician; a daughter, Jennie, sang in European opera under her married name, Van Zandt.

Edgar Allan Poe compared Elizabeth Barrett Browning's poetry to "the hi presto! conjurations of Signor Blitz," which probably pleased the magician, if he was aware of the reference, and distressed Robert Browning's wife.

The Antonio Blitz mixture of magic and comedy was so popular that thirteen other performers took his name, and copied his printed matter. Most called themselves Signor Blitz; one claimed to be a son; another, to be his nephew. As late as January 14, 1899, the *Boston Post* carried a moving article about the talent and grace of the wonderful Signor Blitz who had performed so often in the city. Blitz, the article said, was really David Batents, then confined to an insane asylum, where the poor fellow sometimes asked for a pack of cards to amuse his fellow patients. This was one of the imitators!

Foreign magicians dominated the scene when Blitz arrived in the United States in 1835, but during the ensuing decades American performers presented shows on a par with their European rivals. The two best-known native performers of this period were Jonathan Harrington and John Wyman, Jr., both of whom specialized in ventriloquy.

Harrington was twelve years old when he caught the magic bug. In 1821, at the Washington Gardens Amphitheatre in Boston, he saw Mr. Charles, a French ventriloquist, who was billed as "Professor of Mechanical Sciences to the King of Prussia." Just five years later, Harrington himself gave a performance at the Castle Street Hall. His parents discouraged this venture in show business, and got him a job at Samuel May's hardware store. The personable young man who could make voices emanate from a keg of nails and produce iron hinges from empty bags soon returned to the stage billed as "the second American ventriloquist." This was an exaggeration. Richard Potter had been the first, and by 1822 a Mr. Nicols had also performed. Still, Harrington was an outstanding entertainer with his vocal illusions, conjuring, and automaton band. A critic writing in the

Boston Bee once called him "the funniest man alive." In 1855 he inaugurated a tradition—an annual Fourth of July show for children. He gave seven performances in the Boston Public Garden; an estimated fifty thousand people attended. After a run at the Tremont Street Temple in 1862 he signed with P. T. Barnum for an engagement at the Boston Acquarial Gardens. By 1864 Harrington had gained "time-honored popularity and fame." That Fourth of July he slowed his pace; he gave only five shows, but in three different places —the Boston Theatre, Faneuil Hall, and Tremont Temple.

Fourteen years later Harrington still continued the custom, though that year there were only four shows, all in Tremont Temple. He was then sixty-nine, and affectionately known as "Old Harrington." Fathers brought their sons and daughters to see the feats they had enjoyed as children. He caught a cold in April 1881, while performing in York, Maine. Pneumonia developed, and "New England's Favorite Magician" died at his home in Revere, Massachusetts, on May 4, 1881.

The biggest American moneymaker of the period, John Wyman, Jr., was born in Albany, New York, on January 19, 1816. After his graduation from Albany Academy, his father, a merchant, arranged for him to work in a Baltimore auction house. Wyman however, had already developed a talent for ventriloquism and conjuring. Once away from parental domination, he played an engagement at the Baltimore Museum. With his twin skills and a knack for getting his name into print, he rose rapidly in the profession.

Traveling up the Mississippi from New Orleans to St. Louis on the steamer, *The Goddess of Liberty,* Wyman heard that Signor Blitz, whom he had never met, was aboard. The story of their encounter, considerably embellished, no doubt, is in *Jokes and Anecdotes of Wyman, The Magician and Ventriloquist,* published in Philadelphia in 1866.

Blitz, pressed by the passengers to do a show, agreed and, shortly afterward, began his performance in the forward salon. He singled out a studious young man (Wyman), who until then had been reading a book. Blitz pulled several slices of bread from Wyman's hat, then reached in his coat and drew out a guinea pig. Roars of laughter greeted these productions. Blitz was entertaining with ventriloquism when he heard the buzz of a wasp. He ignored the buzz and continued his act. Then, while creating the illusion of a barking dog in the cabin, he sensed the wasp coming closer, buzzing near his ear. He took a swat at it, but missed.

Someone suggested that Blitz sing an amusing song. No sooner had he begged off, saying that singing was not one of his accomplishments, than "Should auld acquaintance be forgot" emanated from his closed lips. Blitz's usually happy expression turned to bewilderment. Only when the wasp resumed buzzing did he realize what was happening. While he had been having fun with the audience, the studious young man—Wyman, of course—had been having fun with him.

For the remainder of the trip the two ventriloquists kept the steamer in an uproar. Blitz had passengers running to the rail with the sounds of fire alarms; Wyman's imitation of the ship's boiler exploding terrified several old women; and invisible cats and dogs mewed and barked in the corridors all the way to Missouri.

Wyman, Blitz, and Harrington were in New York in the summer of 1856 when P. T. Barnum advertised the first American appearance of Lionel Goldschmidt, the famous British mimic and ventriloquist, at the American Museum. The three magicians went to the opening show; there was standing room only. At curtain time the orchestra played an overture; there was a long pause; then the musicians played again. A distraught Barnum meanwhile had rushed to the back of the house. Explaining that Goldschmidt had not arrived, he pleaded for one of the three to take his place.

Harrington told Barnum he wasn't prepared to perform. Blitz begged off on doing a whole evening of ventriloquism without his magic apparatus, canaries, and rabbits to help fill the program. Wyman reluctantly volunteered.

But what about the difference between his appearance and Goldschmidt's? Wyman asked as Barnum hustled him into a dressing room; Goldschmidt was a large man with a full beard. Barnum uncorked a bottle of spirit gum, and fastened a moustache and a set of enormous false whiskers on Wyman's face.

Wyman stepped out on the stage as the signal bell rang. In an assumed accent, he apologized for the delay and got to work. He imitated crying babies, squealing pigs, crowing roosters, and other barnyard animals. He even mimicked the noise made when a knife was being ground, then went into a ventriloquial routine conversing with imaginary people in the cellar.

A grateful Barnum thanked him profusely after the show. "I must compliment you especially on one remarkable imitation," the producer enthused. "Which one?" Wyman asked, as he peeled off the whiskers. "Goldschmidt!" Barnum answered.

Wyman toured with a gift show in the 1860's; in this show, the stubs of the admission tickets were numbered, giving each customer a chance to win "Gold Watches, Silver Watches, Table Sets, Family Bibles" or "Silver-plated Ware" in a drawing held after the entertainment. Other magicians offered similar lures. J. M. Macallister gave away furniture, bolts of cloth, barrels of flour, opera capes, and live pigs. Zera Semon's prizes ranged from hams, lamps, and butter-

Jonathan Harrington, a Blitz
competitor in New England.

John Wyman, Jr., performed on
four occasions for Lincoln.

knives, to a set of French chinaware—fifty-six items—and a three-piece living-room suite. Allyne advertised "150 Beautiful Gifts, Many of Which are Rich and Costly." Logrenia toured with "Sam Sharpley's Silver Show and Carnival of Croesus," which promised "Elegant Presents and $100 in Gold and Silver Coin."

Jack Shed, a gambler whose only sleights were done at the faro table, saw the chance to make some easy money. He filled halls in New England advertising that Blitz, Wyman, Macallister, or some other currently popular conjurer would appear, and that expensive gifts would be given to all who attended. After the last possible dollar had been taken at the box office, Shed would skip town.

Another more audacious swindler of the period inundated small towns with posters and heralds, carrying the words "He is Coming." Eventually a signboard would be erected at the principal hall, reading "He is Here." When spectators drawn by the unusual advertising campaign filled the hall, the janitor, who had been paid for the extra work, pulled the ropes which opened the curtains. On an otherwise bare stage was a large placard—"He is Gone."

Wyman was honest; if he promised to give away a gold watch, he did—and not to a member of his family. For most of his professional career he lived in Philadelphia, where his money was well invested in various business enterprises, including publishing. As spiritualism spread from New York State across America, he duplicated the tricks many mediums used in his programs. He died at his home in Burlington, New Jersey, at the age of sixty-five on July 31, 1881.

Wyman was invited to conjure at the White House more frequently than any of his contemporary magicians. He performed for Martin Van Buren, baffled Millard Fillmore and his cabinet with the "Inexhaustible Bottle," and entertained Abraham Lincoln and his guests on four occasions.

Blitz, however, was better remembered, and made a more lasting impression on the art. Years after they had seen him, critics in their reviews of other conjurers still mentioned the little magician who could evoke hearty laughter from even the most solemn audiences.

Signor Blitz

8

The Great Wizard
of the North

JOHN Henry Anderson, the Barnum of nineteenth-century bafflers, plastered his gaudy showbills all over the world—even on the sides of the pyramids in Egypt and on the cliffs of Niagara Falls in America. "Anderson is coming," Londoners going to work read stenciled on the pavements. "Anderson is here," proclaimed pats of butter served at mealtime to travelers in hotels and inns after he arrived.

Other publicists were often satisfied with a single large poster on the side of an abandoned building or blank wall; Anderson's printed matter filled every available inch with exciting descriptions and dazzling illustrations of his "Acatalectic Wonders."

Returning to Britain from a tour across Europe, Anderson outdid himself with a spectacular poster based on the painting *Napoleon's Return from Elba.* Dominating the scene was the "Great Wizard." Loyal British followers clasped his knees, as a huge crowd roared an ovation. Over his head fluttered a banner: "The Wonder of the World." In the background, emperors and kings looked on with approval. Famous London landmarks welcomed the mighty magician home. The statue of Lord Nelson in Trafalgar Square, hat in hand, bowed in deference; the towering dome of St. Paul's Cathedral tipped toward him. Blazing letters across the bottom of the lithograph hailed him as the "Napoleon of Necromancy."

Anderson's street parades set a pattern for later circuses. Prancing stallions pulled four carriages festooned with colorful pictures.

They were followed by twenty-four marchers, each holding aloft a pole topped with a giant letter of the alphabet. Viewed from one side the message read "The Celebrated Anderson!!!"; from the other, "The Great Wizard of the North."

Anderson published his own newspapers during some theatre engagements, advertising a guaranteed circulation of a hundred thousand. He held riddle contests, and printed the entries in books. He built Scotland's largest theatre. As an entrepreneur, he presented operas in Glasgow, balls in London, Sydney, and Melbourne, and an elaborate modern version of Shakespeare's *The Tempest,* in New York.

The magician, who was to conjure with "Solid Silver" apparatus, was born in July 1814. Sometimes he said the date was the fourteenth, sometimes the fifteenth, but the birth register shows the sixteenth. His father was a tenant farmer who lived in a small house on the estate of the Laird of Craigmyle in the parish of Kincardine O'Neil, twenty miles from Aberdeen, Scotland. At six, young John's work was turning freshly laundered clothes in the fields where they had been spread to dry. From his earliest years his great ambition was to be an actor. By seventeen he was traveling with touring shows, and he had seen the magic of Signor Blitz. Conjuring appealed to the brawny, almost six-foot-tall youth. He began to present his own brand of magic, displaying some digital skill and the greatest of confidence. By March 1837 he had received ten pounds for a performance at Brechin Castle for Lord Panmure, and an endorsement, which he quoted on his handbills: "I have no hesitation in saying that you far excell any other Necromancer that I ever saw, either at home or abroad."

"The Caledonian Conjuror," as he billed himself then, spent most of what he made for better equipment and flamboyant propaganda. Thirty heavily advertised performances at the Assembly Rooms in Aberdeen drew twenty-eight thousand spectators; twenty-four at the theatre in Dundee attracted twenty-one thousand. The Irish appreciated Anderson's entertainment as much as the Scots. His show ran twenty-four nights in theatres in Belfast and Cork; he played two hundred evenings in the Rotunda Rooms in Dublin.

Then, after forty nights in the Monteith Rooms in Glasgow, Anderson moved into a building he named "The Palace of Enchantment," for the annual fair. During the first season in 1838, one hundred performances drew one hundred thousand paid admissions. The following year he added twenty more shows for the fair; and at the end of four months announced that 170,000 people had seen his production.

Anderson's feature trick in Glasgow was bullet-catching. David Prince Miller, another showman, offered the same feat for a penny in his booth, while Anderson was getting sixpence in the theatre. Anderson denounced Miller as a petty imitator, and Miller prospered; he said later that if Anderson had ignored him, his receipts wouldn't have been nearly as high. In the cities of northern England, Anderson's publicity campaigns paid off. He filled theatres in Sunderland, Stockton, and Preston; halls in Huddersfield, Bradford, and Sheffield. Between shows he taught card tricks to would-be conjurers, and sold magic apparatus as well as a "Magic Dye" that would turn men's gray locks to glossy black in less than a minute.

Early in 1840 the twenty-five-year-old "Great Wizard of the North" opened at the New Strand Theatre in London. His playbill for February 10 carried a woodcut of him springing cards from hand to hand, backed by three tables filled with exotic "Solid Silver" apparatus. Two ancient mystics, wands in hand, rose from smoke on the sides of the stage to acclaim him.

In the course of his performance a pair of ladies' gloves was burned. He produced two eggs, one with each hand, and offered the audience a choice. He cracked the shell of the selected egg; the gloves were inside. A man's watch disappeared, and was found "in a loaf from any baker's shop in town." Rings and trinkets from the audience were deposited in a small box; the box was covered by a cloth and held by a volunteer. Anderson took what he called a "Double-sighted Telescope," placed it to one eye, trained it on the shrouded box, and accurately described the objects inside. Then a case was brought out. A wave of his muscular hand, and the borrowed objects were found in the case. Everyone thought this sequence was over, until he took one corner of the cloth, which still covered the box, flicked it, and the box disappeared.

Ten dead canaries were put in a pan and baked. When the lid was lifted, ten live birds popped up. The magician cut the crown from a spectator's hat, then restored it. From another hat he produced a "menagarie." Rabbits appeared from a spectator's topper. The rabbit-from-hat feat was still new; it had first appeared in the programs of magicians in the late 1830's. (The originator of the feat is unknown; previously, birds were favored.) "The Gun Trick" (bullet-catching) was still Anderson's feature attraction.

There were at least two other contemporary "Wizards of the North," E. W. Young and H. Hall. A Monsieur De Saurin advertised as "The Wizard of the West," and Barnado Eagle was being billed in 1840 as "The Royal Wizard of the South." Eagle, who said his French grandfather came to England after the revolution in Paris, was the son of an innkeeper who lived near Barnet, Middlesex.

As a boy he had seen Breslaw, Blitz, Moon, Gyngell, Rovere "the Persian enchanter" and "Chi Cho Lu La, the original Chinese

John Henry Anderson—one of the first magicians to pull a rabbit from a hat.

Juggler" perform at his father's inn. His first public performance was in a library at Brighton. King William IV heard about his skill, Eagle reported in a souvenir book, and commanded him to perform "in the music saloon, at the Pavilion."

Anderson, who had a fiery temper, did his best to destroy this competitor who, he charged, copied his original billing material and newspaper advertisements. Anderson had a poster made depicting "Barney alias 'The Imposter Wizard' obtaining royal patronage on Ascot Heath Race Course." Eagle, cards in hand, cups and balls, and linking rings near his feet, stands on a slightly raised platform, below King William, who looks down from an enclosure, while one of Eagle's assistants beats a drum to attract attention and a clown passes a tambourine to collect money.

Anderson also had a playbill printed while Eagle was performing in Birmingham, attacking his "System of Imposition." In the woodcut at the top, Anderson pulls aside the drape of his rival's table to reveal a concealed boy operating the "mechanical" figure over his head, and raising the rabbits that would appear from under ornate covers. The text says that Barney "can neither pronounce nor understand" the magical phrases he stole from Anderson, and concludes with a threat: "Barney, when we last met, I merely ruffled your feathers, this time I'll pluck you clean, not one shall be left thee to spread thy [Eagle] wings of imposition."

Anderson on stage was a perfect gentleman; after the show he occasionally drank too freely. One night in Glasgow he staggered late through the streets, trying to find his lodging place. Unsuccessful, he called to a boy to help him. The youth looked up at him in awe: "You're John Henry Anderson, the Wizard of the North!" "Yes, I know," the magician mumbled. "But where do I live?"

Anderson's wife, Hannah, the daughter of a showman named Scott with whom Anderson traveled as a young man, worked backstage. Their first son, John Henry Anderson, Jr., was born in Manchester in September 1843. They were to have four more children: Helen Elizabeth, Alice Hannah, Oscar Longhurst, and Columbia Harriett. All, at one time or another, were to act as their father's assistants.

Anderson repeated his successes in London and the other principal cities of the British Isles, then poured the profits into the construction of a magnificent 5,000-seat theatre in Glasgow. It was 130 feet long, 70 feet wide, and 50 feet high; the stage was 50 feet deep.

The opening of his City Theatre coincided with the start of the city fair in July 1845. The "Great Wizard" starred on the first bill, supported by a company of "Ethiopian Minstrels" and a troupe of bell ringers. In the succeeding weeks the proprietor-producer presented operas, dramas, and farces, featuring prominent British players.

But Anderson's career as a producer did not begin happily. Some actors were annoyed when he insisted that they also appear as extras during the operas; they refused to double up. Sims Reeves, a noted tenor, who was featured in *Lucia di Lammermoor*, stalked off the stage one night, enraged by the orchestra's sloppy accompaniment. That Saturday, producer Anderson docked Reeves's salary and those of the balky actors. They told "Mr. Hankey Pankey" they would not leave the theatre until they got their full pay. In that case they would be locked inside until Monday, Anderson countered as he walked away. They stayed until midnight. Then as the last door was being bolted, the protesting performers fled out on the green, cursing "Signor Squallissimo."

There was more trouble in November. Anderson was charged with assaulting Charles Le Clerq, a dancer. Le Clerq testified that Anderson had called him to his office. The magician seemed to think the dancer was planning to leave before the end of his three-month contract. Words led to blows; Anderson knocked the dancer to the floor. Le Clerq appeared in police court with his head bandaged and bruises under his eyes. Someone suggested that the dancer must have fallen down the stairs that led to Anderson's room. The doctor who treated Le Clerq and another physician who examined him at the magistrate's suggestion agreed it was doubtful that a fall could have caused the injuries. Nonetheless, the judge ruled that the assault charge had not been proven; the case was dismissed.

Fifteen minutes after midnight on November 18, fire broke out in the City Theatre. A man crossing the green saw the blaze and gave the alarm. Soon police, fire engines, and a mob of spectators were on the scene. The fire quickly spread. Firemen managed to save the nearby Adelphi Theatre, but Anderson's new building was gutted. The magician shouldered his way through the crowd like a madman, trying to enter the burning building; policemen had to hold him back. He had some insurance but far from enough to cover the tremendous loss. His elaborate scenery, expensive costumes, and stock of conjuring apparatus were totally destroyed; only the scorched brick walls of the City Theatre were left standing. Benefit performances were staged for him at the Adelphi and other theatres by sympathetic show people.

Wide newspaper coverage of the spectacular blaze made him a bigger box-office attraction than ever; soon he was on the road again with new equipment. In Aberdeen, Anderson met an old friend—P. T. Barnum, the American showman, then on tour with General Tom Thumb, the celebrated midget.

Anderson saw the performance in the hall where he was to appear the following week, then joined Barnum for supper. Barnum was keenly interested in conjuring. A magician, Henry Hawley, had once been his partner. Barnum admired Hawley's poise, ready flow of words, and his ability to extricate himself from embarrassing situations. He had seen Hawley speechless only once. That was when, after producing eggs from a small cloth bag, he reached in for "the old hen" and came up with a rooster, a new assistant having loaded the bag with the wrong chicken.

Anderson was in a merry mood. He introduced Barnum as "The Wizard of the North" to strangers in the hotel and kept asking him which tricks he planned to perform. At first Barnum went along with the prank; then he announced he would give everyone present a pass to his show. He had issued more than thirty before Anderson realized what was happening. "Hold on!" he shouted. "I am the 'Wizard of the North.' I'll stand the orders already given out, but not another one."

Anderson made a European tour in 1847. The climax was a command performance for Czar Nicholas at the Winter Palace in St. Petersburg. Anderson claimed he was the first British performer to entertain in Russia, and said the Czar permitted him to use the Imperial Theatre for public shows without charge. He also appeared before King Christian VIII of Denmark in Copenhagen, King Oscar I of Sweden in Oslo, and King Frederick William IV of Prussia in Potsdam.

Anderson's "Triumphant Return to Britain" in 1848 was spoiled by the presence of two strong competitors from the Continent —Carl Herrmann and Robert-Houdin. They were featuring illusions new to London. In Paris, Robert-Houdin had devised a way to suspend a person in the air, and to produce everything from flowers to human beings from a thin portfolio. Herrmann, without Robert-Houdin's knowledge, had duplicated the feats, and he presented them in London before the French magician made his British debut. By the end of the year Anderson also had working models of the equipment, and the pirated creations of Robert-Houdin became his features. He added a few slight variations: Anderson advertised that he used chloroform for the suspension (Robert-Houdin had said ether made his assistant lighter than air), and his productions from the portfolio were not precisely the same.

Queen Victoria must have heard of Anderson's masterly presentations of the new mysteries. He was summoned to entertain at Balmoral Castle on Monday, August 27, 1849, during the festivities the British sovereign had planned to celebrate her son's birthday. Bagpipes swirled, drums beat, and traditional Scottish games were played. Then the doors to a handsome pavilion, which had been erected as Anderson's "Temple of Magic," swung open.

The garlanded stage was covered by thick Turkish carpet and lighted by hundreds of candles in silver chandeliers. Brocades,

Anderson was billed as "The Great Wizard of the North."

The Robert-Houdin suspension feat à la Anderson at a New York theatre.

Broadway Theate

B. A. MARSHALL... LESSEE

The Coolest, Best Ventilated Theatre
IN AMERICA.

EXTRAORDINARY EXCITEMENT ! !

Magnificent Paraphernalia !
Awe Thrilling Necromancy !
Overflowing, Wonder-Stricken,
And Delighted Audiences!

15,000 OF THE TRUEST FASHION
LOUDLY PROCLAIM

PROF. ANDERSON
The Only Immensely Great Wizard.

In freezing climes, or under sunny skies,
"The pa'm's awarded !" every state replies ;
Their homage and their laurel wreaths they bring,
And proudly hail thee as "The Wizard King !"

Crowded every night with Beauty and Fashion from

PIT TO DOME.

FRIDAY, JULY 30th, 1852,

On this occasion will be given the most brilliant entertainment ever attempted in the country. Among the features will be found the following wondrous acts:

THE FAMOUS CHRYSTAL CASKET
The astonishing wonder, the

MYSTIC CABINET
The incomprehensible feat of
THE MYSTERIOUS PORTFOLIO
The seeming miracle of
THE CAULDRON FANTASTIQUE.
The incredible Phenomena with the

SIX WATCHES
Mechanical Amalgam,
Mysterious Disappearance of Two Persons,
Clairvoyance, or the Second Sight

THE CHAPEAU PROLIFIQUE
The wonder of the 19th century,

SUSPENSION MESMERIC
AND THE

Mysterious Laundry
At the conclusion of the first part, the Wizard will produce from a

RED HOT CRUCIBLE
Thousands of Petite Vases of Ice Cream for the Ladies. Confections and Bon Bons showered upon the Youth of the City.

THE INEXHAUSTIBLE BOTTLE
WILL DO ITS WORK

Reserved Seats in Dress Circle.................50 Cents
Parquette, Family Circle and all other Seats ....25 Cents

To commence at a quarter past 8 o'clock.

damask, and velvet drapes added a striking setting for Anderson's "gold and silver" apparatus.

When the Queen, her consort, and the young Prince of Wales had been seated, the show began. White doves were produced from an "Enchanted Cauldron." Steaming hot coffee materialized in silver canisters, and was served to the audience in the cups and saucers a European king had given Anderson. Bowls filled with water and goldfish appeared from under empty scarves, and there were tricks with cards, handkerchiefs, rings, and watches.

Victoria said later that Anderson's "Magic Scrapbook" was her favorite feat. This was Robert-Houdin's portfolio under another name. After the scrapbook, which was forty-nine inches long, eight inches wide, and three inches thick, had been taken to the Queen for examination, it was placed flat on a pair of thin trestles. Anderson opened the cover. Only a moment before the scrapbook had been empty; now he took out hats, bonnets, plates, a bird in a cage, and a live goose.

Again Anderson lifted the cover. This time he removed vases of flowers and bowls of goldfish. Finally, to the delight of the Queen, out jumped the wizard's small son, in full Highland costume. Then from Anderson's "Wonderful Hat" came a toy, a souvenir, or a bouquet of flowers for everyone in the audience.

A hazard of a royal command performance is that the monarch sometimes requests a number not on the scheduled program. Anderson, however, was prepared when the Queen asked to see his "Inexhaustible Bottle." "What would you like?" he asked Lord Portman. "Whisky" was the prompt reply. Out flowed the amber fluid. Another man chose brandy. John Begg of the Royal Distillery preferred his own product—Lochnagar whisky—and he got it. Other guests asked for and received rum and gin from the same bottle. Those who imagined the bottle was a mechanical masterpiece were amazed when Anderson took a small hammer, smashed the glass, and two doves fluttered up from the shattered pieces.

The final mystery was Robert-Houdin's suspension illusion. Young John Henry Anderson, Jr., rested horizontally in thin air, his only support a vertical pole under his right arm.

The young Prince of Wales talked about the magician's tricks for days. A magazine article gave the Prince's view of the magician in the Prince's own words: "He had cut to pieces mama's pocket-handkerchief, then darned it and ironed it, so that it was as entire as ever; he had fired a pistol and caused five or six watches to go through Gibb's head, and all were tied to a chair on Gibb's other side . . . [Gibb was a footman] but papa knows how all these things are done, and had the watches really gone through Gibb's head he would hardly have looked so well. . . ."

*The Great
Wizard of
the North*

Other conjurers had appeared before British monarchs; none capitalized on the experience so effectively. Anderson toured Scotland with a portable pavilion, a replica of the one at Balmoral. His ads promised audiences they would see the same amazing feats that had delighted Victoria and the royal family. He distributed souvenir "Royal Command" programs, printed in red and black on white satin, backed with red silk. He had medals struck with his face on one side and details of the Balmoral performance on the other.

Anderson was still advertising the Balmoral routine when he opened on Easter Monday, April 17, 1851, at the St. James Theatre in London. Competition was stiff. Henri Robin, the French magician, was in the midst of a long run in Piccadilly, and on May 1, the Great Exhibition in the Crystal Palace opened. Anderson played seventeen days at the St. James, fulfilled an engagement at the Theatre Royal in Bath, then sailed for New York.

Anderson's clever advertising and lavishly mounted shows appealed to Americans. By his count, a quarter of a million people saw him during his hundred-night engagement at the Broadway Theatre in New York City in 1851. His reception, he said, was second only to that of Jennie Lind, the Swedish singer.

Anderson tickets were at a premium in Philadelphia. In August he opened at the Howard Atheneum in Boston. For more than a month Signor Blitz had been playing at Amory Hall. Blitz was then featuring trained birds—"Upwards of 500 Canaries"—as well as conjuring, ventriloquism, and plate-spinning. His presentations were delightful, but his tricks—changing the ink in a vase to water, producing rabbits and guinea pigs from a box, and dyeing a man's coat red, then restoring it to its original color—were less spectacular than Anderson's.

Spiritualism was then a subject of intense interest. Only three years earlier the Fox sisters had introduced their weird knocking sounds in upstate New York. When, after three weeks at the Atheneum, Anderson moved to the Melodeon, he produced "spirit raps" on a table, and denounced spiritualists as "conjurers in disguise." Two nights after he closed at the Melodeon, he returned to the Howard Atheneum to play a dramatic role, the title part in *Rob Roy*, at a benefit for the Scots Charitable Society. The urge to be an actor had never been fully satisfied by his "Great Wizard" characterization. In other cities Anderson also played Rob Roy and other Scottish parts in special productions. His magnificent Highland costume, he said, had been given him by Prince Albert after the royal command performance at Balmoral Castle. Anderson put it on display in local shops as advance promotion.

Copies of Anderson's *Fashionable Science of Parlor Magic* were sold in theatre lobbies. First published prior to his London debut in

M. Jacobs, a magician-ventriloquist, competed with Anderson in Australia.

Fanciful woodcuts adorned "The Great Wizard of the North's" posters.

1840, the book was now in its eighty-fourth edition. Also available were song sheets: "The Wizard's Polka," "The Inexhaustible Polka," "The Bottle Polka," and "The Mystic Polka," all with an Anderson portrait, or a drawing of him performing, on the cover. In addition to these and the illustrated programs on sale, there was also a pamphlet for children: *Master Anderson's (The Young Wizard of the North) Little Ladies and Gentlemen's Magic Alphabet: The Whole of His Papa's Wonders Illustrated.*

Anderson's heavily promoted special riddle contest nights invariably drew packed houses—and added more to his income when the entries were printed in books. On February 6, 1852, more than two thousand conundrums were entered in his competition at the Metropolitan Hall in New York. After thirteen judges were chosen from the audience, the submissions were read aloud. A "Silver Breakfast and Tea Service, value 400 dollars" was awarded to the lady who was selected as the winner. "A Silver Pitcher and two goblets, value 250 dollars" went to the male runner-up. The prizewinners were not designated in the 108-page *Wizard's Book of Conundrums,* but here are a few samples:

> *When is a man most in danger of being beaten?*
> When he belongs to a club.
>
> *Why is Professor Anderson's performance like the kissing of a sweet pretty girl?*
> Because you cannot get enough of it.
>
> *Why is Professor Anderson's Magic Scrap-Book like his wife?*
> Because he has got from it a son.
>
> *Why was Lola Montez's career in Bavaria like a Thunderstorm?*
> Because she flashed, reigned and cleared.
>
> *Why is the Wizard of the North like the American Flag?*
> Because, like that glorious banner, he has no equal.

Returning to the British Isles, Anderson at the age of forty announced that he planned to retire after a six-month tour. This may actually have been his intention, or it may have been just another promotional gambit. At any rate, the farewell tour was a long one, extending into the winter of 1855–56. Anderson leased the Covent Garden Theatre in London for the holiday season. Christmas week he played *Rob Roy.* The play and a pantomime ran until early March, though the receipts were less than he had anticipated.

Finally he advertised a "Grand Carnival Benefit and Dramatic Gala," a gargantuan two-day spectacle that encompassed his magic show, an opera, a ballet, a harlequinade, and a drama. A cast of six hundred artists and musicians! Elaborate scenery! Magnificent costumes! The frolic would climax with a masked ball on the great stage on March 4, 1856, beginning at eleven P.M. and lasting until dawn.

Until an hour past midnight the dancers had been gay but well behaved; then the affair became raucous, and most people left. By four thirty, less than two hundred revelers were on the stage. The theatre was illuminated by almost a thousand jets of gas flame in ornate chandeliers. The highest cluster of flickering lights was near a storeroom on an upper level where Anderson kept his scenery and conjuring apparatus, including kegs of methylated spirits that he used for firework effects. At five A.M. there came a shriek from a dancing couple who had noticed a fire by the storeroom door. How the sudden blaze started no one knows. Perhaps a merrymaker accidentally dropped a lighted cigarette. Once the fire began, it spread quickly through the decorations and furniture; and the dancers ran to the exits. The musicians, who had valiantly played through the night, fled too, leaving drums and heavy instruments behind. The London fire brigade responded to the alarm, but the theatre was beyond saving. Before six o'clock, the roof had collapsed. By seven the famous playhouse was a charred heap of rubble. Fortunately no lives were lost.

When the papers covered the story, Londoners learned that this was Anderson's third stage fire. There had been a less serious one during his American tour, as well as the holocaust that destroyed his City Theatre in Glasgow.

Again the insurance was inadequate to cover the damage, and to complete the tragedy, Anderson's bank failed, wiping out his savings. Any thought of retirement now was out of the question. He borrowed money, bought new scenery, drapes, and equipment, and returned to the road. When British theatre owners were no longer interested in booking him, Anderson announced he would circle the globe. He sailed on March 11, 1858, from Liverpool aboard the *Monsoon*. Despite his misfortunes, the ominous name of the vessel did not disturb him. After a voyage of sixteen thousand miles, he reached Melbourne in June.

M. Jacobs, a conjurer-ventriloquist from Canterbury, one of Anderson's principal competitors in the British Isles, had arrived earlier. By then he was an established attraction in Australia. Two of his tricks were singled out for frequent comment in reviews. In one he passed a borrowed banknote into an egg; in the other he stood his assistant on a table, covered him with a giant cone, and converted the man into a goose. Jacobs' equipment was not as bulky as Anderson's; his staff was considerably smaller. The "Great Wizard" traveled with his wife, his children, four assistants, and a private secretary.

For six weeks Anderson filled the Melbourne Theatre Royal to capacity. In Sydney, after six weeks at the Lyceum, he moved to the Prince of Wales Theatre. Undeterred by the Covent Garden fiasco, he staged a gigantic theatre ball in each city. These ventures made money, and the theatres were still intact after the dancing ended.

As there were gold rushes in Castlemaine, Ballarat, and Bendigo, Anderson took his show to the mining camps. Diggers packed the crude halls to see the same "Royal Entertainment of Magic" that had pleased the Queen.

Jacobs attended Anderson's masked ball in Sydney; later in Brisbane, Jacobs was booked at another theatre there. Anderson met the challenge by advertising that, in addition to his regular program, he would perform any feat the audience requested.

During Anderson's tour of Australia more than £18,659 ($93,000) was taken in at the box office, but the overhead was fantastic. His net profit for nearly fifteen months was $15,000.

Most of this was sent to creditors in England, who had advanced him funds after the Covent Garden Theatre fire. By the time he boarded the ship to sail for California, via Hawaii, there was $1,055 left. He arranged for the vessel to anchor for ten days in Honolulu, and performed there in a wooden building, which, he said, "when well packed (which it was during my stay) held five hundred people."

The night Kamehameha IV and the Hawaiian Queen attended, the "Great Wizard" performed in Highland regalia. The Queen, told that the kilt was a Victorian plaid, wanted to know if Victoria wore a dress that short. A Scot in the royal party assured her that the British monarch's skirt was considerably longer. Kamehameha, who had seen Anderson's show in London, gave the magician a pearl set in gold. Anderson reciprocated with several pieces of conjuring equipment, and an electrical device that amused the king: it was fitted into one of a pair of gloves. When anyone shook Kamehameha's hand, the concealed battery was switched on, and the man received an unexpected jolt of electricity.

Anderson landed in San Francisco in December 1859. The finest theatre in the city was Thomas McQuire's Opera House. The magician had helped Mrs. McQuire book London attractions for her husband years earlier, and had promised to perform there if he ever came to California. Now he had to wait a month before the current attraction closed. It was worth the delay; McQuire said Anderson could write his own contract—he could even have the house for nothing, if he wished, "for if there is anything on earth I like more than another, it is a man who *keeps his word.*" Business was excellent in San Francisco, as it was later in Sacramento and elsewhere in the state. Though Anderson paid $2,570 for his passage on the *Golden Gate* via Panama to New York, he was able to bank the bulk of his California profits—$25,000.

In July 1860 Anderson began to appear again in the cities that

Cover illustration from one of
Anderson's American song sheets.

Another song sheet depicted the
conjurer performing in a palace.

had received him cordially on his first American tour. There were two performances at the Academy of Music in Boston on opening day, the Fourth of July: one in the afternoon at three o'clock, another after the public fireworks display in the evening.

Two weeks later, he went the spiritualists one better by producing raps from the living as well as the dead. The raps sounded on the stage and on seats in various parts of the house.

With interest mounting in the forthcoming national election, someone asked if the spirits could name the next President of the United States. Anderson said he would see.

"Lincoln, are you there?" A rap sounded in the dress circle.

"Douglas, are you there?" Another rap came from somewhere in the middle of the house.

"Lincoln, who's to be President?"

Seven raps answered. The Republicans cheered; there are seven letters in the name Lincoln. The Democrats might have rejoiced, too, if they had thought about it, since there also are seven letters in the name Douglas.

Anderson misjudged the gravity of the crisis shaping up in America over the slavery issue. Business was bad in New York, Philadelphia, Washington, and Baltimore, yet he invested five thousand dollars in new posters and advance publicity, and sent an agent south to book a route that would culminate in New Orleans. The first sign of trouble, for him, came in Virginia; furious Richmond citizens ripped down his advance billings. How dare a "Wizard of the North" even consider invading their city! It was useless to explain that he was from the north of Scotland; North was an incendiary word. Anderson packed his equipment, and scooted back across the Mason-Dixon Line.

When the Civil War broke out in March 1861, Anderson noted in one of his later souvenir books that "all schemes for public amusement were paralyzed." Thinking the conflict would be quickly over, however, he decided to wait it out in New York. After three months, with battles still raging and his bank account steadily diminishing, the "Great Wizard" took the show west to Louisville, Cincinnati, St. Louis, Chicago, and then north to Canada. But the war seemed to affect attendance everywhere; he lost money on the trip. Returning to New York, he gambled the last of his savings on a mammoth topical extravaganza.

He hired Charles Taylor, a popular author, to write a burlesque of Shakespeare's *Tempest* with a strong pro-North slant; five hundred performers were engaged for the production. *The Wizard's Tempest* opened, the magician said later, at the New York Winter Garden to a full house on the night General George McClellan's Federal forces marched on Richmond; a Union victory seemed imminent. Anderson, playing the role of Prospero, implied as much to his daughter, who took the part of Miranda.

> Good gracious, daughter, do you doubt my star?
> Doubt everything but that, doubt Secretary Welles
> And all the *whacks* we've suffered through his *sells.*
> Doubt that the North must be victorious ever;
> Doubt when Jeff Davis dies, we'll hang a felon.
> Doubt that to-night our troops in Richmond are,
> Doubt one! Doubt all! but never doubt my star.

There were cheers and encores for this speech; it seemed obvious that the "Great Wizard" was a hit. Then the morning newspapers appeared on the streets, with boys shouting "McClellan retreating!" The reviewer from *Frank Leslie's Illustrated Newspaper* said: "The plot of the burlesque defies description, and is luckily so deliciously involved as to be beyond the need of it . . . success is certain." However, rave reviews were no salvation. More news of Union reversals came in daily; few people chose to go to the theatre to see a play with the opposite story. *The Wizard's Tempest* played several weeks to few spectators. Anderson, forced to let his huge cast go, abandoned the elaborate production in favor of the old standby, *Rob Roy.* This too, though it received fine notices, was a financial failure.

He was three thousand dollars in debt. "Writs were out against me on every side," he later wrote. "My property was seized, and I experienced all the trouble and difficulties attending to such a disaster." He fled to Canada to escape the bailiffs, "made a second tour there, but met with no success."

He returned to New York, called a meeting of his creditors, gave them promissory notes, and said he would go to England and try to raise money to pay them off. His wife's jewels were sold to finance the passage for himself and his assistants. She stayed in America with three of their children.

Waiting for the wizard in England were old debts, dating back to the Covent Garden Theatre fire. He gave up all hope of ever meeting his massive obligations on both sides of the Atlantic, and went into bankruptcy in October 1866. He still continued to conjure, but the days of extravagant Anderson spectacles were over. The gold and silver apparatus gave way to brass and tin. He was never to see his wife again.

Anderson had covered more than 350,000 miles during his travels around the world; some £157,000 (about $785,000, but the equivalent of more than $3,000,000 today) had slipped through his fingers or been consumed in flames. In addition, his benefit performances for public institutions and charities had netted more than $20,000. While performing in Russia, he had sent a donation of 1,000

Anderson riding high on the waves of popularity.

Topping the shows of his imitators and rivals.

Teaching the Queen how to catch cannon-balls in her teeth.

silver rubles to Dublin to help feed victims of the Irish famine; in New York a single show raised $5,000 for the widow of Police Sergeant Michael Kelley, who was murdered while on duty.

Anderson wrote, after the bankruptcy proceedings were over, that despite his many difficulties he still enjoyed good health. That, too, began to fade relatively soon; he died on February 3, 1874, at the age of fifty-nine, in Darlington, England, and was buried in Aberdeen in the same plot where earlier he had erected a simple tablet over his mother's grave.

Two of Anderson's daughters toured in the British Isles after his death, and John Henry Anderson, Jr., played for many years in the United States and Canada. When the son appeared at the Boston Melodeon in March 1864, a critic called his second-sight routine equal to, "if not superior" to, that of his famous father. Though a good magician, John Henry Anderson, Jr., was never to be an outstanding showman.

A far more flamboyant "Great Wizard of the North," Phillip Anderson, claimed to be the original's son, and to have inherited his equipment. This imitator, probably a former Anderson assistant named Holmes, worked with his personable American wife, who was billed as Louisa Maude Anderson, in Australia in 1881. She performed "Mental Telegraphy," assisted in "The Pillory Test," "The Arabian Sack Mystery," "The Famous Indian Basket Trick," and it was probably her head that was lopped off in "Beheading a Lady." The comedy highlight of the show came during a pie-eating contest between four boys from the audience. With their hands tied behind their backs, they gobbled up as much as they could before the allotted time expired.

This Anderson, like his predecessor, was a great advertiser and a shrewd promoter. He used the gift-show approach to insure full houses, giving away gold and silver watches, furniture, and pianos to holders of winning ticket stubs. In Sydney a horse was paraded through the streets with a banner on his back saying the steed would be presented to a patron.

Two days before Christmas 1881, Phillip Anderson sailed for India. When he came back to Australia three years later, he said he had been in Rangoon, Moulmein, Penang, Singapore, Shanghai, Hong Kong, Batavia, and Manila, as well as Calcutta. Then he had gone on to Glasgow, Edinburgh, and Liverpool, and toured through Africa.

This time he also performed in New Zealand, before he sailed with South America as his announced destination. On his final Australian tour, which began in 1899, Phillip Anderson was accompanied by a new wife, Blanche De La Cour. Robert Kudarz, a New Zealand magician who attended the show, talked with him after his performance at the Wellington Opera House on November 14, 1900. Kudarz never saw him again, nor have records of later performances been discovered. Phillip Anderson, however, was by far the most successful of the many magicians who traded on the name and worldwide fame of the "Great Wizard of the North."

9

Robert Houdin—

Innovator

THE French clockmaker who is justly acclaimed as the father of modern magic reached this eminence almost in spite of himself. Jean Eugène Robert-Houdin delayed his first stage appearance until he was approaching forty, then rashly opened his *Soirées Fantastiques* in a small theatre in the old Palais Royal on the same evening as the gala premiere of the new Paris Hippodrome.

Not a single critic covered Robert-Houdin's July 3, 1845, debut. This was just as well. The perfectionist who built his own equipment confessed in his memoirs that the show had been a disaster. Panicked by stage fright, he talked too fast and in a monotone. By the time the final curtain fell, he was so distraught he did not know what he was saying or doing.

Robert-Houdin returned home in a fever. Tormented by self-doubt, he rolled and tossed throughout the night. When morning came, he was too exhausted to rise. He notified the theatre to rip down his posters. Then, relieved of the ordeal of facing another audience, he slept soundly until the following day.

When an acquaintance who had seen the first night fiasco dropped by to congratulate Robert-Houdin for having had the good sense to close his show before he was forced to by lack of patronage, the slightly built, square-jawed magician glowered. Refreshed by the long rest and irked by the man's effrontery, he coolly said he had no intention of abandoning magic; he would perform again that evening.

Each succeeding performance Robert-Houdin was more at ease on the stage. *Charivari* and *L'Illustration* agreed that his mechanical marvels and artistic conjuring compared favorably with the feats of his most celebrated predecessors, Philippe and Bosco, but few people came to the show during the summer months. Determined to keep the theatre open for the fall and winter seasons, the struggling showman sold three houses in Blois he had inherited from his mother, to meet expenses.

Seven months after the opening, on February 12, 1846, he added a provocative new feature to his program—"Second Sight." While his blindfolded, fourteen-year-old son, Emile, sat in a chair on the stage, the magician walked down the aisles and invited spectators to hand him any unusual objects they had with them. The boy would then describe coins, snuffboxes, and pieces of jewelry as accurately as if he had had them under a microscope.

News spread rapidly of the child's uncanny talent. Soon seats were at a premium. Skeptics came, armed with books written in German and Greek, and odd tools; Emile correctly identified a peculiar piece of metal as a thread counter. Once seated, the audience enjoyed the magic and the automata, but it was the simulated clairvoyance, not the intricate apparatus he had labored so long to perfect, that brought Robert-Houdin success. Later he introduced and presented superbly the best stage illusions of the mid-nineteenth century; he also wrote the first worthwhile manual on conjuring, as well as a fascinating autobiography that is still in print.

France's greatest magician was born Jean Eugène Robert in Blois on December 7, 1805, a day after the date given in his memoirs. His watchmaker father sent him to a college (the equivalent of an American secondary school) in Orléans; then the graduate entered the family trade.

Three years later, while working as an apprentice in a cousin's shop, Jean Eugène prepared to study Ferdinand Berthoud's treatise on horology. Unaware that a busy bookseller had given him by mistake an illustrated encyclopedic dictionary of scientific amusements, he went to his room, lit a candle, and began turning the pages. Annoyed when the expected diagrams of timekeeping mechanisms did not appear, he soon became fascinated as he scanned page after page of conjuring secrets. "How often since," he recalled in his memoirs, "have I blessed this providential error, without which I should probably have vegetated as a country watchmaker."

Conscious that the explanations told how the feats were done but not how to do them (there is a difference!), Jean Eugène paid ten francs for a series of lessons from a Blois pedicure, named Maous, who entertained with sleight of hand at fetes and celebrations.

Maous taught his pupil juggling to coordinate his eye and

hand, then explained the intricacies of the cups and balls. Words, gestures, or glances diverted attention as the conjurer secretly loaded balls into, or extracted them from under, the inverted cups. Digital dexterity, Maous stressed, came only with constant repetition.

Jean Eugène practiced faithfully on his way to work, manipulating balls and coins, his hands out of sight in the capacious pockets of his overcoat. He mystified his friends with his newly acquired skill, but he had no thought then of performing professionally.

He was twenty-three when he met the seventeen-year-old daughter of a prominent Parisian clockmaker at a party in Blois. Hired soon afterward by her father's firm, he moved to the French capital. Jean Eugène Robert married Josèphe Cécile Eglantine Houdin on July 8, 1830; the first of their children, Jean Jacques Emile, was born the following May. The talented craftsman opened his own studio with the backing of his father-in-law and added the Houdin family name to his own to become Robert-Houdin.

After a chance visit to Père Roujol's magic shop on the Rue Richelieu, he began stopping by frequently to purchase equipment and to talk with amateur and professional magicians. He met Jules de Rovère, an aristocrat, who coined a new word, *prestidigitation,* to describe his own elegant exhibitions of sleight of hand. The professional whom Robert-Houdin admired most, however, was Comte, "The King's Conjurer," owner of a theatre in the Passage Choiseul.

Born in Geneva on June 22, 1788, Louis Apollinaire Christien Emmanuel Comte was twenty-six when he first performed for King Louis XVIII at the Tuileries Palace. Later another monarch, Louis Philippe, made the popular magician a Chevalier of the Legion of Honor. Comte, Robert-Houdin observed, flattered the ladies in his audience, while the men—royalty always excepted—were the targets of his humor.

Adept at sleight of hand, apparatus magic, and ventriloquism, Comte excelled as a publicist. During slow seasons he issued family tickets that admitted four people for the price of one. When a family ticket was presented at the box office, the holder was offered, for a mere two sous, a gilded coin with Comte's name and theatrical address on one side and the purchaser's name—stamped then and there—on the other. The profit from the sale of these inexpensive personalized souvenirs paid the theatre's lighting bill. Parents of boys and girls who won scholarship awards were invited to sit with their children in the royal box—if they paid the price of a regular seat. Late arrivals could get choice seats if they entered the hall through a side door in the adjoining café and paid extra for the privilege.

Robert-Houdin undoubtedly first thought of becoming a professional magician himself in Comte's theatre. Thereafter the clockmaker tried to see every conjurer who came to Paris. Their faults as

Robert-Houdin
—Innovator

Robert-Houdin's favorite portrait.

First illustration of his stage.

well as their accomplishments served as object lessons. Naturally, Robert-Houdin was in the audience when the celebrated Bosco played to full houses in a theatre on the Rue Chantereine in 1838.

Giovanni Bartolomeo Bosco had been born in Turin, Italy, on January 3, 1793. Wounded by a Cossack lancer at Borodino, while serving with Napoleon's army in Russia, the nineteen-year-old soldier played dead on the battlefield. When a scavenger took his few possessions, Bosco lifted the Russian's purse and profited by the exchange.

Bosco entertained fellow prisoners and guards in Siberia, then conjured for the rulers of Russia, Prussia, Sweden, and France after the war. Performing extemporaneously in markets, taverns, and on coaches as he traveled to publicize his skill, he attracted immense crowds to his shows.

In Paris, Bosco's stage had no front curtains. Spectators could see conjuring equipment, numerous lighted candles and a human skull on a long, three-tiered, black-draped table near the back—a decor more suitable for a funeral than a place of amusement, in Robert-Houdin's opinion. At center stage stood a square table covered with a long brown cloth and holding five brass cups and a wand. Hanging from a chain several feet above the table was a large copper sphere.

Bosco, a plump man with dark, curly hair and moustache, was dressed entirely in black, except for a white ruffled collar on his short-sleeved jacket and white lace edging on his trousers. He acknowledged the applause, picked up the wand, wiped it with a white handkerchief, then struck the copper globe above his head three times, solemnly intoning, *"Spiriti miei infernali, obedite."* Whether invisible infernal forces aided him or not, Robert-Houdin found Bosco's cup-and-ball manipulations marvelous.

The personable Italian decapitated two pigeons, one white, the other black, asking if the audience wished to see the blood flow. If someone said no, he pressed firmly on the artery in the bird's neck before his blade descended. When yes was the choice, he released his grip, and the blood spurted out on a white saucer. The white head and the black body were deposited in one box, the black head and the white body in another. Uttering a few mysterious words, Bosco flipped open the lids and took from each container a live bird with a mismatched head.

He also loaded a canary into the funnel-shaped barrel of a pistol, passed the weapon to a spectator, then brandished a sword. With a lunge forward as the pistol was fired, Bosco impaled the yellow missile on the blade. These barbaric feats disturbed Robert-Houdin. When the time came for him to present his own show, he resolved never to include anything objectionable on the program and to wear the fashionable evening dress of a gentleman.

Robert-Houdin
—Innovator

A year later Robert-Houdin exhibited an automaton cup-and-ball player and a "Mysterious Clock" at the Products of French Industry Exposition. The timepiece attracted considerable attention. The hands moved on a transparent dial, which was supported by a glass rod attached to a metal base. There were no visible works. He received a bronze medal, but the judges wondered why a man of his ability constructed frivolous rather than practical machines. The reason was clear. He enjoyed devising unusual pieces and had found a ready market for them at the shop of Alphonse Giroux, who catered to wealthy curio collectors at No. 7 Rue de Coc-Saint-Honoré. Still, Robert-Houdin's greatest pleasure came from watching the big magic shows that came to Paris.

Philippe, the conjurer who was to have the strongest influence on the clockmaker's subsequent career, opened at the Salle Montesquieu in 1841. Born Jacques André Noël Talon in Alais on December 28, 1802, he had crossed the channel to the British Isles as a confectioner, and become an entertainer in Aberdeen. Taking Philippe as his stage name, he had toured Scotland, Ireland, and the English provinces with an increasingly more elaborate production before returning to France. Philippe's sensational feats at the Salle Montesquieu made him such a great attraction that a new theatre was built to his specifications in the Bonne Nouvelle bazaar in Paris, while he played an interim date in Vienna.

Robert-Houdin hastened to the impressive new theatre when Philippe opened. Pleased by the attractive, fresh decor, he waited impatiently for the overture to end, then settled back in his comfortable seat to enjoy the show. To his surprise the stage was dark as the curtain rose. A man in a black suit apologized for not having had time to light the scene. Saying he would take care of it at once, he fired a pistol. Instantly hundreds of candles burst into flame, and it was obvious that this was Philippe—not the theatre manager as some had thought. The impact of the brilliant, unexpected opening produced tumultuous applause.

This feat represents the first-known application of electricity to conjuring. Though new to Paris, it had been introduced by Ludwig Leopold Doebler, an inventive Viennese magician. Hydrogen jets ignited when a current traveled through a thin, vertical insulated wire with gaps for the candlewicks. Since the wicks had been dampened by turpentine, they flared up immediately.

On rare occasions, the trick failed. Robert-Houdin believed a magician should be infallible; he resolved never to present this or any other feat that was not mechanically perfect.

He was keenly interested in Philippe's automata. A realistic peacock spread its plumage and pecked at the grain in the magician's

Bosco—Italy's greatest cup-and-ball
conjurer of the nineteenth century.

Frontispiece from the 1861 French
edition of Robert-Houdin's memoirs.

Philippe, in "Chinese" costume,
producing a bowl of goldfish.

hand. A "Cossack" grimaced in a lifelike manner. A harlequin jumped from a box, smoked a pipe, then hopped back inside. A little mechanical man also entered a miniature confectionary shop to fetch refreshments for the spectators; Robert-Houdin later built a similar device, but he did not mention in his memoirs that he had seen Philippe present this routine.

The second half of the production featured two feats Philippe had learned from a troupe of Chinese jugglers in Britain. The conjurer now wore a magnificent robe and a tall conical cap. One Parisian critic said the costume was Egyptian; another identified it as the garb of an ancient sorcerer. After solid eight-inch metal rings had been examined by the audience, Philippe linked, unlinked, and combined the glittering circles into complicated designs. "Then suddenly, when it seemed impossible for him to unravel his handiwork, he blew upon them and the rings fell separately on the floor," Robert-Houdin enthused.

For his spectacular finale, Philippe stood on a low platform just high enough above the stage to convince the audience that trapdoors could not be used. He flourished a spangled shawl, showed both sides, threw it down, then lifted it to reveal an immense glass bowl, filled to the brim with water and goldfish. As the applause mounted, he produced a second, then a third bowl of fish. Finally, with a shake of another shawl, he filled the platform with chickens, rabbits, and ducks. Philippe gave seven hundred performances in Paris. Imitators, dressed in pointed hats and voluminous robes, toured the smaller cities.

Robert-Houdin meanwhile continued to support his family by constructing "Mysterious Clocks" and expensive mechanical singing birds. His wife, who had been ill for many months, died at the age of thirty-two on October 19, 1843. Only three of eight children had survived; Emile, the eldest, was twelve. Somehow the versatile craftsman managed to complete his most complex machine—a smaller than life-size automated man—in time for the May 1844 opening of the Universal Exposition.

On one of his visits to the Palace of Industry, King Louis Philippe asked the android how many people lived in Paris. The mechanical figure put his pencil to a sheet of paper and wrote, "Paris contains 998,964 inhabitants." Wouldn't the new census produce a different total? the king inquired. The answer came from Robert-Houdin. "Sire, I hope at that period my automaton will be intelligent enough to make any necessary corrections."

The judges awarded Robert-Houdin a silver medal. P. T. Barnum, the American impresario, purchased the android for seven thousand francs, then shipped it to London where he put it on display.

Robert-Houdin married François Marguerite Olympe Braconnier in August. She took over the management of his household while he constructed conjuring equipment—not for sale now, but for the theatre of magic he was determined to open.

He had weathered several financial storms in Paris. He and his first wife's father had been swindled by a lawyer who mishandled their investments. Robert-Houdin also lost money on a friend's get-rich-quick scheme, and before he sold the writing automaton, he had been heavily in debt.

As Robert-Houdin worked in his shop at 13 Rue de Vendôme to finish the apparatus for a two-hour show, he occasionally took time off to demonstrate a new trick for a wealthy neighbor who had purchased a "Mysterious Clock." Intrigued by the conjuring, the Count de L'Escalopier invited him to entertain at private parties. Convinced Parisian theatregoers would enjoy the ingenious presentations as much as his guests had, the count invested fifteen thousand francs in Robert-Houdin's theatre project.

A choice site was found near the Comédie Française in the old Palais Royal. Once the residence of Cardinal Richelieu, the building housed shops and cafés on the street level and restaurants, clubs, and assembly rooms on the floor above. Robert-Houdin leased the assembly rooms at 164 Galerie Valois. Carpenters tore down walls, remodeled the interior. The walls were painted white with gold trim. Exquisite drapes, candelabra, and stage furniture in the style of Louis XV gave him an elegant drawing-room setting on the well-equipped stage.

There was a touch of novelty in every number Robert-Houdin presented. A borrowed handkerchief appeared within one of the oranges which materialized on a mechanical tree. The fruit split into four sections as two butterflies came from nowhere to unfold the handkerchief in the air. A silk handkerchief was covering enough for him to produce colored plumes and then a basket filled with flowers to be tossed to the ladies in the audience.

While his "Pastrycook of the Palais Royal" looked like Philippe's "Confectioner," the method and presentation were different. Contemporary magicians believed the "Pastrycook" to be purely mechanical. Actually, Robert-Houdin's small son was concealed inside the miniature building; he controlled the turntable which sent the little man in and out of the doorway, carrying buns, tarts, ices, and liqueurs on a tray. One offering was a cake containing a ring which had been borrowed from a spectator for an earlier trick.

Philippe had produced three bowls of water and goldfish under the cover of a spangled shawl. The sealed bowls, with removable airtight tops, were in special canvas holders attached to the strong belt he wore beneath his robes. Robert-Houdin thought he height-

Any drink called for flowed
from Robert-Houdin's bottle.

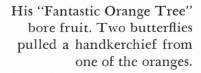

His "Fantastic Orange Tree"
bore fruit. Two butterflies
pulled a handkerchief from
one of the oranges.

Though blindfolded, his son
accurately described objects
offered by various onlookers.

Stewpans, birds, cages, and bonnets came from the empty portfolio. Then his young son was lifted out.

"The Pastrycook of the Palais Royal" darted inside his shop to fetch cakes, ices, and buns.

Rather than take souvenirs from a hat, Robert-Houdin produced them from a cornucopia.

ened the mystery by concealing a single bowl under the coattails of his evening coat, but his bowl was far smaller than Philippe's, and his version lacked the climactic shower of birds and animals.

Nor was "Second Sight," the feat that finally made Robert-Houdin a major theatrical attraction, completely original. Contrary to his memoirs, he did not invent "Second Sight." As early as 1784, Pinetti's blindfolded wife had identified the objects that were handed to her husband by members of the audience. An eight-year-old, kilt-wearing, Scottish boy, Louis Gordon M'Kean, exhibited "Double Vision," with his eyes bandaged, in London in 1833, and "The Mysterious Lady" amazed spectators with a "Second Sight" routine in the United States in the early 1840's.

Robert-Houdin said in his autobiography that he used a spoken code to convey information to his son, but he did not explain his system. M. F. A. Gandon, a French rival, however, published *La Seconde Vue Dévoilée* (Second Sight Revealed) in 1849, three years after Robert-Houdin first presented the mystery.

Like Robert-Houdin and his son, Gandon and a young nephew memorized lists of coins, cards, jewelry, and other categories of objects. Cue words indicated the category, then the specific object in that group. Though Gandon's French cues are not practical in English, these key words and the numbers they signal illustrate the technique: Give (1), Will (2), Can (3), Now (4), If (5), Try (6), Tell (7), See (8), Would (9), Please (0).

"Will (2) you concentrate?" indicates the second category. "Give (1) a description of this object, please (0)" specifies the tenth article on that list. The same key words may be used to transmit letters of the alphabet or numbers. "Will," the cue for 2, indicates the second letter of the alphabet—B. "Now," the cue for 4, signals D. After long practice, the sender speeds up the process by using abbreviations for words to convey data quickly.

When other performers imitated his presentation, Robert-Houdin varied his routine by ringing a hand bell rather than speaking. Still his son called out the items promptly.

The simplest of the many silent methods uses a prearranged series of objects. For instance: purse, spectacles, tie pin, wedding ring, and cane. The receiver doesn't merely say purse when he hears the bell ring; he begins: "This belongs to a lady. She has it with her whenever she leaves the house. It is the convenient receptable for her cosmetics, handkerchief, change, and door key. Yes, I see it quite clearly. It is her handbag." The other items are handled in the same way.

By combining an oral code and a silent system, Robert-Houdin bewildered those who guessed his conversation played a vital part in the feat. His digital skill enhanced the mystery.

I opened boxes, purses, pocket-books, etc., with great ease, and un-noticed, while appearing to be engaged on something quite different. Were a sealed parcel offered me, I cut a small slit in the paper with the nail of my left thumb, which I always purposely kept long and sharp, and thus discovered what it contained.

Established as a Parisian attraction, Robert-Houdin closed his theatre for the summer. He played engagements in Brussels and Liège, then concentrated on devising new wonders for the fall.

Probably inspired by articles about the levitation performed by two conjurers in India, he worked on this incredible illusion. European papers had carried stories of a Brahmin who suspended himself in thin air. Two years after this performer's death in 1830, another magician of the same caste, named Sheshal, duplicated the feat.

Sheshal carried his equipment in a bag and performed in the open or in the homes of his patrons. He displayed a four-legged stool, a length of bamboo, and a roll of antelope hide. His assistants held up a cloth to shield his preparations. When it was pulled away, She-shal was seen, sitting cross-legged, four feet above the ground. His right wrist rested near one end of the horizontal cylinder of antelope hide as the far end of the cylinder touched the top of the upright bamboo pole, which in turn was balanced precariously on top of the stool.

Some Indians claimed controlled breathing was the secret. A European observer, who had seen the performance four times, offered a more rational explanation. Inside the antelope hide and the hollow bamboo were two iron rods. The one in the bamboo fitted neatly into a socket concealed in a brass decoration at the top of the stool. The other, in the rolled hide, was fixed to the upper end of the bamboo. Under his robes, Sheshal wore a metal device that provided him with a place to sit. Attached to the device, an iron support extended down his sleeve as far as his wrist. The tip of this piece of bent metal was inserted into a hole in the hide-wrapped bar. The Indian added two showmanly fillips to his presentation. He held his free arm straight up in the air, while his right fingers counted the beads of a necklace. When the cloth was lifted a second time to cover Sheshal's descent to the ground, a weird sound like the noise of air being forced from a squeezed bladder was heard.

Robert-Houdin took the suspension concept and improved upon it. He devised a method that eliminated the shielding cloth and brought the miracle out to full view. Then he added a ratchet, so that an assistant could be raised progressively higher until his body was parallel with the stage. Robert-Houdin presented his revamped version of the Indian mystery as "The Ethereal Suspension," thus taking advantage of a controversy that had erupted in Paris that fall over the side effects of ether, which surgeons were beginning to use for anesthesia.

Conjurers in India had amazed
audiences by "sitting on air."

Robert-Houdin topped them by
suspending his son vertically.

Six-year-old Auguste Adolphe Robert-Houdin stood on a stool and extended his arms; upright poles were placed under them, close to his body. "When this liquid is at its highest degree of concentration, if a living being breathes it, the body of the patient becomes in a few moments as light as a balloon," the magician said as he uncorked a bottle filled with a yellowish solution and held it under his son's nose. Excitement grew as the unmistakable odor of ether drifted out to the audience.

The boy's eyes closed, his head sagged. Then, very slowly, his knees bent slightly and his feet left the top of the stool. Robert-Houdin reached down and took away the stool. The child hung in the air, supported by the rods under his arms.

Working with exquisite care, Robert-Houdin bent his son's right arm until the hand touched the boy's head, then gently removed the rod from under the child's left arm. The remaining rod didn't topple; the son slept quietly—leaning on the single pole. Effortlessly, with a single finger, the magician lifted the boy's feet until his body was horizontal. To create the proper atmosphere, as the magician removed the cork from the bottle, an assistant backstage poured ether over a hot shovel and fanned the fumes toward the audience.

"This," Robert-Houdin wrote in his autobiography, "was the first time I tried to direct the surprise of my spectators by gradually heightening it up to the moment when, so to speak, it exploded."

Less sensational than the suspension illusion, but just as carefully plotted, was Robert-Houdin's "Enchanted Portfolio." An artist's portfolio, just 1¾ inches thick—obviously too thin to hold anything but pictures—was placed on a pair of slender trestles, its spine toward the audience.

From the portfolio the magician first took out pictures and then objects related to their subject matter. For example, the portrait of a bareheaded woman was followed by two sizable hats, one for winter, the other for summer. Robert-Houdin lowered the top flap of the portfolio after each production, then opened it again for the next. The sketch of a bird led to the production of a stuffed bird, seemingly crushed pancake flat by being in the portfolio, then four live doves. A cartoon of two cooks battling with pots preceded the appearance of three large metal pans containing beans, water, and fire.

Almost as an afterthought Robert-Houdin raised the top flap of the portfolio and lifted out a large square cage filled with canaries. As he walked forward, the audience applauded, thinking the feat was over. He bowed and went back to the still-open portfolio. "Nothing here now—neither anything, nor anybody," he stated emphatically as he rapped on the upright flap. Instantly a small head peered over the edge. His youngest son complained it was stuffy inside. Obligingly the magician lifted the boy out.

The loading of the youngster was a masterpiece of misdirection and timing. While the audience's attention was centered on the cage of canaries, an assistant who had been standing by the open portfolio let the inner cloth lining of the case fall; this covered the space between the portfolio and the stage. A stagehand pulled a lever shooting the boy, who sat in a boxlike elevator under the flooring, up through a trapdoor. When he was level with the bottom section of the portfolio, the child quickly climbed into it. The assistant then casually tucked the cloth lining back inside. In his *Secrets of Stage Conjuring*, Robert-Houdin said this carefully rehearsed loading process took just four seconds. So effective was the misdirection that most spectators were not even aware that the cloth had dropped and been replaced.

The 1848 Revolution closed Parisian theatres. When Robert-Houdin traveled to London for a May opening at the St. James Theatre, Carl Herrmann, an excellent showman, was featuring pirated versions of the French innovator's "Second Sight" and "Ethereal Suspension" in a competing playhouse. Despite this, Robert-Houdin scored a major triumph. He appeared before Queen Victoria at a charity fete in Fulham and was invited to entertain her at Buckingham Palace.

A *Punch* reviewer, who was particularly impressed by "The Inexhaustible Bottle," from which flowed "an ocean of champagne, port, claret and curaçao," warned the magician not to be too liberal with his free drinks, otherwise "his audience may be carried off to the stationhouse and locked up, on the dreadful charge of inebriety."

There was a mad scramble for the magic wine at the Theatre Royal in Manchester in September. Glasses were smashed, and a man ran forward, cupped his hands and insisted that the magician fill them. The idea caught on. Cupped hands were extended on all sides. More demanding spectators threw back their heads and signaled for the conjurer to pour the potions directly down their throats.

Despite the unruly crowd at the opening performance, business was excellent. Bookings followed in Liverpool, Birmingham, Bristol, and other cities. The transition from the small stage in Paris to the larger theatres in Britain brought Robert-Houdin more money than he had ever earned before.

After a year and a half abroad, he returned to France and bought Le Prieuré (The Priory), a country estate, a few miles from Blois. There he relaxed and experimented with new mechanical and electrical devices until May 1849 when he played for a second time in Brussels. In October he reopened his "Soirées Fantastiques" in Paris. Two years later, as his forty-sixth birthday approached, Robert-Houdin announced that Hamilton, a former pupil (whose real name was Pierre Etienne Chocat), would take his place on the stage. The choice was a good one; crowds continued to fill the hall.

January 1852 was a memorable month for Robert-Houdin's pro-

Robert-Houdin, after retiring to his home in Saint Gervais.

London playbill featuring his mechanical trapeze performer.

ROBERT-HOUDIN,

ST. JAMES'S THEATRE.

LAST THREE PERFORMANCES

The celebrated M. ROBERT-HOUDIN will give his Incredible
Delusions and Extraordinary

FANTASTIQUES

AT THE ABOVE THEATRE

MODERN   **MIRACLES.**

LA VOLTIGE DU TRAPEZE

ON

TUESDAY EVENING, MARCH 6,

Last Day Performance

WEDNESDAY MORNING, March 7

COMMENCING AT HALF-PAST TWO O'CLOCK,

AND

FAREWELL REPRESENTATION,

THURSDAY EVENING, MARCH 8

DOORS OPEN AT EIGHT O'CLOCK.

PRIVATE BOXES, ORCHESTRA STALLS, AND TICKETS, MAY BE SECURED AT
MR. MITCHELL'S ROYAL LIBRARY, 33, OLD BOND STREET,
Mr. Sams' Royal Library, St. James's Street; Messrs. Eden's, Hookham's, Allcroft's, Andrews', Leader and Cock's, Hammond's, Chappell's, and Olivier's Libraries,
Bond Street; Cramer's, and the Carlton Library, 12, Regent Street;
And at the BOX OFFICE of the Theatre, which is open Daily, from Eleven till Five o'clock.

PRINTED BY W. S. JOHNSON, 6, PATINER STREET, LEICESTER SQUARE.

tégé. Hamilton became the director of the theatre in the Palais Royal and married his mentor's sister-in-law. Possibly Robert-Houdin conjured for Queen Victoria again that year. His bills at the Waterloo Rooms in Edinburgh in June announced a limited engagement "under the immediate patronage of Her Majesty the Queen, H.R.H. Prince Albert, & the Royal Family," for whom he had appeared "at the Palace in St. James."

The lease at the Palais Royal was not renewed in December. Instead a new Théâtre Robert-Houdin was opened in January at 8 Boulevard des Italiens. The founder of the show gave the inaugural performance and wished his successor well. Robert-Houdin went to England again to entertain at Buckingham Palace for Princess Louisa's birthday party on March 18, 1853. Easter week he opened at St. James' Theatre, beginning a London season which ended in May at the Sadler's Wells Theatre.

Following engagements that fall in Belgium and a few months' rest in Saint Gervais, he began what was billed as his farewell tour: Baden, Wiesbaden, Bad Homburg, Aix-la-Chappelle, Spa, and eventually Berlin, where he stayed four months and drew the largest and most enthusiastic audiences of his career.

Back home in Saint Gervais with his family—there had been four more children by his second wife—he devoted himself to scientific research. His exhibits at the 1855 Universal Exposition in Paris were quite different from those he had displayed at earlier fairs. Among other practical devices were a control mechanism, designed to stem the flow of electricity at night and release it in the morning, and a regulator that kept the current at constant level.

An incipient rebellion brought Robert-Houdin back to the stage. Algeria was in ferment. The Marabouts, a sect of wonder-working religious fanatics, were advising the leaders of the principal tribes to break their ties with France. The troubled head of the French political bureau in Algiers convinced the master magician that by performing his feats there for the assembled chieftains he could counteract the Marabouts' influence and perform a great service for the homeland.

Napoleon III's envoy extraordinary sailed from Marseille in September 1856. The day he arrived in North Africa a revolt erupted in Kabylia. As a result, the scheduled fetes for the Arab chieftains had to be postponed. Meanwhile, Robert-Houdin presented his show twice weekly at the Bab-azon Theatre in Algiers. Then on the evening of October 28 he performed for the potentates of the desert tribes. Interpreters were stationed throughout the audience to translate the conjurer's words. He produced cannonballs from an empty hat—visual evidence of France's limitless armaments. Flowers from the same headpiece suggested his magic controlled nature. The invisible passage of silver coins from his hands to the interior of a closed, suspended crystal chest implied that the strongest fort could be penetrated by French ingenuity.

If the audience suspected he had supernatural power, they were right, Robert-Houdin asserted. He could "deprive even the most powerful man of his strength." Anyone who doubted this should come forward.

A muscular Arab responded to the challenge. At the magician's suggestion, he easily lifted a wooden cash box from the floor, then replaced it. "Behold!" the conjurer cried. "Now you are weaker than a woman; try to lift the box." The man confidently grasped the handle again, but this time he couldn't budge the box. Furious, his face red, he braced his legs for support, gripped the handle firmly and exerted himself to the limit. Suddenly for no apparent reason, he shrieked, fell to his knees, then got up and ran from the stage.

The wooden box was not as innocent as it appeared. There was a sheet of iron in the bottom, camouflaged by a brown paper surface that matched the mahogany sides and lid. Beneath the cloth which served as a carpet for the stage, a strong electromagnet had been implanted in the floor. Wires from the magnet ran to a switch backstage. When the current was on, it was impossible even for a Hercules to move the box. The Arab's cry of agony? He had received an electric shock, generated by an induction coil, through the metal handle.

For his final mystery, the ingenious French conjurer lifted the drapes of a four-legged table to show there was no hiding place concealed by them. A young Moor who stood on the tabletop was covered with a huge cone made of cloth. Robert-Houdin and an assistant slid a plank under the cone and brought the covered Moor forward. One moment they were struggling to support their heavy burden; the next, the board tipped and the cone fell—empty—to the stage. There was pandemonium in the theatre as terrified spectators rushed to the exits.

This illusion had been performed by George Sutton, a British conjurer, long before Robert-Houdin turned professional. In Sutton's version, a girl vanished under the cone as she stood on a table, and reappeared later in the center of an immense imitation pie.

There was a secret compartment behind the drapes of the table. A wooden panel, with collapsible, pleated cloth sides was fastened flat against the tabletop when the drapes were lifted. When they were in place again, the assistant, under cover of the cone, opened a trap, pushed down the panel, climbed inside the expanded compartment, and closed the door over her head.

Robert-Houdin's procedure with the plank increased the impact of the disappearance. As soon as he and his aide lifted the board,

Advertisement for Robert-Houdin's theatre under Brunnet's direction.

Imps aid in the production of liquids from the magic bottle.

They also assist in producing the "Light and Heavy Chest" illusion.

bearing the cone and presumably the Moor, they walked forward, and curtains closed behind them. The vanishing then took place on an empty stage.

Four days after Robert-Houdin's first performance for the chieftains, he was invited to the governor's palace. There the Arab leaders, wearing red robes—symbols of their loyalty to France—presented the magician with a scroll extolling his baffling demonstrations; nothing they had seen before approached his marvels.

Mission completed, Robert-Houdin sailed for France. He gave his last public performances at the Grand Théâtre in Marseille, then returned to his home at Saint Gervais. Never one to be idle, he continued to experiment with new applications of electricity, and to construct clock mechanisms. He also wrote books.

Confidences d'un Prestidigitateur was published in 1858. The English translation, *Memoirs of Robert-Houdin: Ambassador, Author and Conjurer,* appeared a year later. Since then many editions have been printed in numerous languages. This is an exciting tale, as engrossing as a novel—and parts of it are fiction. There was, for instance, no Count de Grisy, who performed as Torrini and gave the young man from Blois an insight into stage conjuring and the histories of his predecessors. Robert-Houdin approached his autobiography the way he did magic; his object was to entertain.

His textbooks were another matter. *Les Tricheries des Grecs Dévoilées* (1861), issued in England as *The Sharper Detected and Exposed,* was as felicitously written, but it is a sound treatise on card handling. *Les Secrets de la Prestidigitation et de la Magie* (1868) (The Secrets of Conjuring and Magic) went further. This is the first really thorough manual on sleight of hand and the psychology of deception.

The sixty-five-year-old master magician who revolutionized stage conjuring with his many innovations died on June 13, 1871, of pneumonia in his home at Saint Gervais. The book on which he was working at the time of his death was published six years later—*Magie et Physique Amusante* (Magic and Amusing Physics). The English title *The Secrets of Stage Conjuring* is more descriptive of its contents.

Robert-Houdin's principal French-born competitor, Robin (Henri Joseph Donckele) though six years younger performed professionally before the clockmaker became a conjurer.

After building a reputation in Europe, Robin played two long engagements in England—the first extending from the winter of 1850 into the spring of 1853; the second ending after his 309th performance at Egyptian Hall in London in 1862. He featured Robert-Houdin's "Second Sight" and "Ethereal Suspension," and Hamilton's curious feat of lifting a small boy by grasping a single strand of his hair.

Later Robin opened a theatre on the Boulevard du Temple in Paris, where his prime attraction was a scientific spectacle depicting the creation of the world in forty-five minutes. Colored pictures projected on a large screen by an "Agioscope" told the story.

After seven successful years in the French capital, Robin retired to the hotel he had purchased on the Boulevard Mazaz. He died there at the age of sixty-three on February 24, 1879.

Though Robert-Houdin had been dead four years, the Théâtre Robert-Houdin still flourished. Cleverman (François Lahire) replaced Hamilton; then Emile Robert-Houdin, himself busy with clockmaking, arranged for Pierre Edouard Brunnet to present the show. Brunnet added the "Malle des Indes" to the theatre repertoire. In this illusion, an assistant dressed as a Hindu, mysteriously escaped from, then reentered, a locked trunk that had been laced in a heavy canvas cover.

Emile Robert-Houdin's widow, the last of the founder's family to control the business, sold the theatre in 1888 to Georges Méliès, the twenty-six-year-old son of a wealthy shoe manufacturer.

Eager to modernize the theatre where he had been enthralled by magic as a boy, Méliès refurbished the by-now dilapidated house. He painted the walls, bought new curtains, and designed new illusions and scenery.

Méliès, who had performed at the Musée Grévin and at a theatre at the Galeries Vivienne, was determined to bring the shows back to Robert-Houdin's standard. The theatre prospered under his management.

When Méliès saw Louis and Auguste Lumière's "animated pictures" at a private showing in December 1895 he immediately tried to buy exhibition rights for the Théâtre Robert-Houdin, but he was outbid. Learning that R. W. Paul, a British inventor, had a similar projector, Méliès purchased a bioscope through David Devant, the English magician who was Paul's distributor.

The enchanting flickering images on the screen of the Théâtre Robert-Houdin inspired Méliès. He purchased a camera and began shooting movies on the grounds of his country home in Montreuil. On film, Méliès performed illusions that were impossible on stage. His head left his shoulders, floated in the air, and multiplied into many heads while the set was brightly lighted. In another sequence, a hose was attached to his decapitated though living head, and when air was pumped into it, the head expanded to enormous proportions. In a "Cremation" episode, his clothes melted away and his flesh dissolved until finally only his skeleton was left. Méliès introduced many trick photography techniques still in wide usage; his "Trip to the Moon" was the pioneer film saga of a journey to outer space.

World War I closed the Théâtre Robert-Houdin and swept away the profits Méliès had earned from the syndication of his films. After the armistice, the theatre reopened, but the great days were

TREMONT TEMPLE
POSITIVELY FOR ONE WEEK ONLY.
COMMENCING MONDAY EVENING, January 22d, 1866.
Doors open at 6 3-4 · Curtain rises at 7 3-4 o'clock.

Tickets 30 Cts. Reserved Seats 50 Cts.
Tickets can be secured at the Office from 10 o'clock, A. M., to 1 P. M.

The Unique and Wonderful MECHANICIEN, VENTRILOQUIST, and PRESTIDIGITATEUR,

HOUDIN!

En route from CHINA, JAPAN, EAST INDIES, and the SANDWICH ISLANDS, with his extraordinary daughter

CAROLINE HOUDIN,
—and the—
Arab Boy, AL-RASCHID,
WILL APPEAR IN THEIR
MARVELLOUS, LAUGHABLE and STARTLING FEATS,
EASTERN NECROMANTIC ILLUSIONS, with
HOUDIN'S Mirth-Provoking Automata!

Immense success, and crowded and delighted Audiences have greeted Houdin everywhere, making a triumphant ovation to his extraordinary skill, with an elegant Stage, Orchestra, and all the necessary appliances to give satisfaction to the vast assemblages.

THE SLEEPING ARAB OF THE DESERT!
OR, "SUSPENSION IN THE AIR" OF THE ARAB BOY.

HOUDIN'S WONDERFUL FEATS
Are performed after the style of the East India Jugglers, on the naked Stage, without the aid of Tables, Traps, or Confederacy of any kind. One thousand dollars reward will be given for the production of any confederate from the Audience.

Everything Advertised Performed.   Crowded Houses.   Triumphant Success.

Everywhere greeted with SHOUTS OF APPLAUSE AND ENTHUSIASTIC DELIGHT, BY VAST CONCOURSES OF PEOPLE.

Eclipsing Everything of the Kind ever Presented to the American Public.

The Great East India Deception,

El Chapeo de ta Travulo!
Will be introduced.   OVER FIVE HUNDRED FAIRY PRESENTS—Bon-Bons, Exquisite Toys, Souvenirs, Flags, Mementos, Trained Canaries, &c., &c., distributed from AN EMPTY HAT!

12 Lighted Chinese Lanterns.   A Menagerie of Animals, &c.

CAROLINE HOUDIN in her unaccountable, investigation-defying, startling phenomena, called

SECOND SIGHT

That astonishes, puzzles, bewilders, and confounds scientific elucidation and learned exposition—Seeing, Reading, Decyphering, describing anything and everything seen by her Father, with an accuracy that defies detection, performed before brilliant and fashionable assemblages with unprecedented success.

☞ Ministers of the Gospel, School Teachers and Superintendents of Sabbath Schools, Soldiers crippled in defence of the Banner of our Fathers, are invited free.   They will please procure tickets at Houdin's hotel during the day.

☞ Houdin's extensive Repertoire of Enchantment enables him to teach and supply with apparatus, gentlemen who may desire, for their own gratification or for public performances, for a fair compensation, any one or more of his extraordinary deceptions.

PROGRAMME CHANGED NIGHTLY.

No Money taken at the Entrance.
Houdin will not be responsible for any bills unless contracted for by his authorised Agent, or a written order by himself.

☞ A Grand Matinee on Wednesday and Saturday Afternoons,
Commencing at Three o'clock.

Attentive Ushers will Seat the Audience.   Houdin's Books, explanatory of his Wonderful Feats, for sale in the audience.   Ladies and Gentlemen will please favor Houdin with articles needed without hesitancy.

Programme of Feats To-night.
OVERTURE · ORCHESTRA

Dream First.	Dream Second.
1. "HOUDIN'S" BANNER FEAT.	1. BENGAL MISER.
* Its Stars were born in glory,	2. WEIRD AUTOMATONS
To Form a free, to Friends a Festal Robe; | Of Freedom's proudest over all the globe."	3. MAHOMET'S CHEST.
2. LESSON IN CARDS.	4. SYMPATHETIC TURTLE DOVES
3. EGG-CHING-CHING.	5. EL CHAPEO DE TA TRAVULO.
4. BIRDS OF THE PALACE.	6. CONVULSIVE SPECTATOR.
5. HINDOSTAN CHAINS.	7. SLEEPING ARAB OF THE DESERT, or Suspension in
6. INCOMPREHENSIBLE WATCHES.	Mid-Air of the ARAB BOY.
7. CAROLINE HOUDIN IN HER SECOND-SIGHT.	☞ There will be an interim of TEN MINUTES between Dream First
8. SPIRIT DRUM.	and Second.

HOUDIN'S Wonderful and Laughable Automata!
F. A. Searle, Plain and Ornamental Job Printer, Journal Building, (up one flight) 114 Washington Street, Boston.

Robert-Houdin never came to the United States, but an imitator used his name in Boston in 1866.

over. The building which housed the most famous magic show in France was demolished in 1924 as the Boulevard Haussmann was widened.

It is unlikely that Robert-Houdin, whose performing career spanned only eleven years, ever imagined that a theatre bearing his name would last nearly eighty years, or that streets would be named for him in Paris, Blois, Bourges, and Caen.

There is now a Robert-Houdin museum in his hometown by the side of the road leading up to the Blois castle. This was opened in April 1966 by the magician's grandson, Paul Robert-Houdin, a distinguished innovator himself. His "Sound and Light" spectacles dramatize history at the Tower of London, the Great Pyramid at Gizeh, and the Acropolis in Athens. On display in the museum are the volumes from which the young clockmaker learned his first magic secrets, the handsomely inscribed scroll presented to him by awed Arab chieftains in Algeria, and some of his conjuring, clockmaking, and scientific equipment. Watching over these treasures is a life-size wax image of Robert-Houdin holding the electric light he made at Saint Gervais years before Thomas Alva Edison produced a commercial bulb.

Robert-Houdin
—Innovator

10

England's Home
of Mystery

JOHN Nevil Maskelyne, Britain's great producer of conjuring entertainments, opened new horizons for magic when he presented original tricks and illusions in dramatic sketches. For almost half a century, his London shows, first at Egyptian Hall in 1873 and later at St. George's Hall, set a world standard of excellence.

The son of a saddlemaker, Maskelyne was born in Cheltenham on December 22, 1839. Intrigued as a boy by an entertainer's "Dancing Dinner Plates," he practiced until he could keep several dishes whirling simultaneously on a tabletop. He also sang in a church choir and learned to play the cornet. Maskelyne was working as a clockmaker's apprentice when at the age of nineteen he constructed his first piece of conjuring equipment: a small chest with a secret panel. He could lock a borrowed ring inside, bind the chest with tape, and secretly extract the ring as he gave the box to a spectator. Similar chests had been used by earlier magicians, but Maskelyne's concealed the release mechanism so ingeniously that the box could withstand the most rigorous examination.

The slender amateur conjurer, who wore a brush moustache and combed his brown hair straight back, attended an afternoon séance at the Cheltenham Town Hall on March 7, 1865. Heavy curtains fastened over the windows darkened the hall. Lamps illuminated the stage where trestles had been erected to support a three-doored wooden cabinet, similar in size and shape to a large clothes wardrobe.

The three doors were open. Plank seats had been nailed inside at either end. A guitar, a violin and bow, and a trumpet hung on the back wall of the cabinet; two hand bells and a tambourine lay on the floor.

A lecturer introduced the Davenport Brothers—Ira Erastus and William Henry Harrison—whose "inexplicable manifestations" had caused a furor in London at a time when interest in spiritualism was at a peak. The lecturer called for volunteers; Maskelyne and several other men hurried up to inspect the paraphernalia. The committee-men lashed the American mediums' wrists behind their backs and tied their ankles as they sat face to face inside the cabinet. Then the lecturer closed the doors and signaled for the lamps to be extinguished.

Almost immediately bells rang and flew out to the floor of the stage. Pale, ghostly hands waved through diamond-shaped apertures in the doors. A tambourine jangled, a guitar strummed and a violin played as eerie music filled the air. Yet, when the lamps were relit and the doors opened, the somber-faced brothers sat tightly bound—exactly as they had been when the séance started.

England was embroiled in a controversy over whether the Davenports were authentic mediums or crafty Yankee tricksters. Purely by chance, Maskelyne discovered they were frauds. A ray of sunlight from an insecurely draped window flashed briefly on the stage. From his vantage point at the side, Maskelyne could see into the cabinet through a partially open door. Ira Davenport was vigorously ringing a bell. Aware that he had been observed, the startled medium quickly threw the bell forward and thrust his free hand behind his back. If one brother could release himself, Maskelyne reasoned, the other could too.

Maskelyne told the audience what he had seen, but a clergyman who had been watching on the far side of the stage scoffed at this explanation. Determined to prove his point, Maskelyne persuaded George Alfred Cooke, a fellow cornetist in the Volunteer Rifles Band to help him build a cabinet so they could work together to duplicate the Davenports' trickery.

Once they learned the technique of slipping their hands out of and back into tightly knotted ropes, producing "spirit music" was a cinch for the two instrumentalists. After three months of practice, the twenty-five-year-old Maskelyne and the thirty-nine-year-old Cooke appeared at Jessop's Gardens on June 19, 1865. Trick by trick—and they stressed that the marvels were tricks—they went through the complete Davenport séance.

Five days later, the *Birmingham Gazette* ran a long account of their triumph, headed "The Davenport Brothers Outdone." The "outdone" was justified. Maskelyne, who was five feet eight inches tall, squeezed himself into a box three feet long, two feet wide, and nineteen inches deep. Volunteers locked the lid, tied a fifty-foot length of rope around the box, then lifted it and stood it on end in the cabinet. The *Gazette* tells what happened next:

> Bells were placed upon the box and the doors of the cabinet were closed, but the click of the bolt had scarcely died away ere the bells began to be tremulous . . . till at length they were pitched through the apertures on to the platform . . . and in less than ten minutes from the closing of the doors they were again thrown open, and Mr. Maskelyne was seen cooly seated on the box, and smilingly bowing his acknowledgements of the applause with which he was greeted. This is a trick which the Davenports never attempted, and (as Barnum has it somewhere) "it must be seen to be believed."

Maskelyne had proved conclusively that spirits were not necessary for a lively séance, and he had introduced an epic box mystery—the forerunner of Houdini's trunk and packing-crate escapes.

After successful exhibitions in nearby towns, Maskelyne and Cooke went to Lancashire, where William Morton, a young promoter, arranged an extensive tour of the provinces and booked them for an engagement at the Crystal Palace in London in 1869. A private showing for the Prince of Wales at Berkeley Castle enhanced their reputation.

Before "the Royal Illusionists and Anti-Spiritualists" returned to London four years later, Maskelyne had introduced another milestone in magic—a levitation that surpassed Robert-Houdin's suspension feat. *The Times* described Maskelyne's great illusion:

> The lady simply rises directly off the floor, where there is no trap, and remains suspended, full in the light, with nothing under her feet, over her head, or in any way visibly connected with her.

While Maskelyne and Cooke were playing at St. James' Hall in April 1873, Maskelyne signed a three-month lease on a theatre in Egyptian Hall. Originally designed as a museum to house William Bullock's "16,000 natural wonders" in 1811, this building on Piccadilly near Bond Street was ornamented with scarabs, sphinxes, and hieroglyphics.

Showmen took over the hall after Bullock's collection of mammals, reptiles, birds, insects, art, and armory was sold in 1819. Louis Gordon M'Kean, "The Double-Sighted Phaenomenon," appeared there in 1831; in later years "The Mysterious Lady," Henri Robin, Alexander Herrmann, and other famous mystifiers amazed audiences in the templelike surroundings.

Colonel Stodare (Alfred Inglis) introduced "The Sphinx" illusion during his three-hundredth performance in the hall on October 16, 1865. He carried a small box to an undraped table and unlatched the front. Inside was a disembodied head wearing an Egyp-

John Nevil Maskelyne, the founder of
a conjuring dynasty in Great Britain.

Plate spinning, automata,
and illusions were among
Egyptian Hall features.

tian headdress. At the magician's command, "The Sphinx" opened his eyes, smiled, then solemnly delivered a twenty-four line verse. "This is certainly one of the most extraordinary illusions ever presented to the public," *The Times* reported.

Thomas W. Tobin, who built the equipment, employed the same optical device he had used several years earlier, when he made a "Proteus" cabinet for Professor John Henry Pepper's lectures at the Royal Polytechnic Institute hall. Two mirrors met at a forty-five degree angle under the three-legged table, reflecting the side curtains of the recess in which the table stood, and creating the illusion that spectators had a clear view through to the back curtain. The V-shaped mirror screen concealed the body of "The Sphinx."

Shortly before Maskelyne signed his lease for Egyptian Hall, "The Fakir of Oolu" (Alfred Sylvester) drew capacity crowds with "The Denizen of the Air, or the Last Link Severed." Wearing a jeweled turban and a shimmering Indian robe, the hefty, bearded English magician demonstrated the wonders of "human magnetism." First, a wand adhered to his fingertips, then he lifted an assistant, whose elbow rested on a five-foot pole, and draped her body with various costumes as he repeatedly shifted her position. The stage lighting changed for each "living picture." When the girl's body was horizontal in the subdued red light, the fakir pulled away the pole and supported her with the palm of his outstretched hand.

A pole within a pole was the key to this variation of Robert-Houdin's suspension feat. The outer polished shell was removed; the inner, solid black rod that remained was invisible under the red overhead lamps and against the black velvet background.

Maskelyne was irked when another conjurer, Dr. H. S. Lynn (Hugh Simmons) was booked into the second of two theatres in Egyptian Hall a week before the previously announced Maskelyne and Cooke opening. Lynn had left the British Navy to begin his career as a magician in Australia. After working there as Washington Simmons, he toured the Orient, Europe, and the United States, where he was billed as "Professor Simmons, the Great Basilicothaumaturgist," before going to London. As adept with words as with his fingers, Lynn drew excellent reviews from the British press.

Consequently, Maskelyne and Cooke opened with some trepidation on May 26, 1873. Lynn had had the gall to present an imitation of the Maskelyne box mystery and pass it off as a Lynn invention. He carried the attack further in *The Adventures of a Strange Man,* an amusing book about his experiences as a magician. The book included a fictitious letter from a man who mentioned Lynn's "would-be imitators in London and the provinces" and testified to having seen the doctor perform the box escape "in China and Japan (I think about 1862 or 1863.)"

When Lynn ignored his rival's fiery letters of complaint, Maskelyne issued a rebuttal pamphlet, *The History of a Mystery*. Maskelyne wrote that he had devised the principle of the box in 1859 and first performed the feat in Cheltenham when he duplicated the Davenport séance. Maskelyne confidently offered five hundred pounds for documentary evidence—a dated program or newspaper review—which would prove Lynn had even attempted the box escape prior to his appearance at Egyptian Hall. This was a safe challenge.

The competing magicians were seated rows apart in the Cavendish Rooms on Sunday, June 15, 1873, when George Sexton, a crusading spiritualist, delivered an impassioned attack on conjurers. This was later printed as a tract. Lynn's "pretended imitations of spiritual phenomena," Sexton charged, were so transparent he had seen through them all on a single visit.

Lynn's sleight of hand, Sexton continued, played an important part in what was purported to be a replica of medium Charles Foster's "blood-red writing." In this feat bits of paper on which members of the audience had written words were crumpled and mixed on the top of a hat. One was chosen and pressed against the sleeve of the conjurer's coat. Lynn pulled up his sleeve to reveal the selected word printed in bold crimson letters on his bare arm.

"This miserable buffoonery" could not compare with the American medium's awe-inspiring blood-red writing, Sexton shouted. He said Lynn simply switched the chosen paper for another bearing the word he had earlier painted on his skin.

As for Maskelyne and Cooke's cabinet séances, Sexton asserted that they were no match for the Davenports' spirit manifestations. True, a man disappeared in one of Maskelyne's cabinets, but if you looked closely, you could detect how this was done. The man climbed up on a shelf and let down from the top a hinged mirror that covered his hiding place and reflected the ceiling.

Maskelyne's woman assistant floated a few feet above the stage, but this hardly compared to the feats Sexton attributed to D. D. Home, the great Scottish medium, who had supposedly soared up to the ceiling in many London homes—and without machinery. Maskelyne's levitation, Sexton explained, "consists of a girl raised on a pedestal hidden behind a looking glass, or rendered invisible for its being painted of the same colour as the background, and the stage partially darkened; or a woman lifted by a lever at the back of the stage." The jerky movement of the rising woman, Sexton said sarcastically, was as much like Home's smooth floating "as is the ascent of an eagle to an acrobat climbing a rope."

Other observers of Home admitted he soared *only* in dark rooms; they said no one had ever actually seen him rise to the ceiling.

Still, most of them were convinced he had, since his handwriting was found there after the lamps were turned up.

Spurred on by tall tales of Home's ascensions, Maskelyne later invented and performed a "Levitation Extraordinary." Standing erect, he rose from the front of the stage to the top of the dome high over the audience's heads. Once there he turned gracefully until his body was lengthwise, then drifted back to the stage. Two lanterns focused on him throughout this remarkable aerial maneuver.

This skillfully presented feat involved perfect timing, an ingenious rigging, and a substitute. It was not Maskelyne who floated but a dummy in matching clothes with a face exactly like the magician's. Invisible wires, chemically blackened so they would not shine when the lanterns zeroed in, hauled the figure aloft, made it turn in the air, then lowered it.

Maskelyne added spectacular new features each season at Egyptian Hall. By now he could escape from his locked box in seven seconds after it had been laced inside a canvas cover. For novelty he reversed the procedure, starting by showing the open box, cover, and rope. Then, behind a screen, he locked himself inside the box, covered it with the canvas, and laced and tied the canvas with rope. At least that's how it appeared to the audience.

The box and Maskelyne's version of the "Proteus" cabinet were the principal props in "Will, the Witch and the Watchman," the most popular of his new playlets. The characters disappeared and changed places, and after the tail of a "gorilla" (a man in an animal suit) was cut off, the tail danced about on the stage. In another scene a walking stick hopped across the stage. Maskelyne kept his fingers nimble by spinning six dinner plates at once.

Four mechanical figures provided variety: "Zoe," a girl who drew pictures; "Fanfare" and "Labial," two men who played musical instruments, and "Psycho," an automatic whist player. John Algernon Clark, a farmer, brought the idea for "Psycho" to Maskelyne, but he made many modifications in the design before the Oriental figure, twenty-two inches high, seated on a box atop a column of glass, appeared onstage early in 1875. There was no room in the clockwork android for even a midget to hide, yet the figure turned its head to study the cards, lifted the ones to be played from a rack, and occasionally puffed on a cigarette. "Psycho" also spelled out words with alphabet cards and solved mathematical problems with number cards.

Air pressure from beneath the stage, forced up through the transparent cylinder, activated the machinery. "Psycho" gave more than four thousand performances. After retirement, the automaton was placed in a display case at the London Museum where it may be seen today.

London's Egyptian Hall had
been a museum in other days.

Egyptian symbols often appeared
on Maskelyne's souvenirs.

Dr. Lynn kept trying to surpass Maskelyne's "Modern Miracles" at Egyptian Hall. Cooke was decapitated in a comedy skit; Lynn countered with "Palingenesia"—cutting off an assistant's head and limbs, then replacing them "without putty or ligature." The *Standard* complimented the doctor on his "excruciatingly funny patter," but most theatregoers who came to the hall chose tickets for the Maskelyne and Cooke show.

After a run of two years, in May 1875, Lynn rented his theatre to Dr. de Buatier, an expert conjurer from France. Early in July the newcomer's show was presented by Maskelyne and Cooke, and they advertised themselves as "the sole hosts of England's Home of Mystery."

The magician then billed as Dr. de Buatier was to become world-famous as Buatier de Kolta. Born Joseph Buatier in Lyons on November 18, 1845, he had been intended for the priesthood by his father, a silk merchant. Buatier left the seminary at the age of eighteen to study art with Eli Laurents, a painter. Buatier's artistry was more evident with cards than with oils and canvas. He was mystifying friends with card sleights in a Lyons café when he met Julius Vido de Kolta, an eccentric Hungarian impresario, who was stranded in the city. De Kolta convinced Buatier he could earn a fortune in Europe as a conjurer. With De Kolta as his manager, the magician set off for Switzerland, where he gave his first professional performance in Geneva. As they crossed the Alps to Italy, Buatier presented shows in taverns and schoolrooms.

A priest from Lyons, rather than De Kolta, got the magician his first substantial fee by arranging a private show for high church officials in Rome. Then, still accompanied by his manager, Buatier toured Spain, Germany, Russia, and Holland, where he invented "The Flying Cage," which he thought was a strong enough attraction for London. De Kolta lived in constant fear of losing his life while traveling. Whenever he rode in a coach, he wore three pairs of trousers, one over the other, and an equal number of vests, coats, and pairs of stockings to protect himself physically. Now De Kolta refused to cross the Channel; he was sure the voyage would make him violently ill.

The British papers gave the French magician with the bushy, black beard high praise for his performance at Egyptian Hall. The *Daily News* of May 10, 1875, said he conjured with "ease and grace"; his "cards diminish in size till they disappear, increase to a size which would render them fit only for the use of Titans, fasten on the walls, flit in the air like birds."

The climax came when "an iron cage with a canary inside, held high in the air, suddenly disappears, without even the melodramatic lightning flash, which, according to all tradition, should accompany such a mysterious flight."

After other performers copied his most startling feat, Buatier

163

*England's
Home of
Mystery*

presented it on a larger scale as "The Captive's Flight." A small wooden platform was passed into the audience for examination, then placed flat on the stage. A girl in a bright yellow canary costume spread her arms, fluttered a pair of silken wings, then knelt to enter the three-foot-high domed cage Buatier had placed in the center of the platform. Covering the cage with an opaque silk cloth, he counted "One! Two! Three!" When he pulled the cloth away, the cage and the human canary had disappeared. Later, he stacked giant playing cards around the sides of the covered cage and carried the platform, with the aid of an assistant, down among the audience. Following his usual count to three, the silk and the cards collapsed; the cage was gone.

"The Vanishing Lady," Buatier's final version of this illusion, was the most imitated stage feat of the 1880's. He opened a newspaper, then spread it on the stage. A young woman sat in the chair he placed on the paper. He covered her from head to toe with a piece of purple silk, lifted the cloth to show her feet, then let it fall again. Grasping the woman through the silk, he with a mighty heave threw her into the air. Instantly she *and the silk* disappeared.

Trapdoors had been concealed by both the early platform and the later newspaper. A light wire form held together by threads fitted on the top of the domed cage. This made it appear that the cage and its human prisoner were still under the cloth, although they had already been lowered through adjacent trapdoors in the platform and stage.

The equipment for "The Vanishing Lady" was more complicated. A marvel of ingenuity, the chair could be shown back and front. When Buatier concealed the woman with the cloth, a light, wire head-and-shoulders form flipped forward from the back of the chair, and two extensions from the front of the chair opened out to take the shape of knees. While it appeared the assistant was still under the silk, the seat of the chair—spring-hinged to the frame—dropped, speeding her down through the trapdoors.

Strapped to the performer's right wrist was a leather band. From this a strong cord, as long as the distance between his wrists when his arms were outstretched, ran up the right sleeve, across the front of his body (under the stiff front of his dress shirt), and down the left sleeve. A thread, attached to a loop at the end of the cord, passed through a pulley (held in position by another strap around his left wrist), then up the left sleeve, across his chest and down his right sleeve. A loop in the end of the thread fitted loosely over the magician's little finger.

Before Buatier picked up his covered "assistant," he removed the loop from his little finger with his left hand, pulled until he could grasp the cord firmly with his right fingers, then fastened the cord loop to a metal hook in the silk shroud. Perfect timing and coordina-

Maskelyne floated up to the
dome of the theatre in 1875.

The American Davenport brothers
and their "Spirit Cabinet."

tion were vital for the disappearance. Buatier's foot tripped a lever which snapped the head, shoulder, and knee forms out of view as he, with a throwing motion, extended his arms wide, and yanked the silk up his sleeve. This is one of few feats in magic that are actually quicker than the eye.

Only a very skillful performer can mask the preparatory moves with natural actions and create a perfect illusion. Several modern magicians have caused concealed assistants to disappear, but none in many years has made the cover disappear along with the girl.

Buatier introduced "The Vanishing Lady" in Paris in August 1887. It was a sensation. Maskelyne bought the British rights for Egyptian Hall, and since Buatier was booked on the Continent through November, Charles Bertram was engaged to present the illusion. Several other performers capitalized on the acclaim the trick had received; only Bertram's presentation compared with the originator's.

The bearded and portly Bertram (James Bassett), who was almost a double for Edward VII, gave twenty-two performances for the King and the royal family during his long career. Convivial by nature, he was as relaxed in a palace drawing room as on the stage. Bertram ended each trick with a smile and the question, "Isn't it wonderful?" This catch line was the title of his autobiography. Another Bertram book, *A Magician in Many Lands,* was a posthumously published account of his world tour.

While Bertram and other Egyptian Hall conjurers performed abroad, Maskelyne limited his travels to the British Isles. He was too busy with his inventions, shows, and appearances in court to take extended trips. One of his associates said he "had a positive love for litigation."

Maskelyne believed it was his duty as a responsible citizen to censure and expose charlatans. He testified at the Bow Street Police Court in 1876 that Henry Slade, a notorious American medium, could produce messages on slates without the aid of spirits. Maskelyne demonstrated the trick in the witness box. Slade was sentenced to three months for vagrancy, but he appealed and a technicality kept him out of jail. He wisely left England before a second trial could be held.

Maskelyne criticized Washington Irving Bishop, a celebrated American entertainer, who made the mistake of claiming he could read thoughts. Bishop retaliated by charging that Maskelyne was "devoid of honorable instincts." Bishop said he could prove the conjurer's "infamy" and "villainous conduct" in court. Maskelyne immediately sued for libel and "the thought reader" fled to France. Though neither Bishop nor his lawyer was present, the court awarded Maskelyne ten thousand pounds, a sum he could not collect as the American never returned to the British Isles.

In turn, Maskelyne was sued by two clerks who worked in an

engineer's office. For years the magician had offered five hundred pounds to anyone who could duplicate his famous box mystery. The young men had made a box which they claimed entitled them to the award. The case of E. Stollery and F. G. Evans versus J. N. Maskelyne started on June 20, 1898. Two boxes were offered in evidence—Maskelyne's and the claimants'.

An assistant escaped from the claimaints' box after it had been laced in a canvas cover. Most of the jurors thought Stollery and Evans were entitled to the challenge money, but they could not reach a unanimous decision. A second trial ended on October 21 with a verdict in favor of Stollery and Evans.

Maskelyne took the appeal all the way to the House of Lords. The challengers frankly admitted they did not know the secret of Maskelyne's box, but they had presented the feat exactly as Egyptian Hall audiences saw it. Maskelyne lost; grudgingly he paid the award money and court costs. He said his mistake had been in the wording of his challenge; in the future he would be more precise. Then the magician issued a new dare to anyone who could *prove* he knew the secret of the Maskelyne box. This thousand pounds was never collected.

A fellow conjurer, who admired Maskelyne's ingenuity, received permission to inspect the box thoroughly for as long as he wished. Reasoning that any mechanical release would have to be oiled occasionally, this magician, who had a keen sense of smell, sniffed every inch of the box, hoping to detect the telltale scent of the lubricant. After more than an hour, he gave up as baffled as everyone else.

When not onstage or appearing in court, Maskelyne was busy in his workshop. He invented and built a typewriter, which he never used himself; he preferred to dictate his letters or answer his correspondence by hand. He also devised several vending machines and patented mechanical devices designed to count fares and passengers on buses. None of these inventions was profitable. His most ambitious nontheatrical undertaking was a grandstand, built to provide visitors to London a comfortable vantage point for Queen Victoria's Diamond Jubilee procession. He had planned to erect this stand on the top of an old building in the courtyard of St. Paul's Church. When the building was ruled unsafe, he tore it down and constructed the grandstand on the site. He promised to demolish the grandstand and reassemble the building after the parade.

Workmen were hard to find. The grandstand was only partially completed when the procession passed; the few people who bought the expensive seats complained about their accommodations. The loss on the venture was enormous.

Fortunately by then Maskelyne had added a magician to his Egyptian Hall company who proved to be a sound businessman, as well as a marvelous showman. David Devant, who had been born David

*England's
Home of
Mystery*

Dr. Lynn, Maskelyne's rival, makes a production from an empty hat.

Each evening Dr. Lynn cut up a man, then put him back together.

Lynn's variation of "The Indian Basket Trick."

Wighton across the road from the Boston Arms pub in Holloway on February 22, 1868, was performing at the Trocadero Music Hall in London when Maskelyne saw him present the first original Devant illusion, "Vice Versa." A man was tied around the waist with an extremely long ribbon. The knots were sealed, and the ends of the ribbon were tossed to two spectators in the stalls. The assistant backed into a narrow cloth-sided cabinet. Devant closed the front curtain. When he pulled it open, a woman stood where the man had been, with the knotted, sealed ribbon around her middle. Maskelyne invited the tall, moustached conjurer to submit a feat for possible production at Egyptian Hall. In less than two weeks Devant completed a scale model of "The Artist's Dream" in which a full-length portrait of a woman came to life. (Later Alexander Herrmann featured this illusion in the United States.)

Maskelyne signed Devant to a three-month contract, and Devant showed this feat for the first time in August 1893. Meanwhile he kept working on new ideas in his home. He made tiny models of the props he intended to use and put them on a miniature stage with figures representing his assistants and himself. Trying different backgrounds, shifting the positions of the lights, he blocked out the staging and solved the production problems before he invested in full-scale equipment.

Ten months after his first appearance Devant became a permanent member of the Maskelyne company. Maskelyne attended a special showing of the Lumière brothers' new "Cinématographe" at the Royal Polytechnic Institute Hall in 1896; he dismissed the flickering movies as a passing fad. By contrast, Devant saw their potential for mass entertainment and bought a similar projector and films from R. W. Paul, a British inventor, for five hundred pounds—the amount the Lumières were asking just for a week's rental of their machine.

Maskelyne paid Devant an extra five pounds weekly to test the films at Egyptian Hall; they became a strong attraction. Devant purchased two more projectors, and as Paul's representative, sold others to showmen in Europe. At first the extra projectors were rented at high fees for private screenings, but soon three road companies of "Mr. David Devant's Animated Pictures, direct from Maskelyne and Cooke's Egyptian Hall, Piccadilly," supplemented by live variety acts, were playing to standing-room-only audiences in the provinces.

Devant advised Maskelyne to form a new company to present Egyptian Hall illusions on tour. Maskelyne was not enthusiastic. He said he had learned from experience that provincial tours lost money. After he studied the profit sheets of Devant's film shows, he changed his mind and approved the project. The Devant-produced illusion show opened on July 31, 1899, at the Town Hall in Eastbourne. Maskelyne had been content with a single musician, a pianist who operated a "mechanical orchestra" at Egyptian Hall; Devant hired a small musical group for this production.

From the beginning the show was profitable, but when Devant himself headed the cast the second year, the receipts almost doubled. He was on tour when Cooke, Maskelyne's longtime assistant, retired at the age of seventy-six in 1902. The proprietor of "England's Home of Mystery" was distressed when the Crown Estate Commissioners informed him that the old hall would be razed to make way for a modern commercial building. Maskelyne supervised his last show at Egyptian Hall in the fall of 1904. Months before, he had begun remodeling St. George's Hall in Langham Place and started preparing for his first show there—the most elaborate and expensive production of his life.

Martin Chapender (Harold Martin Jones), a conjurer from Liverpool who had scored a hit with his sleight of hand on the final Maskelyne bill, rented Egyptian Hall for the last Christmas season before the building was torn down.

"Maskelyne's New Home of Mystery" opened on January 2, 1905, with *The Coming Race*. Based on Bulwer-Lytton's satirical novel, this full-length play told the story of an American who traveled to a strange land peopled with fantastic creatures, whose scientific achievements far outstripped human knowledge. Flying monsters, an earthquake, and other elaborate scenic effects replaced the traditional comedy skits and illusions Egyptian Hall fans had enjoyed. Prominent actors and actresses played the leading roles, but audiences were disappointed. This was not what they expected to see at a Maskelyne show.

Chapender played to fine returns at Egyptian Hall, while eight weeks of nearly empty stalls for the science-fiction play almost bankrupted Maskelyne. In desperation, he asked David Devant, who was still making money in Edinburgh with their road show, to return to London for a conference. Devant advised Maskelyne to post closing notices immediately and to go back to the kind of magic entertainment they knew people would pay to see.

Devant agreed to book the supporting acts and to star in the show as soon as he filled his advance commitments. The sixty-five-year-old Maskelyne closed the play, rented St. George's Hall for concerts, and waited impatiently for Devant's arrival.

Sold out far in advance, the April "Feast of Magic" lived up to its name. Devant's "Golliwog Ball" rolled up and down an inclined plank with no visible motivating force. He poured free drinks for the spectators from an empty "Magic Kettle." His "Burmese Gong" cued a fast-paced series of human disappearances and reappearances. Maskelyne revived "Oh!" an Egyptian Hall favorite in which a volunteer held an

Buatier de Kolta causes a human canary and a large cage to disappear.

Buatier's "Vanishing Lady," as the illusion was pictured in a cartoon.

The climax of Buatier's "Cocoon"— the appearance of a girl in an egg.

assistant's hand as it extended through a slit in a canopy until a moment before the canopy dropped and the assistant disappeared. "The Hermit of Killarney," a magic playlet, topped off the evening.

In August Devant was named managing partner of the hall, and the billing of the show was changed to "Maskelyne and Devant Mysteries." They sent out touring companies to the provinces, Europe, and the United States. There were problems. Max Sterling in New York reported that a crate of special glasses for the "Magic Kettle" had not been shipped with his paraphernalia. The Paris show had to be postponed when an indispensable part of the scenery was left behind in London. There were no such troubles for the British touring company; this was headed by the meticulous Maskelyne himself.

In London, Devant spent his offstage hours devising new illusions. Sometimes ideas developed as he tinkered with old equipment; often ingenious presentations came as flashes of inspiration. Once he dreamed a plot. Late one night his wife awoke to find him sitting in a chair, staring at a lighted candle. She decided not to disturb him. Next morning he told her he had had a vivid vision. Dressed as Satan, he had tempted a human moth with the flame of a candle. The moth flew too close and suddenly disappeared. He solved the production details and presented "The Mascot Moth" in August 1905.

Another of his novel concepts was staged by his partner the next year as "The New Page." A uniformed bellboy was strapped in an upright cabinet just large enough to hold him. When the door was closed, Maskelyne lifted a small doll, a replica of the assistant, and turned it upside down. When the magician opened the cabinet, the strapped page was in the same topsy-turvy position.

Maskelyne was soon back in court again—this time as a result of a controversy with a clergyman. Archdeacon Thomas Colley offered the magician a thousand pounds if he could reproduce the spiritualistic phenomena the clergyman claimed to have seen twenty-nine years earlier in his Stockton rectory. As Colley told the story, the manifestations took place as a medium stood under a chandelier with three jets of gas burning brightly. A "spirit" extruded from the medium's left side, stood erect, talked, ate a baked apple, and returned to the medium's body. The medium then spat out from his mouth the apple core and skin.

When Maskelyne investigated, he found Colley was talking about Francis Ward Monck, a former Baptist minister. Maskelyne reminded the archdeacon that Monck had been sentenced for fraud after being exposed by a magician, who discovered his "spirit" props in the medium's luggage and turned them over to the police.

The *Daily Express* reported the running battle between the archdeacon and the magician. Finally Maskelyne was goaded into accepting Colley's challenge. A packed house came to see "The £1,000

The January 28, 1893, *Moonshine* devoted a page to the Maskelyne entertainment.

Mystery—The Side Issue" at St. George's Hall on October 6, 1906. As Maskelyne stood under a chandelier with three glowing electric bulbs, "from his left side came a vapour; then a 'spirit' hand appeared; a little later a materialized spirit . . . began to grow head first and horizontally out of the body of the 'medium' amidst clouds of smoke," *The Times* stated. The "spirit," fully developed, walked to the footlights and asked, "Where am I?" Though regular patrons recognized this "spirit" as Cassie Bruce, a veteran Maskelyne assistant, *The Times* was convinced that the magician had been successful. "We conclude that he has won £1,000," the story ended.

The archdeacon did not see the show, but friends told him about it. "I was not on stage with my arm around Mr. Maskelyne," Colley said, "and therefore my conditions have not been fulfilled. . . ."

The *Daily Mirror* summed up the situation: "The £1,000 challenge money has not been paid. Mr. Maskelyne thinks he has won it—the spiritualists say he hasn't. The point now is—who shall decide?"

The magician sued Colley for the award; the clergyman countersued for libel. The jurors attended the show and decided Maskelyne had produced only half of the marvel Colley had described; the "spirit" had not returned to the magician's body. The court found Maskelyne guilty of libel and ordered him to pay damages of seventy-five pounds plus costs.

The publicity helped to fill the theatre for many months, and "The Side Issue" was incorporated into Maskelyne's "Spectres of the Inner Sanctum" sketch. This illusion was based on "Black Art." When shielded lights are overhead and directed to the front of a stage with a black velvet backdrop, white objects covered by matching pieces of material seem to materialize as the shrouds are pulled away by invisible (black-clad and hooded) assistants.

Buatier de Kolta had introduced "Modern Black Magic" at Egyptian Hall in 1888. Earlier a German magician, Ben Ali Bey (Max Auzinger) had discovered the principle when he watched a Negro actor play a scene set in a dark dungeon. Only the man's white teeth were visible on the stage of the Berlin theatre.

Once the excitement of the controversy faded, Devant again dominated the St. George's stage. His popularity put his name on the bill of the first Royal Command Variety Performance at the Palace Theatre on July 1, 1912, along with some of the greatest stars of the British music halls, including Harry Lauder and Anna Pavlova. Devant had hoped to stage at least one spectacular illusion, but the time allotted to him was too short. Instead he performed a hat trick with his daughter, Vida, and Maskelyne's grandson, Jasper. From an empty derby hat, Devant produced eggs and passed them to Vida, who gave them to Jasper until the boy's arms became so overloaded the eggs began dropping and breaking on the stage.

David Devant, Maskelyne's partner, was an outstanding illusionist and creator.

Window card advertising Maskelyne and Devant's St. George's Hall.

The next year Devant concluded a private show for King George V and Queen Mary with "The Chocolate Soldier." An assistant, wearing a busby, scarlet coat, and white trousers, was lifted to the top of a platform where he stiffly marched to martial music. A column of white lights was at the back of the platform; vertical rows of reds and blues shone at the sides. Assistants placed three British flags on staffs at the tops of the lighted panels to form a triangular enclosure. At a signal from Devant, the flags dropped. The soldier still marched back and forth, but he had shrunk to the size of a doll.

After ten years of partnership with Maskelyne at St. George's Hall, Devant withdrew from the firm in 1915. He said he had been close to a nervous breakdown due to the strain of performing and running the business side of the theatre; his physician advised him to give up the management responsibilities.

Following a long rest in the country, he headlined in the principal variety theatres and earned far more than he had as Maskelyne's partner. During the Christmas season of 1916, he returned to London for a series of magical matinees at the Ambassador Theatre. Featured illusions included "The Burmese Gong," "The Dissected Messenger," "The Great Indian Rope Trick" and "The Giant's Breakfast." In the latter a huge egg burst through the tissue-paper center of a suspended frame. When the magician cracked the egg, a girl dressed as a chicken hopped out.

One of the most applauded feats was "The Magic Mirror." A tall, full-length, framed mirror was center stage as Devant and a volunteer from the audience donned black robes and hoods. The illusionist led the man around the mirror, then asked him to gaze intensely into the glass. As the stage lights dimmed, a small red flare appeared in the mirror; the spot grew larger and larger until the figure of Satan materialized. Satan beckoned to the spectator, then faded away.

Once more Devant instructed the spectator to gaze into the mirror. This time a streak of white expanded and developed until it became a girl in a wedding gown. At a whispered cue, the man on stage reached toward the lovely image. Devant stopped him, saying this was a vision of things to come. Both men pulled the hoods of their robes over their heads and circled the mirror. Then they knelt before it. The third misty form that took shape in the glass was Devant in evening clothes. The hooded figure by the spectator's side stood up and flung off his cloak—he was Satan!

Science, strategy, and a switch blended in this unusual illusion. The back of the mirror was only lightly silvered. Two black-lined doors were concealed at the rear of the mirror frame. These were opened by the people whose images appeared in the glass. Shielded tubular electric bulbs fitted into the side wooden panels of the framework to illuminate the figures behind the glass. As the lights grew more brilliant, the mirror became transparent. The black-robed and hooded Satan was behind the closed doors of the frame when Devant and the spectator circled the mirror for the second time. Once they were out of the audience's sight, Satan replaced Devant and took the volunteer's arm and brought him back around to the front. Devant quickly removed his hood and robe, opened the doors, and stood behind the glass as the concealed lights were turned on, dimly at first, and then full force.

Devant continued to tour during the years of World War I, while most of the younger British magicians, who had always been so eager for a chance to appear in a Maskelyne production at St. George's Hall, were in the armed forces. Maskelyne had been devoting most of his energy to constructing new equipment and writing magic sketches; now he came out of semiretirement to work with his son, Nevil, in the show.

By late July 1916, Maskelyne was back onstage playing in his favorite skit, "Will, the Witch and the Watchman," and he proved that at the age of seventy-six he was still a skillful plate-spinner. Later a new illusion devised by his son, Archie, was presented. In "The Four Elements of Alchemy," the magician produced a soldier, sailor, and aviator; they, in turn, united to conjure up Cassie Bruce—dressed as the symbol of peace.

Maskelyne missed twice in his plate-spinning routine on the night of May 2, 1917. Despite this, he seemed in good spirits as he climbed the stairs to his apartment above the theatre. The next day he apologized for not coming down to the stage. He said he had suffered from indigestion and a chill during the night and didn't have the strength to get to his feet. For sixteen days he battled pneumonia and pleurisy. Then on May 18, 1917, the seventy-seven-year-old founder of the longest-running magic show in British history died.

Maskelyne's former partner, meanwhile, was still touring in variety houses. One December night in 1919 during his four-week engagement at the Midlands Theatre in Manchester, Devant told the small boy who volunteered for a "Lesson in Magic" to hold a handkerchief and cut it exactly as he did—just as the magician had done with hundreds of other children. The boy followed instructions and shook the handkerchief from side to side. Devant looked down in horror at his own trembling hand and quickly brought the feat to a close. This was the end of his career as a performer. He was found to be suffering from paralysis agitans, a nervous disorder.

With Devant's permission his "Artist's Dream" and "Magic Mirror" were presented at St. George's Hall by Claude Chandler. Retirement gave Devant time for writing. His *Lessons in Conjuring,* one of the best introductions to practical magic ever written, was published in the fall of 1922. His remaining years were spent dictating other

Political cartoon with Russia, rather than Maskelyne, exhibiting "Psycho."

One of the many political cartoons using "The Vanishing Lady" theme.

Charles Arbré presenting a pirated version of "Psycho" in Stockholm.

excellent books, devising new mysteries, and coaching the conjurers who visited him at the Royal Hospital for Incurables in Putney.

Birthday magic shows were staged there in his honor by admiring performers. On Devant's seventy-second birthday, Queen Mary sent a message saying she hoped the performance for him "will in some way repay the great pleasure you have given to so many by your wonderful conjuring tricks and mystifications." When Devant died at the age of seventy-three on October 12, 1941, *The Times* called him "the greatest magician of all times."

"Maskelyne's Mysteries" had continued at St. George's Hall under the management of the founder's son, Nevil, with the assistance of Oswald Williams, a first-rate performer, inventor, and stager of illusions. When Nevil died in 1924, he left his four sons equal shares of the business. Clive, the new managing director, departed from the Maskelyne tradition by working abroad.

After a tour of South Africa, Clive quit the family business and started his own company. He was on his way to India and Tibet to produce films when he died of pneumonia at the age of thirty-three. He was buried at sea on September 17, 1928.

Nevil's youngest son, Jasper, succeeded Clive as the managing director at St. George's Hall. He, too, made a tour of South Africa, and in May 1932 he appeared at the London Palladium in the "Royal Variety Performance." When "Maskelyne's Mysteries" celebrated its Diamond Jubilee the next April, Jasper was not on the bill; his older brothers, John and Noel, had won a two-to-one vote to oust him four months earlier.

The British Broadcasting Corporation took over St. George's Hall late in 1933 and converted it into a radio studio. Noel moved "Maskelyne's Mysteries" to the Little Theatre for the Christmas season. The last performance of the oldest magic show in London was given there the following year.

Jasper Maskelyne, however, was still busy. He was topping the bill when I saw him at the Shepherd's Bush Empire Theatre in March 1937. Two male assistants in red uniforms were center stage as the curtains opened. One held an empty tray, the other a red foulard. Tall and slender with a neatly trimmed moustache, Jasper entered briskly to stirring music. He waved the foulard over the tray and produced four large metal spheres. He talked amusingly as Devant's "Golliwog Ball" rolled mysteriously up and down an inclined plank to indicate the number of spots on playing cards selected by members of the audience or the number of fingers they extended in the air.

In Oswald William's delightful laundry sketch, the shirt of a volunteer was removed, shrunk by a washing machine, stretched in a wringer, and burned in a dryer. Then Jasper held up the tattered shirt between his hands and visibly changed it back into its original condition. He closed the show with a Maskelyne box made of glass panels and mahogany; a lovely girl escaped after the box was locked, roped, and covered by a canopy.

Britain entered World War II in 1939, and Jasper volunteered for the Royal Engineers. Major Maskelyne tells how he camouflaged tanks, cannon, and ships, and gave performances for the troops in Africa, Europe, and the Far East in his postwar book, *Magic—Top Secret*. After seven years in uniform, Jasper returned to the British variety stage in 1946 and that Christmas season starred in a magic show at the Westminster Theatre. His last holiday season in London at the Whitehall Theatre ended in January 1949. In *White Magic: The Story of the Maskelynes,* Jasper said his ambition was to retire to a Cotswold farm. So no one was surprised when he bought a farm, but they were amazed that he chose one in Africa.

As a Kenyan police officer he fought Mau Mau terrorists in 1954 and occasionally gave magic performances. Then he settled down to farming and invested in an automobile agency. Jasper Maskelyne died at his home in Kenya at the age of seventy on March 15, 1973.

London's Egyptian Hall and St. George's Hall are long gone. Today The Magic Circle clubhouse in Chenies Mews is "England's Home of Mystery." Playbills and photographs of John Nevil Maskelyne, the first honorary president, are on display along with mementoes of David Devant and Nevil and Clive Maskelyne, all of whom served as presidents.

Each year The Magic Circle presents England's best conjurers and noted performers from other lands in a week of Christmas magic in a London theatre. During the intermissions, gray-haired spectators reminisce of the golden days when "Maskelyne Mysteries" at St. George's Hall was a year-round attraction.

11

The Great Herrmanns

For more than eighty years the name Herrmann drew crowds to theatres. Carl, the first of the family to achieve international acclaim, was slender, satanic in appearance, and wore a black moustache and goatee. His artistic sleight-of-hand, continental manner, sly sense of humor, and ability to project his personality in the great opera houses of the world made him an attraction, critics said, on a par with the most talented actors, singers, and dancers of the nineteenth century.

Alexander, Carl's younger brother by twenty-seven years, and Leon, his nephew, perpetuated the devil-in-evening clothes characterization. Adelaide Herrmann, Alexander's widow, topped big-time variety bills with her husband's tricks and illusions, and was still amazing audiences at the age of seventy-five.

Carl (Compars) Herrmann, the eldest of Samuel Herrmann's sixteen children, was born near Hanover, Germany on January 23, 1816. As his father's assistant he learned to conjure and imitate birdcalls. When Samuel Herrmann entertained the pupils of Carnet's school near Versailles, the proprietor volunteered to admit the personable youngster tuition free. This led to the boy's first royal command performance.

On a holiday trip to Fontainebleau with his classmates, Carl played on the palace grounds. Aware they were trespassing, his friends fled as a calvalcade came up the road; Carl climbed a tree. Hidden by the thick foliage, he trilled birdcalls. Two young princes, hoping to glimpse the birds, reined their horses, reached up, and parted the leaves. King Louis Philippe and the ladies in his carriage were so amused when they saw the grinning schoolboy that they invited Carl to entertain them at the palace.

A quarter of a century later, the Duke of Montpensier still remembered this incident. He was visiting Queen Isabella II of Spain when Carl Herrmann, then the most celebrated conjurer in Central Europe, performed for the court in Madrid. Montpensier said he deserved at least a share of the credit for the magician's success since he and his brother had discovered Herrmann in a tree at Fontainebleau.

Despite his early skill as an entertainer, Carl, who lived in Paris as a young man, tried to please his father by earning a living away from the stage. He was in his twenties, out of work, and desperately in need of money before he turned to magic. Progressing from school shows and private performances to theatre exhibitions, he finally earned enough to buy equipment for a three-hour production and took the show to London.

At the Adelphi Theatre and later at the Haymarket, he billed himself as "the Premier Prestidigitateur of France and the First Professor of Magic in the World." The *Illustrated London News* critic, who covered the thirty-two-year-old conjurer's performance in April 1848, said Herrmann was not only adept at the tricks his predecessors Philippe and Doebler had shown, he also introduced several striking new mysteries of his own: an empty bottle from which he poured an endless flow of drinks, a portfolio from which he made an immense production, and a "Second Sight" demonstration that was far superior to the one "the Mysterious Lady" had exhibited at Egyptian Hall. Herrmann's last feat was his most dramatic. He lifted a young girl who rested an arm on the top of a rod until her unsupported body was floating horizontally in space.

Those who praised Herrmann's originality did not realize that his most marvelous feats had been created by Robert-Houdin in Paris. Later, one of Robert-Houdin's trusted workmen, a man named LeGrand, served a jail term for having made and sold replicas of his employer's equipment.

Herrmann's run at the Haymarket Theatre ended in May, a few days after Robert-Houdin made his London debut at the St. James' Theatre. They played in competition again in August; the French innovator returned to the St. James', and Herrmann performed at the Princess Theatre. This time "the Premier Prestidigitateur of France" was dropped from Herrmann's billing, but he still claimed to be "the First Professor of Magic in the World."

Following a tour of the British Isles, Herrmann took the

Carl Herrmann, first of the family to win fame on both sides of the Atlantic.

Caricature from the cover of a song sheet: "Herrmann's Polka & Quadrille."

Herald announcing Herrmann's first appearance at a New York theatre.

pirated illusions to Germany, Austria, Italy, and Portugal, and along the way he acquired a remarkable collection of jewels as gifts from his royal patrons: Emperor Franz Josef I of Austria, King Ludwig I of Bavaria, King Dom Pedro V of Portugal, King Frederick VII of Denmark, and Queen Isabella II of Spain.

The child Herrmann suspended at the palace in St. Petersburg in 1852 was his eight-year-old brother, Alexander, who later acted as his blindfolded medium in the "Second Sight" routine. Czar Nicholas I added an engraved gold watch adorned with diamonds, pearls, and amethysts to the trophies in Carl's jewel case.

Usually Herrmann presented the entire show himself, but in Dublin he included a troupe of "Ethiopian Minstrels" on the bill, and he shared the stage of the Vestebros Theatre in Copenhagen with Philippe, the French magician who had been one of his early idols.

Years later in England, Herrmann read that Philippe was to perform at a hall in Cheshire and took a woman assistant to see the show. The box-office attendant recognized the famous magician and offered him free admission, but Herrmann insisted on paying.

The curtains opened on a drab setting, and the man who a few minutes earlier had been selling tickets appeared as Philippe. Carl was furious. He jumped up, interrupting the performance and shouting that the man was an imposter. "Monsieur Philippe is my friend," Carl said. "You are not a Frenchman at all—you are one damned Englishman!"

As the audience hooted Herrmann, the woman with him stood up and tried to explain. "Monsieur Herrmann means nothing disrespectful—he love the English, they have been so good to him; he did not know how to express himself. He is excited and most angry that this man should impose on you and injure his friend."

Herrmann, meanwhile, had hurried down the aisle and climbed up on the stage. He lifted the long cloth which covered the magician's table. A boy sitting under the table, ready to push a rabbit up through a trap when an empty cone was placed over it, scurried on his hands and knees into the wings. The spurious Philippe took a jab at Herrmann and missed. Herrmann struck back; his punch landed. By the time a constable arrived, the imposter-performer had a black eye and a bloody nose, but the agile Herrmann was unscathed.

The imposter's name was Harry Graham; later he posed as Robert-Houdin and other European conjurers. Graham fancied himself as a Shakespearean actor. He boasted his Richard III was second only to Edmund Kean's. His greatest ambition was to play the role in London. The opportunity came when C. W. Montague booked Graham as a magician at the Cabinet Theatre. During that run Graham appeared as Richard at a benefit show. "The excitement caused by his realization of his dream of years was too much for him," Montague said later. "He died, poor fellow, a few days afterwards."

Carl Herrmann was content to play a single part—master magician. Most of his contemporaries enlarged their productions each season. Herrmann took the opposite course. After he became established, he replaced the feats requiring heavy equipment with sleight of hand. He was not the first to do this. Wiljalba Frikell traveled with mechanical boxes, canisters, special tables, and an elaborate setting in Germany early in the 1840's. When a theatre fire destroyed the equipment and the Turkish costumes he wore on stage, Frikell by necessity conjured in conventional clothes, with everyday objects, and without scenery. To his utter amazement, audiences enjoyed these starkly staged shows even more than the spectacles he had earlier presented.

Whether Herrmann was influenced by Frikell's experience or discovered the appeal of magic without apparatus on his own is a matter of conjecture. His new approach brought him triumphs in Brazil, Uruguay, and Argentina. He was presented with a diamond-and-sapphire–studded gold wand, which had his portrait along with an inscription engraved on the staff, in Havana in January, 1861. He needed no wand to work his inimitable wonders, Herrmann's admirers said, but they thought he merited the finest one ever made.

From Cuba, Herrmann sailed to New Orleans, where he gave his first twenty-four performances in the United States at the St. Charles Theatre. When the outbreak of the Civil War terminated the run, he packed his bags hastily and caught the last through train to the north.

B. Ullman, the most prominent New York opera impresario, arranged for Herrmann's debut at the Academy of Music on Fourteenth Street. Ullman told reporters that Herrmann's artistry in magic was as much acknowledged in Europe as Jenny Lind's in music. Preposterous newspaper stories were printed telling of Herrmann's phenomenal feats: He ordered fish at a fashionable restaurant on the Continent, lifted the silver cover, and astonished the waiter by producing a live rat on the platter. He borrowed a diamond ring while entertaining in an Austrian mansion, threw the ring out a window, then whistled a tune that caused a parrot to fly in with the ring in its beak. In the bird's claws were the powdered wigs of two servants, who had been sent outside to search the grounds. The publicity buildup reached a crescendo when the gifts Herrmann had received from kings, queens, and other famous patrons—"The Spoils of Magic" —were put on display in a locked glass case at Tiffany's jewelry store.

The fantastic advance promotion, plus thousands of heralds and hundreds of posters, drew the largest crowd in the history of

The Great
Herrmanns

Doebler lithograph made in Russia.

Doebler played for three months in London on his first visit to Britain.

Doebler's candle-lighted stage and his display of paraphernalia.

the Academy of Music. More than three thousand New Yorkers were turned away from the door of the packed hall on September 21, 1861. "The opening night was a perfect jam," the Herald reported. "The success that has attended these entertainments is unexampled."

The *Leader* said that Herrmann

> prestidigitated with such dexterity and so many prestidigitorial graces, that we all fell in love with prestidigitation . . . with his naked hands, and under your very nose, he actually rolls two live rabbits into one; produces from his person at a moment's notice, and without any apparatus of any kind, six large vessels of water, each alive with goldfish; links and unlinks, with perfect ease, any number of solid brass rings, as if they were made of paper . . . takes out of a single hat, fancy goods enough to set up a country store; catches in a plate the balls from a pistol you have examined, loaded and discharged with your own hand . . . and does a score of other tricks equally as marvelous.

Comparing Herrmann to John Henry Anderson, the Scottish magician, the same critic said Herrmann relied solely on his own fingers, while Anderson was dependent on those of his mechanic. "I don't mind a man's pulling wires, but he should have the politician's skill of keeping them out of sight."

Herrmann's magic was accompanied by a full "Italian Opera Orchestra" in the pit, but the music was forgotten in the rave reviews. Five weeks of full houses brought him receipts totaling thirty-five thousand dollars.

One of Carl Herrmann's specialities was hurling playing cards with amazing accuracy into all parts of the house. Sometimes he threw out small photographs of himself or of Rosalie Levy, whom he later married after divorcing his first wife, Rosa Czillag, a Viennese diva. Miss Levy was a concert pianist who played between his conjuring numbers.

Despite the Civil War, which Anderson claimed ruined his business, Herrmann drew huge crowds in Brooklyn, Philadelphia, Newark, Boston, and Chicago. Herrmann performed for Abraham Lincoln and an assemblage of high government officials, ambassadors, and military men in the East Room of the White House in Washington in November 1861. News accounts said the magician asked the President to shuffle a pack of cards before one of his feats. Lincoln shook his head, passed the deck to Simon Cameron, the Secretary of War, saying "This gentleman shuffles the cards for me at present." After the show Lincoln gave Herrmann a pair of perfectly matched dueling pistols in a polished wooden case.

Herrmann returned to England in 1863. His engagement at the Princess Theatre in London was a sensation. Minus the paraphernalia he had featured fifteen years before, he captivated audiences with his flawless sleight of hand and witty talk.

Then, after another British tour, he bought a mansion in Vienna and furnished it with the antiques and curios he had collected during his travels. Baron de Rothschild, one of his closest friends, took private lessons in magic from him and advised him how to invest the fortune Herrmann had earned. Another intimate, Johann Nepomuk Hofzinser, an official in the Ministry of Finance, had a conjuring salon in his home where three nights each week Hofzinser presented an hour of mystery. His programs were changed frequently to show off the new feats he had devised. Card tricks were to Hofzinser "the poetry of magic," but he also displayed novel tricks using equipment made of fine wood or silver. Hofzinser invented several of the routines Herrmann presented in his later years.

Among Hofzinser's notable creations were "The Card Star," (when a pack was thrown at it, selected cards appeared at the tips of the five points); "The Crystal Clock Dial" (after the single silver hand was spun, it stopped at a thought-of number); "The Ink Vase" (the black fluid in a transparent container changed into water—complete with goldfish—at the performer's command), and "The Floating Wand" (a slender rod mysteriously adhered to the magician's fingers as he shifted the stick from hand to hand).

Hofzinser died in the spring of 1875. His wife followed his deathbed instructions and destroyed the notes he had made about his inventions and presentations. Fortunately George Heubeck, his pupil, continued to perform Hofzinser's masterpieces, and years afterward another Viennese magician, Ottokar Fischer, collected Hofzinser's letters and equipment. From these and Heubeck's recollections, Fischer offered conclusive evidence in two scholarly books that Hofzinser was Austria's most inventive conjurer.

Hofzinser's interest in magic had been sparked by Ludwig Leopold Doebler, a fellow Viennese magician. Doebler, who had been born in 1801, was in his twenties when he first appeared before Prince Metternich and Emperor Francis I of Austria. A handsome man, Doebler performed in a Faustian costume. His startling opening—lighting a hundred candles with a single pistol shot—was later featured by Philippe.

Doebler toured in Austria, Germany, Russia, and France. He played his initial British engagement at the St. James' Theatre in London in April 1842. In his most applauded trick, he fired a pistol to cause two borrowed handkerchiefs to vanish from vases on a table and reappear dangling over the spectator's heads at the dome of the theatre. He fired a second shot, and the handkerchiefs dropped, sometimes directly into the hands of the owners.

The popular conjurer set the style for men's cravats, hats, and

Alexander Herrmann in the costume he wore for the bullet-catching feat.

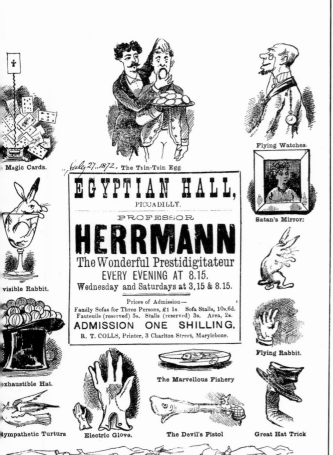

Advertisement listing Herrmann's tricks, Egyptian Hall, London, 1872.

gloves in Vienna, which named a street in his honor. Doebler left the stage at the height of his fame and moved to his estate near Turnitz, Austria. He wished the public to remember him as he had been in his prime. He died at his home in 1864 at the age of sixty-three.

Carl Herrmann had continued to perform regularly until 1870 when he concluded a farewell tour of the United States and retired to his home in Vienna. However, the financial panic of 1874 wiped out his savings and investments. Forced to sell his home and his antiques, he salvaged only the mementos of his shows, the jewels presented to him by his admirers, and his conjuring equipment. At the age of fifty-seven, Herrmann went on the road again. In thirteen years he saved an estimated $150,000 and bought another house in Vienna.

In one of the front rooms at 8 Nibelungen Strasse he set up a private museum to display his decorations and trophies. His once thick dark hair had all but disappeared, but he retained his bristling moustache, imperial goatee, and elegant manner. Nor had age impaired his skill.

While touring Russia in 1884, he slipped on a theatre runway in Kiev and fractured a bone in his foot. Refusing to allow a Russian doctor to treat him, he returned to Austria, wearing a splint. An old friend, a famous Viennese surgeon, reset the break, but the accident left the magician with a permanent limp. Herrmann's seventieth birthday brought greetings from Queen Marie Henrietta of Belgium, his most famous pupil. Her message assured him she had not revealed any of his secrets.

His wife, Rosalie, took the ailing conjurer to Carlsbad for a liver cure in May 1887. Carl Herrmann died there of lung inflammation on June 8 at the age of seventy-one and was buried in Vienna.

The Herrmann name was carried on by Alexander, who had achieved great acclaim with his own magic production. Introduced as Carl's successor-to-be in New York in 1869, he sailed for England while his brother toured America. Thoroughly schooled in Carl's techniques, Alexander played a record-breaking "thousand consecutive nights" engagement at Egyptian Hall in London and appeared in the principal British cities before returning to the United States.

En route he met Adelaide Scarcez, a twenty-two-year-old dancer, who had seen him at Egyptian Hall. Born in London to Belgian parents, the titian-haired, bilingual Adelaide had been planning to marry an American actor. Before the ship docked, she changed her mind. She became Mrs. Alexander Herrmann on March 27, 1875, in Manhattan, the Mayor of New York performing the ceremony. Even on this solemn occasion, Herrmann couldn't resist

Herrmann's mansion at Whitestone Landing on Long Island in New York, and two of his horses.

Herrmann's yacht, *Fra Diavolo,* which was moored near his house during the summer.

Lower left, the lounge.

Right, his cabin.

an impromptu trick; he pulled a roll of greenbacks from the Mayor's beard.

Alexander delighted in extemporaneous magic. He reached in the air, not his pocketbook, for cab fares. He produced cigars from the whiskers of President Ulysses S. Grant. Wine glasses vanished at his fingertips as he drank with friends. Occasionally one of his little jokes backfired. Dining with Bill Nye, the American humorist, Herrmann lifted the lettuce on Nye's plate to reveal a diamond ring.

"Dear me, how careless," the magician said. Nye agreed; he claimed he was always "leaving little things like that around." He picked up the ring and gave it to a waitress. Herrmann had to call on the owner of the hotel to intercede before he retrieved his property.

Deciding to make his home in the United States, Herrmann applied for American citizenship in 1876, but he continued to tour abroad from time to time. Emperor Dom Pedro II of Brazil attended *nineteen* of his performances in Rio de Janeiro in 1883, and King Alfonso XII of Spain invited the conjurer to his palace in Madrid in 1885. Herrmann gave the king an Argentinian saddle trimmed with silver. Alfonso asked if he could do something in return. "Yes," Herrmann replied, "come to the theatre again tomorrow night, and when I call for a spectator to write something on a piece of paper, volunteer to assist me."

The next night when the magician, as usual, asked for a volunteer from the audience, the king stood up in the royal box. Herrmann displayed a blank sheet of paper, passed it to Alfonso, and asked him to sign it for later identification. Herrmann took the sheet and commanded the spirits to produce a message. Words materialized above the signature. He asked the king if this was the same paper he had signed. Alfonso laughed as he read the words, then said: "I will not deny my signature to this document, which appoints Alexander Herrmann prestidigitator to the King of Spain, and, as the spirits have done so, I heartily acquiesce."

While Carl discarded his heavy equipment and specialized in magic without apparatus, Alexander gradually added big-scale illusions to his show. By the 1890's there were three, sometimes four, spectacular scenes in every program. One season he featured "Cremation": his wife was burned alive, then ghostly forms appeared above her casket. Another year the main attraction was "After the Ball": Adelaide vanished as she stood before a large mirror. He performed several variations of the levitation which John Nevil Maskelyne had introduced in England; in the most dramatic version, he played Svengali to Adelaide's Trilby.

When American papers editorialized about the admission of Orientals to the United States, he staged "Ya-Ko-Ya, or Solving the

Chinese Immigration Problem." A man in Chinese costume entered one of the two large cages on the stage. Curtains were closed at the front, then opened. The Chinese immigrant was gone; a customs official stood in his place. Just then the Oriental reappeared at the back of the theatre and ran down the aisle. He was put in the second cage, which was raised from the floor. Herrmann fired a pistol. This cage was shown empty, and the man reappeared in the cage from which he had vanished initially. Scarcely a solution to the immigration controversy, but exciting theatre! Several years later he changed the costumes and setting, and presented "Escape from Sing Sing."

He duplicated the feats of mediums and offered twenty thousand dollars for any marvel he couldn't reproduce on the stage in his spirit séances. He relished playing a mad doctor in a Maskelyne comedy skit. Fitting a helmet, similar to those divers use, over a patient's head as the man sat in an upholstered chair, Herrmann decapitated him, then carried the helmet to the top of a nearby cabinet. After a conversation with the disembodied head, the magician replaced the helmet on the man's shoulders and restored him.

Bullet-catching was performed on special occasions with typical Herrmann flare. Rather than have a single marksman fire at him, he faced five or more sharpshooters and caught their bullets on a china plate.

Herrmann announced in May 1896 that he would attempt the dangerous feat at Palmer's Theatre in New York to raise money for the *Herald's* "Free Ice Fund." Edmund P. Schmidt, manager of the Connecticut Indemnity Association quickly issued a public statement. Herrmann's life-insurance policy with his firm would *not* be in effect when the magician tried this trick. Herrmann had not mentioned the bullet-catching number when he applied for coverage.

A month later when the *World* asked Herrmann to face another squad of riflemen on the stage of the Olympia Theatre for its "Sick Babies' Fund," a woman reporter was dispatched to Herrmann Manor at Whitestone Landing on Long Island for an interview.

An eight-foot-high, spiked wire fence enclosed the property. A herd of cattle and several goats grazed in the pasture as she walked up a winding tree-lined road to the dark red mansion "with countless arches, gables and quaint windows." She pressed the front doorbell; instantly the door swung open. She walked into the entry hall. "What do you want?" a voice asked. She spun around. A black bird, sitting on a perch, was speaking. Heavy tapestry drapes swished open across the hallway, and an animated skeleton sprang out. The reporter's shriek brought a maid into the hall to usher her into the sitting room where the magician and his wife were waiting.

Whenever her husband faced a firing squad on stage, she

Elaborate stage set for Adelaide Herrmann's "Cagliostro" act in 1910.

Léon and Adelaide Herrmann.

As she appeared offstage later.

locked herself in her dressing room, Adelaide Herrmann confessed. She couldn't bear the sight of loaded rifles aimed at him. "Nonsense," Herrmann broke in. He reminded her he had already caught bullets successfully six times—twice in New York, and once each in San Francisco, Paris, Mexico City, and Havana. "Seven, you know, is a lucky number," he said reassuringly.

As Herrmann predicted, he survived the ordeal a seventh time. After the June tenth performance, he was free to spend the summer months relaxing on his yacht, the *Fra Diavolo*. In the fall he traveled from one theatre to another in his private railway car; costing forty thousand dollars, it had once been owned by Lily Langtry, the English actress. Attached to this palatial home on wheels, special baggage cars carried his equipment, scenery, four horses, and a carriage.

He lived on a scale in keeping with his position as one of the biggest box-office attractions in America. Herrmann the Great's annual income, according to the newspapers, ranged from sixty-five thousand to a hundred thousand dollars. He admitted losing half a million dollars speculating in cotton futures on Wall Street. An investment in the Broad Street Threatre in Philadelphia was another fiasco. The roof of a theatre he was building in Brooklyn caved in before the opening, and Herrmann's Theatre at Broadway and Twenty-ninth Street in Manhattan, which he rented for plays and musicals, soon shut down. He dismissed these disastrous investments with a shrug and a lifted eyebrow. He confessed that he also liked to gamble with cards, though he rarely won.

Never too absorbed in personal pleasures to ignore luckless strangers and hard-pressed friends, Herrmann was the first magician to stage a show for the inmates of Sing Sing prison; when David Henderson, manager of the Chicago Opera House, needed three thousand dollars to meet a debt, the conjurer sent him a check. Moved by a letter from an agent, who wrote Herrmann while he was playing at the Lyceum in Rochester, New York, pleading for money to meet overdue hotel bills and to buy railway tickets back to Manhattan for a stranded theatrical troupe, the magician paid their expenses.

After his last show at the Lyceum, Herrmann was feted at the Genesee Valley Hunt Club. Following a late supper, the fifty-two-year-old conjurer performed with cards and told amusing stories about his worldwide adventures. Almost casually he mentioned that his nephew, Leon Herrmann, who was then in Paris, would be his successor when he retired.

As he boarded his private car, Alexander waved good-bye to the friends who had ridden with him in his private carriage to the railroad station. The show was off to Bradford, Pennsylvania, where he was to open the next night. The morning of December 17, 1896, as the train approached Great Valley, New York, America's most popular magician died of a heart attack. His obituaries were the most extensive ever published for a conjurer. For days afterward the newspapers ran columns of stories about the marvelous tricks Herrmann had performed for celebrities.

Adelaide cabled Leon to come to the United States at once. She had to keep the show on the road. Her husband had left her little money. His extravagances had matched his income, and the well-publicized huge life-insurance policies were fables.

Leon Herrmann gave a press preview at Hoyt's Theatre in New York on January 11, 1897. The twenty-nine-year-old entertainer had assisted his Uncle Carl in Europe and South America, and his manipulations with coins, balls, and cards were reminiscent of his Uncle Alexander's. He wore the family trademark: a black moustache and goatee. His French-accented English was charming. The new "Herrmann the Great Company" starred Adelaide and featured Leon. In the finale, "A Night In Japan," they worked together.

The Herrmann name still drew audiences, but Adelaide and Leon parted company after three seasons because of a clash of temperament. Leon further antagonized his aunt by taking out his own full evening show under the billing of "Herrmann the Great." Later he trimmed the program down and played in vaudeville until his death at the age of forty-two on May 16, 1909, during a holiday visit to Paris.

Adelaide Herrmann's serpentine dances and her work in her husband's illusions had been outstanding; on her own, she too became a variety headliner. She appeared at the Folies-Bergère in Paris, the Hippodrome in London, the Wintergarten in Berlin, and made a tour of Cuba, but she preferred performing in the United States. "The Haunted Studio," Alexander's version of "The Artist's Dream," which David Devant had introduced in London, was one of her most effective presentations. Costumed as a male artist, she covered a model with a cloth, pulled the cloth away, and the girl was gone. When the artist sat in an easy chair and fell asleep, Satan materialized in a burst of flame by a fireplace. He gestured toward the artist's portrait of the model, and the picture came to life. The girl gave the rose in her hand to the sleeping artist. The artist awoke and danced with the model as Satan watched. Satan and the artist rolled dice for the girl. The artist lost and fell senseless to the floor. As the devil turned to claim his prize, he—and the audience—discovered that the girl was once more a portrait.

In the fall of 1917, Adelaide, then sixty-four, appeared as Cleopatra in an Egyptian setting with her "Palace of Illusions." She opened a "Temple of Magic" at Luna Park on Coney Island the following summer. *Billboard,* the show-business weekly, said she had "discovered the fountain of youth."

"Noah's Ark—Where Do They Come From?" was the billing

for her act on the Keith circuit in 1919. Pairs of pigeons, roosters, cats, ducks, "lions" and "tigers"—the two latter, dogs with appropriate headpieces—were produced after an ark-shaped box was shown empty, then filled with water. Finally the front and back doors opened. The water was gone; a reclining girl filled the interior.

A fire at the Progressive Transfer Warehouses on West Forty-sixth Street in Manhattan in September 1926 killed nearly sixty of Madame Herrmann's trained animals, along with most of the magic equipment that she had inherited from Herrmann the Great. As firemen fought the blaze, she saw Magic, one of her kittens, trembling on the ledge of a fourth-floor window. "Magic," she shouted; the cat jumped and was saved. Two of the dogs which wore lion and tiger masks in "Noah's Ark" were also rescued. The newspapers said the fire ended her long and glamorous theatrical career.

They were wrong. By November, the seventy-three-year-old "Queen of Magic" was on tour again with "Magic, Grace and Music." And two years later, at Keith's Orpheum in Brooklyn, she was still astounding her fans by converting the water in a canister to flags, producing cages of doves, taking girl assistants from empty palanquins and chests, changing a young woman into a flowering tree, and filling the stage with hundreds of colored silk scarves from her "Wonder Screen."

Failing health forced her to retire. The walls of her Manhattan hotel suite were decorated with her husband's lithographs, photographs, and handbills. Piles of his clippings were heaped on a sideboard. The initialed silver case Alexander had been holding when he died was on a small table. The case contained the shredding cigarette he had been raising to his lips. Adelaide spent her days sorting through the stacks of posters, playbills, newspaper stories, and pictures as she made notes for a book she planned but never completed about his life. Four years after her last performance the world's most famous woman magician died of pneumonia and arteriosclerosis on February 19, 1932, at the age of seventy-nine. Adelaide Herrmann had performed magic longer in the United States than either Carl or Alexander; her career spanned half a century, thirty-one of those years with her own show.

Many contemporaries who saw Carl Herrmann in Europe said he was the finest magician who ever lived. Those who watched his brother perform in America made the same claim for Alexander. As a family of conjurers, the Herrmanns have never been surpassed.

12

Around the World with Kellar

H ARRY Kellar performed on five continents before he was accepted as the virtual king of American magic. Taller and brawnier than his principal rival, Herrmann the Great, the balding Kellar relied more on carefully planned presentations than virtuoso dexterity. Herrmann improvised brilliantly when a trick failed; Kellar struggled to control his quick temper and went on to another feat. The morning after his vanishing lamp failed to disappear in Philadelphia, an assistant set it up on the stage for repair. Kellar scowled when he saw the faulty device. Seizing a hatchet in his powerful hands, he chopped the mechanism to pieces. His fury spent, he calmly said he would build one that worked. Long after his retirement, this lamp still functioned perfectly in another show.

Born Heinrich Keller in Erie, Pennsylvania, on July 11, 1849, the globe-circling illusionist was called Henry or Harry by his friends. Later he changed the spelling of his surname to Kellar.

Young Harry enjoyed dangerous games. He won the admiration of other boys by standing motionless in the middle of the railroad tracks as a train approached, then jumping aside moments before the engine roared by. Apprenticed to a druggist named Carter, he experimented with chemicals until an explosive mixture of sulfuric acid and soda blasted a hole in the floor of the store. Rather than explain how he had lost the job to his German father and to his stepmother, who had shown little affection for him, the ten-year-old youngster hopped aboard a freight train bound for Ohio.

There is little about Kellar's early life in his *A Magician's Tour Up Down and Round About the Earth,* published in Chicago by R. R. Donnelly and Sons in 1896. Letters, diaries, contemporary newspaper stories, and the notes Houdini made during conversations with the man he idolized, are more informative. Kellar told the escapologist he worked in Cleveland at the DeForest dry-goods store and "fed the presses" for the *Herald* before he moved on to New York in another baggage car.

Kellar recalled selling newspapers on the corner of Canal and Centre streets in lower Manhattan and sleeping in the office of the Earle Hotel, in exchange for helping a night porter "sweep and clean the place." Robert Harcourt, a British-born clergyman, took the newsboy to Canandaigua in upstate New York, offering to adopt him and to pay for his education if he would study for the ministry. One evening they went to see a traveling show in Penn Yan, a nearby town. "The Fakir of Ava" gave an enthralling performance. He produced silver coins from nowhere; changed paper shavings into milk, sugar, and steaming hot coffee; smashed a borrowed watch, loaded the parts into a wide-mouthed gun, then fired at a target where the watch appeared —restored. Kellar told Houdini he "immediately got the urge to go on the stage . . . became very restless, bought books on magic and finally left my friend and benefactor."

While employed as a "chore boy" on the farm of Henry C. Fiske in Buffalo, Harry read an exciting ad in a local paper; "The Fakir of Ava" needed a boy assistant. Terrified that someone else would get there first, Harry ran the two miles to the magician's home in the suburb of Cold Spring. The plump, moustached fakir said there had been dozens of previous applicants, but none was suitable. His black and tan dog, an excellent judge of character, had barked or snapped at them; now he was wagging his tail in approval.

Despite his billing, this "Fakir of Ava" had never been to the old capital of Burma. Born Isaiah Harris Hughes in Essex, England, on Christmas Day 1810, he had taken the exotic stage name used by his former employer, William Marshall. If Kellar worked conscientiously, Harris said, he too might become a conjurer. Skill was essential, but "quickness of mind, gumption, mother wit and the power to take the audience with you from the start" were more important.

Harry gave evidence of quickness of mind when he missed a cue in Ohio. He had forgotten to hang a watch on the back of a mechanical target which would cause it to appear before the magician took aim with his blunderbuss and fired. The sound of the shot triggered a rapid response backstage. The boy picked up an envelope, ran out behind the footlights, then up and down an aisle, shouting "Telegram for Major De Quincy Jones." With everyone's attention on the "telegram," he dropped the timepiece into a spectator's pocket. Hurrying back into the wings, Harry whispered to the performer that the watch was in the possession of a fat man in the aisle seat on the sixth row.

Hughes announced that he would find the missing watch by a "Spirit Bell"; it would ring once for yes, twice for no. The bell confirmed his statement that the watch was somewhere in the audience, in the pocket of an onlooker. "Which row?" The bell sounded six times. "Give the number of the seat." A single loud clang brought the feat to an effective conclusion.

With the fakir's reluctant permission, Kellar gave his first show in Dunkirk, Michigan, at the age of sixteen. He went on to Westfield and other small towns before he returned to Hughes, admitting the venture had been a failure. Two years later, Kellar tried again, appearing with humorist John C. Whiston, one of the fakir's old friends, at the St. James Hall in Buffalo. Kellar told Houdini that he was so anxious to make a good impression that he had gone to a barbershop that afternoon to have his long reddish-brown hair trimmed. With his hair slicked back, he waited tensely for the curtain to rise. Whiston rumpled his hair, gave him a shove, and said "Now, go out and show them." Kellar's nervousness disappeared; afterward, Hughes and Whiston agreed he had given an excellent performance.

Subsequent solo shows in various Michigan towns were so sparsely attended that Kellar had to labor for three weeks, paving streets in Detroit, to raise capital. Stranded again several months later, he worked briefly as an assistant to John Henry Anderson, Jr., the eldest son of "The Great Wizard of the North." A glib promoter named Bailey offered to act as Kellar's manager in South Bend, Indiana. Bailey publicized the show, sold tickets at the box office, then skipped town with the profits. While a sheriff was busy attaching the magician's property, Kellar pulled a cloth from a table, threw it over his head, and ran through a snow storm to the freight terminal where he climbed into a baggage car just as it was pulling out. In Chicago Kellar boldly took a seat in a passenger train leaving for Milwaukee. Thrown off by a conductor at Rose Hill, the dejected performer plodded through the snow to Waukegan, Illinois.

A sympathetic Irish bartender, moved by Kellar's story of his troubles, lent him a topcoat and a pair of overshoes. Encouraged, the magician talked the manager of the Phoenix Hall into letting him reserve it for two performances, without a deposit. Kellar was equally effective in persuading a printer to provide him with ten-dollars worth of handbills on credit.

That afternoon a traveling salesman tried to sell the magician stock in a lightning-rod company. Kellar described the marvelous show that he, the protégé of the great "Fakir of Ava," would give. The in-

Harry Kellar followed Herrmann as the dominant magician in North America.

Kellar's wife, the former Eva L. Medley, first saw him perform in Melbourne in 1882.

While traveling with the Davenport brothers, Kellar learned the secret of their "spirit manifestations."

trigued salesman traded two shares and sixty dollars for the receipts of the first performance. Kellar sold the stock to the owner of a hotel for fifty dollars, bought a license to perform, and paid for the hall and the printing.

Now he had to find the equipment for his entertainment. From the friendly bartender came two packs of playing cards and an opaque bottle. One of Kellar's favorite feats was to make a ring disappear, then find it tied to the neck of a guinea pig when he broke open a bottle. As no guinea pigs were available, Kellar gave passes for the show to a small boy who brought him a kitten and a length of clothesline for rope tricks. The child's mother supplied a set of baby clothes to be produced from a borrowed hat. Metal cups for the coffee, milk, and sugar trick were made by a tinsmith, who also constructed a special pan and bucket for a laundry feat and cut the metal disks Kellar would pluck from the air as silver dollars.

Phoenix Hall was almost filled for the first performance and sold out for the second. Kellar was back in business. He bought new clothes, luggage, and conjuring apparatus in Milwaukee, then began a tour of the smaller Wisconsin towns.

For a few weeks he prospered, but by the time he reached Beaver Dam he was broke again. The people who came to his show on the second floor of an old building were mostly creditors. As soon as the front curtain was lowered for the intermission, Kellar packed his gear, tied a rope to a piece of scenery near the rear window, and lowered his luggage and himself to the street.

The printer Kellar approached for credit in Horicon had read a newspaper story about the magician in Beaver Dam who disappeared in the middle of his performance, but he was willing to gamble that the hard-pressed conjurer's luck would change. It didn't.

Disheartened by his efforts to earn a living, Kellar went backstage at the principal hall in La Crosse, Wisconsin, in the spring of 1869 and applied for a job with "The Davenport Brothers and Fay."

Ira Erastus Davenport, born in Buffalo, New York, on September 17, 1839, and William Henry Harrison Davenport, born there on February 1, 1841, were the first successful stage mediums. Shortly after the Fox sisters, the founders of modern spiritualism, produced uncanny sounds in a Hydesville, New York, farmhouse in 1848, similar weird noises erupted in the Davenport home. The boys from Buffalo improved upon the Hydesville girls' technique by permitting themselves to be bound to seats in a large wooden cabinet before unseen forces strummed guitars, played solos on horns, and hurled bells and tambourines into the darkened halls. William Melville Fay, an older showman, joined them as a lecturer and worked in the cabinet when one of the brothers was ill.

After a long and triumphant American tour, the producers of "startling wonders" sailed for England in August 1864. Hailed as valid communicators with the dead by spiritualists, they were denounced as tricksters by John Henry Anderson, John Nevil Maskelyne, and other prominent conjurers. British newspaper critics, while skeptical, admitted to being thoroughly baffled. Riots occurred in Liverpool, Huddersfield, and Leeds as hostile spectators cried fraud and stormed the stage. There was another fracas at the Salle Herz in Paris. Despite this, Emperor Napoleon III invited the mediums to perform at his palace in St. Cloud, in October 1865 and the King of Saxony and the Russian Czar were puzzled by their manifestations elsewhere on the Continent.

Returning to the United States in 1868, after four tempestuous years abroad, the brothers wrote to *The Banner of Light,* a Boston spiritualist paper:

> Before leaving Europe, rumors from time to time reached us from this country, that many of the American newspapers, taking the cue from their equally truth-loving brethren of the English press, were representing us as having "giving up all pretensions to being spiritualists." Now, these statements, as ridiculous as they are false, we treated with silent contempt, thinking them unworthy of notice.
>
> We did believe that our career as mediums for the past fourteen years was sufficient answer to all such reports. . . . It is singular that any individual, skeptic or spiritualist, could believe such statements after . . . the riots . . . where our lives were placed in imminent peril by the fury of brutal mobs, our property destroyed, and where we suffered a loss of seventy-five thousand dollars, and all because *we would not renounce spiritualism,* and declare ourselves jugglers, when threatened by the mob and urged to do so. In conclusion, we have only to say, that we denounce all such statements as base falsehoods.

Hired as an assistant for the Davenport show, Kellar was promoted to advance agent and later to business manager. He had been inclined to believe the Davenports were sincere until he had a friend tie him up and found he could release a hand, use it to produce "startling wonders," then slip it back into the knotted rope.

The Davenports never knew of his discovery, but Fay came into the room while Kellar was practicing one day, winked, and left. Not long afterward, Kellar was ordered to take William Davenport's pets, a monkey and a dog, to his seat on a train in the parlor car. The young man hesitated; he said the conductor would insist that the animals be put in the baggage car. "You do as I tell you," Davenport stormed. "You may as well know that you're my servant."

"I quit the concern then and there," Kellar told Houdini, "and Bill Fay went with me." Featuring the Davenport séance and

Robert Heller, noted pianist
and composer, excelled as a
humorous conjurer.

Haidee Heller, though billed as
the magician's sister, was not
related to Robert Heller.

"The Fakir of Ava," his former
employer, visited Harry Kellar
in Philadelphia during his
long run in 1885.

Kellar's magic, the new team toured Canada in the summer of 1873. That winter they worked their way south, and in December they opened at the Teatro Albisu in Havana. When a Cuban interpreter demanded an exorbitant fee for his services, Kellar fired him and set about memorizing his patter in Spanish. In less than five weeks he was, in his own words, "good enough to make people understand and bad enough to amuse them."

The theatre in Veracruz, Mexico, where Fay and Kellar appeared following their Cuban tour, was packed nightly, but receipts were slim. One evening Kellar counted 213 more spectators seated in the gallery than admission had been paid for at the gallery entrance. Clearly the gallery ticket seller had been pocketing most of the money. Thereafter before each performance Fay checked one box office, and Kellar kept tabs on the other.

En route to Mexico City on the only railway line then in the country, the Americans stopped off to perform at Orizaba, Puebla, and Pachuca. Roving bandits were raiding the trains so frequently that soldiers were posted in the cars to protect the passengers. The showmen faced an attack of another sort in the Mexican capital. Newspapers charged their feats were produced with demonic assistance and warned readers to stay away from the show.

Branding the foreigners as charlatans, two conjurers from Puebla, José Bouila and Eduardo Novos, opened a rival attraction and advertised that they would duplicate the controversial marvels. Public interest mounted. By June 1874 Fay and Kellar had accumulated ten thousand dollars in gold doubloons. Rather than risk robbery crossing the mountains from Guadalajara to Colima with so much cash in a strong box, Kellar bought two large cans of black asphaltum, a mineral pitch used in paving. He poured the coins into the sticky solution, sealed the lids, and packed the cans with his conjuring apparatus in a zinc trunk. They were traveling with a minimum of equipment, since, as Kellar said, "Transportation was so high and difficult . . . that we found it cheaper to have a new cabinet [for the Davenport séance] built in every city rather than carry it with us."

A boy named Pancho was hired to lead two pack donkeys, one with the trunk, the other with the rest of the baggage. He set out two days before Fay and Kellar departed by stage coach. Pancho was in tears when they met at Colima. One of the donkeys—the one with the trunk—had wandered off the previous night. Fay was frantic; Kellar went with the boy to the valley where the animal had last been seen beside a stream. Reasoning that the donkey had gone in search of food, Kellar spent two frustrating hours in the area before he heard a faint clinking sound in the distance. "There was a chain on the zinc trunk and the motion of the donkey was swinging it against the metal. . . . Bill Fay was the happiest man in Mexico," Kellar said.

Spicy Mexican food played havoc with Kellar's digestion. Suffering from stomach pains and a raging fever, he spent three weeks in bed under a doctor's care in Mazatlán. Though still weak in Acapulco, he helped Fay remove their golden hoard from the asphaltum and load it into a small chest with their more recent profits, before they boarded a ship for Panama, Ecuador, and the west coast of South America.

Kellar was arrested on the stage of the Teatro Principal in Lima in September 1874. Someone struck a match during the séance blackout, and the magician shouted for him to put it out. Kellar's offense? He had spoken directly to the audience without asking permission of the *juez,* a theatre official who sat in a special box. The receipts, approximately fifteen hundred dollars, were confiscated, and Kellar paid a hundred dollar fine. He never made this costly mistake again. There were theatre judges in all the Spanish-speaking countries of South America; an advance bribe insured their cooperation.

A sudden flare of light in a dark auditorium could reveal the secret of the "spirit manifestations," but there was a greater danger—fire in the theatre. Indian stagehands at the Teatro de Talca in Chile, struggling to raise a heavy curtain without a windlass, accidentally upset an oil lamp in the wings. As the side drapes ignited, screaming spectators rushed to the exit. Kellar averted a panic by standing at the front of the stage and calmly giving precise instructions. Those in the back rows were to leave first; then, row by row, the others would follow. When an orderly exodus was under way, he whipped off his tailcoat and used it to battle the blaze. Once the fire was out and the people were back in their seats, they gave the coolheaded conjurer an ovation.

Fay and Kellar sailed from Valparaiso, through the Strait of Magellan, to the east coast of South America early in February 1875. Professor Jam, a magician from Barcelona, challenged Kellar in Montevideo; Jam boasted he could tie the American so securely that not even a dozen ghosts could release him. Kellar accepted the dare. The loser was to give the equivalent of two thousand dollars to charity. Jam brought his own rope and lashed Kellar's hands behind his back. In seven seconds a hand waved from the cabinet; moments later, the doors swung open and Kellar stepped out.

Later, in the Teatro de la Opera in Buenos Aires, Jam and another conjurer sought to challenge Kellar again, but Kellar told the audience that the Barcelonian had not given a single peso to charity after the episode in Uruguay. The man with Jam, Kellar went on, had asked him, as a fellow professional, to pay an overdue board bill in Montevideo and advance money for his passage across the River Plate to Argentina. This Kellar had done. Now these rascals were trying to impose on him again. Audience reaction was swift; several husky spectators seized the troublemakers and ushered them out into the street.

Ticket speculators sold seats for triple box-office prices in Rio de Janeiro; Emperor Dom Pedro II had attended the opening night and he returned twice during the run. Following bookings in Bahia and Pernambuco, Fay and Kellar played another engagement in Rio, then boarded the Royal Mail steamer *Boyne* en route to England.

Seventeen days later, on the morning of August 13, 1875, the vessel struck a rock in the Bay of Biscay. Two stokers were drowned, but the rest of the crew and all the passengers reached the island of Moleno. Lost in the wreckage were Kellar's show, clothes, and more than twenty thousand dollars worth of curios, uncut Brazilian diamonds and gold and silver coins. When the magician and the other survivors were picked up by a French warship and taken to Brest, Kellar had only the clothes he was wearing and a diamond ring.

"I am too feeble to write," Kellar confessed in a letter to his father from Brest, "but hope to see you soon." Three days later, Kellar wrote again from the Craven Hotel in London with "still sadder news." He had learned that Duncan, Sherman and Co., his bankers in New York, had failed. Desperately in need of money, the magician sold his diamond ring for a thousand dollars—while his partner, Fay, left to rejoin the Davenport brothers.

A visit to Maskelyne and Cooke's Egyptian Hall revived Kellar's spirits. Intrigued by Buatier de Kolta's new vanishing cage and canary, he went backstage, determined to add the sensational feat to his repertoire. Buatier sold him a spare cage for $750. Nearly broke again after buying a new wardrobe and luggage and paying his living expenses, Kellar had an inspiration. There was just a chance the last $3,500 bank draft he had posted to New York from South America hadn't arrived in time to be credited to his account before the bank failed—ship mail from Brazil was notoriously slow. Kellar presented his case so convincingly to Junius Spencer Morgan (J. P.'s father), that the American banker, then in London, lent him $500 to go to New York.

With the aid of the Manhattan judge who was the assignee of the bankrupt firm, Kellar salvaged his $3,500. Then he traded the secret of the vanishing cage to Henry Stone, a New York mechanic who constructed illusionary devices for professional magicians, for conjuring props to replace the equipment lost in the shipwreck.

Returning to London, Kellar paid his debt to Morgan, formed a new show troupe, then sailed for the West Indies. Advertised as "The Royal Illusionists" (the billing Maskelyne and Cooke were using at Egyptian Hall) Kellar, A. Litherland Cunard, and George Dale Donaldson opened at the Gymnasium Theatre on the island of St. Thomas in November 1875. Cunard took Fay's place in the séance sequence; Donaldson was the manager of the company. After performing as far south as Chile, Kellar returned to New York for a holiday in April 1876.

Joining forces with Ling Look and Yamadeva (two Hungarian brothers, Ferdinand and Louis Guter), one a fire-eater and the other a contortionist, he set off for the West Coast of the United States under the direction of impresario Al Hayman. Cunard traveled with the show in California, Nevada, and Utah; Hayman's younger brother, David, took his place and his name when the troupe sailed for Australia.

The "Flying Cage" was a show-stopper at the Victoria Theatre in Sydney in September 1876. One moment the small oblong cage with a live bird was between the magician's outstretched hands; the next it was gone. "The applause was deafening, and shouts of 'bravo' resounded from all parts of the house," the *Herald* reported. Later an anonymous letter to the newspaper charged the magician with cruelty, claiming "the canary is killed every time this trick is performed, or so maimed it has to be destroyed."

"I will satisfactorily prove to the editor of the *Evening News* and the editor of the *Herald*," Kellar wrote in reply, "that I have had only the one and same educated bird since I came to the colony. . . . I will perform this trick in any place, and at any time, the gentlemen referred to may decide upon. I thank the writer for the very tender regard he evinces toward my pet canary."

A special showing was arranged for members of the Society for the Prevention of Cruelty to Animals and the press. One SPCA official examined the bird; another tied a silk thread to its leg. Kellar placed the canary in the cage. It pecked at the unfamiliar binding until coaxed to jump up on the perch. Then—instantly—bird and cage vanished. Before the gasps had died away, Kellar produced the canary again. The SPCA officials attested this was the original bird, and that it had not been injured. The identifying thread was removed, and the lively canary hopped about, until Kellar told it to return to the large cage it occupied between shows and the bird immediately obeyed.

The October fourteenth issue of the Sydney *Punch* featured the much-talked-about trick in a full-page cartoon. A member of Parliament displayed a caged, birdlike politician. The caption read: "Do not be alarmed, Ladies and Gentlemen; I do not kill the little animal; I simply make him disappear. One! Two! Three! (Poor P-g-t disappears.)"

For two months "The Royal Illusionists" drew large crowds

Kellar's Egyptian Hall opened in Philadelphia on December 15, 1884. He gave 267 shows there.

PROGRAMME

COMEDY THEATRE
Broadway and 29th Street.

GEORGE C. BROTHERTON.....................Proprietor and Manager.
JOHN W. RYCKMAN.............................Assistant Manager.
THOMAS ASHTON.......................,.............Treasurer

MONDAY EVENING, SEPTEMBER 21.
INAUGURATION OF THE SEASON BY
✳ KELLAR ✳
The greatest Magician in the world; who has mystified and astonished the people of all nations with his

Grand Illusions, Unique Surprises, and Extraordinary Experiments in

High Class Prestidigitation.

PROGRAMME:
PART I.
The Spiritual Decanters. Visible Transformation. Obedient Cards. The Mikado's Handkerchief. The Fairy Flowers. El Sombrero del brucho. Marabout Mocha. The Enchanted Casket. Spirit Writing Extraordinary. Thought Reading by Mechanism, and the Mesmerized Hand.

THE INCOMPREHENSIBLE AUTOMATON

P S Y C H O.
The Knight's Tour.   Spiritual Table Tipping.

PART II.
MISS DORA WILEY,
The Charming Prima Donna, in Operatic and Popular Selections.

THE TISSOTS,
In their Novel and pleasing musical entertainment, entitled:
MARIONNETTES VIVANTS (Living Pictures).

PART III
KELLAR AND THE WONDERFUL CABINET,
Introducing startling and unaccountable phenomena by invisible agencies, which, through ignorance and superstition, have been attributed to witchcraft and demonology. First time of the

Davenport Dark Seance. The Katie King Mystery. The Great Holding Test. The Marvelous Livitation Act. The Floating Guitar, and The Fay Spirit Circuit. [EVENINGS ONLY.]

Mr. FRED. W. ZAULIG and his Grand Orchestra.

SPECIAL NOTICE.—Kellar's short methods of arithmetical calculations, including his several tours of the globe, for sale at the box office. Price 25 cents per copy.

THE WEBER PIANOS ARE USED IN THIS THEATRE.

General Admission (Lower floor) .. $ 50	Parquette . . . . $ 75
General Admission (Upper floor) .. 25	Balcony (Two front rows) 1.00
Orchestra Chairs 1.00	Balcony (Other rows) 50

Kellar's 1886–87 season at the Comedy Theatre in New York established a new house record—179 performances.

Robert Heller gave the Globe playhouse on Broadway a new name when he opened there; he called it his "Wonder Theatre."

in Sydney; then they played in Brisbane, Melbourne, Adelaide, and the smaller cities. As David Hayman stayed behind in Australia, Yamadeva performed with Kellar in the séance when the troupe went to Indonesia. The magician wrote his father from Batavia in June 1877 that business was good, despite competition from an American circus, a traveling opera company, and an attraction that featured a ghost illusion. Kellar learned to speak Dutch in Java, and before he sailed for the Straits Settlements, he gave a command performance—for the Sultan of Soerakarta.

The Maharaja of Johore, who saw "The Royal Illusionists" in Singapore, entertained them one evening at his palace. After a late dinner he took his guests to a small amphitheatre to watch a tiger and an elephant fight. The elephant won. "It was a fearsome spectacle, and rendered more wildly barbaric by the red light shed by two torches," Kellar said.

Kellar conjured in English at the Lyceum Theatre in Shanghai, but he began to add several Chinese phrases to his vocabulary. His hotel gave him several small cards on which were printed Chinese characters and approximate translations. If his attempt to pronounce the words properly failed when he gave a ricksha man directions, Kellar could point to the Oriental symbols and hope that the man could read.

After Yamadeva broke a blood vessel, while bowling in Shanghai, Ling Look filled in during the séance. Several nights later, on October 7, 1877, Yamadeva died in his cabin aboard the P. and O. steamer *Khiva*. He was buried in the Happy Valley Cemetery after the vessel docked at Hong Kong. There the grieving Ling Look entered a hospital to be treated for what he thought was a minor kidney infection. He died, following an operation, on April 14, 1878, and was buried beside his brother.

Kellar engaged two British performers to replace Ling Look and Yamadeva. John Morris presented a quick-change-of-costume act. John Hodgkins played the "Cunard" role. The show was publicized in Manila as being "from England's Home of Mystery, the Egyptian Hall, London."

While performing at the Theatre Royal in Calcutta and at the Grant Road Theatre in Bombay early in 1878, Kellar studied the methods of Indian mystifiers. Later he was to tell tall tales of the marvels he had seen, but, among magicians, he confessed that few feats had impressed him. One roadside performer, however, had shown something new. This fakir swallowed powdered sugar of various colors, opened his mouth wide to prove it was empty, then pursing his lips, he blew out a stream of *dry* red sugar followed by clouds of white, green, yellow, and black. The method was ingenious. Small capsules, filled with sugar in several hues, were secreted between the performer's gums and the walls of his mouth. After he closed his mouth, the magician flipped one of the capsules with his tongue until he could bite off the tip. Holding the capsule to one side with his tongue, he opened his lips slightly and puffed strenuously to blow the sugar out and into the air.

On their way to Africa "The Royal Illusionists" visited Baghdad, Bassorah, and Aden, and they performed on the palace grounds in Zanzibar for the Sultan, his court, and as many of his subjects as could crowd into the plaza. The Sultan's wives, with faces heavily veiled, watched from windows of the adjacent harem.

When a spiritualist named Kehoe challenged Kellar at the Athenaeum Theatre in Capetown in June 1878, the *Evening Star* said "at least as many people were turned away as would have sufficed to again fill the Hall." Kehoe arrived with his own eleven feet six inches of heavy rope. He tied Kellar in a way that won approval from several ship's captains in the audience. Fifty seconds passed as Kehoe, smiling confidently, stood to one side of the closed cabinet. His smile sagged as a hand waved from the cabinet, and disappeared seventeen seconds later when Kellar, free of his bonds, stepped gingerly down to the stage. His wrists had been cut by the ropes, but he ignored the injuries as "he was cheered and applauded to the echo, the Hall ringing with shouts of 'Bravo Kellar,' until one was almost deafened."

Kehoe claimed later the rope had been cut, but a *Star* reporter examined it after the show, and reported it was still in one piece. The following Saturday, despite a heavy downpour of rain and muddy streets, "the largest crowd which has even been seen in the Exhibition Building" attended a special Kellar matinee.

"The Royal Illusionists" sailed for England in July. From London, the twenty-nine-year-old magician wrote his father that he had invested twelve thousand dollars of his profits in new equipment. After another world tour, he planned to settle down in London or New York and open a theatre of magic similar to Maskelyne and Cooke's Egyptian Hall.

Kellar was in Paris in August visiting the "Grand Exhibition," "seeing all the shows," taking a ride in a balloon, and learning how to "jabber French." Following an engagement in October at the Philharmonic Hall in Southport, England, he sailed for Havana. Six weeks of mounting losses in Cuba prompted Kellar to cancel his bookings in South America and return to New York. When he arrived, he was told that Robert Heller, then the dominant magician in the United States had died.

Born William Henry Palmer on August 11, 1826, in Canterbury, England, where his father was the cathedral organist, Heller became a gifted pianist himself, but abandoned music for magic after he saw Robert-Houdin. Taking the name of Robert Heller, he boldly appeared at the Strand Theatre in London in 1851 with a replica of the great magician's program. A year later, Heller came to New York and leased a hall at 539 Broadway for his show. Posing as a Frenchman, with a black wig over his reddish hair and his light moustache darkened, he gave two hundred shows. Then, after a fifteen-week season in Philadelphia and appearances in several other cities, Heller stored his apparatus and went on tour with the Germania Musical Society—as a concert pianist.

After marrying the daughter of a prominent German banker in 1857, he settled in Washington, D.C. For four years Heller wrote music and gave occasional recitals before returning to the stage with an entirely different magic style. His natural wit, elegant manner, and effective advertising brought him immediate acclaim. While performing in Paris during the 1867 Exposition, Heller gave a command performance for Napoleon III.

Billed as an American, the following year he appeared for a hundred nights at the Polygraphic Hall in London. Between the magic and second-sight routines, he played classical music and hilarious variations on popular themes. *The Times* said Heller had few rivals as a mystifier, "but as humorist and conjurer combined, he certainly stands alone."

With Haidee Heller, a British girl who was introduced as his sister, he sailed to Australia in September 1869, then continued on around the world with, in addition to his usual program, "the first Punch and Judy Show ever seen in Australia and the only one ever seen in India and China."

"Heller's Wonder Theatre" opened at the Globe on Broadway in New York in late November 1876. His eye-catching posters, "Go to HELLer's," shocked clergymen, but he enjoyed a six-month run. He was at the peak of his popularity when he gave his last performance at the Concert Hall in Philadelphia. Though Heller was ill, the critics who praised the show the following day had not known it. Doctors said later that Heller had been suffering from a cold which led to "organic exhaustion." The magician, who had begun as an imitator of Robert-Houdin but achieved fame when he performed as himself, died in Philadelphia two days after the opening night on November 28, 1878.

Eleven days later Kellar began a four-week engagement in Boston at the Horticultural Hall. The *Post* called him "a master of his profession," and said "Psycho" (Kellar's copy of Maskelyne's card-playing automaton) completely baffled the audience. The *New York Sun* took a different view. "Heller is scarcely dead before we read of 'Kellar the Wizard.' Of course 'Kellar' aims to profit by the

Lifelike bust of Harry Kellar played an important part is his "Blue Room" feat.

Paul Valadon toured with Kellar before Howard Thurston became his successor.

Ben Ali Bey (Max Auzinger), a German performer, invented the "Black Art" act.

Alexander Herrmann was firmly established as America's leading magician by 1880.

reputation that Heller left, by adopting a close imitation of Heller's name. This is not an uncommon practice."

Kellar protested, saying his real name was Keller and that he had changed the spelling while in the Orient to avoid being confused with his old friend Heller. Box-office receipts fell off. Business in Boston, according to Kellar's records, was "fair." In Philadelphia it was "miserable," in Washington "very bad," and in Richmond it hit rock bottom, averaging eight dollars a night.

He canceled his advance bookings in the United States, and borrowed money from a longtime friend, Colonel Willard P. Tisdell, to pay his passage to Brazil where, during his previous visit, he had made the biggest profits of his career.

Before sailing in April 1879, Kellar wrote the London firm that supplied him with bills and posters for advertising. If they would send $150 worth of them to Pará or Rio de Janeiro, he would pay them when he could. The hoped-for shipment did not arrive during his stay in Pará; without proper advertising, the show netted just enough to cover his first-class fare to Rio, where four times the number of posters he had expected awaited him. Emperor Dom Pedro II attended the opening at the Imperial Theatre and returned to see three other performances. Kellar paid his debts and went on to Montevideo and Buenos Aires as the upswing continued. Though heavy seasonal rains washed away his chances for profit in Rio Grande and Pelotas on his return to Brazil, Kellar sailed on the S.S. *Potose* for Liverpool in late August 1879 "with pockets full of money."

At Egyptian Hall he admired Maskelyne's automaton sketch artist and his two mechanical musicians. Purchasing the plans from another source, Kellar arranged for facsimiles to be made while he booked a British tour. Meeting Haidee Heller and her new partner, Warren Wright, by chance, he booked their "Second Sight" act as a special feature for an engagement in Edinburgh. The most memorable night on this tour came on April 29, 1880, when Kellar was summoned to Balmoral Castle in Scotland to entertain Queen Victoria.

Though the show played four weeks in Liverpool, and as close to London as Brighton and Southport, Kellar stayed away from the British capital. Obviously he didn't relish a confrontation with Maskelyne.

Kellar's second round-the-world voyage was made in the reverse direction of the first: Gibraltar, Malta, Egypt, then to Spain, Portugal, and Madeira before South Africa. Arriving in Cape Town on New Year's Day 1880, the troupe performed in eight cities, then began the long overland trek to Kimberley.

"If anything will try a man's temper," Kellar said later, "it is to ride for a month in a wagon of any kind; but when that wagon is without springs and is dragged by eighteen bullocks, the man's anatomy, as well as his temper, is likely to reach a stage of collapse."

The diamond center—with crude homes built from sheets of galvanized iron and roads littered with trash—was unlike any city he had seen in his travels. Yet for six weeks the theatre was sold out, which was why he had come there. Kellar lost another "Cunard" in Kimberley; John Hodgkins left the show to work as the secretary of the Royal Stock Exchange.

After eight months in South Africa and an engagement on the island of Mauritius, Kellar crossed the Indian Ocean to Bombay. Bookings in Allahabad, Cawnpore, and Lucknow went by without incident, but in Delhi the chief of police ordered Kellar to remove the gaudy posters that had been plastered on walls throughout the city to herald the magician's appearance. Instead, the American packed his equipment, canceled the booking, and sent the chief a sarcastic note telling him to rip down the posters himself.

His return to Calcutta was a triumph, Kellar said, second only to the fantastic success he had enjoyed in Rio de Janeiro. *The Asian* of January 3, 1882, expressed a popular sentiment:

> For many a day
> We've heard people say
> That a wondrous magician was Heller;
> Change the H into K,
> And the E into A,
> And you have his superior in Kellar.

A virulent fever kept the traveler in bed for several weeks in Batavia. Following an engagement in Surabaya, Kellar began a tour of Australia and New Zealand at St. George's Hall in Melbourne on the evening of May 6, 1882. This time the mechanical figures appealed even more to his audiences than "The Flying Cage" and his "Dark Séance." The *Herald* said:

> Skilful as Mr. Kellar is as an illusionist, it is, however, as the inspirer and director of the wonderful automata that he is greatest of all. The sight of these neatly dressed figures, obeying with unerring accuracy the most difficult instructions of their lord and master—giving without hesitation the squares and cube roots of any four figures . . . sketching the features of our gracious queen, and playing with unusual correctness and brilliancy, the most difficult and popular airs—was worth tramping miles to see.

After one of the performances during the show's six-week run in Melbourne, Eva L. Medley, a nineteen-year-old fan, came backstage to ask for the thirty-four-year-old magician's autograph. He promised to send her an occasional postcard or letter, if she would reply. He wrote frequently from New Zealand, then chose Melbourne

Two imps appeared on the letterheads Kellar used in later years.

Even after he retired, Kellar sent Christmas
cards with a magic theme to his friends.

as a perfect place for a vacation early the following year. The correspondence continued as he traveled to China, Japan, and Vladivostok, Siberia. From Bangkok he wrote of the four performances he had given for the King of Siam and his court at the great palace across the road from the temple that housed a gigantic reclining Buddha.

Wearing a thick moustache (perhaps to compensate for the rapid retreat of hair on the top of his head), Kellar appeared before an American audience for the first time in five years at the New Park Theatre in New York on September 22, 1884. A month later he realized a long-standing ambition when he leased the old Masonic Hall in Philadelphia and gave it a new name. Opening at Kellar's Egyptian Hall on December 15, he began the longest run he had ever made— 267 performances. His friends, Edwin Booth, the great actor, and Mark Twain, the celebrated humorist, came to see his show in Philadelphia.

When spectators recognized John L. Sullivan in the audience one night, they urged the heavyweight boxer to tie Kellar before he entered his spirit cabinet. Once bound, the magician invited the fighter to step inside the enclosure with him.

"I was never so surprised in my life," Sullivan admitted in an interview published in the March 18, 1885, *Philadelphia Times.*

> The next thing I knew my overcoat was gone . . . then I was chucked out of the cabinet on to the stage, as if I had been shot from a cannon. My inside coat was turned inside out, and I lay sprawling on the stage as if someone had tucked me in the jugular. I'll be blank if Kellar isn't the strongest little man I ever saw.

Kellar established a new house record at the Comedy Theatre in New York during the 1886–87 season with 179 consecutive shows; then he toured the Midwest, breaking attendance records in Cincinnati and Chicago. On November 1, 1887, his dark-haired Australian admirer, Eva L. Medley, whom he had wooed and won by correspondence, became his wife at the Congregational Church in Kalamazoo, Michigan.

While Kellar was abroad, Alexander Herrmann had risen to the top of the conjuring profession in the United States. Kellar could scarcely hope to surpass his rival's magnificent sleight of hand, so he set out to offer a more lavish and spectacular show. He hired William Ellsworth Robinson, one of the most ingenious younger American magicians, to present his "Black Art" act and encouraged him to devise new illusions for the program.

Herrmann met the competition by adding a similar scene; white objects materialized and faded away in front of a black curtain. Robinson built "Astarte, the Maid of the Moon," which Kellar featured. A girl in tights, standing alone on the stage, rose several feet

John Grdina, one of the many magicians who patterned their shows after Kellar.

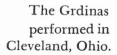

The Grdinas performed in Cleveland, Ohio.

and turned heels over head in the air. Herrmann countered with "Cremation," setting a woman afire, then causing spectral forms to rise from her coffin.

Eventually Herrmann secured Robinson's services by giving him a substantial salary boost. Robinson's "The Mysterious Swing," later billed as "How to Get Rid of a Wife" or "The Divorce Machine," was an instant hit. A woman, seated in a suspended chair, vanished when a pistol was fired, and the empty chair crashed down to the stage.

The Kellar-Herrmann rivalry plumbed the depths of pettiness in Canada. Kellar's agent hired men to cover Herrmann's posters with those of Kellar. Herrmann's staff retaliated by pasting on third layers; then Kellar's people obscured these with more of his bills.

Impresario M. B. Leavitt signed Kellar for a tour of California and Mexico in 1888. Herrmann learned of the contract and cajoled Leavitt into booking him ahead of his competitor. Kellar won this round by going to Mexico City weeks before the announced date of his opening and getting the owner of the Teatro Nacionale to let him share the stage with a Spanish opera company by offering half of his profits.

Rather than play in direct opposition, Herrmann toured the smaller cities below the border. After a profitable run in the capital, Kellar moved on to San Luis Potosí, Mexico. A telegram arrived there, saying Herrmann had opened in the capital and was boasting he had forced his competitor to return to the United States. Realizing Herrmann had two more Mexican cities left to play, Kellar immediately rented the two best theatres in Puebla and the principal playhouse in Veracruz. This left Herrmann with his company trapped in the capital, where he was beginning to run out of customers. Finally Herrmann offered 60 percent of his receipts to a Puebla theatre company for the privilege of using their stage on alternate evenings, and ended his Mexican tour in the red.

Later when Herrmann and Kellar became friends, they agreed on the ridiculousness of the cutthroat feuding, which had caused them both heavy losses; North America really was big enough to support two outstanding magic shows without needless booking conflicts. After Alexander Herrmann died in 1898, his widow, Adelaide, and his nephew, Leon, attempted to keep his show in the running, but from then on, Kellar had no real competition.

Totally bald now and minus his brush moustache—he shaved it off after his manager told him he looked like a burlesque comedian —Kellar invested his profits wisely and bought an annuity, which would pay him a sizable monthly income in later years.

His wife was featured in "Karmos"; blindfolded, she rapidly solved intricate mathematical problems and performed other mental feats. She also disappeared in "The Divorce Machine" and appeared in "The Queen of Roses," another big-scale illusion. Until ill health interfered, she played as vital a part in Kellar's presentations as Adelaide Herrmann had in Herrmann the Great's.

Kellar bought a home in Yonkers, New York, and took Eva to Europe during their summer vacations. In 1904 they saw Paul Valadon, a German magician, performing with Maskelyne at Egyptian Hall in London. Eva was less impressed than her husband, but she didn't object when Kellar told her he was booking Valadon's act for their fall tour. After Valadon had toured with the show for three seasons, it seemed obvious he was being groomed to take his employer's place. Kellar's eyesight was failing; he knew his performing days were almost over.

Howard Thurston, a young American, whose personality and card manipulations had delighted Kellar and his wife earlier in Paris, wrote that he had taken an illusion show to India. People he met there often spoke of Kellar. Thurston had heard Kellar was thinking of retiring. If this was true, Thurston said, he would like to make a bid for the show. Encouraged by Kellar's reply, Thurston arrived in New York in May 1907. He saw the Kellar-Valadon program, then joined the Kellars for a late supper.

In the fall Kellar began his farewell tour with his successor-to-be—Howard Thurston—and a conjurer Thurston had brought with him from India. In most cities, critics said Kellar was still the master, but they thought Thurston, who plucked cards from the air so skillfully and produced a woman from a small trunk that expanded until it was large enough to hold her, a worthy disciple.

A Buffalo writer, however, devoted most of his space to Thurston's brilliant performance and mentioned Kellar only in passing. Kellar told Houdini that several years earlier he had refused to explain his new levitation to the writer, John Northern Hilliard, and from that moment on, the reviewer had roasted him.

On the evening of May 16, 1908, on the stage of Ford's Theatre in Baltimore, Kellar made a brief farewell speech. Then he called Thurston to his side, put his arm around his friend's shoulder, and wished him well.

After a few-weeks rest in Atlantic City, the Kellars went to New York for the annual banquet of the Society of American Magicians. The society presented to its first dean a gold medal, diamond studded with the initials SAM.

Harry and Eva traveled to California to live in a mansion, which had been built to the magician's specifications, at 495 South Ardmore Road in Los Angeles. Within two years she was dead. Annie Marie Buck, one of Kellar's nieces, and her husband moved in with her favorite uncle. Ching Ling Foo, Charles Carter, and Houdini were his guests whenever they performed nearby. Kellar set up a garage workshop where he experimented with new illusions and devised close-up feats to entertain his visitors.

Houdini persuaded Kellar to return to New York on October 17, 1917, to star in a mammoth benefit show staged by the Society of American Magicians for the families of the first American casualties in World War I—the men who lost their lives when the U.S. transport *Antilles* was sunk by a German U-boat.

Kellar levitated a table and escaped from ropes, after bells had rung and tambourines had played in the cabinet where he had been tied. There was a roar of applause as the tall, tanned magician bowed and started to walk toward the wings. Houdini ran out and brought him back to the center of the stage. America's greatest magician should be carried off in triumph after his final public performance, Houdini said. Members of the society helped Kellar up into the upholstered seat of a sedan chair. Twenty-four men and women hurried onstage with baskets of red roses and yellow chrysanthemums and showered the old magician with flowers as the sedan chair was raised. The 125-piece Hippodrome orchestra played "Auld Lang Syne" and the six thousand spectators rose to their feet and sang the nostalgic words as Kellar was slowly borne away.

The greatest traveler among magicians died five years later on March 10, 1922, following a pulmonary hemorrhage brought on by an attack of influenza. A few days before the end, Kellar sat up in bed to read a French grammar. He was brushing up on his languages, he told his niece, because soon he might be taking another trip.

13

Thurston—The Wonder Show of the Universe

WHEN Howard Thurston purchased Harry Kellar's show in 1908, he was more interested in the business advantages to be gained as the designated successor to America's most prominent magician than in the older man's equipment. Most of Kellar's feats, in Thurston's opinion, were too small for large theatres; Thurston was determined to present the biggest mystery production the world had ever seen. Kellar rarely included more than five big-scale illusions in a single program; Thurston was to offer eighteen in his "Wonder Show of the Universe."

Though Thurston retained only two of Kellar's specialties, a levitation and a spirit-cabinet routine, eventually three railway baggage cars were needed to transport the massive equipment, and a staff of forty people aided him in the production and presentation of the spectacle.

In early press releases Thurston said he had learned his magic from Muhammadan mystics, who had kidnapped him at the age of three in Algiers, where his father was American vice-consul. This story, of course, was too good to be true. Born in Columbus, Ohio, on July 20, 1869, Howard Franklin Thurston was the son of a carriage maker. Thurston's father also made beef pounders, mallets for tenderizing meat, that Howard and his brothers sold in the streets. Later the boy worked as a bellhop in the American House hotel and sold newspapers on the Columbus-Akron commuter train. As a teen-ager he dreamed of becoming a famous jockey. So he ran away from home to follow the races as they moved seasonally from city to city. He worked in the stables, exercised horses, and sold programs in the grandstands. During the winter months he supported himself with other jobs.

At the age of twenty, the 5½-foot-tall Ohioan was selling newspapers in New York when he heard a businessman-evangelist deliver a stirring sermon at the Broome Street Tabernacle. Inspired by W. M. F. Round's words, Thurston joined the crusaders who stood on soapboxes in the Bowery and pleaded with all who would listen to give up booze and lead Christian lives. Mrs. E. E. Thomas, one of Round's wealthy patrons, was moved by the handsome young man's avowed new goal—to further the cause as a medical missionary; she volunteered to pay his tuition at the school Dwight L. Moody, the famous evangelist, had founded in Mount Hermon, Massachusetts.

Four years later, on his way to take an entrance examination at the University of Pennsylvania in Philadelphia, Thurston visited the Burnside Industrial Farm at Canaan, New York, a reform project for delinquent boys directed by his friend Round. Hired as an assistant, Thurston stayed eighteen months before he started off again for Philadelphia. In Albany, New York, a Herrmann the Great poster caught his eye. Acting on a sudden impulse, he went to the theatre.

He had seen Herrmann in Columbus, and later he had learned to do several tricks from Professor Hoffmann's book, *Modern Magic*, for a Christmas party at Mount Hermon, but Thurston had forgotten how exciting an evening of sleight of hand and illusions could be. The desire to perform overwhelmed him. When he left the theatre, he checked in at a hotel and spent a sleepless night trying to reach a decision—magic or the ministry. He went to the railway station early the next morning, determined to continue his studies at the university. Then he saw Herrmann and his wife boarding a Pullman car on a train that would shortly leave for Syracuse. Thurston asked the man at the ticket window for a ticket to Philadelphia. Hearing a last call for Syracuse passengers, Thurston glanced at his ticket; it was for Syracuse! Without stopping to wonder how this mistake had been made, he ran for the car he had seen Herrmann enter.

Thurston paid extra for a seat in the Pullman car in order to sit near the man who, just the evening before, had levitated an assistant; the young man fully expected to see a marvelous trick at any moment, but the magician's only activity during the hours Thurston watched him was to light one cigarette after another as he chain-smoked while talking with his wife.

Thurston sat mesmerized through Herrmann's performance in Syracuse. All thought of spreading the gospel to savage tribes faded. A few months later, the young man from Columbus made his first appearance as a professional magician in Nelsonville, Ohio, with the "Great London Sideshow" of the Sells Brothers Circus—salary, six dollars a week.

Not long afterward in Boston, Thurston met Dr. James William Elliott, a bearded physician who spent more time working out new card tricks than treating patients. Other magicians of the period made cards disappear by maneuvering them to the backs of their hands, where the cards were held clipped between closed fingers. Elliott added a new move. With a reverse manipulation he could show both sides of his hand empty. He taught Thurston the "Back and Front Hand Palm."

The conjurer was working with a variety show in a small southern hall when he noticed that one of "The Butterfield Sisters," a song-and-dance act, stood in the wings each evening as he performed the intricate card sleights he had mastered after months of arduous practice. Grace Taxco was fifteen and Thurston twenty-eight when they married in Sparta, Mississippi, on August 21, 1897. Pert, personable, and slightly less than five feet tall, Grace immediately went to work as his assistant.

They spent their first Christmas together in an old hotel in Cripple Creek, Colorado, forbidden to leave the premises because of a smallpox epidemic. When the quarantine was lifted, they traveled with a wagon show to Montana.

According to Grace, it was she who discovered the principle for one of Thurston's finest tricks. After sewing together lengths of red flannel to make a background for their act in a mining-town saloon, she stepped to the front to admire her handiwork. She noticed a thread dangling over her head, a few feet in front of the curtain, when she left the stage; from the front row it was invisible. Grace suggested to Howard that if he tied a card to a thread it would appear to be floating. The idea appealed to him, but there were difficulties. If the thread came from above, he could not pass his hand over the suspended card. If, however, the thread extended horizontally across the stage he could wave his hand over *and* under it. With two assistants, hidden in the wings, holding the ends, he could cause the card to rise, but he had only one assistant. Perhaps the left end of the thread could be tied offstage, and Grace could pull the right end? The card rose, but it wobbled and veered to the right.

Eventually he ran a long thread up through an eyelet offstage to the right, across and down through another eyelet on the left. The eyelets were placed so the thread would be just above his head. To the ends, which hung several feet below the eyelets, he tied weights. At first the weights were too heavy and the card shot up too fast. With lighter weights, the ascent was smooth and mysterious.

He glued tabs to the backs of several cards. Standing onstage with the taut thread above him, Thurston held the pack in his left hand, tapped the cards with his right fingers, then raised his hand as if to indicate that the card should follow his motion. Catching the thread with his fingers, he brought it down and, as he squared the cards, passed the thread under the tab on the rear card. Raising his right hand again, he gracefully wiggled his fingers. When he loosened his grip on the pack, the tabbed card slowly floated up to his hand.

For Thurston's version of the rising cards, the stage must be lighted so the thread casts no shadow. The thread must be thin enough to be invisible to the spectators, yet strong enough not to break mid trick. In later years Thurston devised another use for a horizontally suspended thread. In one of the funniest bits in his show, the hair of a man from the audience periodically flipped up, as though a spirit hand had ruffled it. Two hidden assistants in the wings put the thread under the hair, then, with a quick pull, sent it up. The startled victim always swung around, but there was no one there.

Thurston opened in a small variety house in Denver the week Adelaide and Leon Herrmann, the wife and nephew of the late Herrmann the Great, appeared at the Tabor Grand. Thurston was in the lobby one day, studying a poster which showed Leon Herrmann's hands in various positions as he manipulated balls, when a stranger tapped him on the shoulder and introduced himself. William Ellsworth Robinson, the stage manager of the Herrmann show, asked Thurston if he wasn't the magician with the new rising-card trick? Leon Herrmann had heard about it and had said he would like to see it. Thurston volunteered to perform backstage before the evening performance —if Robinson would permit him to make certain advance arrangements.

A two-column story in the Sunday, October 23, 1898, *Denver Post* told about the demonstration. According to the reporter, Leon and Adelaide Herrmann and several members of their company gathered on the stage at 7:30 P.M. and watched Thurston as he stood with his back toward the closed curtain. Four cards were chosen and they floated up, one by one, to the magician's hand. "Afterwards Herrmann acknowledged the trick was a winner and offered to purchase it. Thurston was especially gratified at the fact that this trick was not seen through by the Herrmann party. He had mystified the mystifier."

Thurston, however, found it easier to fool a famous magician than to get work in New York. Few bookers would even talk with him. Tony Pastor was more cordial. He sat behind his desk as Thurston showed him card tricks, then signed the act for an August 21, 1899 opening at Pastor's Fourteenth Street theatre. By then Grace had gone on the road with a stock company; Thurston's new assistant was a nine-year-old Negro boy. The act was a hit. Agents who had ignored Thurston earlier now offered him contracts. Grace and Howard were divorced a few years later; George White, the boy who had taken her

225

Thurston—The Wonder Show of the Universe

Thurston's costume for his first
big-scale illusion act.

Kellar's successor, Thurston, presented
"The Wonder Show of the Universe."

A pistol shot, a puff of smoke; Whippet car and its girl passengers disappeared.

place on the stage, went with "the man who mystified Herrmann" as he played the Keith circuit in the East, the Orpheum circuit in the West, and the Théâtre Français in Montreal.

Thurston began a four-week engagement at the Palace Theatre in London in November 1900. Critics acknowledged his artistry, originality, and showmanship, and his skill at hurling cards with amazing accuracy to all parts of the house. They had seen rising cards before, but not cards that soared up several feet through the air to a magician's hand. The four-week booking extended to six months.

The Prince of Wales visited with Thurston backstage; later the American conjured in Europe for Emperor Franz Joseph and the kings of Denmark, Greece, and Belgium. Leon Herrmann and Harry Kellar, both on holiday from the United States, congratulated him at the Folies Marigny in Paris. Had he chosen to, Thurston could have been booked for years without varying his routine, but he had other plans. He rented a workshop in London, and hired carpenters, painters, and several more assistants. When his new act was completed, he engaged the Princess Theatre for rehearsals. Until this time, Thurston had always appeared onstage in white tie and tails. For this production he dressed as an Oriental prince: silk turban; dark, close-fitting jacket; light riding pants, and black boots. Paul Keith, on a booking tour abroad, saw a run-through and signed the attraction for the United States.

Thurston was nervous at Keith's Theatre in Boston on May 4, 1903. A review in *Mahatma,* the conjuring periodical, said the new routine depended too much on elaborate scenery and special lighting effects and not enough on Thurston's skill. He presented the "Floating Ball," produced inflated balloons from a hat, took eggs from George White's mouth, and a hen from his midsection. Then a statue changed into a living woman and a torrent of water poured down into a large urn from the inverted half-coconut shell Thurston held high in one hand.

By June, when the act reached Keith's Theatre in New York, the show was running smoothly. After a year on the road he signed for the summer season of 1904 at the Willow Grove Amusement Park near Philadelphia. Earlier Thurston had added a levitation to the program; there he introduced new tricks and illusions each week. Thurston returned to vaudeville in the fall, and in the spring of 1905 sailed for Australia with his own show. Critics who saw him in Sydney at the Palace Theatre in July said Thurston presented the most opulent mystery production they had ever seen.

Following a ten-month tour of Australia, the show moved on to Manila and Hong Kong. The pace was too fast for the Chinese audience at the Tai Ping Theatre in Kowloon. A man stood up and politely asked the magician to pause between tricks so the spectators could discuss how they were done; Thurston acquiesced. Another objection came after he covered a glass-sided, water-filled tank, then pulled away the cloth to reveal a bathing-suit-clad girl floating inside. Angry shouts brought the manager to the stage; he told the American that females were taboo in Chinese theatrical productions. Thurston had an "explanation," which the manager translated to pacify the crowd. The magician said he used women assistants because they were more susceptible than men to hypnotism—and the assistants had to be in a trance in order to perform. With the slowed tempo and the interruptions, this show lasted five hours.

Business had been excellent in China, but the Japanese, in the midst of a war with Russia, were in no mood to patronize foreign entertainment. After a single performance in Kobe, Thurston sailed for Saigon; then, after stops in Java, Singapore, and Rangoon, he went on to India.

Unwittingly he offended his audience at the Classic Theatre in Calcutta by producing an egg from a Hindu boy's mouth. Eggs were unclean, the magician was informed; the boy would have to do penance. Thurston dropped the egg trick, and put a comedy routine in its place. This skit ended with a pig being fed from a baby's bottle. One night the pig wriggled free from Thurston's arm and jumped over the footlights. Rows of spectators fled to the streets to avoid being contaminated by the despised animal.

Thurston performed in a specially made 6,000-rupee tent in Benares. Though the newspapers reported several cases of bubonic plague in the area, he played to large audiences. He also appeared in the tent in Lucknow, then sold it for a sixth of its cost; he knew there were theatres large enough for his attraction in Delhi and Agra. The plague was spreading; corpses lay uncovered in the streets. Thurston closed the show and wrote Harry Kellar he was coming back to the United States. Thurston asked to talk to Kellar before he made a final decision on his successor—if the reports of his impending retirement were true.

Thurston arrived in New York in May 1907, a little more than two years after he had sailed from San Francisco on the world tour. He saw the Kellar show at the Lincoln Square Theatre, then went backstage. Early that fall Kellar announced the coming season would be his last. In each city on his farewell tour, he would introduce Howard Thurston as his successor.

"The World's Greatest Magicians"—Kellar, Thurston, and Bella Hassan, a conjurer Thurston had brought from India—drew immense crowds. Kellar had hoped to give his last performance in New York. When no theatre was available, he played an extra week at Ford's in Baltimore, where he took his final curtain call on Saturday, May 16, 1908.

During the summer Thurston built new equipment for the fall, and became engaged to Beatrice "Tommy" Foster, who appeared and disappeared in his principal illusions; they were married two years later.

The new opening for the show presented Thurston as the inheritor of a great tradition. A giant book was seen at center stage. Assistants turned the huge leaves to display paintings of Robert-Houdin, Philippe, Herrmann the Great, and Kellar. Thurston, in evening dress, stepped from the final page. Though he still manipulated playing cards early in the evening, the emphasis was on big-scale deceptions. A girl appeared in an empty trunk after the interior had been lined with sheets of glass. A man, strapped right side up in a narrow box, was found upside down a moment later. Curtains were closed on four sides of an immense platform and then drawn back to reveal "A Bridal Chamber." "The Lady and the Boy" changed places inexplicably in a truck and a box. Ghostly forms appeared, as well as made noises, in Kellar's spirit cabinet, and Kellar's levitation was staged in an Oriental setting.

The program ended with "The Triple Mystery." After two empty boxes were nested, a girl materialized in one of them. She was enclosed in a mummy case and this was suspended above the stage. Thurston fired a pistol. The girl disappeared from the case, and a spotlight zeroed in on the roped trunk which had been hanging over the heads of the audience throughout the evening. A second shot, and the trunk slid rapidly down a long rope to the stage. The large trunk was opened. Inside was a smaller one, and inside that, a still smaller one. The top was unlatched; the girl who had vanished from the mummy case jumped out.

Season by season the Thurston show expanded. Some of the new illusions took only a few seconds. In "The Appointment," assistants closed the drapes around a small framework cabinet. Thurston looked at his watch and asked, "Where are you?" "Here I am" was the immediate reply as a girl pulled open the drapes and walked forward.

"The Phantom Piano" was a heavily advertised feature in 1912. A girl stepped up on a platform, sat in front of an upright piano, and began to play. A canopy, with cloth sides and a solid top, was lowered from the flies. The front was open; the audience could see the assistants as they attached chains to the instrument and the player's armpits. The front of the canopy was closed; the stagehands hoisted the piano and the musician a dozen feet into the air. The music could still be heard coming from the covered piano. Thurston fired his pistol. The music stopped. The sides of the canopy dropped; girl and piano were gone.

Hearing is the easiest of the senses to deceive. The upright "piano" was a realistic, hollow shell; the girl pretended to play, but the sound came from a real piano backstage. While fastening the chains,

229

Thurston—The
Wonder Show
of the Universe

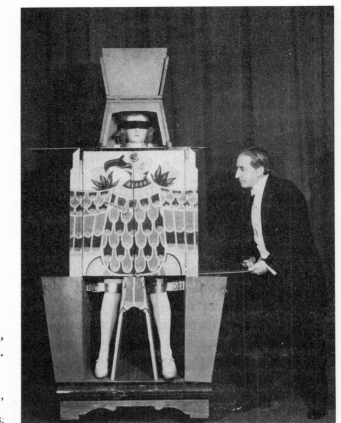

Blades divided a girl in three pieces,
then her midsection vanished.

"The Levitation of the Princess Karnac,"
one of Thurston's greatest illusions.

"The Mystery of the Water Fountains"—
closing spectacle of the 1923 show.

The last illusion devised for Thurston
—a three-part miracle.

the assistants also released staying pins, thus permitting the sections of the piano to be folded inside the platform after the front of the canopy closed. The girl also concealed herself in the platform, which was so ingeniously designed that it did not appear to be thick enough to hide a person, let alone a piano. Assistants wheeled the platform off while attention was focused on the rising canopy; as a result, the disappearance occurred on an empty stage, which made it seem all the more marvelous.

Thurston's four-week run at the Globe Theatre in New York in September 1919 disproved predictions that Broadway audiences would not pay Broadway prices for a magic show, according to *Variety*, the theatrical weekly. The closing spectacle was an elaborate version of an Oriental feat that Ten Ichi, the great Japanese magician, had introduced to American vaudeville. Streams of water spurted up from everything Thurston touched with his wand. He caused water to gush five feet in the air from an assistant's fingertip, from the toe of another's shoe, and from the bald pate of a third. Finally a dozen fountains played simultaneously as the curtain fell.

During his engagement at the Belasco Theatre in Washington in December 1924, Thurston was invited to perform at the White House. His staff erected a stage, curtains, and wings in the East Room. The master magician arrived the day of the show with twenty-two assistants, an orchestra, and truckloads of equipment. Other illusionists have appeared at the White House, both before and after Thurston. He gave by far the most elaborate performance, yet it was a small trick that received the greatest applause. He smashed Calvin Coolidge's gold pocketwatch to bits, made the pieces disappear, then asked Mrs. Coolidge to carefully slice in two a loaf of bread that had been brought in by the butler from the White House kitchen. "Yes, dear, be careful," the President cautioned. Inside was the watch, completely restored.

That week five hundred children from Washington orphanages were Thurston's guests at the theatre. In every city he played he invited service organizations to drive patients from nursing homes and other institutions to see his performances, and he made frequent visits to bedsides to entertain those who were too ill to come to the theatre. As a young man he had longed to be a medical missionary; in later years he helped people forget aches and cares, at least briefly, with his magic.

Thurston paid annual visits to Ford's Theatre in Baltimore, where I grew up. Unfailingly kind to small boys who were interested in becoming magicians, he attended a yearly luncheon given in his honor by the Pyramid Magic Club. He was fifty-seven when I first met him there. One year he apologized for not eating and distributed printed diet cards, saying they would add years to our lives if we followed the suggested food combinations. He had sworn off cigarettes, but still smoked small cigars.

He was eager to get our reactions to his new illusions. We were especially enthusiastic about "Iasia." A girl stood in a "prayer cage" as it was pulled up and out over the heads of the spectators. Curtains dropped on the four sides, then the girl threw souvenir Thurston good-luck cards from a slit in one panel until the magician fired a pistol. At that second, the side curtains fell and the hinged bottom of the cage dropped open; it was empty.

We were asked which of two versions of his vanishing automobile we preferred. One season the Whippet car and its passengers disappeared as flickering lights played on the slatted-front garage; the next, the car vanished in a cloud of smoke. Unanimously, we preferred the smoke.

Thurston's third wife, the former Nina Leotha Fielding, sat in a box taking notes at most performances. After the show Thurston would assemble his assistants on stage, adjust his glasses (never worn while performing), and read the jottings on his wife's pad: A silver cloth used during the goldfish bowl production needed pressing. Curtains had closed too quickly after the sawing-in-two illusion. There had been a spot on the left sleeve of Abdul's Indian jacket as he spouted fire. Thurston himself sometimes had occasion to pause over a note and perhaps remark: "Yes, I do need a haircut"—and turning to his secretary—"Make an appointment with the barber at eleven tomorrow morning." These "school" sessions, as the staff called them, kept the presentation razor-sharp.

Thurston limited his engagements to cities in the East and in the Midwest, but a rising demand for his magic in other sections of the country led him to send out additional shows. He chose Harry Jansen, a Chicago illusionist, to head the first road company and gave the Danish-born showman a new name—Dante. The Dante show debuted in Pittsfield, Massachusetts, on September 3, 1923. After playing four years in the United States, Dante sailed for Puerto Rico; this proved to be the start of an around-the-world tour.

Raymond S. Sugden, a Pittsburgh magician, headed the second Thurston unit, billed as "Tampa, England's Court Magician." Press releases claimed he had performed for King George V. Tampa's equipment, like Dante's, had been constructed in the workshop Thurston maintained on his estate at Beechhurst in Queens, within commuting distance of Manhattan.

Howard's brother Harry presented a third Thurston show. Though similar to him in appearance, Harry lacked Howard's charm and skill. After traveling with Thurston in the Orient, he had worked as a circus advance man and booked carnival attractions. He had a sizable steady income from the store-front curio museum and burlesque theatre he owned in Chicago. After building illusions from

Thurston—The Wonder Show of the Universe

the blueprints Howard gave him and studying his brother's presentations, Harry bought a circus tent, hired supporting acts, and opened "Thurston's Mysteries of India" in Harvey, Illinois, on May 18, 1931.

An hour before the show it began to rain. The clatter on the canvas continued during the opening musical and dance numbers. A torrential downpour drowned out the introductory speech by Eugene Laurant, an adept magician from Denver. Long before time for Harry Thurston to present his illusions, leaks in the "waterproof" big top brought the opening performance to an end. It rained on all but one of the twenty-one days that "Mysteries of India" toured.

The next summer Harry went on the road with Percy Abbott, an able Australian magician who had been on the original bill as his coworker. This time the unit fared better and played until Labor Day. The show opened at the Capitol Theatre in Bowling Green, Kentucky, in January 1933 and closed in St. Augustine, Florida, that March. Two years later, Harry took his show out again. After eight summer weeks under canvas, he gave up. Harry Thurston was seventy and living in retirement in West Palm Beach, Florida, when he died on May 6, 1941.

Jane Thurston, Leotha's daughter by a previous marriage, made her first appearance with Howard Thurston in September 1928. Blonde, shapely, and versatile, she sang "My Daddy Is a Hocus-Pocus Man," danced, and produced silk scarves and a stack of glass bowls filled with water and goldfish. There was to have been another addition to the show that season: "The Appearing Baby Elephant on a Fully-Lighted Stage," but the 700-pound Indian pachyderm died before the feat was perfected.

Thurston spent the summer of 1929 putting the finishing touches on his autobiography, *My Life Of Magic,* and arranging for the production of his mystery play, *The Demon.* He sat near the back of Poli's Theatre in Washington for the October 21 premiere. "The frightened screams of the audience in the first act must have made him swell with pride," Ernie Pyle reported in the *Daily News.* "The play was not Thurston at his best, but even bad Thurston is worth seeing." Noting in the *Post* that the opening "went off well," John J. Daly said he would have been happier if Thurston had been on the stage. Andrew R. Kelley in the *Times* said onlookers "were thrilled to the point of hysterics. Ghosts came out into the auditorium, fiendish things with green eyes swirled out of the darkness, and a monster descended from the air and then mysteriously vanished aloft. . . . the audience loved it." Yet he found the work more "a masterful piece of theatrical hokum" than a tightly constructed play.

The Demon went on to Wilmington, Delaware, and New Rochelle, New York, before Thurston changed his mind about taking it to Broadway. Instead he returned to the nation's capital with

"Hypnotizing a Duck" and "The Indian Rope Trick"—Thurston specialities.

A horse and rider in a stall were hoisted up; the empty stall fell.

"Spirits" returned at every show to the cabinet on Thurston's stage.

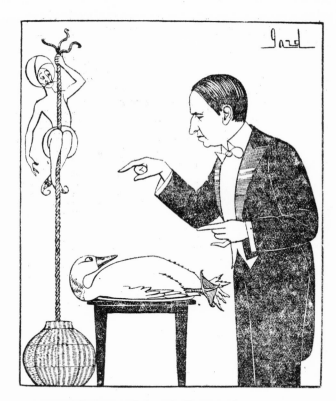

his "Wonder Show of the Universe" and played to unanimous critical praise and full houses.

The depression that followed the 1929 stock market crash had a disastrous effect on the high-priced attractions in legitimate theatres; Thurston's final full evening of magic was presented April 20, 1931, at the Tremont Theatre in Boston. His career, however, was far from over. He signed for a Publix tour of presentation houses—large theatres offering stage shows and feature films at a price the public was willing to pay. With an hour of his best mysteries, Thurston set new box-office records at the Michigan Theatre in Detroit, the Chicago Theatre in Chicago, and the Minnesota Theatre in Minneapolis. The next year a tour of RKO houses took him to Los Angeles and San Francisco. After the long trek ended at the Palace Theatre in Cleveland, Thurston went immediately to Chicago; then, beginning on November 3, 1932, he became a star in another medium —radio.

Sponsored by Swift and Company, the meat packers, his twice-weekly dramatized adventures were broadcast over the NBC-WJZ network. Thurston's compelling, magnetic voice captivated listeners even though they could not see the wonderful feats around which his plots were built.

On Easter Monday 1934 he entertained on the White House lawn for the thousands who attended the traditional egg-rolling party. Newspapers across the United States carried pictures of him presenting rabbits to two of Franklin D. Roosevelt's grandchildren as the First Lady smiled.

The third Mrs. Thurston, who had been ill for many months, suffered a severe heart attack at their home in Beechhurst while her husband was performing at Loew's Valencia Theatre in Jamaica, New York, in April 1934. Howard received the news between shows. He instructed Herman Hanson, an accomplished magician, who supervised the construction of new illusions for the show, to take over for him on stage. Leotha died before Thurston reached her bedside; Hanson substituted for him the rest of the week.

In the fall of 1934 Thurston said he would begin his farewell tour early the next year, but when spring came, the sixty-five-year-old magician married one of his assistants, twenty-seven-year-old Paula Mark, and left for a Florida honeymoon instead. The newlyweds sailed from New York aboard the *Shawnee*. Paula told reporters she had seen Thurston for the first time in Chicago. As a girl of twelve she had gone on stage to help him and was given a white rabbit as a souvenir. The newsmen were astonished by the magician's youthful face. "It's all mental," Thurston told them. "I learned it from the Yogi in India . . . believe it or not, gentlemen, I expect to live to be

Will Rock toured with Harry Thurston's illusions featuring "sawing" à la Howard.

Mayor Broening of Baltimore with the magician, his wife, daughter, and Hindu assistant.

125." No one except his most intimate friends knew two plastic surgery operations had removed Thurston's wrinkles.

The delayed farewell tour began at the Fox Theatre in Philadelphia on Friday, August 23, 1935. Missing were the card manipulations he had excelled in for so many years, but the other tricks and illusions were as swiftly paced and as entertaining as ever. From a giant opera hat, Thurston produced a dozen parasols, followed by several girls. The center of an assistant disappeared after she had been fastened in a form-fitting upright box, and wide blades were thrust through her neck and hips.

"Vivisection" was shown for the first time. A large but narrow drumlike container, with closed back and front, stood broadside to the audience. A girl was inserted horizontally through an opening in one rim until her feet extended from the right side and only her head could be seen at the left. A chopper sliced through her neck and above her ankles; then the rim was turned until her head was at the top and her feet dangled at the bottom. When the assistants removed the front and back "drumheads," the girl's body was still horizontal—despite the strange positions of her head and feet. The opaque disks were fastened back in place; the rim was turned until head and feet were again in line with the body; and the girl was removed—still in one piece. The magician revived the colorful water fountain scene for his finale. *Billboard* reported Thurston's magic, not the accompanying film, *Charlie Chan in Egypt*, drew the largest Fox attendance of the season.

There were still doves, ducks, and rabbits in the show, but none of the large-animal illusions, such as "The Vanishing Horse and Rider" or "The Lady and the Lion." He had first performed the lion feat shortly after taking over the Kellar show. In this illusion, two huge empty cabinets were set several yards apart on the stage. A girl entered one; curtains were dropped around both. The girl vanished; in her place was a lion in a cage. She reappeared in the second cabinet, perched like a canary in an oversized, suspended birdcage.

Thurston had intended to feature this mystery on a vaudeville tour, but he had difficulty finding a lion. Finally he bought one with the aid of a dentist who knew an importer. The animal, shipped to the Philadelphia theatre where Thurston was then playing, was, according to Herman Hanson, "not a tame, shaggy-maned African lion, but a wild, slinky tree animal," and far too unruly to use. Hanson suggested that Thurston could get good publicity from a bad purchase by giving the lion to a public zoo. Within a few days press agent John Northern Hilliard called to say the Philadelphia zoo and those in other cities had declined the offer. Hanson came up with another idea: "Let's crate the lion and the cage and ship them to your dentist friend—with no return address on the label." Thurston agreed. And that, Hanson said, was the last they heard of the lion.

On Sunday night, October 6, 1935, after their fourth show at the Kearse Theatre in Charleston, West Virginia, the Thurstons, Hanson and his wife, Lillian, ate a late supper at the Idle Hour restaurant.

"We are all tired," Thurston said when they had finished. "Why don't we get a good night's sleep?" He stood up and started for the door. After three steps, he collapsed. "What's the matter with me? I fell down," he said with difficulty. No, he told Hanson, he did not wish to be taken to a hospital; he would go to the hotel. The doctor, who was called to examine him, sent him at once to St. Francis Hospital. Wire-service stories the next day said Thurston had suffered a paralytic stroke.

Following the magician's instructions, Hanson and Jane Thurston completed the engagement in Charleston, then returned to New York where Thurston said they should work out a new routine and continue on tour without him. Meanwhile, the magician's wife took him to a sanatarium at Briarcliff Manor, New York.

By mid-November, Thurston could walk with a cane. He told reporters he would soon produce a new mystery drama, *The Creeps*, for the stage. He even danced a few steps as he said he and Mrs. Thurston were going to Biloxi, Mississippi, to spend a month in the sun. From Biloxi they traveled to Miami Beach. Meanwhile his equipment had been stored; theatres weren't interested in booking the Thurston show without its star.

Rajah Raboid, a vaudeville crystal gazer, visited him frequently in Florida. Thurston talked of touring with Raboid when he regained his health. He would appear in a short act; Raboid would present the major portion of the program and perform exploitation stunts, such as driving a car while blindfolded. This proposed partnership never materialized. Thurston was stricken with a cerebral hemorrhage late in March. Pneumonia followed, and he died at the age of sixty-seven in Miami Beach on April 13, 1936.

Thurston had earned more than a million dollars with his magic, but most of his money had been lost through investments in unproductive Canadian gold mines and unlucky speculations in Florida real estate and orange groves. Jane Thurston sold several of his illusions, but neglected to pay long-overdue storage charges on others. Gerald Heaney, an Oshkosh, Wisconsin, magician, acquired these props from the warehouse owner for a pittance.

Will Rock, a Detroit magician, purchased some apparatus from Jane and the equipment Harry Thurston had used with his ill-fated tent production. For several years the Rock show was advertised as "Thurston's Mysteries of India." To most people, however, there was only one Thurston: the dexterous young man from Ohio who had pioneered with a card-manipulation act in vaudeville, who had gone on to present a magic show on a scale never before attempted, and who had maintained his position as America's greatest illusionist for twenty-eight years after being chosen as Kellar's successor.

14

Ching Ling Foo,
Chung Ling Soo,
and The Great Lafayette

CHING Ling Foo, who billed himself as "the Court Conjurer to the Empress of China," quickly caught the fancy of the American public after he came to the United States in 1898, appearing first at the Trans-Mississippi Exhibition in Omaha, Nebraska. So successful was the Oriental magician that he soon spawned a host of non-Chinese imitators, several of whom were excellent magicians in their own right. They included The Great Lafayette and William Ellsworth Robinson, who as Chung Ling Soo became even more famous than his Chinese prototype. Ironically, both these imitators were to have tragic deaths; Lafayette in a theatre fire and Robinson in the most dangerous of all magic tricks, one that the man from Peking never attempted—the bullet-catch. Ching Ling Foo (Chee Ling Qua), tall and bald—except for a pigtail—spiraled colored streamers from between his lips; the whirling paper strips caught fire and exploded. He pulled a six-foot-long pole from his mouth and produced plates of cakes and nuts under the cover of an empty cloth.

His most sensational feat was so old that it appeared new: Standing at the center of an Oriental rug, the forty-four-year-old conjurer displayed both sides of another cloth, lowered it until the bottom touched the rug, then threw it aside to reveal an immense porcelain bowl, brimful with water, and with several red apples

241

*Ching Ling
Foo, Chung
Ling Soo,
and The Great
Lafayette*

bobbing on the surface. After tossing the fruit to waiting assistants, the master showman hefted the ninety-five-pound container and tilted it so the water splashed down to fill three pails.

A year later, while touring Keith theatres as a headliner, "the strongest attraction of the season" added another show-stopping mystery. Following the bowl production, he materialized a three-year-old Chinese girl—his daughter, Chee Toy.

Oriental magic became the rage. An obscure quick-change artist, The Great Lafayette (born Sigmund Neuberger in Munich on February 24, 1872) perfected a marvelous imitation of Ching Ling Foo, which critics said was better than the original, and was signed as a Keith headliner himself. This medium-sized, square-jawed, thin-lipped man of many talents had struggled for years to attain recognition. Now he invested in new costumes and equipment and went on to win international acclaim.

Lafayette was driven across the arena to the stage in a motor car at the London Hippodrome in August 1900. Attired in a large beret and shimmering smock, he rapidly dipped brushes in various paints and splashed color on six wooden panels. These were fitted together in two rows of three in a gilded frame. What seemed at first to be haphazard daubs blended to form a painting of a rural scene. Bowing off at the wings, Lafayette immediately returned as Ching Ling Foo. From a spangled cloth, embellished with dozens of tiny glowing electric bulbs, he produced a bowl of water, a flock of pigeons, a dog, a turkey, and a Negro child in diapers. The youngster disappeared after being covered with a tapering cone, then reappeared with a second child by his side.

"Ching Ling Foo" shuffled off behind a three-fold screen at the rear of the stage. Curtains opened in the center panel, and Lafayette, in a red uniform and military cap, appeared as John Philip Sousa, "the American March King." Rapping for attention with his baton, "Sousa" led the Hippodrome band.

The costume changes were made with incredible speed. Beneath the smock, Lafayette wore a Chinese robe with the lower portion folded and held in place by a pinned tape around his waist. Under the robe was the bandmaster uniform.

Lafayette tossed the artist's attire aside in the wings. One assistant fitted a bald wig, with a pigtail at the back, to the performer's head, and another loaded the covered water bowl into a sling between Lafayette's legs. The magician yanked the robe release pin at his waist, then reached for the foulard. All this happened in a matter of seconds. Lafayette altered his gait for the Ching Ling Foo role; because of the heavy bowl under his robe, he, like Ching, walked slowly. The final change, made behind the onstage screen, was less hectic.

Off came the wig and the robe; he jammed a visored cap on his head and picked up a baton.

Later in his career Lafayette used more complicated props: trousers, snap-fastened rather than sewn at the sides, and reinforced coats which opened at the back and were held snugly to his body with concealed strips of flexible metal. Often a double took Lafayette's place as he darted behind a piece of scenery. While the double performed, the magician changed costumes, then popped up where least expected.

The most startling of Lafayette's transformations came during the final moments of "The Lion's Bride," an illusion he introduced in the United States in 1901. The setting for the act was the interior of a circus tent. An African lion paced restlessly in a cage while fire-eaters, jugglers, and contortionists exhibited their specialties. As the band played the wedding processional music from *Lohengrin,* a young woman in a lace veil and white satin gown walked slowly onstage and entered the cage.

Once she was inside, the lion roared and the girl screamed. The beast reared up, ready to pounce. Suddenly the animal skin was ripped away, and The Great Lafayette swung around to face the footlights.

The actual switch was over before the audience knew it had begun. The circus performers momentarily blocked the spectators' view of the cage as the spotlight focused on the entrance of the girl in white. At that instant, a revolving panel swept the lion into a second cage concealed behind the first, and moved Lafayette, covered by an animal skin, into the first cage. He played lion until the script called for him to stand erect and fling off his disguise.

The live lion invariably roared on schedule. Not because he had been trained, but as a protesting reaction to a jolt of electricity sent through a metal plate on the floor of the hidden cage. The secret of the shock-producing device leaked out in Pittsburgh; Lafayette paid a fine for his inhumane treatment of the animal but did not change the routine.

In 1906 Lafayette expanded the lion illusion into a two-act play, *The Medicine Man.* Midway through the blood-and-thunder first act, Lafayette galloped out astride a white horse, shouting that the Indians were on the warpath. Hardy settlers barricaded their families in a log cabin and loaded their rifles. Guns fired, arrows streaked across from the wings, and spears were hurled before the Indians captured the white men.

Act Two had a realistic mountain setting. The Indian chief ordered his braves to throw a hostage from the cliffs. When the heroine still spurned his advances, the chief signaled for her to be locked in the lion's cage. As the gate closed, the girl remembered a mystic talisman given to her by an old medicine man. She waved the amulet. It worked. Practically in mid-leap, the lion changed to her lover—The Great Lafayette.

The lion illusion presented problems almost from the start. During a 1902 matinee at the Orpheum Theatre in Brooklyn, the gate to the cage came loose and fell on Lafayette's head. The scalp wound was serious enough for him to cancel the evening show. A year later at the Grand Opera House in Indianapolis, the lion seized one of the magician's pet dogs which had slipped through the bars of the cage. Armed with a pistol containing a single round of blank ammunition, Lafayette went to the rescue. The lion dropped the dog, sprang at the illusionist, and knocked him unconscious to the floor. The beast bit Lafayette's shoulder and clawed his chest and abdomen before stagehands drove it away with red-hot pokers.

Another near tragedy occurred at the Palace Theatre in Turnly, England. The lion battered two bars in the cage loose from their sockets and jumped to the floor of the stage. Lafayette's assistants fled, but a conscientious stagehand lowered the front curtain before he, too, ran to the street. Alone with the beast, Lafayette stood his ground. By sheer force of presence he backed the animal into the cage, then rolled a cart in place to cover the gap between the bars. As the illusionist relaxed and turned away, the lion reached out and raked his arm with its claws.

While he had no qualms about torturing the lion with electric shocks to make him roar on cue, the bachelor entertainer lavished tender care on his favorite dog, Beauty. Houdini, the escape artist, gave him this fawnlike creature of uncertain origin when they played on the same bill at the Opera House in Nashville, Tennessee, in 1899. Lafayette invented a pedigree for his pet. He said she was a rare gheckhundt from the island of Gheck in the Azores. Printed forms, enclosed with Lafayette's requests for reservations at leading hotels in Europe and the United States, specified that the dog must stay with him in his suite. Beauty wore a wide leather collar festooned with silver strips on which were engraved the names of the hotels where she had been a guest.

Beauty traveled in her own compartment in her master's private railroad car in the United States. Her bedroom, furnished with a dog-sized settee and a miniature porcelain bathtub, adjoined his in Lafayette's London townhouse on Tavistock Square. A plaque on one wall proclaimed, "The more I see of men, the more I love my dog." A metal statuette of Beauty, holding an American flag, served as a radiator ornament for the magician's limousine, and an engrav-

Harry Kellar greets Chinese
magician Ching Ling Foo.

The Great Lafayette making
a Ching Ling Foo production.

Lafayette astride one of the horses in his stage show.

ing of the dog and two sacks of gold appeared on his checks with the caption, "My two best friends."

Aside from Houdini and William Ellsworth Robinson, who was starring in British theatres as Chung Ling Soo, Lafayette spent little time with other magicians. Less successful conjurers gossiped about him, his dog, his mauve motor car, and the two black footmen, who saluted him on the streets, attended him wherever he went, and stood at attention until he dismissed them.

At least one man believed the eccentric star was more interested in women than he pretended to be. The husband of Lalla Selbini, a vaudeville performer whose form-fitting, scanty costumes shocked some patrons of the two-a-day, sued Lafayette for alienating his wife's affections. The magician testified in court that he was "a bachelor at heart as well as in deed." He admitted he admired the glamorous Lalla, but said he was only one of her legion of fans. The jealous husband never collected. The publicity only served to increase the public's interest in the highest paid variety artist in England. Lafayette's salary rose to four thousand dollars a week.

The 1909 edition of the "World's Greatest Entertainer's" spectacle opened with a trumpet fanfare and pulse-quickening music. Entering in a satin court costume, Lafayette snared six white doves as he waved a net at the end of a long pole. Cyril Yettmah, a British magician-inventor, had approached him earlier with the idea. "Visualize the effect," Yettmah enthused. "Catching live canaries in thin air!" "Canaries, hell, we'll catch eagles," Lafayette responded. They compromised on doves. To give the trick a finish, the illusionist picked up a sequined cloth and shook a dozen birds from its folds. Then, to cap the routine, he produced a goat.

Lafayette donned artist's attire as a black assistant stood behind an open window in the central panel of a three-section screen. The magician painted the man's face and added bits of hair to convert him into a living image of the President of France. To make sure everyone recognized the features immediately, a French flag opened out under the window. Using a beard, a robe, and a crown, the magician changed the French leader into King Edward VII as a Union Jack unfurled.

Lafayette left the stage as "the King" approached the footlights and removed his disguise. Under the robe, crown, whiskers, and makeup was The Great Lafayette. The magician sped to a covered basket that had been in full view near one side of the stage. He flipped open the lid; out stepped the missing assistant.

Later Lafayette brought a statue of "Leda and the Swan" to life; fountains sprung up around the base of the pedestal, and colored lights played on the cascading water. The funniest scene featured a travesty band that Lafayette directed, making five speedy clothes changes, as he parodied the styles of well-known conductors. Few shows in England could equal the finish of the first act. Lafayette, in plumed hat and gold-braided uniform, rode out on a white horse followed by a cavalcade of twenty mounted musicians. Cannon boomed offstage as the riders played martial music and gigantic flags unfurled from the flies.

Lafayette opened a two-week engagement at the Empire Theatre in Edinburgh on May 1, 1911. Four days later, Beauty died of apoplexy. The magician was inconsolable. He performed that night with tears streaming down his cheeks. Beauty was laid out on a silk pillow in his bedroom at the Caledonia Hotel, surrounded by lilies. The silver-tagged collar was by her side along with a newer ornament with the names of the hotels where she had stayed in recent years. Pierhill Cemetery refused permission for Lafayette to bury the dog there until he signed a document stipulating that the $1,500 vault under a weeping willow tree would eventually be his final resting place too.

On Tuesday, May 9, four days after Beauty's death, three thousand spectators jammed the Empire Theatre for Lafayette's second evening show. As he came forward for a bow after "The Lion's Bride," an Oriental lamp high above a Persian tent burst into flame. At first the audience was not alarmed; they expected unusual scenic effects in a Lafayette production, but when the orchestra abruptly began to play the national anthem and the asbestos front curtain started to descend, they hurried to the exits. The curtain jammed two feet above the floor. By then the stage was an inferno, and clouds of smoke puffed out into the auditorium.

Firemen brought the blaze under control before 2 A.M., but smoke still rose from the ashes at dawn. Ten people lost their lives in the fire. An eleventh died of severe burns.

Lafayette's charred body was found near the lion cage. Identified by the sword he had carried in his last scene, his corpse was sent to Glasgow for cremation. Witnesses said he had escaped to the street, then returned to the stage trying to save his horse and dogs. The lion, its mane on fire, reportedly got loose and blocked the stage door. It was also said that the exit on the far side of the stage had been locked, as it always was during a Lafayette show to protect his secrets.

Lafayette's lawyer was puzzled when the diamond rings the great magician always wore were not on the fingers of the corpse. Searchers returned to the gutted theatre. In the basement beneath the stage, they found another body, this one with diamond rings. It was clear then that the man who had been cremated was Lafayette's double.

Houdini sent a floral representation of Beauty to the funeral.

247

Ching Ling
Foo, Chung
Ling Soo,
and The Great
Lafayette

Chung Ling Soo (W. E. Robinson),
most successful Ching impersonator.

The warrior costume Chung Ling Soo
wore for his bullet-catching act.

Chung Ling Soo, his wife, and the
daughter of an assistant.

The attached card read: "To the memory of my friend from the friend who gave him his best friend." Later the escapologist said Lafayette fooled the public "in life and in death. I envy him."

Lafayette had impersonated Ching Ling Foo only long enough to establish himself in vaudeville. The other performer who rose to variety stardom with an imitation of the prestidigitator from Peking carried on the characterization for eighteen years.

William Ellsworth Robinson was born of Scottish parentage in New York City on April 2, 1861. He gave his first magic show at the age of fourteen. Twelve years later, using the name Achmed Ben Ali, Robinson introduced the first American "Black Art" act. He copied from Ben Ali Bey (Max Auzinger) who earlier had devised the technique in Germany, but never demonstrated it in the United States.

In "Black Art" the magician, dressed in white, stands in a black recess, rimmed with lights that are directed toward the audience. As he waves a staff an invisible helper, clad in black coveralls, pulls black cloths from white objects to make them appear, or covers them to effect disappearances. Vases and tables "float" as the unseen aide lifts them. Robinson later married his deft assistant, Olive Path, nicknamed Dot, because she was so small.

Working as a performer and illusion-builder, first with Kellar, then with Herrmann the Great, and eventually with Adelaide and Leon Herrmann, Robinson acquired a thorough knowledge of magic and stagecraft. He naïvely applied for the thousand-dollar award newspapers said Ching Ling Foo would pay to see a duplication of his sensational water-bowl feat, but found that this was just a publicity stunt after the Chinese magician refused to see him in New York.

An international vaudeville agent, Ike Rose, aware of the demand for Chinese magic in Europe, offered Robinson a month's engagement in Paris—if he would imitate Ching Ling Foo. Robinson promptly shaved his head and moustache, engaged a Chinese juggler, Fee Ling, and headed for France.

Billed as Hop Ling Soo, Robinson opened at the Folies-Bergère on May 17, 1900. Unhappily, the water bowl slipped and spilled during his featured trick. Charles De Vere (H. S. G. Williams), a former English professional who owned a magic shop in Paris, reported in *Mahatma,* the conjuring monthly, that the American was "out of his element" in Chinese garb and would have been more effective in evening clothes. This was a minority opinion. Rose booked the act for a month at the Alhambra in London to follow the Parisian run.

Robinson made his British debut on May 17 as Chung Ling Soo—the name he was to use for the rest of his life. He shook bran between two plates and converted it into a pair of white doves. Water poured into a jar changed into dozens of flags, then the flags com-

249

Ching Ling
Foo, Chung
Ling Soo,
and The Great
Lafayette

bined into an immense Union Jack. Colored ribbons spurted from Chung's mouth, followed by a long pole. As he displayed the pole with one hand, an open parasol appeared in the other. Four live goldfish were caught at the end of a line cast out into the audience. (Professor Mingus, a New Jersey performer, had invented the feat; new to London, "Aerial Fishing" drew hearty applause.)

The lights dimmed as Fee Ling twirled two bowls of fire, attached to the ends of a long chain, in ever-widening circles over his head. The lights went up again as the Chinese juggler threaded his pigtail over a pulley let down from the flies and then raised himself above the floor by literally pulling his hair.

Chung's production of the big bowl of water brought down the house. The booking was prolonged for three months. Before the run ended, he signed contracts to play in Britain and on the Continent for the next five years.

In Brussels, Berlin, and other European cities, Chung was distressed to find many performers calling themselves "the Great American this and that," and featuring the Stars and Stripes on their printed matter, though they could not speak a word of English. This was ironic; the American now claimed to be Oriental and gave interviews in "Chinese" with Fee Ling "translating" his remarks.

Chung's act at the London Hippodrome in January 1905 surpassed his earlier routine. He opened with one of Kellar's favorite feats: producing two flower bushes from an empty cone. Suee Seen (Dot) stood on a platform, and, under the cover of a tapering cylinder, changed into a flowering tree. Later she was inserted in the barrel of a cannon, and "shot" to the back of the house. In a death-defying bullet-catch, marked ball ammunition was loaded into an old-fashioned, powder-charged musket and fired at the magician's heart. With a sweep of his hand, Chung caught the bullets on a china plate.

That week the original Ching Ling Foo made his first appearance in Britain, playing in opposition to his imitator at the Empire Theatre. Ching's manager, Leon Mooser, issued a challenge in the Chinese magician's name:

> I offer £1,000 if Chung Ling Soo, now appearing at the Hippodrome, can do ten out of my twenty tricks, or if I fail to do any one of his feats.

Chung brashly replied that he, "Conjurer to the Dowager Empress of China," would not stoop to compete with a lowly street performer. Irked by his impersonator's gall, Ching pointed out that it was he, not his rival, whom the Empress had honored with an appointment; Ching charged that the magician who called himself Chung Ling Soo was an American opportunist, who had been cashing in on his (Ching's) worldwide reputation.

The editor of the *Weekly Dispatch* invited the disputants to stage a battle of magic at his office. Chung arrived, eager to match his skill against that of the man who had had him turned away from the stage door of Keith's Theatre in New York. The American worried only that Ching might expose him by pulling off his fake pigtail. However, Chung won the match by default when the challenger failed to appear. The Chinese magician played four weeks at the Empire; the American stayed at the Hippodrome three months.

By then even the imitator was being imitated. Chung Ling Sens, Chung Ling Hees, and Ching Ling Fees flourished. Oriental conjurers were so popular in Europe and the United States that agents imported several troupes from Asia. Among them the companies of Tschin Maas and Tan Kwai. Long Tack Sam, of the Tan Kwai Company, outdid Ching's water-bowl production; the young entertainer turned a somersault without spilling a drop of water as he brought his bowl into view.

Chung Ling Soo toured Australia in 1909, his four-hundred-pound weekly salary was twice that of the Governor General. The fifty-minute act at the Tivoli Theatre in Sydney ended with four illusions, each more spectacular than the last. Chung shot an arrow, attached to a long, slender rope, through Suee Seen and into the bull's-eye of a target. He stacked four eighteen-inch square dice and lowered a long four-sided cover over them. When he raised the cover, the dice were gone; Suee Seen stood on the otherwise empty platform.

An empty octagonal cabinet with glass sides was hauled up into the air and spun rapidly around. As the enclosure slowed down, Suee Seen materialized within it. Finally the magician poured water into a large caldron that was suspended from a tripod. Assistants lighted a metal gas ring on the stage and, as the water began to bubble, tossed dead pigeons, ducks, and rabbits into the pot. Chung clapped his hands, dipped them into the caldron, and took out live birds and animals. Philippe and other mid-nineteenth-century performers had shown this feat, but Chung had a new finish: He reached inside and lifted out his wife. She had been ingeniously loaded. The center of the gas ring was open and lay directly over a trapdoor. She was raised by a lift in the basement and entered the caldron through a concealed opening in the bottom—after the boiling water had been drained away. The flames from the gas ring masked her passage.

After playing to capacity business in other Australian cities, the show returned to Sydney in July with a new feature, "The Birth of a Pearl." A mammoth empty oyster shell (resting on a pedestal) opened and closed. Water gushed up from pipes in the base of the stand, and colored lights played on the spray. When the shell opened again, a human pearl—Suee Seen—was in the oyster shell.

Fred Culpitt, a British conjurer-comedian, worked on the bill

Li Sing Foo, a British magician, toured briefly with Chung's equipment.

Striking lithograph of Chung Ling Soo —under the eyes of his audience.

A GIFT FROM THE GODS
TO
MORTALS ON EARTH
TO AMUSE AND MYSTIFY.

CHUNG LING SOO

No scene in the show was as imaginative as the one on this poster.

CHUNG LING SOO

"Mosaic" Chung Ling Soo lithograph; another carried a portrait of "Dot."

with Chung in Sydney. The American frequently stood in the wings to watch him perform. One day Chung gave Culpitt a handsome Oriental drape for his table. Culpitt asked a professor friend the meaning of the Chinese characters on the cloth. "They indicate," the scholar explained, "that you are a fully paid-up member of the Foochow Undertaker's Union."

Lafayette had stayed apart from magicians; Chung reveled in their company. Culpitt and other conjurers were welcome at the workshop in Australia where Chung constructed new illusions. He had opened in Melbourne in February with thirteen feats; by the end of the tour in September, he had performed thirty.

Chung worked as usual with other acts on the bill when he returned to England. By 1911, however, he was presenting special once-a-week all-magic matinees—two hours of visual mysteries without speaking a word. (The conjurer who talks can give a show of this length with a fraction of the equipment a pantomimic performer requires. Talking magicians add time to their routines by telling anecdotes about their travels and the history of their illusions. Chung's silent matinees included thirty-eight feats, ranging from sleight of hand and small apparatus tricks to big-scale illusions.)

Chung constantly experimented with new devices. He perfected an elaborate variation of the dice-to-girl mystery. Six twenty-four—bottle cases of beer changed into a single massive bottle; then the hinged label opened, and Suee Seen hopped out.

In "The Dream of Wealth" at the London Hippodrome in 1912, Chung Ling Soo poured milk into a small metal box, heated the liquid over an oil lamp, then tipped the box toward a tray held by an assistant. A shower of silver coins spilled out. Another shower filled another tray, and five-pound banknotes materialized—by the hundreds. He tossed them in the air as assistants scrambled to pick them up. Two lines from above were fastened to a hidden object in the box. When the lines were pulled, up came a gigantic silk replica of a thousand-pound note; it filled the entire back of the stage. Suddenly, instantly, the huge bill disappeared, disclosing a mammoth gold sovereign hanging at the center of the stage. Triangular sections, hinged at the sides, sprung open to reveal a girl dressed as Fortune. She carried a cornucopia. From it came a seemingly endless stream of gold coins.

Shortly after World War I began on the Continent, Chung presented a patriotic spectacle at the Holborn Empire in London. A massive globe was shown empty, then closed. From holes in the curved surface, he produced the flags of nine nations. As each country's flag was displayed, the globe opened, and an appropriately costumed man or woman stepped forward. Britannia emerged last, and uniformed servicemen marched out to escort her to the footlights.

After playing the Alhambra Theatre in Paris in October 1916,

254

Ching Ling
Foo, Chung
Ling Soo,
and The Great
Lafayette

the magician and his company prepared to sail on the *Medina* on January 5, 1917, for what he announced would be a five-year world tour.

Chung's bullet-catching created a sensation in India. One night a rajah came to the theatre in Bombay, accompanied by his many wives. The women were sequestered behind the curtains in his box, until intrigued by the magic, they threw open the drapes for a better view. The angry potentate sent them back to his hotel, though he himself stayed until the end of the performance.

Since the Shanghai Red Cross had taken over the principal theatre, Chung was forced to play in a Chinese movie house. Finding it impossible to get all his larger equipment on the narrow stage, he substituted smaller tricks for several illusions. Chung wrote an American friend from Hong Kong that the backlash of the war was being felt even in the Orient; he intended to bypass Australia and come to the United States for the first time in more than seventeen years. U-boat raids in the Pacific made him change his mind; the show returned to England in September. The projected five-year world tour was over in eight months.

With skilled mechanics and metal, too, in short supply, Chung no longer built massive conjuring equipment in his British workshop; he experimented instead with model airplanes. Wounded soldiers and troops at training camps welcomed his frequent afternoon visits, though they thought the magician who entertained them in street clothes without makeup was not as Oriental in appearance as he had been on the stage.

Through friends in the armed forces, Chung still managed to get gunpowder for the bullet-catching feat. He seldom saw his wife except at the theatre. Another woman shared his house at Barnes. Since the United States had entered the war, sea travel was less precarious, so the magician planned a tour of South Africa. Meanwhile he continued to perform in England.

His second show, like his first one, on Saturday, March 23, 1918, at the Wood Green Empire in suburban London drew a full house. At 10:45 he held a china plate in front of his chest and braced himself for his most dramatic feat—"Defying the Bullets." Two assistants across the stage took aim as a drumroll increased the tension. They fired.

Chung staggered back, fell to the floor, and rolled over. "My God," he gasped when his assistants reached his side. "I've been shot. Lower the curtain."

MUSIC HALL STAGE TRAGEDY
CHINESE MAGICIAN SHOT
DURING A TRICK

That was the stark headline in the Monday *Daily Express*.

Ching Ling Foo, Chung Ling Soo, and The Great Lafayette

Willow-pattern coasters carried the likeness of Chung on one side, details about his show on the other.

Memorandum from

CHUNG LING SOO

MARVELLOUS CHINESE CONJURER

19

PLEASE ADDRESS
YOUR NEXT TO

There was scarcely room for a message on Chung's business stationery.

The story said Chung Ling Soo had "died from his injuries Sunday morning." Then rumors started to spread. One had it that his jealous wife had murdered him. According to another, heavily in debt and suffering from an incurable illness, the distraught performer had arranged a spectacular suicide.

The inquest opened March 28 at the Wood Green Town Hall, with East Middlesex Coroner A. M. M. Forbes presiding. Two Town Hall officials and a journalist augmented the usual seven-man jury. They established that the conjurer had died after a bullet passed through his right lung. Dot Robinson, who had ridden with him in the ambulance to the hospital and massaged his feet when he said they were cold, testified that her husband, an American, would have been fifty-seven years old in April.

No, she was not familiar with the mechanism of the guns. He prepared them in his dressing room before each performance. On that last Saturday night when she came for the guns, her husband had asked her to return later. He was talking with a visitor, a man in uniform. The serviceman was still there when she picked up the guns, but her husband had gone to the stage to check some production detail with the carpenter.

The visitor, Lance Corporal Cecil Lyle, identified himself as a magician. Chung, he said, had prepared for the bullet trick while he was present, but Lyle had turned his head away out of courtesy to a brother professional. Since Lyle had never seen the bullet-catch, he went to the front of the house before the second show.

Mrs. Robinson testified that she had taken two bullets (round balls, not cartridges as some newspapers had reported) down into the audience. She carried them in a special metal cup. The bullets to be marked were in an upper removable section; two others, previously marked to match a third pair which Chung concealed in his hand when he picked up the plate, were hidden in the bottom of the cup. On her way back to the stage, Dot palmed out the upper section and gave the cup to a committee who noted the identifying marks on the remaining bullets before they were loaded.

The crucial evidence came from Robert Churchill, a gun expert who ran a shop on Agar Street just off the Strand. The guns, he testified, were muzzle-loading muskets. They were at least twenty years old and might have been made for the Persian Gulf gun-running trade. In the place of the usual ramrod tubes under the barrels, long steel cylinders, smaller in diameter than the barrels, had been soldered on each weapon. Chung charged these cylinders with gunpowder before each performance in his dressing room. The main barrels, which were charged and loaded with marked bullets during the show, had been blocked off years before so they could not be fired. The ammunition balls, Churchill emphasized, were so large that they would not fit in the smaller "trick" cylinders.

While testing the barrel of one of the muskets, Churchill had found that hot water poured into the barrel percolated down into the cylinder beneath it. When he took the gun apart, he saw that one of the screws holding the cylinder to the barrel was loose. The metal threads of the screw had corroded enough for water to leak down from the upper chamber to the lower. He said it was obvious that after years of loading, tiny bits of gunpowder had filled the space once occupied by the threads and trickled so near the flash hole of the cylinder that finally the charge in the loaded barrel, which was never intended to be fired, had exploded along with the charge in the cylinder.

The gunpowder was still in the barrel of the second musket though the cylinder attached to the barrel had been fired, Churchill testified. The bullet from the first gun had killed Chung.

Dan Crowley and Jack Grossman, the assistants who fired the guns, swore they did not know the secret of the trick. Crowley recalled that on the night the magician was shot, his gun kicked against his shoulder much harder than ever before.

Police Inspector Cornish told the jury he had taken the muskets to a gunsmith after the shooting. A screw hammer had been necessary to turn the rusty screws in the breechblock. He was certain those screws had not been removed in years. This, he said, ruled out any possibility that Chung or anyone else had tampered with the guns. The other woman, who, newspapers said, had phoned the theatre after the magician had been shot and whom some papers erroneously identified as Mrs. Robinson, was not called to testify. No motive for, or evidence of, suicide or murder was established. The coroner's jury, convinced that the shooting had been an accident, brought in a "misadventure" verdict.

No doubt, Churchill's explanation was correct. The lethal grains of gunpowder had seeped slowly from barrel to cylinder. Chung Ling Soo had been drawing closer and closer to death with each performance of this, the most dangerous feat in all of magic—the bullet-catch.

15

The Selbit Sensations

P.T. SELBIT, a tall, lean Englishman with impeccable manners, delighted in driving spikes through females, stretching their arms and legs, and crushing them. Sawing through a woman, he was at his best. Of course, no blood flowed while Selbit was at work, nor did his victims complain. He was the most prolific inventor of modern stage illusions, and his diabolical tortures were confined to the vaudeville stage.

Selbit was born Percy Thomas Tibbles in London in 1879. His English father was a social worker; his Scottish mother believed she could foresee the future; and his brother, an artist, professed to have the same ability. P. T. himself was dubious. It seemed to him that coincidence, not psychic insight, accounted for their few accurate prophecies of things to come.

Maskelyne's magic at Egyptian Hall intrigued the thin-faced, keen-eyed youth. He was thrilled when Charles Morritt, who sometimes appeared with Maskelyne, rented the basement of the wholesale silversmith shop where P. T. was employed to use as a workshop. The boy planned to sneak down the stairs and get a closer look at the magician's paraphernalia, but Morritt always locked the door when he left in the evening.

P. T.'s mounting curiosity led him to pick the lock to gain entry. Thereafter he made frequent clandestine visits, inspecting the parts of a new illusion then being constructed. When Morritt produced several girls from the innermost of two empty cages for the first time publicly, P. T. was almost as elated as the inventor by the trick's success.

The audience hadn't suspected that the edges of two mirrors met behind the bar at the far right corner of the inner cage. One mirror ran back to a bar of the outer cage; the other extended diagonally to the far right corner of the larger cage. From the front the cages seemed to be empty. Each time Morritt lowered a canopy around the inner cage and raised it, a girl appeared. The canopy only covered the front and two sides of the inner cage. The back of the cage and the first mirror were spring-hinged. The assistants came one by one from their V-shaped hiding place between the mirrors.

Mirrors had been used in many ways since Thomas Tobin constructed a "Protean Cabinet" for Professor Pepper's demonstrations at the Royal Polytechnic Institute hall and "The Sphinx" for Colonel Stodare's Egyptian Hall show in the 1870's, but Morritt's cage illusion, brilliantly staged, produced an entirely new effect.

Later the boy, who had followed the work in progress, would use a mirror passageway in one of his most ingenious presentations. As he grew older, Tibbles sold several articles to Fleet Street newspapers and entertained at parties with sleight of hand and hypnosis. Realizing that Tibbles was scarcely an impressive professional name, he reversed it, dropped a "b," and became Selbit. His picture ran on the cover of the initial issue of *Magic,* the first British conjuring monthly in October 1900; editor Ellis Stanyon predicted the twenty-one-year-old performer would have a "brilliant" career. Five years later, Selbit edited and wrote most of the copy for a rival publication, *The Wizard.*

The Wizard made frequent mention of a new Egyptian conjurer. Joad Heteb's showing at The Magic Circle's "Grand Séance" at St. George's Hall in April 1905 led to a booking with the regular Maskelyne and Devant production. During the year-and-a-half run of "The Wizard of the Sphinx" at St. George's Hall, he sometimes doubled at other theatres. He introduced "A Shocking Surprise" at the Metropolitan Theatre in London: a "convict," strapped to an electric chair in a cabinet, disintegrated in a puff of smoke. By the time Joad Heteb returned to England, after a tour of French, German and Russian theatres, most agents knew that "The Wizard of the Sphinx" was P. T. Selbit—in Egyptian costume, beard, and dark greasepaint.

Selbit worked as himself in June 1909 when he topped the bill at the Oxford Theatre in London with "The Selbit Mystery." Center stage, several feet in front of the backdrop sat a three-foot-square box on four bamboo legs. Two angled mirrors, extending from rods on the sides of the box, gave the audience a view of the back. A pull on a cord opened or closed the doors of the box.

First came phenomena of the sort usually associated with séances: loud raps from inside the closed box, messages on blank slates, and the production of flowers. Selbit lifted a heavy block of stone and put it in the box. Chipping sounds were heard. When he opened the doors, a chiseled bust of a celebrity, previously chosen by the audience, stood where the stone had been. He took this out and put handbells and tambourines inside. Once shut off from view, they began to ring and jangle. The next time he opened the door, a girl, bent forward in a sitting position, filled the interior. The magician helped her down to the stage and then turned to flip open the doors and reveal a second girl. Finally Selbit curled up inside the box himself. His assistants opened the doors; inside, in his stead, was a third girl. The smiling magician hurried in from the wings to bow with his assistants.

The basic idea for Selbit's "Delphos" came from Julian Wylie, who devised special effects for the Maskelyne show. A bearded "mechanical" figure, dressed in Oriental clothes, carried out near human actions. Even conjurers were puzzled to read that Selbit was presenting "Delphos" in London while Joad Heteb was touring the provinces. The explanation was simple. Selbit had sent another performer out on the road with his "Wizard of the Sphinx" act.

Selbit bought the American rights to Dr. Wilmar's "Spirit Paintings" in 1910 and agreed to pay a weekly royalty. Wilmar (William Marriott) had read about the marvelous paintings produced during séances by a pair of Chicago psychics, the Bangs sisters. He wrote David P. Abbott, an amateur magician and investigator of alleged psychic phenomena, who lived in Omaha, Nebraska, asking if by chance he had solved the mystery. Abbott replied that not only had he duplicated the marvel, he also had added several touches to make the feat effective onstage.

Abbott described the routine in detail. Two framed blank canvases were examined. Before placing them in a large box with an open front, the magician switched one of the canvases for a painting. He put this canvas upright in a holder inside the box near the back and inserted the other one at the front. A strong light at the rear of the box penetrated the painting and diffused the colors so only a glow of white appeared on the front canvas. By slowly moving the painting forward, hazy colors appeared and became more intense on the front canvas as the painting "materialized." When the magician removed the two canvases, the spectators thought the picture on the front canvas had been "painted by spirits."

Without asking Abbott's permission, Wilmar staged the act in the Maskelyne show. It was an immediate hit. Selbit made a coast-to-coast tour of the United States with "Spirit Paintings" in 1911. Abbott came backstage to see him at the Orpheum Theatre in Omaha, and showed Selbit copies of his correspondence with Wilmar. By then Selbit had paid the "originator" ten thousand dollars in royalties.

The following year Selbit perfected a "Wrestling Cheese."

P. T. Selbit, The Great
Levante, and London
reporters at lunch.

Roy Carter, a British
magician, exhibiting
Selbit's "crushing."

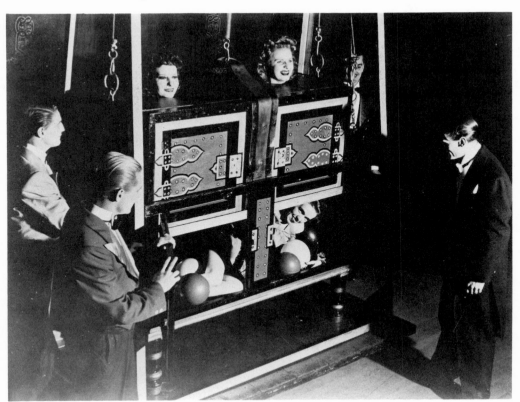

This in many ways was the most unusual act he presented in vaudeville. Six strong volunteers from the audience attempted without success to turn a large round of cheese on its side. They couldn't, of course, unless the performer wished it done. Inside the imitation cheese was a gyroscope.

"Shadow People," first shown at Maskelyne's theatre, was Selbit's big attraction in 1913. Silhouettes of men and women acted brief pantomimic scenes when a light from the back of the stage played on a translucent screen. Spectators examined the screen, the framework around it, and the spotlight, before and after the images appeared; but they found no clue to the mystery. Selbit called the illusion "The Haunted Window" when he took it to the United States for his second American tour.

A prime example of Selbit's ingenuity was "Walking Through a Wall," which he introduced in June 1914 at Maskelyne's theatre. Assistants spread a large sheet of canvas to cover the stage and to "prove that trap doors do not play a part in this mystery." They pushed a brick wall, mounted in a metal frame on rollers, to the center of the canvas and placed it with one end facing the audience. A committee of theatregoers examined the wall and two threefold screens, then they stood on the sides and at the back of the stage as the illusionist led a young woman in a satin dress and a broad-brimmed hat to the left side of the wall. One screen hid her from the spectators' view; the other was put in place on the far side of the wall. At Selbit's command, assistants folded and took away the screen at the left. The girl had vanished. Selbit opened the side panel of the second screen; the girl was back. It was impossible, he stressed, for the girl to climb over or under the barrier, or to walk around it—so she must have walked through the wall.

Sidney Joselyne, a London performer who had never before presented an illusion, immediately claimed he had invented this marvel. Joselyne used a steel plate, rather than a brick wall, in his version. Houdini bought the American rights from Joselyne and featured the feat—with a brick wall as in the Selbit presentation—at Hammerstein's Roof Garden in New York in July. This killed any opportunity Selbit might have had to make a third American tour with something new.

When a new illusion receives great acclaim, other performers often contend they have been doing it for years. The Great Alexander, a California mentalist-magician, said he had "walked through" solid objects sixteen years before Selbit staged his mystery in London. Alexander claimed he had penetrated walls made of wood, sheet metal, and even blocks of ice. Sellers of magical secrets offered a method for a dollar: a trapdoor. When the door was opened, the floor covering sagged down just enough for the performer to crawl under the barrier.

Selbit nevertheless argued it would be good for magic if all the old tricks were discarded; then conjurers would be forced to think of something novel. The inventor was confident he could create mysteries faster than they could be copied. Still, he was not averse to capitalizing on someone else's illusion, which had hitherto only been seen by a limited audience. "The Golden Gypsy," presented by Selbit at the Victoria Palace Theatre in London in 1916, had been shown earlier at Maskelyne's as "The Yogi's Star." In this trick a girl in Romany attire stood at the center of a square sheet of glass, supported on four glass candlesticks. Though apparently insulated from any attempt to communicate information to her, she described accurately objects that had been borrowed from the audience and locked in a basket suspended in the air at the side of the stage. This was probably the first use of radio in a mental routine.

Three years later when the *Sunday Express* offered a £500 award for genuine spirit manifestations, Selbit boldly entered the contest "on behalf of a lady who did not wish her name to be known." Bewildered by the first demonstration, reporter Sidney Mosely invited a formal committee to attend another test séance. Sir Arthur Conan Doyle, the editors of *Light* and the *Occult Review,* a Scotland Yard superintendent, and several widely known people assembled in a private room above the Criterion Restaurant. Participants put personal objects in a black cloth bag, which was then tied at the neck and deposited in a tin box. "The Masked Medium" entered the room, her features hidden by a headdress with a heavy veil. She sat facing the committee and held the closed box in her lap.

"There are disbelievers and believers," the woman said, "and these mixed influences make it difficult to get in touch with the spirits." She relaxed, breathed deeply, and began to describe the items. One man had contributed a fountain pen—a black Swan pen. The author of the Sherlock Holmes stories had chosen a ring; it was gold with initials on it. She called them out. She quoted from a letter in the bag and gave the writer's address.

Part two of "The Masked Medium's" demonstration was to be a materialization séance. Two women escorted her to another room, searched her clothes and body, then brought her back. Committeemen tied the psychic to a chair and locked the door. The lights, except for two small red bulbs on the far side of the room, were switched off. A pianist began to play softly.

Soon the medium seemed to go into a trance. A misty luminous form loomed up behind her. One spectator said later this took the shape of an elderly woman. It floated up from side to side, as far away as several yards from the medium's body; then it disappeared.

After the lights were turned up, Sir Arthur Conan Doyle said the medium must be clairvoyant. How else could she have made out the worn initials on his dead son's signet ring? As for the "floating light," he would have to attend several more séances before he would know for sure whether or not this had been a spirit.

Lady Glenconner, one of the investigators, had no doubts; the medium, she said, should be given the award at once. Sir Henry Lunn, another onlooker, was more cautious. While positive the woman had telepathic powers, he was not convinced of the spirit origin of the luminous form. More probably, he said, "unknown natural forces" caused it to appear.

The committee failed to reach a unanimous decision, but the resulting publicity assured good audiences when Selbit publicly presented "The Masked Medium" act. Later he told Reporter Mosely how the test séance had been staged. Selbit had gone to the door with the tin box under his arm to introduce the medium. As she walked in, an assistant in the hall unobtrusively took the box and replaced it with an exact copy. The medium held this duplicate in her lap. In a cubicle down the hall, Selbit's assistant opened the box and the bag, and sent the pertinent data by radio to the medium. She received the information through a set of earphones concealed in her headdress.

When the medium was taken to be searched before the materialization séance, she left the headdress behind in the dressing room. The misty shining form? Just luminous cloth waved by an acrobat dressed completely in black. The committee had locked the door; they never imagined anyone would scale the wall of the building and climb in through an unlatched window.

Four years after the séance. Mosely's article, "How Conan Doyle Was Tricked" appeared in the October 20, 1923, issue of *John Bull*. Sir Arthur said the account was accurate, but he still believed telepathy, not "wireless telephone," accounted for the description of the concealed objects. Selbit had admitted the materialization was just a trick, but Conan Doyle insisted he needed "a better assurance than the word of a showman or of Mr. Mosely, who is the echo of a showman." Sir Arthur asked to attend a second séance with "The Masked Medium" and offered twenty-five pounds to cover expenses.

His wish was granted in early November. "The Masked Medium" came with her magician escort to the *John Bull* office at 93 Long Acre. Again she described the objects the spectators placed in the black bag which was put in a box. Sir Arthur frankly confessed he saw no evidence of deception: "It was done very cleverly if they substituted another box." Nor had he serious doubts about the "yellowish vapor-like matter" that materialized in the dark. In the past, he said, he had seen the spirit of his own mother appear in the presence of six witnesses. "If a man cannot believe the evidence of his own senses and the evidence of every man in the room, what can he believe?"

Conan Doyle might well have seen Selbit produce "The Long

Acre Ghost" at Maskelyne's theatre soon after the *John Bull* séance. P. T. was too good a showman not to make use of such an impressive illusion.

Selbit introduced his greatest creation in London on January 17, 1921. Five long ropes were securely tied around a young woman's neck, wrists, and ankles. She backed into an open box after the ends of the ropes had been threaded through the holes in the sides. Spectators held the free ends throughout the presentation.

Selbit told the audience that the volunteers, by holding the ropes taut, would feel the girl's movements if she attempted to shift her position once she was fastened in the box. Closing the lid, he snapped padlocks in place to secure it. Uniformed assistants tilted the box back and carried it lengthwise to a skeletal wooden support that held the box raised more than two feet above the floor.

Selbit asked the spectators to tighten their grip on the ropes while he thrust three panes of glass down through the box and two steel blades in from the back to the front. It seemed impossible for the woman inside to survive. He removed the sheet of glass at the center and with the aid of a man, who held the front handle of the crosscut saw, dramatically sawed the box in two.

The illusionist pulled away the saw after it severed the last slivers of the bottom of the box and swiftly removed the glass panes and the steel blades. The assistants opened the padlocks and lifted the lid of the box. Selbit looked inside; instantly he turned toward the audience—a look of horror on his face. Then his expression changed to a smile as the woman sat up, and he reached out his hand to help her over the side and down to the stage where she bowed—still in one piece.

"Sawing Through a Woman" drew packed houses at the Finsbury Park Empire in London and standing-room-only crowds in Birmingham the following week. The London correspondent of *Billboard*, the American show business weekly, rated Selbit's latest illusion the biggest hit of the season on the Moss Empire tour. Pointing out that other performers had stolen Selbit's ideas in the past, George Johnson, editor of the British *Magic Wand*, advised the inventor to put the first thief in his box, cut him in two, and leave him divided.

In New York, Horace Goldin, one of Selbit's rivals, read the accounts of the British magician's triumphs and told theatrical reporters he had invented "Sawing Through a Woman." He claimed he had thought of the idea in 1909 and said he had offered to produce the feat for an impresario in New Zealand in 1917, for John Ringling's circus at Madison Square Garden in Manhattan in March 1919, and for J. J. Shubert's Howard Brothers show at the New York Winter Garden in October 1920.

Selbit responded by asking why Goldin hadn't put the illusion

Roy Carter presenting
Selbit's "stretching."

Will Rock, an American,
shows the "stretching."

in his show—if he really had thought of the idea so long ago. Goldin meanwhile moved rapidly to try to justify his ownership claim. He presented his sawing for the first time at the annual banquet of the Society of American Magicians in New York on June 3, 1921. Clearly Goldin had been thinking along different lines from Selbit. Goldin's box, placed on a special base, was shorter than Selbit's. Moreover, his subject's head extended from a hole in one end, while the feet protruded from two openings in the other. He offered no preliminary business with glass panes and steel blades. The American magician sawed the box in two, inserted metal plates close to the cut made by the saw—then pulled the two halves apart!

Selbit had sawed *through* a human being; Goldin sawed a human being *in two*. Goldin made one mistake during his presentation at the banquet; he used a man for his subject. Any show-wise performer should have known it would be more thrilling for an audience to see a woman in this melodramatic situation. Goldin rectified this error when he went on tour with "Sawing a Woman in·Two" in Keith theatres.

Selbit had publicized his act in England by having assistants carry buckets filled with a murky red liquid to the front of the theatre after a performance and pour the "blood" into the gutter. Now, Goldin in the United States set out to top him. Ambulances drove through midtown streets with red-lettered banners on their sides: "We are going to Keith's in case the saw slips." They arrived in front of the box offices just before a show began. White uniformed nurses and interns stood by with stretchers in the theatre lobbies.

"Undertakers" in top hats, frock coats, black ties, striped trousers, and white gloves paraded along the busy sidewalks to attract attention. The somber-faced morticians carried the crosscut saws in to the theatres. In exchange for passes to the show, newsstand dealers stamped "See a Woman Sawn in Half at Keith's Tonight" above the day's headlines in their supply of papers.

Goldin ran provocative advertisements in the dailies: "Girls wanted to be sawn in half at B. F. Keith's next week. Guarantee $10,000 in case of fatality. Only girls having necessary physical qualifications need apply." Sometimes a "local girl" stood up in the audience and challenged the magician to saw her in half. He invited her to come backstage. There was one qualification; she must wear a mask during the act.

Goldin had a three-month lead on Selbit in American theatres. By the time the British inventor arrived in New York, several Goldin road companies were on tour. Keith arranged for either Goldin or one of his staff magicians to play a week in advance of Selbit in every city on his route.

Servais Le Roy, The Great Jansen, Kalma, Joe Dolan, and Henry Marcus headed Goldin units. Le Roy advertised "I came, I sawed, I conquered." Goldin had registered every conceivable name for the illusion with the Vaudeville Manager's Protective Association except "The Divided Woman." That was the billing for Selbit's act.

The sawing fever spread. The Great Leon offered his own variation on the West Coast. Small-town magicians built strange boxes and barrels, trying to cash in on the popularity of the greatest box-office illusion in history. One performer even worked out a way to sever a girl lengthwise. Not as good as the original in audience impact, but at least it was different.

Selbit arranged for nine units to tour under his management in the United States, then returned to England in December. By then two Selbit troupes were playing the provinces in Britain. Others were sent to France, Germany, South Africa, and Australia.

In January 1922 the ingenious showman introduced "Growing a Girl"; in April he presented "The Idol of Blood, or Destroying a Girl." Neither caught on. When he was invited to appear at the Royal Command Variety Performance at the London Hippodrome in December, it was his sawing feat that the family from Buckingham Palace wished to see.

Selbit had a banner year in 1923: four successful illusions, all based on mock sadistic torture.

"The Indestructible Girl, or Living Pincushion" stood in a device facing a metal plate dotted with holes. At her back was an iron panel, bristling with eighty-four sharp-pointed spikes. An assistant drew curtains at the sides, then turned a wheel that forced the spikes forward until their tips extended through the far side of the metal plate. Once the victim was impaled, the illusionist opened small doors in this plate between the ends of the spikes so the audience could see the girl's face and feet.

"The Elastic Lady" entered a tall, very wide but narrow cabinet, sat on a stool behind the upright center panel, and put her head through a hole. When the side doors were closed, her hands and feet extended forward through diagonal cloth-backed slots. Ropes were fastened to her neck, ankles, and wrists; then she was stretched five feet in as many directions.

In "The Fourth Dimension, or Avoiding the Crush," a girl with a parasol reclined in an oblong topless box. Assistants filled the space around her with balloons before they closed the two front doors. Another slightly smaller box, in which two girls sat cross-legged with their heads extending, was slowly lowered by a hoisting device into the first box. Balloons popped as the box containing the two girls continued its descent. Obviously there was no room in the outer box for the girl

The original "sawing-through," as it was devised by P. T. Selbit in 1920.

Zati Sungar, of Turkey, introduced the "thin" box for the Goldin version.

with the parasol—unless she was crushed flat. Assistants raised the second box; Selbit opened the doors to the first. The girl with the parasol stepped out—still three-dimensional.

The eye in "Through the Eye of a Needle" was a two-inch hole in a heavy metal disk studded with rivets. The disk was the size of a street manhole cover. First a rope was tied to a strap around the "victim's" waist and threaded through the "needle," down into an empty barrel and out through a bunghole in the front. Then the metal disk was placed on top of the barrel and the victim (female, of course) on top of the disk. Finally the girl herself was covered by inverting another barrel. Volunteers from the audience gripped the end of the rope extending from the front of the lower barrel and pulled until the girl passed through the two-inch hole in the metal disk and into the lower barrel. At least that is how it appeared to the audience.

Selbit came to New York in September 1924 to present his new mysteries in four succeeding productions at the Hippodrome. Before returning to Britain, he arranged for road companies to show them throughout America.

Selbit's "Man Without a Middle" was in essence a cutting-in-three—with a surprise finish. The man stood in a box just large enough to hold him; three sets of doors were closed; then two wide steel blades were pushed through from the sides. When the lower doors were opened, the man moved his legs. When the upper doors were opened, he moved his head. When the center section was unlatched—the middle portion of his body was gone.

A blindfolded girl assistant, dressed as a toy grenadier, was used in "Seeing Through a Soldier." To the audience the effect was the same, but this variation had one major advantage. It could be presented on a concrete stage, whereas the former version required a trapdoor.

The Egyptian-garbed assistant in Selbit's "Mummy Mystery" survived, though the magician thrust thirty steel blades and a dozen metal rods through the sarcophagus. Equally invulnerable was the girl in his "Cane Cabinet." Though seemingly impaled and held in position by walking sticks pushed through the sides, front, and back of the cabinet, when the lid was lifted and a line let down from above, she was pulled up and away, free of encumbrances.

"The Million Dollar Mystery," shown at Maskelyne's in 1928, was reminiscent of the earlier "Selbit Mystery," though the box was smaller, the supporting legs thinner, and there was a single front door of framed frosted glass. Shadowy images materialized behind the glass, then faded away. Balloons materialized, and were removed when a top door was opened. An empty pail lowered inside was taken out a moment later—filled with water. One of the most fascinating sequences involved a crate three times as long as the box was wide. The crate was shown empty; then a side door was opened in the box, and slowly the long crate was forced inside it. The side door was latched; the front door was opened. Out came the crate—with a man inside it. The funniest touch came when the crate, with the man inside it, was pushed through the box so that a third of the crate extended from each side. The right end of the crate was opened to show the man's head. Then the left end was opened—the man's head was there too! When the crate was removed from the box, the man was gone, and a girl was in his place.

Even the best rehearsed illusions can go wrong. Selbit's most uncomfortable moments on any stage came during the Christmas Eve matinee at Maskelyne's in 1928. There was a full house to see his new "Mile a Minute Mystery." In Chicago, he announced, the police dealt swiftly with gangsters. Moments after an arrest had been made, a special Black Maria arrived on the scene. As he spoke, a roar came from an engine in the wings, and a uniformed assistant drove out with a cell on wheels attached to his motorcycle.

Spectators were invited to examine the portable prison. After they returned to their seats, a girl wearing a mannish suit and a slouch hat was manacled to a chair in the cell. Selbit locked the door. Assistants pulled down four opaque blinds from the top of the enclosure and fastened them at the base. The driver immediately started his motor, then jumped from his seat with a shout of pain. A blast of fire from the engine had scorched his trouser leg. The fire grew in intensity. A woman somewhere in the audience screamed, and several children clapped their hands. A stagehand ran out with a fire extinguisher, but the chemical solution spread the blaze. A fireman lugged a hose from the wings. The stream of water from the nozzle drenched the curtains, sprayed front row patrons, but had little effect on the fire. The stagehand came back with a pail of sand. He emptied the sand on the motor, and the blaze spluttered out.

While all this had been going on, the girl in the cell escaped from her manacles, forced open the door, and leaped out. A man in the audience stood up and insisted on leading three cheers for the girl.

Selbit waited for this din to die down, then said "Ladies and gentlemen, we will proceed." Again the girl was handcuffed and put behind the bars, and the blinds drawn to cover the sides. As the engine of the motorcycle was no longer in working condition, the magician's assistants pushed the cell around and around in a circle. Selbit clapped his hands; the blinds flew up; the cell was empty.

"Apart from the fire," the *Daily Express* reported, "this was one of the most brilliant illusions that Maskelyne's have staged for years." It was even more mystifying when presented as Selbit had planned it. After the girl disappeared, a man—not a stooge—from the audience was blindfolded and put in the cell. The motorcycle drove up a ramp and into a "garage." There was a brilliant flash of light, and the front of the "garage" fell. It was empty—except for the girl who had vanished earlier. Later the man came from the wings to take a bow with Selbit. He admitted frankly he had no idea what had happened. The final showmanship touch came with the magician's brief curtain speech. He told the spectators that the Black Maria had been mysteriously transported to the street in front of the theatre. He said they would see it there on the way out; and they did.

Selbit's "Broadcasting a Woman," first shown in 1923, was presented in later years as "Televising a Girl." Two cabinets were seen on a raised platform. The subject sat in the cabinet at the left; the cabinet at the right was empty. Lights in the left one dimmed gradually, and the girl disappeared. She appeared as bulbs burned with increased intensity in the cabinet at the right.

Reviving his fourteen-year-old "Sawing Through a Woman" in 1935, Selbit sent Leo Martin, another showman, on a tour of British variety halls. A columnist in *The Magic Wand* said the famous illusion was "as puzzling as ever and a decided draw. . . . Audiences haven't such long memories as we conjurers credit them with having."

P. T. Selbit died on November 19, 1939, at the age of fifty-nine in Sonning, a town near Reading, England. Almost every major illusionist since has featured at least one of his big-scale mysteries. Selbit never presented all of his illusions on a single program. Nor is it likely anyone ever will. The show would run five hours—before the first intermission.

16

The Great Vaudeville
Specialists

ORE than four thousand magicians played on vaudeville bills
around the world between the 1890's and the 1930's. At the turn of
the century there were twenty theatres presenting variety shows—
acrobats, jugglers, comedians, singers, animal turns, dramatic skits,
and novelty acts—in and around London, and as many within a thirty-
mile radius of New York City. Acts varied in length from eight
minutes to an hour. Entertainers could work a hundred weeks in
the United States without appearing twice in the same city by playing the Keith circuit in the East, the Orpheum chain in the West,
and other affiliated theatres in the South and Midwest.

There was a constant demand for novelties. Magicians who
presented unusual routines had a tremendous advantage over those
who showed traditional feats without special themes or ingenious
staging.

Joseph Michael Hartz was the pioneer vaudeville conjuring
specialist. Born in Liverpool on August 10, 1836, he appeared in
London at the age of eighteen with a full-evening show, patterned
after Robert-Houdin's. Twelve years later he came to the United
States featuring "Crystal Magic" with transparent boxes, bowls, and
glasses, as well as several automata and illusions. After a three-year
tour, Hartz opened the first "Magical Repository" on Broadway in
Manhattan, supplying equipment for both professionals and amateurs.
His brother, Augustus, aided him behind the counter and in his

workshop, and another brother, George, opened a similar shop in Boston, then set up a rival establishment—Hartz and Levy—in New York. For a short time there was also a Hartz store in Chicago. Michael Hartz sold his thriving business in 1876 and returned to the stage. In the 1890's he perfected an eighteen-minute act for vaudeville—"The Devil of a Hat." From a borrowed top hat, the slightly built, balding conjurer with a moustache produced a hundred yards of sash ribbon, twelve large silk foulards, twenty pint-size red and green tumblers, twenty-four silverplated beer mugs, a dozen bottles of champagne, thousands of playing cards, a skull, a canary in a cage, seven lighted lamps, and a bowl of water and goldfish. With this prodigious production from a single source, Hartz performed in the United States, in Great Britain, and on the Continent.

Thomas Nelson Downs, a specialist of another sort was born in Montour, Iowa, on March 26, 1867. The first and greatest "King of Coins" acquired his manipulative skill while working as a railroad ticket agent and telegrapher in nearby Marshalltown. At thirty-one, Downs "was receiving the largest salary of any of our variety hall performers," according to *Mahatma,* the New York conjuring monthly. His version of "The Miser's Dream"—producing silver coins at the fingertips—was enhanced by original sleights and by his charming personality. In 1899 the clean-shaven showman with brown curly hair was booked for two weeks at the Palace Theatre in London. He stayed six months, signed a five-year contract for an annual ten-week season at the rival Empire Theatre, then went on to top bills on the Continent.

Downs said later that the manager of the Palace had complimented him on his graceful stage deportment and his stately entrances and exits. This leisurely approach had not been planned; he was tired and his feet were sore from sightseeing. So effective was Downs's acting that when he forgot to palm a stack of coins one night at the Folies Marigny in Paris, he pantomimed the production and the completely deceived audience gave him his usual rounds of applause.

Nate Leipzig, who featured a less dramatic coin feat, used ingenious staging to make his "Steeplechase" effective at the Palace Theatre in London in 1907. First he caused the coin to gallop, end over end, across the back of the fingers of his right hand; then under and across again. After this a movie screen was lowered and a close-up film of the action was projected so those in the far reaches of the house could appreciate the dexterity involved. Leipzig repeated the manipulation and bowed off to hearty applause.

Leipzig was born Nathan Leipziger in Stockholm on May 31, 1873. He worked for several years as a lens grinder with a Detroit optical firm before he made his debut in American vaudeville. His

J. M. Hartz delighted vaudeville patrons by making an enormous production from a hat.

Gus Fowler, "King of Watches and Clocks" on the two-a-day.

T. Nelson Downs won international acclaim as the best of coin manipulators.

Nate Leipzig was equally adroit with cards, thimbles and coins.

specialty was performing parlor tricks so cleverly that even on large stages they retained their appeal. A red handkerchief vanished from the transparent glass cylinder he held between his hands. A table knife clung mysteriously to his fingers. He manipulated thimbles and balls, but he was at his best with cards.

Members of the audience were invited onstage to participate. They inserted aces in four different parts of a pack. By simply slapping the card on the front of the pack four times, Leipzig changed it to each of the aces. After a card had been selected, returned, and shuffled into the deck, Nate gave the pack to one of the volunteers and asked him to deal the cards facedown. Whenever the man wished to stop, Leipzig said, the card in his hand would be the one previously chosen. Invariably it was. Two selected cards were found after the pack had been wrapped in a sheet of paper. A spectator thrust a knife through the side of the package. When the paper was torn away, one chosen card was seen under the blade; the other above it.

Gus Fowler, the young librarian of the British Magical Society in Birmingham, had seen Leipzig, and he had read Downs's treatise on coins, Howard Thurston's book on cards, and was aware that Clement de Lion, the Danish billiard-ball specialist, had produced ten balls in his bare hands. What other object, Fowler wondered, could be used for a manipulative act? He took out his pocket watch, glanced at the time, then began handling it as Clement de Lion would a ball.

Fowler was nineteen when he went to London to appear at the "Third Grand Séance" of The Magic Circle at St. George's Hall in 1908. "Anyone can produce a watch," a reporter noted, "but it takes a real good wizard to make one go." Fowler was signed to perform with "Maskelyne and Devant's Mysteries." After 650 performances, he toured Europe, the British Isles, Australia, and the United States. I saw him at the Maryland Theatre in Baltimore during his second American tour. Working swiftly and silently in front of a black curtain, "The King of Watches and Clocks" caused three covered timepieces of different sizes and shapes to change places. Pocket watches appeared on the end of the chain that dangled from his vest almost as rapidly as he could remove them. A watch suddenly became a clock. He flicked a silver cloth over an openwork display stand, and thirty watches instantly filled as many niches. Two wide metal hoops held a piece of tissue paper in place. Fowler tore away the paper to reveal a clock. Then from an empty hat he took several small ringing alarm clocks and many larger, noisier ones. For an encore, Fowler passed a glittering watch bracelet from one side of the stage to the other where it appeared on the leg of his girl assistant.

José Florences Gili, another outstanding manipulator, came to New York, by way of the Continent and South America, in 1914.

The forty-one-year-old Spanish magician performed in a gray court costume, assisted by his wife, Selika. Florences conjured with cards and coins, but the billing "Something New in Magic" was amply justified by his routine with lighted cigarettes. When one was thrown away, another appeared in his fingers, then another, and another. He also produced four bowls of water from as many cloths draped over his arm. The last bowl was covered and thrown up in the air. Only the empty cloth fell into his waiting hand.

The first conjurer to wear gloves as he manipulated was Paul Freeman. The ambidextrous British magician astonished fellow performers in 1913 by the rapidity with which he made five playing cards appear and disappear at his gloved fingertips. Fran-Klint, who arrived in London from Spain nine years later, exhibited sleights with an entire pack while wearing black gloves.

Working behind the magic counter at Gamage's department store at the time of Fran-Klint's arrival in London was a young Englishman who as Cardini would present the finest manipulative act ever devised. Richard Valentine Pitchford, born in Mumbles, Wales, on November 24, 1899, had been wounded in France during World War I. Returned to a Southampton hospital with other casualties, Pitchford was restless. He asked a nurse to bring him a pair of gloves and a pack of cards so he could practice the card sleights he had worked out earlier in the trenches. Gloves? The attending physician thought his patient was mad and had him transferred to a mental ward in Liverpool. There the staff was more understanding and encouraged Pitchford to entertain them with his tricks. After he was mustered out of the service, he tried to earn a living as a conjurer and ventriloquist in Wales. Not succeeding, he came to London. Pitchford had used several professional names: Valentine, Professor Thomas, and Val Raymond. As Val Raymond, he worked at Gamage's. Frustrated because he wanted to perform magic, not sell it, the young veteran signed on as an engine-room worker and made a trip around the world aboard a tramp steamer. Back at Gamage's again, he still found it impossible to interest agents in his act. Working his way to Australia as a steward on a passenger ship, Val Raymond played the smaller halls in Sydney before he was given a showing date at the principal theatre—the Tivoli. The slender performer, who talked as he conjured, made a hit. Signed for a tour at twenty pounds a week, he was asked to take another stage name. The Great Raymond, an American illusionist, had been in Australia and a local Raymond was playing the smaller houses. The booker suggested he adopt a catchy name, one people would remember, like Houdini. Val Raymond's best tricks were with cards—he became Cardini.

In Australia, as Cardini, his act naturally stressed feats of digital dexterity, but he was still a talking magician when he made his first appearance in New York at the Regent Theatre in 1926. His gloved manipulations with playing cards and lighted cigarettes needed no verbal accompaniment, but he joked as he produced thimbles and passed knots from one set of three silks to another.

A year later, Cardini opened at the Palace on Broadway, performing in pantomime. The dark jacket and striped trousers he had worn previously on the stage in the United States were replaced by evening clothes, white gloves, a silk hat, and a cape. His wife, the former Swan Walker, whom he had met in Chicago, assisted him, dressed in a page-boy uniform and a visored cap.

Billboard acclaimed Cardini as "the personification of grace, admirable showmanship and prestidigitorial excellence." The new act was imitated, but not equalled, by hundreds of envious performers who saw it in the United States, Britain, Europe, and South America.

Cardini played the role of a London clubman befuddled enough by drink to imagine he was having hallucinations or being tormented by prankish spirits. "Paging Mr. Cardini! Paging Mr. Cardini!" A spotlight picked up the slightly tipsy, monocled Britisher as he walked unsteadily from the wings reading a newspaper. The page took the paper and used it to catch the fans of cards that began appearing at Cardini's gloved fingertips. Obviously annoyed, he threw aside one perfectly formed fan after another. The page took his cape, cane, top hat, gloves, and cape. Cardini steadied his hand, and after considerable effort fitted a cigarette into the holder he gripped between his teeth. The cigarette disappeared and reappeared several times to his distress. He finally lighted the cigarette with a match from nowhere. Then a sudden blast of fire above his head startled him. The red flower in his buttonhole whirled dizzily. The white silk handkerchief he tried to knot untied itself. Billiard balls appeared between his fingers; they changed colors and multiplied.

Lighted cigarettes plagued him. Sometimes he was so astonished when one appeared that the monocle dropped from his widened eye. Then a lighted cigar materialized from thin air. He puffed on it contentedly as the page brought him his cape, cane, hat, and gloves. As he strolled toward the wings, he tossed away the cigar—and two more cigarettes. Before he walked off, a large, lighted meerschaum pipe startled him by its sudden appearance. Smoking this, he left the stage. Music, lighting, and perfect staging aided in making the act a masterpiece. Franklin D. Roosevelt saw "The Suave Deceiver" four times, as did his successor in the White House, Harry Truman. One of Cardini's engagements at the Palladium Theatre in London extended ten months. He conjured for King George V at the Royal Command Variety Performance in 1933.

Curiously, the week Cardini made his first Manhattan appearance, another magician from abroad opened at the Palace—wearing gloves for his card manipulations and producing lighted cigarettes. He had never seen Cardini, nor had Cardini seen him.

Frakson (José Jiminez Seville) was one of a Spanish family of conjurers. His father, brothers, a sister, and several uncles were magicians. He admired Florences, who had introduced the continuous production of lighted cigarettes to vaudeville. Frakson's style was unlike Cardini's. He performed with a wide smile and made witty asides. He had been billed as "The Man with 100 Cigarettes" in Europe; the number was upped to "1,000" in the United States.

Vaudeville's greatest conjurer with silk, Ade Duval (Adolph Amrein), introduced his "Rhapsody in Silk" in the Midwest late in the 1920's. John Chapman, the *New York Daily News* critic, noted when Duval played the Palace in July 1931 that the "superior" sleight-of-hand artist pulled "enough silk for two editions of the 'Vanities' [Earl Carroll's lavishly staged Broadway revue] from a tube the size of a fifty-cent beer can." On his return from a tour of the British Isles and Europe in April 1937, Duval starred in a production staged to highlight his magic at the Radio City Music Hall. He entered through a panel in a gigantic curtain that pictured a conjurer with outstretched arms. The colored silk foulards he tucked into one assistant's handbag vanished and appeared tied to the bare ribs of a parasol held by another; the parasol cover was found in the handbag. After several sleights with a billiard ball, Duval gestured toward the back of the stage. Two doors swung open, and a giant cage containing the Radio City Glee Club rolled forward. Later from an empty, paper-capped tube, measuring ten inches long by three inches in diameter, Duval whipped literally hundreds of yards of silk. Then he changed white silks to various colors by simply blowing them through a small paper cylinder. Eventually he produced a rabbit from a top hat, and the Radio City Rockettes, garbed as bunnies, hopped up and out of a line of gargantuan silk hats for the show's finale.

Cecil Lyle, England's "Magical Milliner," made his first appearance in British variety in 1913. Lyle displayed a woman's hat, devoid of decoration, on a stand, then put a silk cloth over it. He wrapped bits of white fox fur and an ostrich plume in a piece of tissue paper, then ripped open the package to show the trimmings had vanished. They appeared artistically arranged on the chapeau when he pulled away the silk that covered it. There were other offbeat feats: a golf club disappeared and a gramophone vanished. Strips of silk and torn pieces of tissue paper were converted into stylish headgear, and from an empty hat box Lyle produced a dozen bonnets.

By 1919 Lyle was presenting large-scale mysteries in his "Millinery Shop of the Future." One of the best was a candy-box illusion.

Frakson sent showers of sparks from the ends of the cigarettes he produced.

Cardini devised and presented an act and a style that has never been surpassed.

"Think a Drink" Hoffman poured any potion thought of by his patrons.

The lid of the mammoth carton was lifted so the box could be shown empty. When it was raised again, the box was filled with gigantic chocolates. The third time the cover was removed a girl filled the interior.

Season by season the show grew larger. In September 1941 The Great Lyle opened his Calvalcade of Mystery at the Aldwych Theatre in London. This show featured illusions that had been performed in the past by De Biere, Horace Goldin, and David Devant. Devant, then living in retirement, devised a spectacular number for the production—"Guarding the Crown." A critic in the *Observer* said, "There are no horses in this Calvalcade. . . . but there is everything else a Master Magician may command." The production ran for twenty weeks. Later Lyle added Selbit's crushing illusion, billed as "A Tight Squeeze," and Amac's "Find the Lady," a stage version of three-card monte with a girl appearing and disappearing under the cover of three immense, suspended cards. Lyle had traveled earlier in Australia and the Orient; in 1950 he played the theatres of South Africa. A few weeks before his show was to begin another British tour, Lyle died in London on March 9, 1954, at the age of sixty-three.

Protean, or quick-change, artists had been popular in Europe even before The Great Lafayette came to Britain. The first to win an international reputation was Leopoldo Fregoli. Born in Rome on June 2, 1867, Fregoli performed in London in 1898 with four assistants. Two, wearing red coats and knee breeches, flanked him on the stage; the other two were hidden in the wings, holding wigs, hats, costumes, and props in readiness for his rapid transformations.

The versatile Italian appeared first as an old man singing in court costume, then as a woman, and finally as a girl soprano. He bowed off at the wings. Before the applause had ended, he was back, dressed as an elderly music teacher. He sat at a piano and began to play. The spotlight moved to the wings as a buxom woman in an evening gown walked out. Suddenly the audience realized this was Fregoli; a dummy was now in his place at the piano. The woman trilled a few notes, left the stage. Fregoli strode out from the far side, dressed as a conjurer, wearing a beard and moustache à la Herrmann. He produced flowers from an empty paper cornucopia, exited at the left, came on from the right dancing—in a wig and ballerina's tutu.

A Scot billed as "Mr. Hymack" played British variety halls in 1913 with an "instantaneous change" act that was more puzzling than those of many magicians. As the curtains opened, "The Human Chameleon," dressed in formal afternoon attire—tailcoat, stiff shirt, striped trousers, and top hat—paced back and forth on a station platform. He was on his way to a wedding, but had missed the train. He inserted two coins in a slot machine; immediately strange things began to happen. Until then, his hands had been bare; now he was wearing

282

*The Great
Vaudeville
Specialists*

blue gloves. The small flower on his lapel changed to a larger one of a different color. The cuffs of his stiff shirt dropped off. He reached for his white pocket handkerchief to wipe his brow; a red one appeared. His four-in-hand tie changed to a gaudy crimson bow.

Another pair of shirt cuffs dropped, but these were attached to sleeves long enough to fit a giant. His plain white shirtfront was suddenly slashed by vertical stripes of red. Red gloves appeared on his hands. His top hat grew taller and taller. Handkerchiefs came in profusion from the breast pocket of his coat. The flower on his lapel flew across to the opposite side. Another flower appeared where the first had been. His stiff collar became loose and flipped open. He tore it off; another took its place. He pulled off his gloves; others of various colors appeared as rapidly as he could strip them away. The once well-groomed wedding guest was in sad disarray. Then, instantly, without cover, his clothes changed back to the formal attire he had been wearing when first seen.

The greatest American-born quick-change specialist, Charles T. Aldrich, was one of the stars of the first Royal Command Variety Performance at the Palace Theatre in London in 1912. A favorite at the New York Hippodrome, he also appeared with Fred Stone in *Jack o'Lantern* and in other Broadway shows. Some of his costume switches were made behind a wide screen that hid his body, but his legs could be seen as he moved behind it. The most startling change came when, dressed in tights, Aldrich stood on a pedestal and lowered a canopy until it covered him. The moment the bottom of the curtain touched the platform, the top dropped, and he was seen dressed as a bearded street peddler, carrying a tray. For many years Aldrich, garbed as a tramp, ended his turn with a funny harassing handkerchief skit. Tormented by the red cloth that danced on end around him, the tramp nailed the handkerchief to the stage. It got away. He shot it, buried it under a mound of sawdust, and erected a miniature tombstone. Before the curtains closed, the indefatigable handkerchief wriggled up from the mound, shook off the sawdust, and cavorted as merrily as ever. The last time I saw Aldrich in the early 1930's, he closed his act with "A troupe of educated whiskers." Beards of various sizes and colors took on life and, under his direction, jumped up and down, turned somersaults, and paraded in time to the music.

During the period when Ching Ling Foo's water-bowl production was the talk of two continents, Aldrich gave an hilarious impersonation of him, wearing a robe and a bald wig with the pigtail sticking straight up in the air. Ching had produced a bowl; Aldrich whisked his foulard and conjured up a barrel.

Han Pin Chien, one of several Chinese performers who followed Ching Ling Foo in vaudeville, lifted his cloth to reveal a stack of bowls, one neatly balanced on another. Another Chinese, Long Tack

The Great Vaudeville Specialists

Ten Ichi, Japan's most famous conjurer, featured a "Thumb Tie" and water tricks.

Han Pin Chien and his company from China headlined in Europe and the United States.

Long Tack Sam, magician, acrobat, juggler, comedian, and worldwide vaudeville star.

First as Kuma, and later as Kim, this Oriental conjurer stayed in the United States longer than his rivals.

Sam, came to the West with the Tan Quai troupe from Shanghai, and later fronted his own company, "The Royal Pekinese Troupe." This sub-billing had to be dropped; booking agents thought it was a dog act.

Critics who saw Long Tack Sam at Hammerstein's Theatre in New York in 1915, said the short personable performer who was a comedian, balancer, and contortionist, as well a conjurer, could teach "know-it-all American showmen" a trick or two about putting a show across. During his many years as a headliner in the United States, Australia, Britain, and Europe, Long opened bank accounts in many countries. If a catastrophe occurred almost anywhere in the world, he said, he had enough money in another land to get himself started again. He weathered two world wars and several upheavals in his native China. Long Tack Sam died in Linz, Austria, where he had been living in retirement, on August 7, 1961, at the age of seventy-six.

Long Tack Sam seldom exhibited more than four tricks in his act; Li Ho Chang rarely performed less than a dozen. Chang, as he was billed during his later years, was born Juan José Pablo Jesorum in Panama City on December 2, 1889. He was one-fourth Chinese on his mother's side, half Indian on his father's, and part Spanish on both. He started in show business as an interpreter and assistant to The Great Raymond, the American illusionist, in Central and South America. He gave his first vaudeville performance in New York in 1915, wearing an Arabian costume, and advertised as "The Great Pablo." He was Chang when I saw him at the State Theatre in Baltimore in 1933. His beautifully costumed Chinese act, warm personality, and rapid pace brought him three curtain calls. Later, with a full evening show, he made a fortune in South America, and traveled to Europe, Australia, China, and India.

I saw him again in Havana when, after a profitable tour of Cuba, he was flying to Venezuela with his "Magic Circus." This venture under canvas was a fiasco, but Chang was soon in the money again with an elaborate magic production, which he took to Argentina, Mexico, Spain, and Africa. During his later years, he presented an act, rather than a complete show, in Japan, the Philippines, Thailand, Trinidad, and Martinique. He was still working—at the age of eighty-two—when he became ill in Mérida, Yucatán. Chang died there on April 27, 1972.

Chin Sun Loo, who patterned his Chinese act after Chung Ling Soo, was born John Gerard Rodney Boyce in Toowoomba, Queensland, Australia, on December 4, 1872. As Jean Hugard, he presented the Chinese routine as a part of his full-evening magic show. Hugard sailed from Australia on a world tour in 1913, and performed in New Zealand, the Fiji Islands, Samoa and Hawaii en route to California. When his feature mystery—bullet-catching—was banned in the United States during the years of World War I, Hugard played in vaudeville with his Chinese act; then in 1919 he opened a theatre of magic at Luna Park in Coney Island, New York. Retiring from the stage in 1927, he started a second career as a writer and teacher of magic. His many excellent technical manuals and *Hugard's Magic Monthly,* which he edited and published for seventeen years, made him a world authority on conjuring. Though Hugard was deaf, and had been blind for several years, he was still dictating precise instructions until a week or so before he died in Brooklyn, New York, at the age of eighty-six on August 4, 1959.

Arthur H. (Al) Wheatley, who had been born in Australia and brought to the United States as a boy by his parents, worked as Jean Hugard's assistant, before he too became an expert "Chinese" magician; first as Ching Ling Fu, then as Tung Pin Soo, and eventually as Chop Chop.

Rush Ling Toy, "China's Great Illusionist," and The Great LaFollette, "International Transformist," were at one time in partnership with Hugard in a second Luna Park theatre of magic. Both performers were actually the same man, George F. Reuschling. He was born in Baltimore, Maryland on December 8, 1886. By 1912 Rueschling was being featured in Keith vaudeville as Rush Ling Toy. Two years later he became The Great LaFollette, switching costumes and disguises as he performed as Herrmann the Great, Harry Kellar, Buatier de Kolta, Servais Le Roy, and Rush Ling Toy.

LaFollette toured Cuba with Carl Rosini, another vaudeville magician, and South America with Dr. Carl Hermann, "The Electrical Wizard." In 1923 LaFollette played in *The Main Street Follies* at the Central Theatre in New York. He also appeared with Rajah Raboid (Maurice P. Kitchen), a vaudeville crystal gazer, in *Knights of the Orient* at the Belmont Theatre in New York in 1931, and in *Mysteries of 1931* as the show was called when it moved to the Eltinge Theatre. At the start of LaFollette's transformation act, he sat behind a table and lifted a large "Book of Life" to read. Each time he lowered the open volume, his facial appearance had changed completely. In "The Arrest" he played five parts: an old peddler with whiskers, a woman flower seller, a mysterious man in a black felt hat and cape, a policeman, and Frenchie the Thief.

The split-second changes were made as LaFollette ran around a kiosk. The climax came when the uniformed policeman spun on his heel and was instantly changed into the goateed Frenchman attired in formal afternoon wear and a top hat.

In his later years LaFollette owned a magic shop in St. Petersburg, Florida. On the few occasions he still made an appearance as Rush Ling Toy, he wore a special rubber Chinese mask that could be stripped off in an instant.

Though many Chinese conjurers played in Western vaude-

Chang played in vaudeville, toured with
his full-evening show and his circus.

Cecil Lyle, "The Magical Milliner," later
became a famous illusionist.

The Great LaFollette also appeared as
Rush Ling Toy, "Chinese transformist."

ville, few Japanese performers came to the United States or Europe. The most famous was Ten Ichi (Shokyuku Hattorie). He was the first to produce "Water Fountains" in vaudeville. Jets of water spurted up from every object or person he touched with his magic wand. He was also an excellent showman with "The Thumb Tie." After his thumbs were firmly tied, solid rings tossed toward him passed through the barrier, and encircled his arm. On his return to Japan, with several illusions he had purchased in New York and Chicago, Ten Ichi traveled with his own show. The Great Asahi later played in variety with an act very similar to Ten Ichi's. The best Japanese sleight-of-hand artists, Tenkai and Okinu, manipulated watches, cards, and other small objects. Sometimes Tenkai and his wife performed the same feats simultaneously.

The Oriental illusionist who toured in American vaudeville longer than any other mystifier from the East was billed first as Aki Kuma and later as Kim. Before Japan bombed Pearl Harbor, he said his real name was Kinjiro Tanaka Kumajo and that he had been born in Tokyo. Thereafter, he said his name was Yen Soo Kim and that he had been born in Seoul, Korea, on February 4, 1884.

His principal feat, which he presented with rare skill, was a classical Japanese trick. Two large tubes rested on the top of an un-draped table. He showed them empty, passing the smaller tube through the larger. Then he nested them, lifted the two tubes as one to reveal a large metal jar filled to the brim with water. He scooped out some of the liquid with a cup, then demonstrated the jar was too big to fit into the tubes by trying unsuccessfully to push them down over it. Suddenly the tubes dropped over the jar, and the jar vanished. After again showing the tubes, he nested them a second time. Lines were let down from the flies and attached to something in the jar. The ropes hauled up an immense piece of green silk, which for a moment covered the magician and his assistants. When they stepped out from behind the billowing folds, their costumes had changed from Oriental robes to Western clothes. Aside from an occasional trip outside the country, Kuma performed in vaudeville from 1905 until the variety era ended. He appeared frequently at the Palace on Broadway, and at one time presented various illusions, including a trunk feat and a levitation. He died in New York at the age of seventy-nine on March 27, 1963.

The most colorful of the Indian magicians who performed in Occidental variety was Linga Singh (Dutt). Sent to study medicine in Edinburgh, he joined the dance troupe of Ruth St. Denis instead, and traveled with her throughout the British Isles and on the Continent. He appeared first as a magician in the United States under the name Ram Bhuj. Then, early in the 1900's, he went to England with one of the most lavishly staged acts of the period.

Curtains opened on a dimly lit stage. A weird temple setting could be seen through an entranceway in a painted mountain. A torch-bearer ran out from the wings and darted through the gap in the mountain to light an altar in the temple. The mountain scenery went up to reveal a chamber with gilded elephants at the sides and a curtained platform at the back. Silken folds were drawn aside. The turbaned magician sat cross-legged on a cushion, surrounded by attendants. A dancing girl amused him and the audience, then his magic props were rolled forward. He arose, cut a strip of cloth in two and restored it. From two empty nested boxes, he produced a girl. She vanished in another pair of boxes and reappeared when the curtains of a sedan chair on wheels were closed and opened.

Another assistant was cremated, then reincarnated in the chair. From an inverted half-coconut shell held high in one hand, water gushed down to fill a jar on a table. The overflow ran through a chute into a larger jar, and from there into an ornate tub. Once the tub was filled, the conjurer covered it with a cloth. The water disappeared and "The Bride of the Ganges" stood up and stepped out to the stage.

As Linga Singh, the name he was to be known by thereafter, he was featured at the Coliseum in London. His new act opened with the production of six large snakes, which he draped over the shoulders of a smiling girl assistant. His closing feat was even more striking. Under his direction, one of the attractive young women in his company drew a carriage with three people sitting in it across the stage without touching it—using "the power of her eyes."

I met Linga Singh at the Trocabaret, an intimate night club in the Trocadero Restaurant in London, early in 1937. Though the floor space was limited, his troupe paraded out to Oriental music. An enormous Indian parasol was held over the conjurer's head by an assistant as Linga Singh entered slowly, waving a tasseled ceremonial wand.

His principal tricks that evening were removing colored sands after they had been mixed together in a large brass bowl filled with water (with each dip of his hand, he came up with dry sand of a different color) and the suspension of a reclining assistant on the point of an upright scimitar, held by the hilt in a base on the floor. He said after the show that he had learned his first tricks in the sideshow of the Ringling Brothers circus in the United States. He never told his relatives in India that he was a magician; they thought he was a successful doctor.

Linga Singh died of pneumonia at the age of fifty-three in London on November 27, 1937. After his death, his magnificent costumes and stage equipment were piled in a heap in a contractor's yard in Brixton, and one of his assistants set them afire, in accordance with his final wish.

Vaudeville offered an ever-changing kaleidoscope of wonders. A miniature house was burned at every performance of Hadji Ali, an

Tung Pin Soo was really an Australian-born magician, Al Wheatley.

Fregoli, master protean artist, in London in 1898.

Fred Keating and his aide, The Great Alexander.

Arabian regurgitator of the 1920's. The act began when he swallowed an enormous amount of water, then sent it spouting into a large container across the stage. Next he swallowed nuts, rattled them in his stomach, and brought them up singly or in audience-specified numbers. To prepare for the finale, he swallowed more water, then some gasoline. A small building behind a protective wire-mesh screen was lighted. Standing several feet away, Hadji Ali sprayed the building with the gasoline. Flames leapt high. Then as fire bells rang in the pit, he sent out a stream of water which doused the blaze.

Clarence Willard, "The Man Who Grows," stretched himself until he was eight inches taller. King Braun squeezed his body through the frame of a tennis racket, then a keyhole-shaped opening in a plank. Arthur Lloyd, "The Human Card Index," pulled any playing card called for from one of his pockets—also, as requested, laundry slips, train tickets, menus, and "For Rent" signs. De Roze, a Swiss magician, headlined bills, pouring martinis, manhattans, beer, milk, and sodas from pitchers of crystal-clear water. The American magician, Charles Hoffman became "Think a Drink Hoffman, The Highest-Paid Bartender in the World." De Roze's audiences *asked* for their mystic potions; Hoffman's simply *thought* of them.

Competition from continuous-run, lower-priced feature films at other Broadway houses forced the Palace, the most famous vaudeville theatre in the United States, to present a third, then a fourth daily performance. Fred Keating, a magician whose conversation was as delightful as his tricks, headed the last straight vaudeville bill in July 1932.

Keating became a film star, played dramatic roles in the legitimate theatre, and, as a conjurer, shared the stage with comedian Beatrice Lillie and actress-impressionist Cornelia Otis Skinner.

The Palace, now a legitimate theatre, operated for a time as a movie house, then added hour-long variety presentations to their film fare. The last nonstop stage and screen show closed in August 1957. By then the marvelous era of the two-a-day was just a memory.

17

LeRoy and Goldin—

Trendsetters

Servais Le Roy, a slender bilingual Belgian who learned his first tricks in Britain, and Horace Goldin, a plump Russian Pole who began his conjuring career in the United States, won international acclaim as illusionists. They shared a greater distinction. Both were innovators in styles of presentation and technique. Le Roy, the first magician to use a double in a transposition feat, invented a levitation with a breathtaking climax—the floating woman disappeared in midair. Goldin introduced the ten-tricks-in-twenty-seconds pace to vaudeville, and invented the most sensational of all sawing mysteries —ripping through a woman's midsection with a buzz saw.

Jean Henri Servais Le Roy, the son of a Belgian hotel manager and a British mother, was born in Spa on May 4, 1865. He ran away to England as a boy and was adopted by a British family. In his late teens, he saw Captain Henry Worsely Hill, a retired naval officer, perform with cups and balls. The captain had been drinking heavily; his sleights were easy to follow. After practicing assiduously, Le Roy astonished the conjurer with his own routine. Several years later, Hill, noting the long lines at four London theatres where Buatier de Kolta's "Vanishing Lady" was being performed by as many illusionists, decided to make a world tour with this proven box-office attraction as his feature. He hired twenty-one-year-old Le Roy, by then a professional magician himself, to be his co-worker and to play the role of "Vanishing Man."

Hill's opening night in the fall of 1886 for the British forces at Gibraltar was a shambles. Befuddled by liquor, he failed at his smaller tricks and clumsily spoiled the illusion. Thoroughly disgusted, Hill's younger brother and the "Vanishing Man," who was adept at Buatier's "Disappearing Cage and Canary" and sleight of hand with cards and coins, took the morning ferry for Cadiz, intending to travel on their own in Spain. Hill swore out warrants for their arrest, claiming they had stolen his equipment; they were brought back to Gibraltar to stand trial.

The captain failed to prove his charge, and the young men returned to Spain. Le Roy later said that all he gained from his performances there was experience. Yet on the strength of a handbill printed in Spanish, he was booked for his first London showing at the Royal Aquarium in Westminster. During his six-month run he hired Mary Ford, a personable young English girl, as his assistant and gave her an exotic stage name—Mercedes Talma. Later he married her.

Le Roy's first original stage presentation, "The Three Graces" involved a cabinet of the sort Professor John Henry Pepper had once used to produce a man at the London Polytechnic. Two hinged mirrors met at an upright pole in the center and reflected the interior sides of the box. Le Roy found there was room for three standing assistants in the concealed triangular space at the back. He removed the front door, mounted the cabinet on a round fixed base, and used the pole as an axis around which the cabinet could be revolved.

After spinning the box to show it empty inside and out at the beginning of each production, he held up three cloths, one by one, over the open front and under them conjured up three forms. When he shouted, "Appear!" three girls tossed their shrouds aside and posed as the Three Graces of Greek mythology. The London success of this illusion brought Le Roy his first American tour with the "Boston Howard Athenaeum Star Specialty Co." in 1892. In later years Le Roy rebuilt the cabinet and devised an even more effective presentation. Four covered forms were produced. He and his wife disappeared in the cabinet, and two of the four people who stood up and threw off their cloths were Le Roy and Talma.

Le Roy introduced the second of his creations, "The Flying Visit," at the London Pavilion in 1894. Wearing a tight-fitting red cap, which gave him a satanic appearance, he curled up in a small box and closed the front drape. Almost immediately the curtains opened, and Talma jumped out. "Where are you?" she called. From the top of another box high in the air, supported on four tall legs, Le Roy popped up, shouting, "Here I am." He dropped back out of view as Talma climbed a ladder and pulled aside the front drape. The box was empty. "Where are you?" she cried plaintively when she de-

Servais Le Roy conjured in London
as "The Devil in Evening Clothes."

Le Roy and Bosco in the workshop of
Servais Le Roy's Holborn store.

Talma, Le Roy, and Bosco play cards
as their impish assistants look on.

scended to the stage. "Here!" was the immediate response as Le Roy raced down the aisle and up to her side.

Two doubles and perfect timing produced this seemingly inexplicable marvel. The audience had seen Le Roy put on the red cap as he introduced the feat. They were not aware that another man took his place before "he" climbed into the first box or that still another assistant, with matching moustache, cap, and costume, appeared in the second. Meanwhile the magician was running around from the back of the stage to the front of the house.

Le Roy was playing vaudeville in the United States with his "Flying Visit" when M. B. Leavitt, a theatrical producer, had the idea of combining the acts of three magicians from as many countries in a single show. "The Triple Alliance"—Le Roy, the Belgian; Imro Fox, a portly German-born conjurer-comedian; and Frederick Eugene Powell, an American—opened in Milwaukee in August 1898. The troupe played as far west as Kansas City, as far north as Toronto. During the two years the trio worked together, they intermittently broke up the "alliance" to make individual theatre appearances.

Eager to take a more prominent role on the stage, Le Roy's wife learned sleight of hand. Soon after T. Nelson Downs became a headliner in American variety with coin manipulations, Talma with her husband's help put together a similar routine.

The American "King of Coins" opened at the Palace Theatre in London in April 1899. Four months later, Talma made her debut across town at the Oxford music hall as "The Queen of Coins." A *Daily Telegraph* critic predicted that the beautiful brunette would offer strong competition to the man "who has so long been a potent attraction at the Palace." Talma's hands were so small, another paper reported, that she wore a size five-and-a-half glove. Despite this, she could palm thirty half-crowns to perfection.

She was booked to top bills elsewhere in Britain and in France and Germany. Then Le Roy formed his own star trio—Le Roy, Talma, and Bosco. Leon Bosco, a fat, bald comedian with a moustache and goatee, had been an acrobat until excess weight forced him to seek another occupation. His foghorn voice and feigned clumsiness made his attempts at conjuring hilarious. Le Roy, Talma and Bosco, "The Monarchs of Magic," toured the British Isles, Europe, South Africa, Australia, New Zealand, and North and South America.

So many performers had copied Le Roy's originations that in 1910 he purchased the City Magical Company in London, renamed it after himself and began to manufacture his illusions. "Stolen Jam," the production of two girls from an empty palanquin, with curtains at the back and front, was a best seller. The same was true of his "Costume Trunk." The magician displayed the drawers filled with various costumes and replaced them in the case. As soon as a spec-

Le Roy and Goldin— Trendsetters

tator selected a country, a girl dressed in the national costume appeared from the top of the trunk.

His "Devil's Cage" withstood rigid examination by a committee from the audience. After assistants had locked and roped the cage, the performer stood beside it in a cabinet. The drapes were closed and opened: the magician now stood inside the cage. Once more the assistants shut the curtains; seconds later, the performer stepped out.

Carl Hertz and Arnold De Biere were among Le Roy's best customers. Hertz had been born Leib Morganstern in San Francisco in 1859. He arrived in England in 1884 and picked up choice bookings with Buatier's "Flying Cage," which he boldly claimed as his own invention. Another Buatier creation, "The Vanishing Lady," performed by Hertz in England soon after the French magician had introduced it in Paris, made the American a variety star. Emilie D'Alton, the British girl he hired to disappear, later became his wife.

Following appearances in the provinces, Europe, and the United States, Hertz opened in Melbourne in January 1892. To promote his show, he advertised for "1,000 cats of all descriptions," promising a shilling or a ticket for each one delivered at the stage entrance of the theatre.

The next morning, Hertz said in his autobiography, *A Modern Mystery Merchant*, hundreds of small boys arrived with bags and boxes of cats. His assistants fastened paper collars bearing the words "See Carl Hertz at the Opera House" to the felines' necks and turned them loose downtown.

Though his first tour of Australia was successful, the second—four years later—topped it. Audiences thronged to the Opera House on September 18, 1896, to see his great new "Animated Pictures," projected with the machine invented by R. W. Paul in England. The marvelous projector, the *Referee* critic said, was "a combination of the kinetoscope and a limelight lantern"; there were gasps at the sight of moving London buses, cabs, and the pedestrians, and a roar of laughter when an old man turned in the street to ogle a pretty girl. Harry Rickards, the theatre owner, paid three fines for overcrowding the house with patrons eager to watch the first movie show in Australia.

From Australia, Hertz took his magic and motion pictures to Ceylon, India, China, Japan, the Fiji Islands, and Hawaii. When he returned to England, he presented "The Indian Rope Trick." A boy climbed a suspended rope; Hertz mounted a scaffolding and covered him with a cloth. The magician pulled the covering away; the boy was gone.

Hertz's Oriental settings were less spectacular than the ones

The production of strips of cloth from a puzzled spectator's coat made a hit.

Le Roy found the audience reaction was even better when the cards were larger.

Other conjurers caused billiard balls to multiply; Le Roy used playing cards.

Artistic staging and graceful movements added greatly to Le Roy's original feats.

another American illusionist, Harry Sears, used in England. An elephant, a camel, a horse, several snakes, and forty-five people in costume appeared in Sears's production. Nonetheless Sears soon faded from the magic scene while Hertz, the superior performer and a showman who could turn even adverse criticism to his advantage, continued to draw crowds.

He constantly added new illusions, obtained from Servais Le Roy and other inventors, but Hertz was at his best with "The Flying Cage." In August 1921 while considering a "performing animal" bill, the House of Commons called Hertz to testify before a select committee. Previous witnesses had charged the magician with killing a canary at every performance. Hertz invited any member of the committee to mark Connie, his feathered assistant. James O'Grady, M.P. and a bird fancier, examined the canary and said he would recognize her again without markings.

Hertz vanished cage and canary with a clap of his hands. Tossing his jacket to a member of the committee, he left the room. When he came back with the bird perched on his forefinger, O'Grady testified that this was the same canary and that she had not been even slightly injured. Hertz told the committee Connie had been disappearing twice nightly without mishap for twelve months and some of his canaries had worked in the show for as long as six years.

Servais Le Roy vouched for Hertz's statements. He, too, had performed the feat for many years, and he repeatedly said only bunglers and magicians with improperly made cages injured their birds. As a conjurer and a manufacturer of apparatus, Le Roy knew that both skill and precision-made equipment were vital to a successful performer.

Long before Arnold De Biere, one of Le Roy's best customers, put "The Flying Cage" in his act, he had used birds in another way. A small man with thick, curly, dark hair parted in the middle, De Biere came to England in 1903 when he was twenty-five, two years after his first major success at Tony Pastor's Theatre in New York. De Biere performed in court dress, wearing a cape for his entrance. Producing a canary from an assistant's ear, he made it disappear, reappear, and then changed it into two birds. He put them in a paper bag, twisted the top, and blasted away the bottom with a pistol shot. The canaries reappeared instantly in a cage.

Assistants opened two giant fans behind a girl in Chinese costume who stood on a platform with a parasol over her head. Roller blinds attached to the parasol were pulled down to cover her from view. At a signal from De Biere, the blinds flew up. The girl was gone; in her place was a large bowl filled with ducks.

Billiard balls appeared and multiplied between De Biere's fingers. A man in a slatted box changed into a woman. Rice doubled in quantity when shaken between two mouth-to-mouth bowls, then it turned into water. From an empty box came a girl. The magician slowly tore a strip of paper into bits, then restored it. His closing feat had been introduced into Western vaudeville by Ten Ichi of Japan. A volunteer came up on the stage and tied the magician's thumbs together. After the spectator examined four hoops, he was told to throw them across the stage, one by one, toward the magician. The hoops mysteriously passed through the tied thumb barrier and dropped like giant bracelets on De Biere's arm.

De Biere's show expanded in Europe. Audiences in Paris, Amsterdam, Brussels, and Berlin applauded as he drew curtains around a platform and produced a "Bridal Chamber" complete with a live bride. However, when he shot a girl from a cannon into a nest of suspended boxes, illusionist Horace Goldin charged him with thievery and threatened a lawsuit. De Biere retaliated by running an advertisement in theatrical journals calling the chubby illusionist a "fat-headed bluff." Goldin had patented the feat, but Houdini had told De Biere the trick was so ancient it must have been "invented by Noah on the ark during the flood."

After The Great Lafayette's death in May 1911, De Biere added several of Lafayette's specialties to his show. By 1915 the De Biere act included ten illusions. Most perplexing was the production of a giant tortoise shell under the cover of two large cloths. His assistants lifted the shell, and the magician, who until a moment before had been on the stage, popped out from underneath it.

When his British assistants were drafted in World War I, De Biere returned to the United States. The forty-five minute act that had been so popular abroad was presented with eight American assistants in New York in October 1916; then the show went on tour. As the war dragged on and his American staff entered the armed forces, De Biere stored his heavy equipment. Billed as Arnold, he played with a one-man routine at the Columbia Theatre in New York. For twenty-two minutes he entertained with only three tricks: "The Multiplying Billiard Balls," "The Egg Bag," and "The Thumb Tie." The enthusiastic response brought him an immediate booking with the Loew circuit.

Shortly after the Armistice was signed in November 1918, a sailor volunteer tied De Biere's thumbs so tightly the cord cut to the bone. Unable to work with this injury, he cancelled his dates in the Midwest and soon returned to England with his big show. Critics who saw De Biere during his eight-week season as the featured performer at Maskelyne's St. George's Hall in 1919 said he presented one of the most beautiful productions ever staged there. Perhaps De Biere's most intriguing illusion was shown eight years later in March 1927 at the Wintergarten Theatre in Berlin. Standing center stage with a male assistant by his side, he flourished the large purple foulard the man handed him, held it up to cover the assistant's outstretched arm, then whipped the cloth away to reveal a girl perched on the arm.

De Biere dropped his big-scale feats a few years later and headlined variety bills with a solo act similar to the one he had presented in the United States during the war. Again the program comprised three tricks: "The Flying Cage," "The Cut and Restored Rope," and "The Egg Bag." De Biere was still delighting audiences at the Streatham Hill Theatre in London at the age of fifty-six when he became too weak to work. He died a week later on August 5, 1934.

Le Roy, who had sold De Biere many illusions, continued to perform during the years he owned a magic supply company in London. Bosco, the hefty, bald, bewhiskered comedian, who had worked with him on his first immensely successful visit to Australia in 1905, was in declining health.

Le Roy began to look for another magician-comedian of similar appearance and skill to replace Bosco. He remembered Dr. James William Elliott, a portly, affable Boston physician. Elliott was marvelous with cards, and he had a fine sense of humor. Perhaps he could be persuaded to play Bosco. While performing in America, Le Roy learned that Elliott had teamed up with Barney Ives, another conjurer, after trying a solo act in vaudeville, but no one knew where the dexterous doctor could be found. So Le Roy returned to London without him.

Then one day Elliott paid a surprise visit to Le Roy's shop at 52 Hatton Garden in Holborn. Before the afternoon was over, the doctor had been persuaded to shave his head and trim his beard in the Bosco style. He was the Bosco who played with Le Roy and Talma in England and Scotland in 1914, and he went with them to Australia.

The trio's show on May 2, 1914, at His Majesty's Theatre in Perth, the largest production Le Roy had ever staged, featured "Nero—the most bewildering spectacle ever seen." The twenty-two people in the cast had had only a few days of rehearsal before the opening. Even so, they caused less trouble than the lions. Le Roy planned to use three, but only one was tame enough to be controlled. Backstage problems delayed the curtain for twenty-five minutes. When it finally did go up, there were miscues, stage waits, and lighting errors. Le Roy had been relatively calm throughout the chaos, but he lost his temper when a painted scene of an English pasture was lowered by mistake for the great Roman finale.

By the time the troupe reached Adelaide, the show was running smoothly. A versatile performer, billed for some unexplained reason as "The Great Unknown," received show-stopping applause. Small wonder—in England he was a headliner. Harry (Henry) Cameron, who had been born in Melbourne, worked as a weight lifter, juggler, and contortionist before he went to the British Isles in 1907. In four years with Le Roy's help he topped provincial bills as "The Great Carmo," with an act built around "The Devil's Cage." When Carmo heard his mentor was leaving for another trip Down Under, he volunteered to go along and present his old turn.

Carmo juggled, made quick costume changes, and balanced a long pole with a woman in a small dirigible at the top of it on his chin. The magic began with Le Roy, Talma, and Bosco producing rabbits—six of them—from a top hat. Talma conjured with coins and filled glasses with the beer that flowed from an empty, paper-capped barrel. Le Roy hypnotized his wife, covered her with a white silk cloth, caused her to float up in the air and then to hang in space as he passed a hoop over her vertical body. While he gestured dramatically, she floated higher. Suddenly he whipped away the cloth; she was gone! This was "Asrah," the greatest of his inventions. Less satisfying was the disappearance of a covered Indian boy who had climbed eighteen feet up a suspended rope. Bosco seemingly beheaded a duck and a rooster, restored them with their heads transposed, then chased them off into the wings with an ax.

Le Roy had devised a realistic slip-on rooster head for the duck and a duck "suit" for the rooster. Twelve ducks came from the water Le Roy poured into a large empty tub. He put two of the ducks into a box, then took it apart piece by piece to prove that they had disappeared. The three stars mysteriously changed places in cabinets and left the stage to produce coins, cards, silks, and vegetables in the midst of the audience.

Three illusions were performed before the actor who portrayed Nero in the final scene. Roman soldiers decapitated one Christian prisoner and cremated another. The third, Talma, rebuffed the Emperor's advances and was thrown into a lion cage. Le Roy came to her rescue; with a puff of smoke he made the lion disappear.

The Le Roy, Talma, and Bosco company had intended to continue to the Orient and around the world after the New Zealand stop, but World War I brought about a change of plan. They sailed instead to the United States, opening at the Cort Theatre in San Francisco in December 1914. Then, with a shortened version of their full-evening show, "The Monarchs of Magic" worked in vaudeville. Dr. Elliott left the act in 1917; thereafter at least five other performers played the Bosco role.

After leaving the company, Carmo had returned to England to present a new version of Le Roy's "Vanishing Lion." By the late 1920's he advertised "The Most Gigantic Mystery Act in the World,"

Imro Fox set the pattern for Le Roy's
conjuring comedian, Leon Bosco.

Bosco with Le Roy's first duck pan.
Previously smaller birds were used.

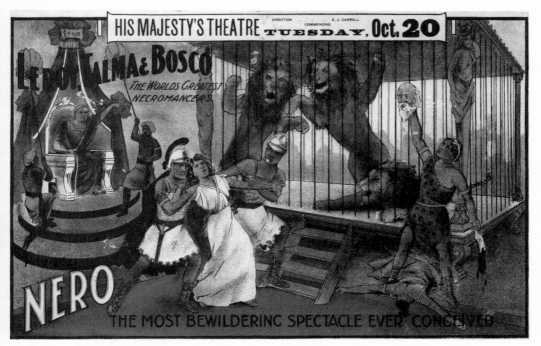

Window-card advertisement for the spectacular lion illusion in Australia.

complete with lions, tigers, bears, horses, two elephants, a camel, and forty people. The "Great Carmo Circus" played a season under canvas in the summer of 1929, mixing a blend of tricks, illusions, dancers, animal acts, and specialty performers. Business was so good that Carmo broke with tradition and kept the tent show out during the winter. This was a bad decision.

In Birmingham the big top collapsed under the weight of a hundred tons of snow. Believing a man had been trapped beneath the canvas, roustabouts slashed it, hoping to rescue him. No one was found. Less than a week later, fire destroyed a second Carmo tent. It was empty, but animals housed nearby panicked. Ten lions went berserk and threw themselves against the metal bars of their cages; M. Togare, the trainer, finally calmed them, but two elephants pulled up their stakes and trampled a man as they bolted to escape the flames.

This succession of catastrophes left the illusionist burdened with enormous debts; he continued to perform, but never again on so grand a scale. During the early years of World War II, Carmo played in variety and entertained British troops. He died at the age of sixty-five at the Municipal General Hospital in Coventry on August 1, 1944, following a cerebral hemorrhage. Rita, his wife, later carried on the Carmo name briefly in vaudeville.

During the years Carmo performed with his big show in Britain, Le Roy limited his tours to North and South America. In 1920 the Le Roy, Talma, and Bosco production played three months at the Casino Theatre in Buenos Aires and for a short while in Montevideo. Periodically the trio appeared at the Palace Theatre on Broadway in New York and at other major American vaudeville houses, but Le Roy was happiest when he was on the road with his own complete program. A Le Roy, Talma, and Bosco production, "The Unseen World," featuring the Zancigs—"Two Minds with a Single Thought"—Memora, the memory expert, and Madame Modjesta, a crystal gazer, ran for a few months.

Le Roy stored his illusions in 1921 and signed a contract to head one of Horace Goldin's "Sawing a Woman in Two" units. Goldin agreed to let Le Roy stage the mystery in his own style. Goldin's assistants had worn traditional brass-buttoned uniforms; Le Roy's dressed as hospital attendants. His magical operation was so realistic that two women spectators fainted during the opening performance. Like Goldin, he established new box-office records in many of the theatres he played.

After the sawing vogue passed, Le Roy presented "Subduing a Woman with Bayonets" in vaudeville. Flanked by five nurses and interns, he displayed a new torture device. A heavy block bristling with bayonets was hauled up and released. The magician drove the blades through a cylinder. The interns raised the block a second time, inserted Talma lengthwise in the tube, and closed the end of the tube. As the drums rolled, the block fell. The gleaming sharp points of the blades extended from the lower side of the container. Despite this ordeal, Talma emerged unharmed. The illusion was well presented, but it lacked the dramatic tension of the sawing.

Le Roy's two-hour show, *New York to Bagdad,* featured "Subduing" with a surprise finish in 1924. Talma entered the cylinder garbed as an old crone; after the bayonets were drawn up, she slithered out in an evening gown. Charles Marion, in the only supporting act, then manipulated his fingers before a spotlight at the front of the stage to produce amusing lifelike shadows on a white screen. Within a few seconds the audience recognized the performer in smock and beret as Le Roy, but as a program note said, "What's in a name, anyhow?"

The sixty-five-year-old illusionist was struck by an automobile near his home in Keansburg, New Jersey, in October 1930. He recovered despite a fractured skull and several broken ribs. A few years later, John Mulholland, the editor of *The Sphinx,* a magic periodical, introduced me to Le Roy in New York. I had first seen him when I was a boy in Baltimore. I remembered how impressed I had been with his "Flying Visit" and complimented him on a difficult card sleight he had performed earlier in the act. "Oh, that," he said. He stood up, poised a pack of cards on his shoe, kicked upward and dexterously spread the cards in a fan as he caught them with his right hand.

Sam Margules, one of Le Roy's admirers, persuaded him to present a final evening of magic. It had been years since the seventy-five-year-old illusionist had given a full show. On June 6, 1940, a packed house at the Hecksher Theatre in New York gave the great Belgian conjurer an ovation when he walked out on the stage, but it was soon apparent he was ill at ease. His fingers trembled; inexperienced assistants brought him the wrong props; the magician forgot his carefully planned but insufficiently rehearsed routines.

The next day—utterly dejected—Le Roy began destroying his tricks, illusions, and the mementos of a long and rewarding career. Until then, he had been working on a book about his adventures and original creations. He never touched his manuscript again after the sad night at the Hecksher. Talma died four years later. Her sister, Elizabeth Ford, who had worked as an assistant in the Le Roy, Talma, and Bosco show, took care of Le Roy in his Keansburg, New Jersey, home until he died at the age of eighty-eight on June 2, 1953.

Le Roy outlived Horace Goldin, his principal rival as an innovative showman, by fourteen years. Goldin was born Hyman

Goldstein near Vilna in Russian Poland on December 17, 1873. He slipped and fell in a well when he was five; after this harrowing experience he stammered. Brought to Tennessee by his parents when he was sixteen, Horace learned his first words of English clerking in an uncle's grocery store in a suburb of Nashville; later, he worked as a traveling salesman for another uncle who manufactured inexpensive jewelry. He stammered less now, but he still had difficulty making himself understood because of his Russian accent. While earning his living as a draper's assistant in Washington, D.C., he went to see "The Incomparable Albini." Albini became the young man's idol. Goldin had learned several tricks from a sign painter-conjurer in Tennessee; he tried to present them in the manner of Albini. Later, when Albini visited Goldin's boardinghouse room in New York City, and found one wall covered with an enormous Albini poster, he taught his admirer how to do "The Egg Bag" the Albini way.

With this trick as his strongest feat, Goldin played dime museums, sometimes giving as many as twenty-five performances a day for ten dollars a week. Gradually he added larger tricks to his routine. Repetition brought perfection. In the first six months of 1888 the twenty-four-year-old magician played six engagements at Tony Pastor's Theatre in Manhattan. Confident of his ability to entertain, Goldin told jokes between the tricks. Alan Dale, the caustic *New York American* critic, reviewed "The Humorous Conjurer" at Koster and Bial's Music Hall. Dale advised those who planned to see the show to stuff their ears with cotton. Only then could they enjoy the promising young magician's performance. Goldin knew his English was atrocious, but he hadn't realized it was that much of a handicap. Stung by the cutting words, he changed his style, hired two assistants, stepped up the pace of his program, and was on his way to stardom.

Goldin's ten-minute turn at the Brooklyn Music Hall in October 1900 was distinguished by speed and smoothness. He rushed out, pulled a bowl of fire from a scarf, blasted a handkerchief from the end of a rifle, then found it tucked in his collar. From a cone of paper came a live kicking rabbit; from a water-filled tub, into which eggs were thrown, four ducks emerged.

His girl assistant stood in a framework cabinet, covered to her waist by a drape. Goldin entered a wire cage on a pedestal, pulled down curtains at the back, sides, and front. His male assistant donned a red robe and a devil mask and fired a pistol. The girl disappeared. Within seconds, she came running from the back of the theatre and up to the stage. Another pistol shot caused Goldin to vanish from the cage. The "devil" took off his disguise; he was Goldin.

Not a word was spoken, though throbbing drum rolls, rim shots, and cymbals pointed up the action.

Arnold De Biere peers through a crystal clock.

Carl Hertz presenting "Vanity Fair—the girl through the mirror" in 1899.

Carl Hertz and his assistants; he wears spats; his wife holds a dog.

The act was signed for the Keith chain, and more eye-catching marvels were added. Goldin caught goldfish at the end of a line flicked out over the heads of the audience. He shot two canaries from a paper bag into an empty cage; vanished and reproduced a lighted oil lamp. In the closing illusion the magician flourished a bedspread-sized cloth, held it up between his raised hands. A whistle blew offstage, three "policemen" hurried out and pulled away the cloth. No one was there. One of the officers tossed off his cap, wig, and coat. Presto, he became Goldin in evening clothes, taking a bow.

On the strength of this run, Goldin was booked for his first appearance in London. The "Whirlwind Illusionist" opened to a large audience and excellent notices at the Palace Theatre in July 1901, and was signed for annual engagements for the next five years.

After filling previously booked dates in the States, Goldin returned to London where he attracted even more favorable attention than on his first visit. He was summoned to Sandringham Palace on November 2, 1902, to entertain King Edward VII, Queen Alexandra, and the visiting Emperor Wilhelm II of Germany. During the next week he gave three more performances for the British royal family.

Edward VII sent the entertainer a diamond-studded stickpin in appreciation; later the Prince of Wales and the Queen of Saxony gave him similar ornaments. He began calling himself "The Royal Illusionist," and adorned his calling cards, stationery, programs, and posters with illustrations of his jewels.

Goldin's fourth appearance at the Palace Theatre in London in June 1904 was cyclonic in pace. In twenty minutes he presented, in addition to the usual fast opening tricks, an enormous production of flags from a small paper-capped tambourine, a table that changed into a suitcase, and five illusions.

A paper cube, on a raised platform instantly expanded to twice its size. A girl leapt from the cube and danced as a huge nickel-plated staff of music was lowered from above. Fastened to it were numerous top hats filled with bells. The assistant's high kicks struck the bottoms of the hats to punctuate her steps with the jingling bells.

Then a giant "weighing machine" was rolled center stage. A girl climbed stairs to step on one tray, where she was covered with a cloth by the illusionist's assistants; the other tray was loaded with weights to balance her. At a signal from Goldin, the girl vanished, and the weighted side of the scales clanged to the stage.

Following a levitation illusion, a lion and a woman disappeared in a cage. The finale was a showstopper. Suspended from an inflated balloon, festooned with electric bulbs, was a passenger basket. Goldin put on a coat and hat, and climbed up in the rigging between the balloon and the basket. An assistant fired a pistol; the empty basket dropped; Goldin vanished, and a second later he reappeared at the side of the stage.

Ellis Stanyon, publisher of *Magic*, a British conjuring monthly, was overwhelmed. He said the production was unique—the "most costly" conjuring act ever seen in England.

The woman who vanished in Goldin's lion cage reappeared in the innermost of three suspended trunks. The Great Lafayette objected so strenuously to his competitor's performing a feat so similar to his "Lion's Bride" that Goldin stored the cage. Thereafter he shot his assistant from a cannon into the boxes. Fasola, another illusionist, later featured the cannon illusion in Scotland; Goldin promptly sued him and lost the case. Goldin also threatened legal actions against Arnold De Biere, who was performing the cannon feat in the United States, and against Carl Hertz, whose "Bridal Chamber" Goldin claimed to have invented. Goldin spent large sums trying to stop other magicians from using the mysteries to which he claimed title.

Goldin's success produced imitators of his style as well as his tricks. An Austrian magician who had seen him in Prague built a similar pantomimic act and played on the Continent and in Britain as The Great Roland. Though he claimed to be an American, Roland could not speak English.

One of Goldin's cleverest routines was used to open and close his act at the Alhambra in Paris in 1909. Four assistants carried a sedan chair onto the stage. A woman stepped down from the chair. The sedan curtains were closed; then they opened again, and Goldin was seated where she had been. After his final illusion, Goldin bowed as though the program were finished. The sedan chair was brought on again. The magician entered it. Halfway to the wings, one of the bearded bearers threw off his turban, beard, and cloak—it was Goldin again.

The Merry Magician, a musical comedy starring Goldin and including two of his most massive illusions, "The Vanishing Piano" and the disappearing tiger, opened at the Theatre Royal in Brighton in April 1911. His fans were disappointed; they had hoped for more magic and less singing and dancing.

The following year at the Alhambra in London, Goldin presented two acts. The first, "A Review of Prestidigitation," had the energetic conjurer playing the parts of Buatier de Kolta, Signor Blitz, Robert-Houdin, Ching Ling Foo, Herrmann the Great—and himself. The second was a "Grand Oriental Illusory Scene," which culminated with the disappearing tiger. In June 1912 the illusionist began a five-month tour of Africa with his own variety company.

Goldin was the first magician to play the new Palace Theatre on Broadway in New York. He opened there in September 1913, then

Should an accident occur during the "sawing" act, an ambulance was at hand.

Horace Goldin, his crosscut saw, and applicants for the operation.

Publicity picture showing circular saw employed in Goldin's "Miracle."

toured across the country with "twenty carloads of equipment and forty assistants" before sailing for the Orient in the summer of 1915.

Fifteen brothers of the King of Siam were so enthusiastic about Goldin's show in Bangkok that he was invited to perform at the palace. There was no room large enough for the proper presentation of his spectacle; a theatre was built on the grounds. The evening of October 25, 1915, shortly after 10 P.M. the King and his party walked from the palace toward the theatre. Goldin, who had been standing near the entrance with his manager, dashed for the stage. He was stopped by a call from the King, who said that Goldin probably didn't remember him, but they had met many years before.

The King, then a prince, and one of his brothers had been in London on their way to enroll at a British school. They had seen Goldin perform several close-up tricks in the Cecil Hotel's American Bar and had asked him to explain them. The King was keenly interested in conjuring. Goldin had been booked for a single royal command performance; he gave three. He constructed a new illusion in Bangkok: the production of a girl from an empty ricksha. Before he left, Goldin gave the ricksha to the stagestruck monarch. The King, in turn, presented the magician with his fourth jeweled stick pin and "an unprecedented fee."

Goldin had to buffet a strong current of anti-German sentiment when he played Colombo, Ceylon, during World War I. Mistaking his accent for German, a spectator interrupted the illusionist's short opening speech by shouting, "What part of Germany do you come from?" "Tell me, which part of the zoo do you come from?" the plump performer shot back angrily. When his temper cooled, Goldin explained he had been born in Russia, but was a naturalized citizen of the United States. He offered to show his American passport to anyone who visited him backstage.

Singapore authorities raised three objections to Goldin's playing at the Opera House. Wild animals were not permitted in the building; the magician's boiler which produced a cloud of smoke to screen the tiger's disappearance might explode; and the trapdoors Goldin intended to put in the stage might cause the flooring to collapse. The harassed conjurer explained that he housed his tiger in a cage and used a safety device to keep the boiler pressure under control. As for the trapdoors, they would be cut on a bias and be reinforced on the under side with iron bars, thus strengthening rather than weakening the floor of the stage. After this persuasive argument, the inspectors allowed Goldin to proceed.

His reception in Tokyo was more cordial. The young lady who introduced Goldin on opening night gave him a bouquet of flowers and told the audience that she had met him when as a child she performed in the United States with Ten Ichi, the great Japanese magician. At Ten Ichi's request, Goldin had taught her several fine feats. After the show Goldin learned that her name was Ten Katsu, that she was the star of her own illusion production and the most popular magician in Japan.

Goldin arrived in Melbourne in May 1916. The *Referee* said the Tivoli Theatre had "a most serious problem"; it was not large enough to accommodate the crowds. An updated version of "Vanity Fair," one of Herrmann the Great's mysteries, attracted considerable comment. In the original a woman stood on a ledge in front of a large full-length mirror. Covered by a threefold screen, she disappeared. Goldin replaced the opaque mirror with a sheet of transparent glass and created the illusion that his assistant "walked through" the barrier. When the screen was removed, she was standing on the far side of the glass.

After filling engagements in other Australian cities, as well as in New Zealand and Java, he reached the Hawaiian Islands early in July 1918. At the end of his engagement at Lahaina, Goldin's equipment was loaded into small boats for transfer to a liner anchored four miles from shore. As the heavy crate containing "Walking through Glass" was being hoisted up to the deck of the ship, the cable snapped and the 780-pound box fell, striking and overturning the small boat. Five illusions and many smaller crates of props sank to the bottom of the sea, and with them went the locked strong box containing most of the profits from the illusionist's long tour.

Goldin arrived in San Francisco in August without "The Tiger God," "The Floating Piano," and other big-scale mysteries. He played the Orpheum circuit in the West with the smallest act he had shown in many years. The magician built a second "Walking Through Glass" and a "Film to Life" illusion before he opened at the Palace on Broadway in June 1920. *Variety* reported Goldin talked and tried for comedy, but "he misses wildly." The new "Film to Life" illusion was novel; he spoke with a woman in a moving picture projected on a screen, then entered the picture to escort her out on the stage. "Goldin's present style of working and illusions can't compare with his speedy method of the past," the critic said. "It will need a revival [for him] to mount again into the headline class."

A few months later Goldin staged "The Phantom Hands." Two disembodied hands resting on the keyboard of a piano, set in a black alcove on the stage, came to life and played whatever popular songs members of the audience whispered to a man who walked down a runway into the audience. Bookers said the illusion was good only for a few minutes, not for a complete act.

Goldin found it increasingly difficult to get engagements. Then early in 1921, he heard that P. T. Selbit's "Divided Woman" had created a sensation in England. He quickly built his own sawing il-

Goldin's hand emerges from the front,
after a hole has been drilled in body.

Water downed by his assistant gushes
out through the opening into a glass.

"The Girl in the Cage," Wintergarten, Berlin.

lusion. In Goldin's version, unlike Selbit's, the victim's head, hands, and feet extended from the box. By July, Goldin had returned to the Palace in New York and scored the biggest triumph of his career with "Sawing a Woman in Two."

At this moment of triumph, Goldin was broke. After the ship-loading accident in Hawaii, he had borrowed heavily to buy new equipment. He filed a petition for bankruptcy, listing liabilities of $38,775 against assets of $1,284. The five road companies sent out with Goldin's sawing act profited his new backers more than the magician. He did phenomenal business at Keith theatres, but he spent almost as much as he made suing other performers who featured similar feats. One illusionist cut through a girl in a barrel; another divided his assistant diagonally; a third made the incision vertically. By the spring of 1922 the sawing craze had run its course.

Goldin arranged a private showing for his next creation, another film illusion. A woman whose image was projected on a movie screen apparently read the minds of the audience as Goldin strolled along the aisles. Unfortunately the sound of her words was not synchronized with the movement of her lips. He scrapped the film and opened at Henderson's in Coney Island with a melodramatic skit designed to appeal to those audiences that had been thrilled by the sawing.

After a few tricks in the fast-paced style of other days, Goldin played the role of a mad doctor in "Tearing a Woman Apart." Fiendishly the plump magician ripped off the arms of a peasant girl as her farmer father stared in horror. The magician forced his armless victim into an open-front cabinet, strapped her in place, then sliced off her head and legs. The dismembered pieces were burned in a steaming cauldron. He loaded the ashes into the mouth of a cannon and fired at the strapped torso in the cabinet. When the smoke cleared away, the girl was intact. Audiences laughed; no one gasped. Bookers found the presentation more silly than sensational.

Goldin tried again in September 1923 with a new version of the cinema mental act, "The Girl with the Celluloid Mind," at B. F. Moss's Regent Theatre in Manhattan. The lip movements on the screen now matched the accompanying sound, but the act was not strong enough for the big time. Yet for this routine alone Goldin rates at least a footnote in the history of talking pictures.

He was reduced to touring as an added attraction with *Step On It,* a burlesque show. His new act included "Shooting a Canary into a Burning Light Bulb," "Film to Life," "The Indian Rope Trick," and "Sawing a Woman in Two." Presented at his old rapid pace with a minimum of words, it reestablished him as a saleable headliner.

Goldin opened to rave reviews at the London Coliseum on his return to England. Once more he was in top form—and broke. He filed another bankruptcy petition, itemizing debts of almost $45,000 and cash on hand of $46.

Then the magician was arrested as a counterfeiter in Birmingham, England, in 1926. To advertise the show, his assistants had scattered thousands of imitation banknotes in the streets. One side carried a perfect facsimile of an American dollar, the other an announcement saying that no one had seen Goldin perform in the United States for less than a dollar. Someone had pasted two of these banknotes together, with the advertisements on the inside, and used the "dollar" to pay for drinks at a pub. A sympathetic judge fined the showman the equivalent of five dollars: a small price to pay for a stunt that garnered thousands of pounds worth of space in the British press.

Goldin added "Boring a Hole Through a Man" to his program shortly afterward. He drilled through a "Hindu" as the man stood at the center of the stage. The assistant gulped down a glass of water, and the liquid gushed out from the hole in his body. When Goldin held an electric bulb behind the man, the rays could be seen at the front; then the illusionist thrust his hand and arm through from the back to the front and wiggled his fingers.

"Sawing a Woman in Two" continued to attract and mystify British and European audiences until the fall of 1931 when "A Living Miracle" replaced it. This was sawing with a difference; no box was used. The girl was halved bloodlessly by a buzz saw as she reclined on a table in full view. Goldin's salary rose at the Palladium in London, the Scala in Berlin, and elsewhere in Britain and on the Continent. Photographs of his latest attraction were published around the world. Canterelli, a German-Brazilian, offered his version with a larger circular saw in Rio de Janeiro; Blackstone, in the United States, severed the girl while she was facedown instead of faceup.

"The Living Miracle" caused at least one death, though not on the stage. Anastasius Kasfikas, a Greek illusionist, and his wife, Valeria, were en route from Salamanca to Tordesillas, Spain, when the truck in which they were traveling with their equipment crashed. The sharp circular blade shot out of the case, severing Kasfikas' neck. Billing herself as Cleopatra, his dark-haired, lovely widow later performed in North and South America. She was the best female illusionist I have ever seen. Not surprisingly, she preferred less dangerous deceptions.

I met Horace Goldin in London in the fall of 1936. At sixty-two he was stout, wore his reading glasses on a black ribbon around his neck, and carried a cane. The tiepin in his cravat sparkled with the jewels he had received from Kings and Queens.

"Confidentially," he said, "I have the best act in the world. You must see it as my guest." I accepted his invitation. Again the next April, when he played at the Regal Palace in East Ham, a suburb of London, I sat in the front row as three curtains parted before he

Sketch of Goldin napping as he sits in the winter sun before his show.

It was a far cry from the decapitation illusion presented in the 1890's in a New York dime museum to Goldin's "Living Miracle" illusion.

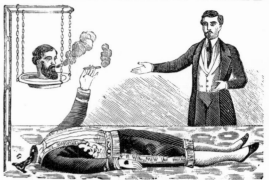

BURNELL'S MUSEUM,
MENAGERIE,
—AND—
THEATRUM,
511 WASHINGTON STREET.
THE WONDERFUL AND MYSTIFYING
DECAPITATION FEAT

Or--LIFE IN DEATH.
A LIVING HUMAN HEAD suspended on a common Tea-Tray, three feet above the Body. The Head Eats, Smokes, Talks, &c.
CROWNING MYSTERY of the 19th CENTURY

Admission to entire Museum, Menagerie and Performance,
25 CENTS.
Children under 10 years of Age, 15 Cents.

F. A. Searle, Printer, Journal Building (up one flight), 118 Washington St. Boston.

Goldin performing on BBC-TV, June 28, 1939.

stepped forward. The flags he pulled rapidly from a small tambourine were gathered up and attached to two lines from above. They blended into an immense Union Jack, large enough to fill the back of the stage. Hand shadows of animals came to life when he broke through paper frames. From the stomach of his pet dog, seemingly sliced open with a knife, Goldin extracted a live rabbit; thereupon the dog jumped from the table, barked, and ran off the stage. Albini's "Egg Bag," to which Goldin had added various comedy touches, delighted the audience.

He caught goldfish on a line cast over the footlights, produced a girl inside a giant balloon inflated slowly on the top of a pedestal, divided another girl in half with a buzz saw and restored her, and looked on as an assistant "walked through" a pane of glass. Then the magician caused a boy to disappear after he had climbed to the top of an upright rope. Before the curtains closed, Goldin caught a bullet, fired at him from a rifle, on the china plate he held in front of his chest.

We talked in his dressing room after the performance. I asked if he was working on a new illusion. "Not one," Goldin chuckled, "four!" We discussed bullet-catching. Week nights he caught the bullet on a plate; Friday night, as a special feature, he stopped it between his teeth.

On Monday, August 21, 1939, Goldin opened at the Wood Green Empire, where Chung Ling Soo had been fatally shot. It was a busy day; in addition to doing two shows he roughed out a routine for his second appearance on the BBC-TV later that week. The sixty-five-year-old illusionist told an assistant he was tireder than usual as he left the theatre. Goldin went to his Queen's Gardens apartment in London where he died in his sleep during the early hours of Tuesday morning.

Then on a holiday in New York, his wife immediately returned to London. Goldin had met Helen Leighton, a drama student, backstage at the Orpheum Theatre in San Francisco in 1912. He asked her to marry him; she rejected him. He proposed again in Chicago in 1914 and a third time in 1922. She finally said yes when they met again in London five years later. Goldin said his marriage was evidence of his tenacity and his will to succeed. His autobiography, *It's Fun to Be Fooled*, which was published in England in 1937, was dedicated to his wife.

Not every new approach or feat Goldin planned worked, but he kept trying. Early in his career the switch from comedy magic to a rapid-fire pantomime presentation brought him fame; later, by constantly experimenting, he topped "Sawing a Woman in Two" with "A Living Miracle."

Servais Le Roy was equally persistent; he struggled for seven years before he perfected the "Asrah" levitation and disappearance.

Even when he finally evolved a practical method, he took the precaution for several weeks of having Leon Bosco stand in the wings with a tray of dishes. If something went wrong, Bosco was to stride out, stumble, and take a comedy fall. This was never necessary.

Dissimilar in style, temperament and appearance, Le Roy and Goldin were trendsetters. Their influence on both magicians of their own day and those who came later was prodigious.

18

Carter, Nicola, and Raymond

THREE American illusionists found it more profitable to work abroad than to compete with Kellar or his successor, Thurston. Carter the Great, Nicola, and The Great Raymond returned periodically to perform in the United States, but they scored their greatest triumphs in Australia, the Orient, or South America.

Charles Joseph Carter was born in New Castle, Pennsylvania, on June 14, 1874; his parents came from Maryland, where one of his ancestors founded the town of Cartersville. He made his debut as a boy magician in Baltimore when he was ten. Later Carter traveled with a Kickapoo Indian medicine show, one of the many road troupes offering entertainment as a prelude to the sale of bottled remedies. Billed as "Master Chas. Carter, America's Youngest Prestidigitateur," he topped a variety bill at a Texas opera house at the age of seventeen.

Carter graduated from Rockhill College in Maryland and studied law in Illinois. He married at twenty and toured with his wife, Corinne, in a music hall act, "The Escape from Sing Sing." A committee from the audience shackled Corinne and locked her in a cage on the stage of Frank Hall's Casino in Chicago in December 1894. A reporter from the *Dispatch* said Carter covered the cage with a canopy and "In less than thirty seconds she makes her appearance at the front of the theatre . . . sitting quietly in her former place, the cage, a desperate-looking criminal is seen."

After the birth of their son, Lawrence, in El Paso, Texas, on

March 9, 1895, Corinne complained that the escape feat was too strenuous. Carter stored the cage. In July he opened with "The Phantom Bride," at Kohl and Middleton's Clark Street Museum in Chicago. Tied to a chair, Corinne was hoisted six feet above the floor. The magician fired a pistol; she disappeared as the empty chair crashed down.

To avoid paying an agent 10 percent of his salary, Carter established his own booking office with Mat Rand in charge. Rand's principal objective was to keep Carter working for the highest possible fees. Lyceum shows were in demand; groups sponsoring lectures, musical evenings, and dramatic presentations found Carter's program of "Psychomany and Telepathy" appealing. Corinne, while blindfolded, described objects shown to her husband as he walked among the audience. A carved wooden hand, isolated on a sheet of glass resting between the backs of two chairs, rapped out answers to questions. Carter, tied hand and foot behind the closed doors of a cabinet, caused various musical instruments to play. The climax came when he escaped from his bonds.

In Carter's *Magic and Magicians,* a book published in 1903, he advised prospective conjurers "to talk glibly, with earnestness, unction and sang-froid"—an apt description of his own style. He said magicians should strive to make their spectators laugh, "for when they laughed you are sure they are pleased."

Carter was thirty-one when he embarked on his first world tour. Thurston's success in Australia and Asia prompted theatre managers in those areas to seek another illusionist with similar skill and showmanship. They were impressed by Carter's fine lithographic advertisements and the enthusiastic American reviews of his show.

Carter opened in Sydney in November 1907. After four weeks, the *Bulletin* said his most astonishing feat was "transforming the Palace Theatre from an empty to a crowded house, which incomprehensible act he has been doing nightly for a month." Five months later the Carter appeal was equally potent at the Zorilla Theatre in Manila. "The boxes were filled with beautifully gowned women and properly attired men. . . . Hundreds were turned away," the *Cable-News American* reported.

A plague ravished China during Carter's stay. In Fuchow a spectator became convulsive and died in his seat during the show. Disease was rampant in India; a Carter assistant died of scarlet fever. "Wherever one goes, one shakes hands with smallpox, elbows cholera, or is quarantined against bubonic plague," the magician wrote in an article on his experiences. There were other hazards; train wrecks, for instance; he and his company survived a crash near Bombay.

While he was appearing at the Printania Theatre in Cairo in February 1909. Carter heard marvelous stories about a snake charmer who produced reptiles from nowhere in the desert near the royal tombs in Upper Egypt. The inquisitive magician went to Luxor in search of a possible explanation. Early one morning Carter crossed the Nile and sat behind a mound near the place where the snake charmer each day performed. Eventually an old Egyptian and a boy carrying a sack arrived. Looking around to satisfy themselves that no one was watching, they took snakes and scorpions from the bag and secreted them in crevices and under rocks. Then they went away. Carter joined a throng of tourists to watch the show that followed. The other onlookers were properly awed as the miracle worker coaxed living creatures from the barren ground.

After covering a distance he estimated to be equivalent to three times the circumference of the earth, Carter returned to Chicago in May 1909. He played several theatres, booked by Edgar Healy, Kellar's former business manager, hired Fritz Bucha, a skilled mechanic who had worked as Kellar's stage manager, then crossed the Pacific again. The show opened in Honolulu in October with Carter featuring Kellar's levitation. Neither Kellar nor Thurston who had become his official successor were aware that Bucha had made an unauthorized copy of the complicated lifting device.

In November, during Carter's second tour of Australia, the Brisbane *Telegraph* reported that he drew even larger crowds than he had on his first visit. This trip he also performed on the west coast of the continent and toured New Zealand. Then, rather than face the discomfort and disease of the Orient, Carter sailed for England. *The Magical World* covered his opening in November 1910, at the Palace Theatre in Manchester. Performing in a setting of crimson and green curtains, he won approval by "sheer merit." A red silk handkerchief vanished from a crystal decanter and immediately appeared in a transparent bottle on a table some distance away. He converted bran, confetti, and sawdust to hot coffee, sugar, and cold milk. A girl materialized after an empty trunk was lined with sheets of glass and spun around. The "Spirit Rapping Hand" provoked the laughs Carter insisted should be included in any program of magic. Kellar's levitation, "a perfect mystery skillfully executed," was followed by a "Spirit Cabinet" routine. Later a girl passed invisibly from one cabinet with slatted sides to another when Carter shouted, "Flyto." The act ended with the disappearance of his wife as she sat in a chair suspended above the stage.

Carter's first performances in Britain were booked through an agent. Positive he could do better himself, Carter negotiated subsequent deals. Christmas week at the Rotunda Theatre in Dublin, he played to capacity business and, sharing the receipts, netted four times the amount he would have made on a straight salary.

After a year in the British Isles, Carter moved on to Europe. The Great Lafayette had died in an Edinburgh theatre fire in May 1911; a

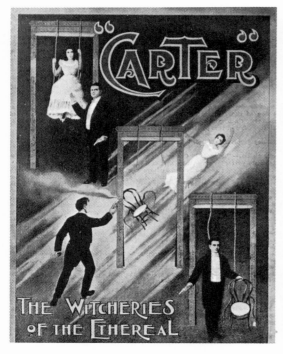

Carter's wife disappeared when he fired a pistol; the chair fell to the stage.

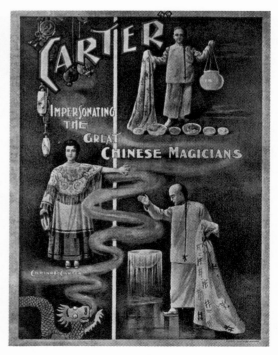

A Chinese sequence in the Ching Ling Foo manner was a part of the Carter show.

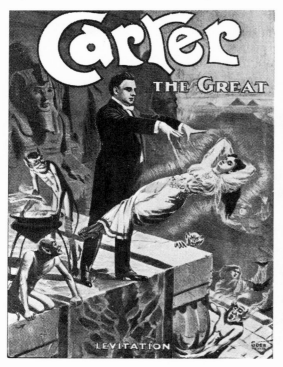

Carter's levitation was a pirated copy of the Kellar presentation.

Like The Great Lafayette, Carter drew immense audiences with a lion illusion.

replica of his "Lion's Bride" illusion was Carter's feature in Liège in November. Carter did not ride out on a white horse as Lafayette had done, but Belgian papers reported the bewildering change of a live lion to a livelier magician had been handsomely staged.

The lion illusion was one of the best investments Carter ever made. It drew five thousand spectators to the Coliseu dos Recreios in Lisbon in January 1912. A few months later, Carter headlined with this feat in vaudeville houses in California; then he performed in Midwest America. His full evening show at the Crown Theatre in Chicago in May 1912 included the mental act he and his wife had used in earlier years and an Oriental scene with Carter and his assistants in embroidered costumes he had purchased in China. The most striking number was the Ching Ling Foo production of a huge bowl of water.

Carter's thirty-minute vaudeville act at Proctor's Fifth Avenue Theatre in New York in 1913 drew standing-room-only audiences and brought him engagements in the principal cities of the East. By the end of 1916 he had enough money to retire. Within a few months he bought the New York firm of Martinka and Co., the oldest magic supply house in America, and the forty-three-year-old illusionist told friends he planned to open branch shops across the United States. He also intended to run a booking agency and to give personal instruction in conjuring.

Carter advertised his "$25,000 show" for sale in 1917. When no one made him a reasonable offer, he sailed in November for a month's engagement in Havana. Then, leasing the Belmont Theatre on West Forty-eighth Street in New York, Carter opened on Broadway on the evening of April 9, 1918. *Billboard* said he was clever and witty; the other reviews were sour. *Variety* found the acting in "The Lion's Bride" skit "almost as atrocious as the lion seems ferocious." The *New York Clipper,* another theatrical weekly, headed its account, "Carter the Great Should Go Back to Vaudeville Again." Carter had hoped to establish a permanent theatre of magic at the Belmont; his "indefinite" run ended in two weeks.

In June the magician tried to sell the Martinka magic shop. Ten months later, Houdini, Alf Wilton, and John Collins bought it. Doomsayers said Carter's career as an illusionist was over; he was not listening. He took his show on the road and formed the Carter Film Corporation in San Francisco. The illusionist attracted "big crowds" at the San Francisco Hippodrome in August 1919, according to *Variety*. He sailed for Australia and New Zealand again the following year, and in February 1921 opened at the Criterion Theatre in Natal, South Africa. A publicity story said Carter's male assistants wore the liveries of the royal household in Britain; the magician had purchased them after King Edward VII's death. Baby, Carter's lion, another newspaper article re-

323

Carter, Nicola, and Raymond

vealed, had been captured in Africa by Manuel II, the deposed King of Portugal.

A tour of Japan late in 1922 was beset by difficulties. The White City Company of Tokyo, which brought Carter there, canceled his show after a nine-week stretch of bad business. Then the Japanese firm entered suit against him for a $28,000 loss. Though the court refused to hear this complaint, the personal possessions of the troupe as well as the stage paraphernalia were seized. Carter's assistants made a surprise raid on the warehouse and carried the crates and baggage to the street. As they were loading them into a truck, warehouse employees rushed out to do battle; they drove the invaders off and lugged the material back into the building.

Carter recovered his property in five weeks and filed a $22,500 damage suit against the White City Company and its officers, which a Tokyo District Court agreed to hear. This in itself was a victory. Other American entertainers stranded in Nippon by Japanese promoters, had tried in vain to get a hearing on their cases. Carter vowed to fight until he collected. This took seven years, but the tenacious conjurer won.

Carter played the Curran Theatre in San Francisco on his return from Japan in June 1923. Then, after other West Coast bookings, he was off again for Australia in 1924, featuring "Beauty and the Beast" and a new version of Horace Goldin's "Sawing a Woman in Two." Carter sliced through the table on which the box rested as well as the box, then pulled the sections apart so he could walk between them.

When Baby, the aging lion, became too ill to work in 1926, "Beauty and the Beast" was dropped from the show. Remembering Houdini's success with "The Vanishing Elephant," Carter decided to build a similar illusion. Models were constructed for several ingenious cabinets, none of which met with his approval. He tried a different approach. As he visualized the feat, an elephant would stand on a platform; curtains would be lowered around it; then platform and elephant would be hauled into the air. The curtains would be raised just enough for the audience to see the pachyderm's feet; then they would be dropped to the level of the platform. A pistol shot from the illusionist would cause the elephant to disappear. Carter built the apparatus, bought an elephant, and began to rehearse. There was an unexpected complication; the elephant would not cooperate. She bolted from the platform as it was being raised. The show opened at His Majesty's Theatre in Brisbane in 1927 with four girls ("The Disappearing Flappers") vanishing on the platform instead of the elephant.

In October in New Zealand Carter read a newspaper item saying the Federal Taxation Department in Sydney had started proceedings against him. Inquiry disclosed that this "Carter the Great" was an Australian imitator who had neglected to pay taxes on the tickets sold for his performance in a village town hall.

Carter performed in South Africa for the third time in May 1928. After a cross-country itinerary, he played in Jerusalem, en route to Germany and other European countries. The last stop was Moscow. On his return to San Francisco in July 1930 Carter stated emphatically that he would never go to Russia again; the Soviet government had imposed a 40 percent tax on his gross receipts.

Billed as "The Last of the Great Magicians," Carter headlined at the RKO Golden Gate Theatre in San Francisco and the Pantages Theatre in Oakland in the fall of 1932. Then, at the age of fifty-eight he began preparing for his most exciting theatrical venture—a "Temple of Mystery" at the Century of Progress Exposition in Chicago. Carter approved blueprints for an all-steel structure 123 feet long, 50 feet wide, and 30 feet high; the area would seat from five- to seven-hundred people. He advertised in the theatrical papers for "East Indian fakirs, Egyptian magicians, beautiful girl dancers and aerialists, Borneo fire eaters, Mexican Marimba musical acts and bands, men who freeze themselves in ice, bury themselves alive, suspend animation, drink gallons of water and gasoline. . . . Electric magnetic wonders. . . . In fact, any attraction of extraordinary merit and magnitude for six months' engagement."

Replies flooded in from sword-swallowers and sideshow performers who danced on broken glass with their bare feet. Acts of "extraordinary merit" in the listed categories were either not available or demanded salaries beyond Carter's reach. He launched a publicity drive to promote his Chicago attraction. He "hypnotized" a girl, placed her in a sarcophagus decorated in the style of Pharaoh Tutankhamen, sealed the lid, and signaled for a crane to lift the "living cornerstone" for his building and deposit it in the ground. Carter told reporters the girl would be buried for five months; then he would breach the tomb, and waken her.

The 1933 Chicago World's Fair attracted millions of patrons. They flocked to the pavilions filled with free attractions but spent little money for the shows on the midway. The "Fort Dearborn Massacre" shut down for restaging. Miller Brothers' "101 Ranch Wild West Show" played to receipts that would scarcely pay for the feed of their livestock. "The Army Show" closed after a twelve-day run.

Carter's "Temple of Mystery" with its exotic Egyptian facade did not attract the throngs he expected. As he was not feeling well, his son, Larry, stepped into the role of chief illusionist. Carter had announced earlier that when the fair was over he would make a present of his building to the Chicago Assembly of the Society of American Magicians, but when his receipts sagged in July, he sold the temple to the Thompson food chain for conversion into a restaurant. Fortunately for the "living cornerstone," her burial was just a skillfully executed trick; otherwise she would have been in the sarcophagus when the fair site was cleared, since Carter never got around to opening the tomb to revive her.

Carter was approaching his sixtieth birthday when he announced his eighth world tour. He could have, if he chose to, stayed in the San Francisco mansion he had built with the profits of previous tours. Furnished with antiques and rare Oriental works of art, it housed a private theatre. The longing to return to the area of his greatest successes, however, was overpowering.

Once more he journeyed to Australia and New Zealand, to Singapore, China, and Japan. His health deteriorated in Hong Kong early in 1935. His son, Larry, took over the presentation of the illusions; Carter himself appeared only in the mentalism portion of the program. He kept traveling—to Calcutta in January 1936 and to Bombay in February. A severe heart attack in Bombay led to his being hospitalized. He made his son swear that the show would go on as usual that night. Carter died the next day, February 13, at the age of sixty-one.

His friend and competitor, Nicola, summed up his career:

> Carter was not only a great magician, but a smart business man. I know because he and I played the same territory and dealt with the same managers. One never had to fear that Carter had run down the price. His show, which he presented in all parts of the world, was a credit to our profession. He mounted it lavishly, billed it like a circus, presented it with dignity and charm, and collected a princely fee for his efforts.

Had Carter been writing of Nicola, he would have said the same thing. Nicola was born William Mozart Nicol in Burlington, Iowa, on December 14, 1880. His grandfather, McNichol, had been a magician in Scotland. His father, John, dropped the *Mc* from his surname and added an *i*—Nicoli—when he, too, became a conjurer. He made enough performing in the United States to retire on a farm in Monmouth, Illinois. Will assisted in his father's shows and gave his first performance on his own in a sideshow at the 1897 Trans-Mississippi Exposition in Omaha, Nebraska. Rather than use the same professional name as his father, he changed the final *i* to an *a*, becoming Nicola.

Three years later, Will, then nineteen, worked his way across the country to Baltimore, carrying two suitcases of equipment. Hired as a cattle-handler on a ship bound for France, he was determined to conjure at the International Exposition in Paris. Luck was with him. Loie Fuller, the famous dancer, whose home was near Will's in Monmouth, introduced him to the producer of the show at the Théâtre Egyptien and he was hired to perform in pantomime in the revue.

Carter's mental feats provoked even more comment than his illusions.

One of the lithographs made for Carter's last tour of Australia and the Orient.

Carter card-game-with-Satan poster, inspired by a Servais Le Roy picture.

During his twenty-six weeks in the French capital, the short, chubby Midwesterner added many new tricks and, on his return to the United States, was ready to present an hour program on lyceum circuits. Like Houdini, then the greatest vaudeville attraction, Nicola escaped from handcuffs and trunks. These feats were only a small part of his repertoire. Gradually he added illusions. A doll placed in a small box became a girl when the box expanded behind the drapes of a cabinet. An assistant in Turkish costume sat on a chair as he used "mesmeric suggestion" to make her superhumanly strong. She extended her arms; heavy weights were attached to her wrists without causing her arms to bend. The secret was in the specially constructed chair. Metal rods came out from each side behind her arms; these, not her wrists supported the weights. Later the girl stood on a table and was wrapped in a sheet. The sheet was pulled away, leaving the tabletop bare. He threw the cloth over "The Throne of Delhi," then pulled it away to reveal the girl seated on the throne.

Nicola escaped from prison cells and, when tied to the Lake Shore Railway tracks in Cleveland, freed himself moments before a locomotive thundered along the rails. He also jumped, while handcuffed, from a St. Louis bridge and made his escape under the waters of the Mississippi in 1909.

Nicola's friend, Vic Hugo, a magician-mentalist who booked circus attractions, formed a syndicate in Chicago a year later to send American shows across the Pacific. Nicola was signed for an eighteen-month tour. The advance man wired from Hawaii, before the company sailed in May, saying the theatre where the show was to have opened had been destroyed by fire. "We play Honolulu regardless," the twenty-nine-year-old magician cabled back. The advance man knew the only other theatre large enough to house the illusion production was occupied by the McRae Stock Company. McRae was not inclined to terminate a profitable run to make way for a rival attraction.

The advance agent posted Nicola's bills on every available wall and fence in the city. "Opening Soon," they were headed; McRae wondered where. The agent told him Nicola carried a gigantic tent to set up in areas that were without a suitable playhouse. This tent would be erected on the vacant lot directly across the road from McRae's dramatic show. McRae made an offer. If the American would pay McRae's traveling expenses, the stock company would move to another city, leaving the theatre vacant. The agent accepted this stipulation; the tent had existed only in his imagination.

From Honolulu, Nicola went to China. When a theatre of sufficient size could not be found in Peking, Nicola built one. Coolie labor was cheap; a workman received the equivalent of ten American cents a day. Six hundred Chinese worked in three shifts around the clock, constructing a massive framework of bamboo by the side of the Hat-a-men Gate; this framework was covered with broad strips of woven, waterproofed grass. In five days a structure with room for three thousand spectators was finished.

In China, as in other countries with a language barrier, an on-stage interpreter was hired—sometimes with unexpected results. One night the audience roared with laughter when they should have been speechless with amazement. The translator had been adding explanatory asides: "I can see a secret compartment in the box"; "You think the lady is under the cloth; I saw her conceal herself in the chair."

Nicola escapes rated columns of praise in the Hong Kong dailies; even when he was stymied, the story made the papers. An insolent elevator operator aroused the mild-mannered magician to such fury that Nicola punched him on the jaw. The man took the car to the ground floor, darted out, slammed the door, and sent the elevator up until it was trapped between two floors. The hotel manager heard Nicola's shouts and came to the rescue.

Business was so good in India that Nicola's brother, Charles, who had been helping backstage, was sent out as Von Arx with a show of his own, using Will's spare equipment.

Private shows for Maharajahs netted Nicola jewels in addition to his fees. The gifts became more lavish as the tour progressed. Each ruler tried to outdo his predecessor's generosity. Nicola played Australia next; then South Africa. Audiences in one of the smaller African cities paid their way into the show with sacks of grain; wheat was the local medium of exchange. An export merchant converted Nicola's grain profits into cash. By the time the magician from Monmouth, Illinois, returned to New York in February 1913, he had circled the globe, and his eighteen-month booking had extended to almost three years.

Nicola went to South America after he bought new apparatus, stage settings, and costumes. In Buenos Aires he used quick-change costumes on the street. Newspaper advertisements said he would give the equivalent of five hundred American dollars to anyone who identified him on the Avenida de Mayo, where he would roam for an hour. The short busy thoroughfare was jammed almost shoulder to shoulder, but using a variety of disguises he eluded recognition.

Crossing the Pacific again in 1916, the magician, in addition to giving his show, became a partner with Vic Hugo and Hugo's brother, Charles, in a new business—supplying wild animals and rare birds to American zoos. Charles Hugo returned first with a cargo of black tigers and jungle birds. He had also bought a herd of Indian elephants, but he sold it at a large profit when his ship stopped in China. Then baby elephants, purchased in British East India for two hundred dollars, were sold for ten times that amount in Chicago. Nicola returned from his theatre tour in 1917 with a consignment of goldfish. Half of the fish had died en route, but he still made two thousand dol-

329

Carter, Nicola, and Raymond

lars on the deal. Charles Hugo later brought back the most fascinating collection of creatures ever unloaded from a single ship in San Francisco: elephants, tapirs, tigers, monkeys, pythons, and hundreds of exotic birds from China, India, Borneo, Sumatra, Siam, and Java. Then Hugo booked a tour for Nicola through the Southern States and the Middle West.

After the armistice was signed in November 1918, Nicola stored his illusions and, with his brother, Charles, who took a new name—The Great Chalbert—went to Europe to entertain the occupation troops with less bulky equipment. Then, in September 1919, Nicola went on tour again with his full-evening show. "Nicola to Be Hanged," posters and newspaper advertisements proclaimed in Natal, South Africa, on April 1, 1921. This was no April Fool joke; the smaller type explained he would be strapped in a straitjacket, then try to release himself while hanging upside down over the city streets. For twenty minutes the following day downtown traffic was at a standstill. There were calls for an investigation at a Town Council meeting. One member said the city's tram cars had lost an hour's revenue. Another proposed the magician make up the loss. A third said the transportation company had made money rather than lost it because more people than ever were riding the street cars to see Nicola's show. For nine months the show played to excellent business in South Africa, then Nicola embarked for Australia. He played to small houses there and in New Zealand. Receipts mounted in Java and for the rest of his itinerary, which like his former around-the-world tour took almost three years; there was no red ink in his ledger.

Not until 1926 when Houdini had progressed from a vaudeville act to a full-evening show did Nicola play in New York at a major vaudeville house. Twice that year he topped the bill at the Hippodrome, receiving, the trade papers reported without specifying the amount, more money than the famous escapologist had made there.

Nicola traveled as a headliner on the Keith, Albee, and Orpheum circuits for two years, then began another world tour. In 1931 he fulfilled an old ambition. On February 15 he opened with his illusions for a three-week engagement at the Studebaker Theatre in Chicago.

Those who thought they had seen all of Nicola's tricks were taken aback the following year when he toured in vaudeville. The act began when six boxes, each bearing a letter of his name, were stacked. The fronts opened simultaneously; Nicola stepped out. From a large bamboo screen, standing on edge and formed in an oval, he produced a gigantic imitation pig that walked on its hind legs, rolled its eyes, and stuck out its tongue. Most publicized of Nicola's feats was "The Vanishing Elephant." Nizey, the elephant, weighed a mere six hundred pounds. Nicola told reporters he had started out with a full-grown

Nicola performed in pantomime at the Exposition in Paris when he was nineteen.

In his later illusion show, Nicola wore exotic costumes and made many changes.

He met Ching Ling Foo in Omaha, then years later visited with him in China.

NATIONAL
THEATRE

Direction - - - J. C. WILLIAMSON LTD.

Sensational
MATINEE
Saturday Afternoon
JULY 1
at 2.30 p.m.

J. C. Williamson Ltd. present
The Acknowledged EMPEROR OF MAGIC:

NICOLA
WORLD'S MASTER OF MIRACLES

And his own BIG COMPANY of
SENSATIONAL MYSTIFIERS
AND
INTERNATIONAL STARS

MATINEE PRICES:
ADULTS: D. Circle & R. Stalls, 6s; Stalls, 4s;
Pit, 2s; Back Pit, 1s -- plus tax.
CHILDREN: 3s, 2s, 1s -- plus tax.
PLANS AT FINDLAY'S.

Thousands of handbills were distributed heralding the Nicola show in Australia.

animal, but each time Nizey disappeared, a few pounds wore off; she was now just a shadow of her former self.

The elephant made the papers regularly. There were pictures of her parading in the street, shaking the Mayor's hand with her trunk, and eating with the magician in popular restaurants. The animal's upkeep was small. In 1932 Nicola paid three dollars a day to house Nizey at the Ben Hur stables in New York and another dollar a day for her food.

Nicola married Marion Eddings, who had been his principal assistant for seventeen years, in New York on January 17, 1938. They spent their honeymoon traveling in England and Europe. Then in November, with the biggest and best show he had ever produced, Nicola opened at His Majesty's Theatre in Auckland, New Zealand. From the start this tour drew packed houses. Three rival attractions made their debuts the night he began an engagement in Melbourne. Six weeks later only the magic show was still running. In Java, Bali, and Singapore, the illusionist prospered, though the shadow of World War II was falling across the Pacific. Entry permits were becoming more difficult to get; there were new monetary restrictions, and sailing schedules were unpredictable. After the third week in Singapore, Nicola canceled advance bookings in Bangkok and Calcutta and engaged passage for Honolulu with his troupe aboard the British-Indian liner *Sirdhana.* Before the vessel sailed, he saw a small army of Chinese laborers being marched up the gangplank and down into the hold where, he heard, they were to be locked in cells. Singapore authorities said the Orientals had entered the Crown Colony illegally; they were to be landed at a Chinese port en route to Hawaii.

Shortly after the harbor pilot had climbed down the rope ladder into a waiting tugboat, a terrific explosion rocked the *Sirdhana;* the vessel had struck one of the British mines laid in the harbor as a protective measure. The fifty-eight-year-old illusionist and the members of his company were saved; lost in the wreckage with many lives were the crates that carried his "$100,000 Mystery Spectacle." Nicola told me later that the courageous action of two men on his staff, Eddie Gaillard (who with his wife starred in American night clubs as Lucille and Eddie Roberts with a telepathy act) and Chuck Vance (a talented young magician), saved more than fifty passengers from drowning.

Nicola sent his company on to the United States, but he and Marion stayed in Singapore. There was a possibility the section of the ship's hold where his baggage had been stored was still intact. He hired a deep-sea diver to fly over the water where the *Sirdhana* had gone down. The diver reported the ship was on her side. Later the diver submerged and probed, though nearby mines made this a hazardous operation. He thought the crates could be removed. Months of pleading with Singapore officials for permission to do this were to no avail. Anything recovered, the magician was told, would be the property of the salvage company. Rumors spread that Nicola had a fortune in precious stones hidden away in one of his trunks. He vehemently denied this. He said he wanted to get the measurements of his illusions. They might be waterlogged, but he could use them as prototypes for duplicates. It had taken him a lifetime to assemble and perfect these devices.

Finally Nicola gave up and returned to the United States. After America entered World War II, he volunteered to perform without pay at military camps and in service hospitals, but he was never to appear again with an illusion show. Nicola died at the age of sixty-five of a heart ailment on February 1, 1946, and was buried in the city where he had learned magic as a boy—Monmouth, Illinois.

The Great Raymond, the third of the American illusionists who won fame abroad, was born Maurice François Saunders in Akron, Ohio, on May 30, 1877. At nine he assisted an uncle who performed magic; a year later he worked with the Forepaugh Circus, driving ponies and performing on the trapeze. Raymond gave his first solo conjuring show when he was fifteen. Ten years later he was releasing himself from handcuffs and chains at Kohl and Middleton's Clark Street Museum in Chicago, advertised as "Greater than Houdini."

Raymond performed in California, Oregon, and Washington theatres in 1904 with an act that included escapology, "The Spirit Cabinet," and "The Substitution Trunk." His wife, Luella, impersonated Anna Held and other glamorous stars of the period.

The tall, broad-shouldered Ohioan met Harry L. Reichenbach, a young circus press agent, at Luna Park in Pittsburgh a few years later. Raymond said he was planning a world tour; Reichenbach, who was eager to travel abroad, became the magician's advance man. Raymond's favorite exploitation feat, an escape from a box made by a local manufacturer, drew packed houses as the show came East. Raymond, shackled and roped, was nailed in a crate. Usually he was out in ten minutes, but he did not always have such an easy time. In Rochester, Pennsylvania, on the night of January 18, 1907, almost an hour went by before his worried assistants dragged the box from the cabinet and told the challengers to rip off the lid.

Raymond, still bound, was pale and motionless. His wife screamed, and several women in the audience fainted as his limp body was lifted out. A doctor at the hospital where the unconscious escapologist was taken told a reporter that if Raymond had stayed in the air-tight container another five minutes he would have died of suffocation. Thereafter Raymond made sure air holes were drilled in all challenge boxes.

The Raymond show sailed for Cuba in the fall of 1907 with a program he described as "two-thirds mystery, one third vaudeville."

The Great Raymond enjoyed presenting full-evening shows but hated playing in vaudeville.

Notice in four languages posted backstage in theatres by Raymond.

From a box with paper sides, a girl materializes. Raymond and his wife help her emerge.

The opening at the forty-five hundred seat Teatro Nacional in Havana "drew the largest audience and the most money" in the theatre's history, Raymond reported in a letter to the *New York Dramatic Mirror*. His escapes from death cells in Cuban prisons sent the Latin crowds into frenzy, he continued; they "unhitched the horses from my carriage and drove me through the streets, cheering and waving hats, canes and handkerchiefs."

When Raymond opened at the Polythema Theatre in Bahia, Brazil, after his Cuban run, men in the audience hired by a rival theatre were less cordial. They came onstage when he asked for a committee, bringing their own chains, locks, and spools of fishline. They bound him so tightly his wrists were cut. Seeing blood trickle down his hands, the shocked audience was incensed. A dozen husky men left their seats, seized the torturers, and dragged them from the stage. "A riot was avoided," Raymond said in one of his letters, "by a squad of forty police."

News of his successful escape despite savage treatment spread. By midafternoon the next day the house was sold out for the evening performance.

Reichenbach, Raymond's press agent, suffered a severe attack of tropical fever in Brazil. He recovered, but his curly brown hair had turned snow white. The show traveled down the west coast of South America, up again, then across the Atlantic to England. Raymond arrived in London in November 1909. His opening week at the Hackney Empire Theatre the following January brought him excellent notices and a tour of the British Isles. A year later he played on the Continent; then he continued on around the world by way of Egypt, India, China, Japan, and Hawaii. Immigration officials boarded the ship that brought the magician to San Francisco in August 1912, and told Raymond his livestock and animals would not be permitted ashore. Despite his strenuous objections, the doves, ducks, rabbits, a trained pig, and several pet dogs were slaughtered and thrown overboard.

"The Globe-Trotting Funmaker, Magician, Humorist and Fantasist" began an American tour with his full-evening show at the Savoy Theatre in San Francisco, and arrived at the Studebaker Theatre in Chicago the following March.

Raymond told stories of his travels between tricks. Alfonso XIII of Spain had occupied the royal box at the theatre in Madrid every Thursday night. He invited the magician to perform at the palace. The orchestra was late. "I'll be the music," the impatient King said. He sat at the piano and played while Raymond conjured.

Chicago critics agreed the illusionist's best feats were catching live pigeons from thin air in a net; a huge production of birds, animals, and then a woman from a "Noah's Ark"; and the masterly disappearance of an assistant floating in the air. The *Record-American*

Carter, Nicola, and Raymond

MAGICIAN

Production of 24 lighted Cigarettes from mouth. The Macbeth mystery, Dove Tub illussion. The Burning watch mystery, Ring mystery Hanging rope trick. Fairy drum illussion and several others too numerous to mention.

Professor - - - - AGNI.

The Worlds' Master Magician Hypnotist and Illusionist in his Numerous and Startling effects.

Is open to ENGAGEMENTS for PRIVATE PARTIES "AT HOME" and evening ENTERTAINMENTS.

Ladies and Gentlemen.

I wish to draw the attention of all who desire to learn Magical tricks. etc., etc. These can be taught in a very short time.

Charges on Application.

Permanent Address :—
Beadon Street Gandanala, DELHI.

Delhi magician Agni performed feats introduced by traveling magicians.

reviewer observed that "Herrmann was taciturn and Kellar was silent as the grave compared to this Niagara of language." The *Tribune* critic was more impressed by Raymond's wizardry than his words: "He breaks an egg into a flaming chafing dish and produces three ducks, and he turns water into wine and pink paper into coffee. Marvelous."

While in Chicago the illusionist sued for a divorce from his wife; she had deserted him three years earlier. Following four weeks at the Studebaker, Raymond topped a vaudeville bill at the Majestic with a shortened version of his show, then signed for the summer season at White City, an amusement park.

His second tour of Latin America was more extensive than the first, including Puerto Rico, Mexico, Central America, Panama, and to quote from one of his letters, "all of South America." On his way across the Atlantic to perform in the Azores, his plans were changed by German submarines. The captain of the ship bypassed the Portuguese islands and went directly to Lisbon. "The kind Kaiser's war craft cost me a nice sum, as we had theatres booked, deposits and rents paid, towns billed and six weeks' lost salary to pay the advance agent," Raymond lamented in a letter to another world traveler, Harry Kellar.

Still luck was with him. The star of the Coliseu dos Recreios in Lisbon was ill; Raymond filled in as a last-minute replacement. After playing to "smashing business" in Portugal, the show went to Spain and France, then to the British Isles, where "The Supremest of Sorcerers" toured the provinces and played thirty-one weeks in and around London alone. He purchased a building, installed a workshop, and hired workmen to make new equipment for the show. On a brief visit to the United States in 1920 Raymond learned that another "Maurice Raymond" was performing in New England. He instructed a lawyer to enter suit against this blatant imitator. The lawyer reported the illusionist had no grounds for legal action; the man's real name turned out to be Maurice Raymond.

Before the illusionist left the British Isles for a tour that was to encompass Europe and South America, Raymond added a harpist to his troupe. Pearl Beatrice Gonser Evans, the beautiful young widow of a British army officer, had seen Raymond perform when she was a girl, and had told a friend that one day she intended to marry the magician with the winning smile and carefree manner. In the intervening years she had studied at the Royal Conservatory of Music in Brussels and had been a soloist with several symphony orchestras. She became the second Mrs. Raymond while the show was in Uruguay in January 1927. An American ship in the harbor at Montevideo was sailing for New York. They boarded the vessel, were married at sea "on American soil" with a Senator from Ohio and the American Vice-

Consul to Uruguay acting as witnesses; then the newlyweds boarded a tugboat and headed back for the dock.

When this tour of Latin America ended in Mexico in June 1930, Raymond performed in California. The following year he headed a Fanchon and Marco vaudeville unit, then came east with a thirty-minute act.

Eight girl trumpeters heralded his mysterious appearance. He materialized in a metal archway from a cloud of smoke. Covering two large glass bowls with cloths, he pulled the cloths away to show the bowls heaped high with oranges. Pigeons were snared in the magician's empty net. Flowers were tossed from a tray into the audience; the tray changed into a pagoda from which ribbons spiraled down to fill a tub. Suddenly three ducks appeared in the mass of ribbons. Displaying a large empty cabinet, Raymond produced eight girls from it; then he stepped inside and disappeared.

The girls marched, played on drums, and danced before Raymond reappeared. He broke through two drumheads to produce rabbits; birds came from the others. The birds vanished in a box; a girl appeared in a framework cabinet with paper sides after Raymond held a lighted bulb behind each panel to prove the cabinet was empty. He tore sheets of tissue paper, crumpled the pieces, and converted them into a paper hat for one of his assistants. A girl vanished from a chair hoisted in the air. His wife, who used the stage name Litzka, put on a coat borrowed from a man who had volunteered to come up on the stage. Raymond reached in the pockets and found a strange assortment of bottles and lingerie. Then Litzka was tied in a sack and locked in a trunk. Assistants pushed a canopied cabinet forward to cover it. Raymond took off his tailcoat, entered the canopy, and in three seconds Litzka came out. The trunk was opened; the sack was untied; he was inside it, wearing the volunteer's coat.

During the ensuing years Raymond played vaudeville, which he disliked because of the many shows a day, and presented full-evening programs, which he thoroughly enjoyed. The Magicians' Guild and *The Conjurors' Magazine* sponsored his last Manhattan appearance at Town Hall on September 10, 1945. He died in New York on January 27, 1948, at the age of seventy.

Raymond survived two World Wars, and several revolutions. A bullet went through his hat during a street skirmish in Portugal; another penetrated a Mexican theatre wall and struck the tip of his bow tie.

Few Americans, even magicians, knew the extent of Raymond's travels, or of Nicola's or Carter's, nor were they aware of their stature in international show business.

19

Houdini

HARRY Houdini, a short muscular man with curly dark hair, an infectious smile and a compulsive drive to succeed, became a legend in his own time. Unexcelled escape artist, silent film star, scourge of fraudulent mediums, and eventually presenter of an illusion show that many critics said was more exciting than Thurston's, he had an almost uncanny understanding of audience psychology.

Will Rogers, the cowboy humorist, in one of his syndicated newspaper columns recalled waiting impatiently in the wings of Keith's Theatre in Philadelphia while Houdini tackled a handcuff challenge. Periodically the manacled showman came from his curtained cabinet "to size up the audience and see just about how they were standing it." When he was in the enclosure struggling to free himself, there "was not a thing going on, a whole theatre full [of people] just waiting." Finally—ninety minutes later—the perspiring Houdini emerged triumphant. After that, Rogers admitted, "I might just as well have got on my little pony and ridden back to the livery stable as to have ridden out on that stage."

The man who billed his vaudeville act as "The Impossible Possible" was born Ehrich Weiss (Erik Weisz) in Budapest on March 24, 1874. Brought to Appleton, Wisconsin, as a child in his mother's arms, he steadfastly maintained in later years that he had been born there on April 7. This was the date on which his mother, Cecilia Weiss, always celebrated the event, perhaps to give him the security of American citizenship. After his beloved mother died, Houdini wrote his brother Theo that he would continue to observe his "adopted" birthday on the date she had chosen.

Houdini's father, Mayer Samuel Weiss, earned $750 a year as Appleton's first rabbi. When the bearded Hungarian was replaced by a younger man, the family moved to Milwaukee. At nine Ehrich performed on a makeshift trapeze in a friend's backyard circus. Three years later he ran away from home, hoping to contribute more to his impoverished parents than he could make shining shoes and selling papers.

Samuel Weiss left for New York shortly afterward; he thought a teacher of religion might do better in a city with a larger Jewish population. Ehrich worked his way East to join his father; between them, they saved enough to bring Cecilia and the other children to Manhattan.

Embedded in the palm of Ehrich's right hand was a bullet. Some time during his wanderings he had been shot. The skin had healed, but he was to carry this reminder of his runaway days for the rest of his life. This led to one of the many Houdini myths: that this injury enabled him to make his hand smaller than his wrist and thereby release himself from handcuffs.

Young Ehrich learned to swim and dive in the East River, a few blocks from the Weiss flat on East Sixty-ninth Street, and he won medals as a junior member of a neighborhood track team that ran on a nearby lot. Determined to keep himself in top physical form, he resolved to exercise each morning to strengthen his muscles—and never to smoke or drink.

Magic was just one of the teen-ager's many interests until he read the *Memoirs of Robert-Houdin*. Enthralled by the story of the small-town clockmaker's apprentice who became France's greatest conjurer, Ehrich confessed to a friend, who worked across the bench from him in the necktie factory of H. Richters' Sons on lower Broadway, that his ambition was to be "like Robert-Houdin." That could easily be done, Jack Hayman (Jacob Hyman) replied, if Ehrich added an *i* to the Frenchman's last name. Hayman admitted he had been thinking of going into show business himself.

So after two and a half years as an assistant tie-lining cutter, Ehrich Weiss left his first steady job, and at the age of seventeen transformed himself into Houdini, the magician. He and Hayman broke in their new act playing single-night dates at fraternal meetings and beer halls. Discouraged when agents refused to book them for longer runs, Hayman quit. Theodore Weiss, Houdini's younger brother, eagerly took his place. Performing for the most part in dime museums on platforms adjacent to snake charmers, fire-eaters, and "human curiosities,"

Houdini—master
escapologist.

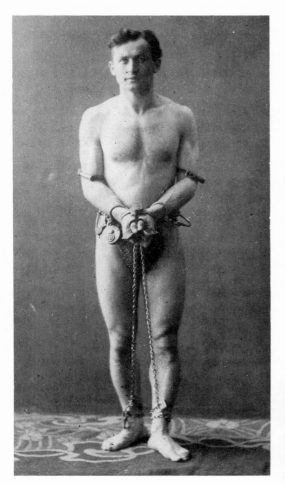

He was stripped and searched
before being locked in jails.

Early lithograph advertised
Houdini's skill with cards.

they traveled as far west as Chicago, where "The Brothers Houdini" worked during the 1893 World's Fair. Theo later explained how Ehrich became Harry. His friends had called him Ehrie or Erie; the transition was almost inevitable.

Though to the public he was Harry, he was always Ehrich to his parents. Before Samuel Weiss died at the age of sixty-three, he called his son to his bedside and had Ehrich swear on the Torah that he would provide for his mother as long as she lived. This vow was unnecessary. Cecilia had made the costumes for his first magic act, and she encouraged him in his chosen career. He loved his mother dearly, and the bond between them grew stronger with the passage of the years.

Houdini prided himself on his skill as a card manipulator, but his most applauded feat was an illusion he called "Metamorphosis." John Nevil Maskelyne had introduced the basic principle in England, and Herrmann the Great's assistants had performed a similar transposition in the United States.

The Houdini version had two strong selling points. Until then, no one had thought of tying the performer's wrists as part of the build-up, and the switch was made with lightning-like rapidity. A spectator bound Harry's hands behind his back with a length of tape, then helped Theo tie him in a bag and lift him into a large wooden box. The box was padlocked and doubly secured with rope. Theo pulled a framework cabinet with cloth sides around the box. "When I clap my hands three times—behold a miracle!" he announced, then stepped inside and closed the drapes. A moment after the third clap sounded, Harry threw open the curtains. Swiftly he removed the rope, opened the padlocks, and raised the lid of the box. Inside the bag, tied exactly as Houdini had been, was his brother.

Theo made this switch rapidly; Houdini's wife, Bess—Wilhelmina Beatrice Rahner—was even faster. Harry was twenty when he met and impulsively married the tiny brunette singer, who weighed ninety-four pounds. Her widowed Catholic mother was furious, but the understanding Cecilia welcomed the newlyweds to her apartment. Bess soon began working with Harry, and Theo went on the road with another girl, "Madame Olga," as the assistant for his featured barrel escape.

Harry and Bess Houdini played twenty-six weeks in 1895 with the Welsh Brothers Circus, a small tent show, which maintained winter quarters in Lancaster, Pennsylvania. When not presenting magic, working with his wife in a mind-reading act, or exhibiting Punch and Judy in the sideshow, Harry sold soap, combs, toothpaste, and other necessities to fellow performers.

He spent his free hours pursuing a new hobby—handcuffs. He discovered they could be opened with a concealed duplicate key or a pick—a small piece of metal or bent wire. A single key would open every manacle of the same pattern. With less than a dozen hidden keys and picks, Houdini thought he could escape from any fetter then in use by the various police departments in the United States. Rare or unusual cuffs required special handling. He read every scrap of information he could find on locking mechanisms; he began collecting manacles and took them apart to study their construction.

Though Harry sent half of his weekly twenty-dollar salary to his mother, by the end of the tour he had saved enough to buy an interest in *The American Gaiety Girls,* a burlesque show. His cousin, Harry Newman, was the company's advance man, traveling ahead of the production, booking theatres, and arranging for publicity.

The investment seemed wise. The Houdinis would be working regularly, and Harry could use his new escape skill to get free newspaper space for the show. The Gloucester, Massachusetts, *Times* reported on November 22, 1895, that Houdini had amazed the officers at the local police station by freeing himself from a pair of their official handcuffs. Items in other papers soon told of similar exploits. The Houdinis appeared to be well on their way to success. Then the show closed abruptly in Woonsocket, Rhode Island; the company manager had been arrested for embezzling the burlesque show's funds.

To fill the summer months, Houdini signed with "Marco the Magician" to tour Nova Scotia. Marco—Edward J. Dooley, a Connecticut church organist—had hoped to emulate Herrmann the Great, but business was so bad in Halifax that the would-be master conjurer gave up and returned to his regular occupation in Bridgeport.

Houdini stayed on in Canada, determined to succeed on his own. He was playing in St. John, the principal city of New Brunswick, when he accompanied a doctor friend on his rounds in a mental institution. Houdini watched in shocked fascination as attendants rolled a patient in sheets and strapped him to a cot to subdue him. In a padded cell a straitjacketed man tried feverishly to free himself. Houdini thought an escape from a leather-and-canvas punishment suit would be effective on the stage. He obtained a straitjacket through the physician and, after a week of strenuous practice, was ready to try his skill before an audience.

Volunteers buckled Houdini in, carried him to his cabinet, and Bess closed the curtains. He had gained some slack by holding his crossed arms rigidly as the sleeve straps were fastened. Straining every muscle, bit by bit, he forced one sleeve and then the other over his head; then he opened the straps with the pressure of his fingers through the canvas. Twisting and turning, he finally squirmed free, threw off the restraint, and came from between the curtains to take a bow. The escape fell flat. The audience hadn't seen him struggle; they thought a concealed assistant had released him. Houdini had not yet

343

Houdini

Houdini's notes describing
how a lock could be opened.

Advertisements in theatrical
publications kept agents
informed of his successes.

learned how to hold a crowd with, as Will Rogers put it, "not a thing going on" on the stage.

On the voyage back to Boston, Harry was violently seasick. This malady intensified with the years; eventually even the sight of a vessel standing motionless at a dock would cause his stomach to churn.

The Houdinis experienced their worst winter season in 1896, and bookings still eluded them in the spring. In August Harry wrote Harry Kellar and Herrmann the Great, offering to work with his wife as their assistants. Kellar said his staff had been engaged; he wished Houdini luck. Herrmann failed to answer. John Nevil Maskelyne refused to hire the Houdinis for Egyptian Hall in London because he had not seen their act.

In the fall of 1897, Houdini toured with a Midwestern medicine show. Dr. Hill, the proprietor, sold bottled cure-alls to the crowds that gathered on small-town street corners to watch the free entertainment supplied by members of his troupe. After the last possible dollar had been made, Hill invited the people to come to the local town hall to see his far-famed "California Concert Company."

When the proprietor mentioned to Houdini that a professional spirit medium had been attracting sizable audiences in that territory, Harry volunteered to stage a séance as part of the performance. The rabbi's son made his debut as a "spiritualist" on January 9, 1898, in the Galena, Kansas, Opera House. Tied to a chair in his cabinet by a committee from the audience, he pretended to go into a trance. Once the curtains were closed, a mandolin played softly and bells and tambourines sounded before they shot over the top of the enclosure and crashed to the stage. When the curtains were opened, he was still firmly tied. Once more the curtains were closed, and he was "freed from his bonds by spirits." Houdini then walked to the front of the stage, closed his eyes, and transmitted messages from the dead.

He had prepared for this, the most convincing part of his performance, by listening to local gossip, reading back numbers of the Galena newspaper, and copying names and dates from tombstones in cemeteries. When Houdini pretended to contact the spirit of a lame man whose throat had been cut and spelled out the victim's name, Negroes in the gallery fled from the theatre. They had no intention of staying under the same roof with a mystic who could talk with a former citizen whose horrible murder had shocked the town.

The medicine show tour ended, and Houdini still found it difficult to book his magic-and-escape act. He and Bess traveled as professional mediums before they were signed to play another season with the Welsh Brothers Circus. At twenty-four Houdini was still on the lowest rung of the show business ladder. One more year, Harry promised his wife, then if he didn't make a hit, he would give up magic and work at some more profitable trade.

A short, plump man with a German accent questioned Houdini after his performance in a small hall in St. Paul, Minnesota, early in 1899. Could he free himself from other manacles? Or just those used in the show? Harry boasted that the restraint had yet to be made that would hold him. The next evening the man returned with his own fetters, locked them on Houdini's wrists, and pocketed the key. When the brash young escapologist justified his boast, the stranger introduced himself. He was Martin Beck, booker for the Orpheum vaudeville circuit. He offered Houdini a trial date in Omaha if Harry would drop his feats of magic and put together a handcuff act featuring challenge releases.

With Beck's aid, Houdini escaped from the small time and began his rise to fame. In Omaha, where he played for a week and received sixty dollars—the most money he had ever earned—the escape artist slipped from five pairs of police shackles and a set of regulation leg irons. By the time he reached California, his salary had jumped to ninety dollars. Stripped to the skin in the office of the San Francisco detective force and thoroughly searched by a police surgeon, Houdini divested himself of ten pairs of handcuffs, a wide leather belt used to subdue maniacal prisoners, and a regulation straitjacket. These escapes took place behind the closed door of a closet. Neither the officials nor a reporter from the *Examiner* had any idea how this was done. The lengthy newspaper account of Houdini's feat did not mention that he had visited the detective's office in advance to inspect the restraints and the closet.

When Houdini's salary soared to $150 a week, he ran large ads in the trade papers to make sure the theatrical world knew of his accomplishments:

> Who created the biggest Sensation in California since the Discovery of Gold in 1849?
> WHY! HARRY HOUDINI! The ONLY recognized and undisputed King of Handcuffs and Monarch of Leg Shackles.

Martin Beck used the stacks of newspaper stories and sheafs of box-office reports from the Orpheum tour to sell Houdini to the Keith circuit in the East as a headliner.

To publicize his first date at the Orpheum Theatre in Kansas City, Harry had escaped from handcuffs at the Central Police Station. When he returned after playing the Keith houses, he introduced his second major publicity stunt. Stripped naked, fastened at his wrists and ankles by five pairs of irons, Houdini was locked in a cell. In less than eight minutes he was free of the manacles—and of the jail. He wrote a new headline for his advertisements: "Champion Jail Breaker." Understandably he made no mention of an embarrassing incident that had happened in the lobby of the Savoy Hotel in Kansas

City. A traveling salesman, E. P. Wilkins, recognized the escapologist as he went into a closet to make a phone call. The salesman borrowed the key to the telephone cubicle from the desk clerk and locked the door. When Harry hung up the receiver and tried to get out, he was furious. He yelled, kicked, and battered at the barrier until a crowd gathered. Then the distraught hotel manager persuaded the salesman to unlock the door. Thereafter whenever Houdini entered a phone booth that could be locked from the outside, he kept one foot firmly lodged between the door and the frame.

Eager to travel abroad, Houdini sailed with his wife for England without a booking. He had to convince a dubious theatre manager that he could escape from handcuffs at Scotland Yard before he received his first contract in Britain.

In July 1900, Houdini opened to acclaim at the Alhambra Theatre in London; then he traveled to the Continent where he set new box-office records in Dresden and Berlin. The demand for vaudeville handcuff acts became so great that he brought his brother Theo from New York and sent him on tour billed as Hardeen. Within a year Houdini was the strongest variety attraction in Europe.

"The Elusive American" did not claim to be the first to escape from manacles. In his press interviews he cited the Biblical account of what took place after King Herod jailed Saint Peter in Jerusalem. An angel appeared and commanded the prophet to rise up "and his chains fell off his hands." However, Houdini never mentioned Samri S. Baldwin, "The White Mahatma," who released himself from handcuffs during a performance in New Orleans, Louisiana, in 1871.

Houdini stated emphatically that he was the first to accept challenges from all comers, and he was ready to back up his claim. When Werner Graf, a German policeman, wrote a derisive article in July 1901, accusing Houdini of lying when he said he could escape from *any* police restraint, Harry sued Graf for slander. Though the American lost profitable playing time as he fought this case through two appeal courts in Cologne, he eventually won the suit. Houdini celebrated by issuing a new advertising lithograph showing himself wearing evening clothes and manacles before the highest German tribunal. "Apology in the name of King Wilhelm II, Kaiser of Germany," he titled the lithograph; there also were a few words explaining that his detractor had been forced to publish an apology in the Kaiser's name and to pay all court costs.

Houdini was not the type to ignore an insult. Engelberto Kleppini, an escape artist with the Circus Sidoli, advertised in 1902 that he had defeated the American in a handcuff competition. When Houdini heard this, he traveled from Holland to Dortmund, Germany, to confront his detractor. Wearing a false moustache, he took a seat in the stands. He sat through the show until Kleppini told the audience he

Wagon bringing Houdini's paraphernalia to the Hippodrome in Poplar, England.

His assistants rode with the equipment to the Empire Theatre in Croydon.

had been the victor in a contest with Houdini; then Harry took a running leap into the ring, ripped off his disguise, and waving a handful of bank notes, challenged the startled performer: five thousand marks said Kleppini couldn't escape from a pair of Houdini handcuffs; and another five thousand said Houdini could get out of Kleppini's "Chinese Pillory."

Prodded by the business manager of the Circus Sidoli, Kleppini agreed to allow Houdini to lock him into a set of French letter-cuffs the next night. Before show time, the business manager had seen the manacles; Houdini had shown him how the five cylinders could be turned to spell out c-l-e-f-s—the French word for keys—and open the cuffs.

Kleppini entered his cabinet confidently. Thirty minutes passed; then the structure was moved to the side of the ring to permit the rest of the show to continue. After the program ended, roustabouts lifted the cabinet again. Kleppini ran across the ring to the manager's office—still shackled. It was almost 1 A.M. before the manager ordered Kleppini to give up. Harry spun the cylinders until the letters F-R-A-U-D fell into place; he had changed the combination before the manacles were snapped on his competitor's wrists.

If the police failed to challenge Houdini, he challenged them. During his engagement at the Establishment Yard, a cabaret in Moscow, in May 1903, the escapologist dared the chief of the Russian secret police to imprison him in one of the "escape-proof" jails on wheels designed to transport enemies of the state to exile in Siberia. Harry had seen one of these strange horse-drawn vans on the street. He had examined it while the horses drank from a roadside trough. Escape was impossible from the front, sides, bottom, or top but the entrance door at the back was fastened by a single padlock—and there was a small barred window within arm's reach of the keyhole.

On the occasion of his challenge, Houdini was stripped, searched, manacled hand and foot, then locked inside the van. The entrance door was turned away from the police as they watched from the far side of a courtyard. Harry was out in twenty minutes. The indignant police refused to confirm his escape, but the news spread rapidly, and soon there was a handsome lithograph showing the American magician outwitting the Russian secret police.

Four thousand spectators jammed into the London Hippodrome for the March 17, 1904, matinee to see Houdini accept a defy from the Daily Illustrated Mirror. A pair of special handcuffs with six sets of locks and nine tumblers in each cuff was clamped on his wrists. A Birmingham mechanic had spent five years constructing these formidable manacles. The cabinet Houdini used to cover his release was considerably smaller than the one he employed in his "Metamorphosis" illusion. He knelt to enter the cabinet at 3:15 P.M. Within twenty minutes his head popped over the top. At first the audience thought he was free, but he just wanted to get more light on the cuffs. He dropped back out of view again. At the end of thirty-five minutes he pushed aside the front curtain and came out. Still shackled, he stood up.

Perspiration dripped from his face. His stiff collar had wilted and broken. He said his knees were sore, and he limbered up as the *Daily Mirror* representative sent an usher to get a pillow. With his knees on the pillow inside the enclosure, Houdini set to work again. After twenty minutes more, he put his head out and asked the *Daily Mirror* spokesman to open one handcuff so that he could take off his coat. This request was refused. Harry then stood up, twisted his manacled hands until he could reach a pocketknife in his vest pocket. He took out the knife, yanked the blade open with his teeth, then pulled the coat over his head until it was bunched in front of his body. Gripping the hilt of the knife between his teeth, he sliced the coat into ribbons and threw the pieces aside before he returned to the cabinet. This dazzling display of determination and skill brought roars of approval from the spectators.

Sixty minutes had passed. As the hands on the timekeeper's watch moved to the hour and ten minutes mark, Houdini suddenly sprang out from the enclosure. His wrists were free; he held the manacles in the air. Pandemonium broke loose. The audience cheered, applauded, and stomped their feet. Some of the committeemen lifted Harry to their shoulders and paraded him around the stage. Then Houdini's composure broke; tears streamed down his cheeks. He wiped them away before he accepted a hearty handshake and congratulations from the *Daily Mirror* man.

Four months after his return to American theatres, Houdini staged his most remarkable prison break at the United States Jail in Washington, D.C. On January 6, 1906, officials locked the nude escapologist in the cell on "Murderers' Row" that had once held Charles J. Guiteau, the assassin of President Garfield, then they locked his clothes in another cell and returned to the warden's office.

Working swiftly, Houdini freed himself. He proceeded to open all the doors and to shift the prisoners from one cell to another. He met no resistance, though the inmates were astonished by the sudden appearance of a naked man. After changing the housing arrangement of the entire block, Harry locked the cells, dressed, and knocked on the warden's door. The entire escapade took less than twenty-seven minutes.

That winter Houdini jumped from the Belle Island Bridge in Detroit and got out of two pairs of handcuffs under the waters below. The most famous of all Houdini legends says the Detroit River was frozen over—that he plummeted down through a hole in the ice and almost drowned before he found the opening and was pulled out.

Actually, though it was a cold day, the surface of the river was not frozen, and the date was November 27, not December 2 as given in later Houdini souvenir books. Like this exploit, his subsequent bridge jumps were front-page news.

Houdini made his first escape from a padlocked water can on the stage of the Columbia Theatre in St. Louis on January 27, 1908. He went offstage to put on a bathing suit while a committee examined a large galvanized container, similar in shape to the milk cans dairies supplied to farmers. The volunteers looked on as the assistants filled the container with water. Gravely Houdini reminded his audience that a man could live only a short time deprived of "life-sustaining air." He suggested that they start holding their breath the moment his head disappeared from view. Entering the can feet first, he submerged. Within thirty seconds most spectators were gasping for air. He stayed under for a minute and a half. This endurance feat alone won him a mighty round of applause, but the most thrilling part of the act was yet to come.

His wrists were handcuffed. Again Houdini slid down under the water. More liquid was added until it ran over the edges of the can. Quickly his assistants jammed the top in place and secured it with six padlocks. They drew a cloth cabinet forward around the can and closed the front curtains. Time ticked by. Thirty seconds; one minute; ninety seconds. Franz Kukol, Houdini's chief assistant, came from the wings with an ax in his hand. He put an ear to the side of the cabinet and listened. Two minutes; two minutes and a half; three minutes. Kukol frowned, raised the ax to striking position. The tension was almost unbearable; something must have gone wrong. Surely, any second, the assistant would slash through the curtains and cut into the can. At this moment, Houdini, dripping wet but smiling, burst through the curtains to a rafter-shaking ovation.

Preparation for his next spectacular achievement took place in Germany. While playing at the Hansa Theatre in Hamburg in November 1909, Houdini bought a Voisin biplane after witnessing a short flight by a pioneer aviator. Within a month the thirty-five-year-old showman had learned to pilot the plane. He had followed the development of aviation with fascination for six years, ever since the Wright Brothers made history near Kitty Hawk, North Carolina. Harry knew no one had yet conquered the air above Australia, and he was bound to be the first. The crated Voisin was stored in the hold of the *Malwa* with his heavy luggage when he sailed on January 7, 1910, to fill contracts Down Under.

Twenty thousand people lined Queen's Bridge and the banks of the Yarra River on February 18 to watch the manacled daredevil jump into the murky water to publicize his engagement at the New Opera House in Melbourne. Few were present one memorable morning less than a month later at Digger's Rest, a field twenty miles from the city. Eager to take advantage of any period of good flying weather, Houdini went to Digger's Rest after his nightly shows and slept in the tent that served as a hangar for his Voisin. Ralph Banks, an Australian sportsman, kept a Wright plane at the same field. Banks got his machine twelve feet off the ground on March 1—then crashed.

On March 16, 1910, at 5 A.M., Houdini's Voisin was wheeled out on the wooden planks that served as a takeoff area. Harry donned a pair of goggles and a cap and climbed up to the seat behind the steering wheel of the machine. He waved to Bess as the propeller was spun and the mooring line was cast off. The engine roared, and the plane shot forward and up. It soared gracefully in the morning sky, skimmed the uppermost branches of a tall gum tree, then circled the field at an estimated speed of fifty miles an hour before heading back to the runway. From nowhere clusters of people appeared on the field and cheered wildly as Houdini came in for a perfect landing after the first sustained flight in Australia.

While playing in England the next year, Houdini worked on the stage device that would take the place of the padlocked water can. In March he sought legal protection for his new idea by presenting it in the form of a play to the Lord Chamberlain. A single spectator paid a guinea for the privilege of watching the show from a seat in the pit of the theatre. Then the magician crated and stored his "Chinese Water Torture Cell" to have it ready when another blockbuster attraction might be needed to bolster his act.

Upon his return to the United States in the fall of 1911, Houdini released himself after being tied to a plank by three sea captains. He also escaped from a deep-sea diving suit after the headpiece had been bolted to the shoulders. Then he accepted his strangest challenge.

A "sea monster"—a cross between a whale and an octopus—had been found on a beach near Boston; the Lieutenant Governor of Massachusetts challenged Houdini to play Jonah. The manacled escapologist was forced through a slit in the embalmed carcass on the stage of Keith's Theatre. Assistants "sewed" the opening with a metal chain, wound a heavier chain around the carcass, and padlocked it. Working under the cover of a huge cabinet, Houdini freed himself in fifteen minutes. He said he would never try a similar release again; he had been almost overcome by the fumes from the preservative arsenic solution taxidermists had sloshed inside the creature.

Escapes from heavy wooden crates, nailed and banded with steel before they were lowered in rivers, kept the showman's name in the papers and drew throngs to the theatres he played in the summer of 1912. Since his water can had been copied by performers in the United States, Europe, and Australia, Houdini introduced "The Chi-

Harry and Bess posed for a picture between shows in Philadelphia.

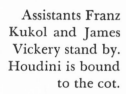

Assistants Franz Kukol and James Vickery stand by. Houdini is bound to the cot.

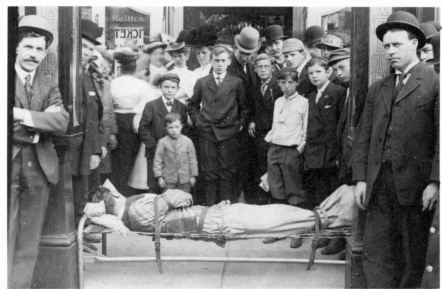

First man to make a successful flight in Australia, morning of March 16, 1910.

nese Water Torture Cell" during his fall tour with the Circus Busch in Germany.

Committeemen examined the metal-lined mahogany tank and a "cage" that was to be lowered into the water-filled tank. After they snapped the cuffs on his wrists, they probed the heavy stocks that were closed on his ankles, and the massive frame that fitted over the stocks. Houdini was hauled up and lowered head down into the water. Assistants locked the top of the tank and pushed a canopy forward to cover it. He could be seen through the plate-glass front of the tank until the drapes closed. Two assistants stood by with axes, ready to break the glass should an emergency arise. Two suspenseful minutes later, Houdini parted the curtains to show-stopping applause.

Eager to see his mother again, Houdini crossed the Atlantic the following summer to play a single month-long engagement at Hammerstein's Roof Garden in New York City. Cecilia Weiss attended his opening performance. The days her son spent with her passed all too quickly. Though frail and weak at seventy-two, she came to his bon-voyage party on the ship the day he sailed. There were tears in her eyes as she waved from the dock.

Two Danish princes were in the audience for the opening of "The Modern Proteus" at the Cirkus Beketow (later the Cirkus Schumann) in Copenhagen on July 16. "The Chinese Water Torture Cell" was a sensation. Next morning in the lobby of the circus building, Houdini was at his confident best as newspapermen interviewed him. Then a cablegram arrived. He ripped open the envelope, read that his beloved mother had died, and fell unconscious to the floor. Breaching his Copenhagen contract and canceling his European bookings for the summer, Houdini returned to New York for the funeral. This was the severest emotional blow he had ever suffered. Not until September could he force himself to resume his European tour.

Houdini was working in the United States when World War I broke out in the summer of 1914. With the European market closed to him for the duration, he perfected a new publicity stunt to insure turnouts at American theatres—a straitjacket escape made while dangling high in the air upside down from a rope attached to the cornice of a tall building. More than twenty thousand spectators turned out to see him wriggle like a barracuda at the end of a giant fishline in Providence, Rhode Island; fifty thousand blocked downtown traffic in Baltimore; and twice that number gathered in the nation's capital. The *Washington Times* said he attracted the largest crowd "ever assembled . . . except for the inauguration of a president." Always the showman, once Houdini squirmed free and let the straitjacket fall, he extended his arms and took a bow upside down in the air.

Houdini registered for the draft in 1917. At the age of forty-three he was not likely to be inducted. So he volunteered to entertain at training camps, appeared in Red Cross shows, and staged his upside-down straitjacket release over Broadway as members of the Society of American Magicians and their wives sold war bonds and thrift stamps in the street. He had been elected President of the Society; under his leadership new assemblies were formed from coast to coast.

Houdini had not lost the old urge to be "like Robert-Houdin." Along with "The Chinese Water Torture Cell," he performed the smallest trick in vaudeville, swallowing several packages of needles and bringing them up threaded. On January 7, 1918, at the New York Hippodrome he went to the other extreme, introducing the biggest illusion ever staged—"The Vanishing Elephant." Charles Morritt, who for years had featured "The Disappearing Donkey" in British theatres, devised the feat. He had mentioned the concept to Houdini during his last visit to England, and the escapologist had immediately purchased the worldwide performing rights.

Jennie, a 10,000-pound pachyderm, lumbered up a ramp into a box the size of a small garage. Houdini fired a pistol. His assistants opened the front curtains and removed a circular section at the back of the box to allow the audience to see through to the stage curtains at the rear. The elephant was gone! With this baffling mystery "Houdini puts his title of escape artist behind him and becomes The Master Magician," wrote Sime Silverman, editor of *Variety,* the principal theatrical weekly.

Envious conjurers circulated a disparaging story. They said *six* stagehands rolled out the box and *twenty* shoved it off. This account was not true, but it is still being repeated.

Houdini had been booked for six weeks with his new illusion. The impact of the elephant disappearance prolonged the engagement to nineteen weeks—the longest run Houdini ever played.

Before he closed at the Hippodrome, the magician signed a contract with B. F. Rolfe of Octagon Films to star in a movie serial, *The Master Mystery.* As Quentin Locke, a Justice Department undercover agent, Houdini worked in the laboratory of a patent firm and utilized his expertise as an escape artist to thwart the efforts of the villain, a partner in the patent enterprise. Though Locke was buried alive in a gravel pit, tied at the bottom of an elevator shaft as a car was slowly lowered to crush him, suspended head down over a pit of boiling acid, and strapped in an electric chair, he always survived. In the last of the fifteen episodes, Locke dramatically revealed that moviedom's first robot monster was a man sheathed in metal.

Houdini broke three bones in his left wrist during one of the early scenes, but production continued at the Yonkers, New York, studio. The magician was wearing a leather wrist support when he returned to the Hippodrome in August.

Despite this handicap, he wriggled free from a straitjacket

Escapes in Houdini's films were even more thrilling than those presented in his stage shows.

Harry Kellar visited Houdini and his director between takes at a Hollywood studio.

After being frozen in a block of ice for many years, Houdini returns to civilization as *The Man from Beyond*.

The odds were against him as usual in *Terror Island*.

while hanging upside down above the stage. It was too soon to repeat "The Vanishing Elephant" so he had devised a spectacular patriotic finale. He poured red and blue liquids into the water in a transparent fish bowl resting on a sheet of glass on a small table. Then he stirred the liquids and capped the top of the bowl with a tissue-paper drumhead. Baring his right arm to the elbow, Houdini broke through the sealed top and whipped out a cascade of silk streamers—four hundred feet long and forty feet wide, followed by a string of giant flags of the Allied nations. He reached beneath the folds of the Stars and Stripes as the music built to a crescendo and produced a live American eagle. The wartime audience gave him an ovation.

Houdini made his first Hollywood feature film, *The Grim Game,* for Paramount-Artcraft Pictures in the spring of 1919. His fragile left wrist fractured again when he fell three feet during a jail-escape sequence. The most breathtaking scene in the picture was a midair transfer from the wing of one airplane to another. The two collided accidentally and crashed in a bean field. This was written into the plot. Press stories said Houdini had narrowly escaped death, but he was on the ground with his arm in a sling at the time. A stunt man had doubled in the air for him.

In 1920, Houdini played British theatres not only as a variety headliner, but as a film star making personal appearances. Theatrical papers said he received the highest salary ever paid to a single performer at the London Palladium—$3,750 a week.

This was a pittance compared to the sums bereaved widows and mothers were spending trying to communicate with their loved ones. Spiritualism had reached a new peak of popularity in postwar England. Foremost among the distinguished men who championed the cause was Sir Arthur Conan Doyle. The creator of Sherlock Holmes believed Houdini to be a powerful medium. How else could he perform such remarkable feats? J. Hewat McKenzie, president of the British College of Psychic Science, shared this view. McKenzie had been onstage when the magician released himself from a padlocked water tank; McKenzie was convinced that Houdini dematerialized, oozed out, then took human form again before he came out from his curtained cabinet.

Houdini, who disclaimed supernatural powers, met many of the prominent British mediums through Doyle. Encountering nothing but trickery and self-deception at their séances, Houdini felt someone must counteract the propaganda being spread by too credulous believers. Ashamed of having masqueraded as a psychic during his medicine-show days, he decided to put his specialized knowledge to good use. He began making notes for a debunking book.

Terror Island, Houdini's second Hollywood film, was still playing in American theatres on his return to the States. Confident he

358

Houdini

could write and produce movies as well as star in them, he formed the Houdini Picture Corporation. *The Man from Beyond* and *Haldane of the Secret Service* followed the pattern of his previous vehicles. Houdini, the hero, triumphed over adversaries using his escape know-how to extricate himself from diabolical traps and snares.

Arriving in New York in 1922 for a nationwide lecture tour, Sir Arthur Conan Doyle saw *The Man from Beyond* as Houdini's guest. Impressed by the exciting scenes, particularly one showing the magician rescuing the heroine from the rapids at Niagara Falls moments before her empty canoe swept over the brink to destruction, Doyle called the picture "one of the really great contributions to the screen."

Harry and Bess, in turn, attended Doyle's Carnegie Hall lecture. When a photograph of Katie King, a "spirit," who materialized in the home of Sir William Crookes, the distinguished scientist, was shown, it seemed obvious to the magician-filmmaker that the "ghost" was a flesh-and-blood woman. How, he wondered, could his friend Doyle believe in such utter nonsense?

In June, when the Houdinis visited the Doyles in Atlantic City, Lady Doyle gave Harry a demonstration of automatic writing. Picking up a pencil, she rapidly wrote a message which, she said, came from his mother. The words, in English, told him to stop grieving, reported that Mrs. Weiss was happy, and suggested he try automatic writing himself.

Houdini was uncomfortable. At the top of the paper Lady Doyle had marked a Christian cross. His mother had always written to him in German; she had known only a few words of English; and though by coincidence it was her birthday, she had not mentioned it.

How did one get spirit messages? he asked Lady Doyle. She told him to hold the pencil, clear his mind of all conscious thought, then write.

He touched the pencil tip to the pad and wrote "Powell." Sir Arthur was thunderstruck. A friend, Ellis Powell, had recently died. This was a message from him! Houdini disagreed. Frederick Eugene Powell, a magician, had been on his mind during the weekend. He had received a letter from Powell about his wife's illness, and Harry and Bess had discussed the Powells' problems.

Houdini launched an all-out attack on psychic fraud that August. Making personal appearances with his film *The Man from Beyond*, at the Rialto Theatre in Washington, he projected slides of famous mediums and denounced the deceptions they performed in darkened rooms. He answered questions about charlatans' methods in a *Washington Times* column, a practice he was to repeat in New York, Philadelphia, Chicago, and other cities. Though he continued to perform in vaudeville, most of Houdini's offstage hours were spent tracking down and exposing "vultures who preyed on the bereaved." His activities received extensive press coverage, but this was not primarily a publicity gambit. Nothing would have pleased him more than to speak with his dead mother.

Doyle's lectures had aroused great interest in spiritualism. The *Scientific American* offered twenty-five hundred dollars for psychical phenomena produced by a medium under rigidly controlled conditions and a similar amount for a spirit photograph made under the same conditions. Houdini served on the five-man investigation team.

At the age of fifty he took time off from more lucrative vaudeville engagements to travel across the country on a lecture crusade. *A Magician Among the Spirits,* which was published in 1924, made Houdini's views crystal clear. Since the time of the Fox sisters who snapped their toe joints to produce raps in 1848, there had never been an honest medium. He admired Sir Arthur Conan Doyle as a man, but the brilliant writer had a closed mind; he refused to believe that the mediums who impressed him cheated.

Nino Pecoraro had astonished Doyle during his first American lecture tour by causing a bell to ring, a tambourine to spin in the air, and a toy piano to play, though he was bound to a chair. Pecoraro applied for the *Scientific American* prize money while Houdini was on the road. A telegram from publisher Orson Munn brought the magician from Little Rock, Arkansas, to New York to attend a test séance. Fellow committeemen planned to tie the young Italian with a single long rope; Houdini literally exploded. Even amateur escapologists could free their hands when trussed up this way. Houdini slashed the ropes into short lengths and secured the medium himself. When an expert did the binding there were no manifestations.

The strongest contender for the award lived in Boston. Margery (Mina Crandon), the twenty-six-year-old wife of a former professor at the Harvard Medical School, was blonde, beautiful, and a versatile medium. J. Malcolm Bird, secretary to the investigation committee and a member of the *Scientific American* staff, thought she merited the prize. The publisher called in Houdini for consultation.

Stunned to think the magazine would even consider approving a medium he had never seen, Houdini took the train to Boston with Orson Munn.

Margery did not perform under test conditions in the Crandon home on Lime Street. The medium and her audience formed a circle in an upstairs room. Those seated to her left and right took her hands and assumed, because she pressed her legs against theirs, that her feet were under control. On the evening of July 23, Houdini took the chair at Margery's left, while her husband—scarcely a disinterested investigator—occupied the one at her right. A "bell box" (the bell would ring only when the lid was pressed) which had been placed on the floor

"The Chinese Water Torture Cell" and "The Needle Trick," as seen by an artist.

between the magician's feet, rang in the dark; a megaphone was levitated; and the threefold screen behind the medium toppled and fell.

Later that night Houdini offered explanations for these marvels. He told Munn he had felt Margery's leg slide as she used her left foot to press down the top of the bell box. He was sure she had used her right hand—the one her husband held—to pick up the megaphone and don it like a dunce cap. A quick toss of her head sent it in any direction she wished it to go. The collapse of the screen she used as a cabinet? With her right hand Margery tilted it back far enough for her right foot to get under the side panel. A later kick upward overturned it. Houdini's verdict: "All fraud, every bit of it."

The following evening Margery gave another séance at the Hotel Charlesgate apartment of committee member David Fisk Comstock. This time the bell box did not sound when placed on a table in front of the medium. Yet the table itself tilted in the dark and sent the box crashing to the floor. Houdini released his left hand from Munn's right as the table moved. Groping under the table in the dark, he touched Margery's head. She was lifting the table as she raised her head. Later the bell did ring when the box was put between Houdini's feet on the floor.

That fall Houdini embarked on another coast-to-coast lecture tour. The Crandons were not in his audience when he appeared at Symphony Hall in Boston on January 2, 1925. Thus they missed his demonstration of megaphone tossing and table tilting, as well as of a deception once practiced by an earlier medium, D. D. Home. A volunteer sat at one end of a table, Houdini at the other. The man put his feet on top of Houdini's feet under the table and held his hands across the top. Still a tambourine jangled and a dinner bell rang under the table. The volunteer assured the audience that the magician's feet were still under his own. An assistant lifted the tablecloth. Houdini had slipped his right foot out of his shoe. His sock had been cut away at the toes. The bell was between his toes. When he shook his leg, the bell rang.

The *Scientific American's* report on Margery came out in February. Hereward Carrington, a prolific writer on the occult, claimed the Boston medium had produced some genuine phenomena. Dr. Walter Franklin Prince, research officer of the American Society for Psychical Research, and Dr. William McDougall, professor of psychology at Harvard, said they had seen no proof of Margery's alleged supernormal powers. Dr. Daniel Fisk Comstock, formerly on the staff of the Massachusetts Institute of Technology, asserted no manifestations had been produced under strict scientific controls. Houdini was blunter. He called Margery a fraud. The four-to-one negative verdict eliminated her as a contender for the award. Nor did any subsequent applicant qualify for the *Scientific American's* money and seal of approval.

A boyhood dream came true for Houdini on September 14, 1925, when he opened in his own full-evening show at the Shubert Alvin Theatre in Pittsburgh. It was a unique program, unlike that of any predecessor. He cast himself in three roles: magician, escapologist, and exposer of mediums. In every city on his route, Houdini offered ten thousand dollars to anyone who could exhibit a spiritualistic manifestation which he could not duplicate. The Cincinnati *Commercial Tribune* critic summed up the new venture: "There's one big difference between Houdini on a vaudeville bill and Houdini in his own show. In the latter instance there's more of him. Ergo, the show is better."

Houdini, paradoxically, underestimated his drawing power as an attraction in legitimate theatres. He had planned a two-week engagement at the Forty-fourth Street Theatre in New York in December; the demand for tickets was so great he played another fortnight at the National Theatre. Booked for four weeks at the Princess Theatre in Chicago in the spring of 1926, the show ran for twelve. When the tour ended in May, he returned to New York, intending to spend the summer months relaxing and devising new mysteries for his fall season.

Instead he was confronted by a new psychic sensation. Hereward Carrington, the only *Scientific American* committeeman to endorse Margery, the Boston medium, espoused an "Egyptian Miracle Man"—Rahman Bey. The slender, bearded mystic displayed the power of mind over body by increasing the pulse rate of one wrist while slowing down the other; he thrust steel needles through his cheeks and metal skewers through the flesh of his chest; and he rested with one sword blade under the back of his neck and another under his heels as a man wielding a sledge hammer cracked a stone slab on his chest. While mystifying to audiences, these stock tricks of fakirs were well known to the magician who had traveled with circuses and performed in dime museums.

In July, Rahman Bey, entranced and enclosed in a waterproof metal box, remained under water in the Dalton Hotel swimming pool for an hour. Challenged to duplicate this remarkable feat of endurance, Houdini allowed himself to be sealed in a container of the same size—six feet six inches long, twenty-two inches wide, and twenty-two inches deep—and lowered into the Shelton Hotel pool. An hour and a half later assistants took the box from the water and opened it. Fatigued but otherwise in good condition, the fifty-two-year-old magician told reporters there was nothing supernatural about the stunt. The secret, he said, was to remain calm, move as little as possible, and breathe with regular, short intakes of air.

The Houdini full-evening show began its second season in September in Paterson, New Jersey. Bess became ill with ptomaine poisoning in Providence, Rhode Island. Harry called a doctor immediately and arranged for a nurse to come from New York to travel with her. He was less concerned about his own health. A sudden pull on the lifting lines snapped a bone in his left leg after his ankles were locked in the heavy stocks of the "Chinese Water Torture Cell" on the stage in Albany. A Dr. Brannock, who came up from the audience, advised him to go at once to a hospital. Houdini thanked the physician but finished the show before stopping at Memorial Hospital for an X ray and treatment. Wearing a leg support, which he fashioned himself, he went on to Schenectady and Montreal.

On Friday morning, October 22, two McGill University students visited the magician in his dressing room at the Princess Theatre. One young man was drawing a portrait of Houdini when a third visitor, J. Gordon Whitehead, another McGill student, came in and questioned the American showman about Biblical miracles. Houdini was more interested in his morning mail. Whitehead asked if Houdini could withstand punches to his midsection without injury. If so, Whitehead said, he would like to take a few trial jabs. Relaxing on the couch and reading his mail, the magician gave his permission. The student struck with four quick jabs before Houdini could brace himself. The artist and his friend thought Whitehead had gone mad; they were about to pull him away when Houdini signaled for him to stop.

By show time the magician's stomach was sore, and the throbbing pain worsened as he performed. Once in his hotel room, he could not sleep; Bess, believing he had a stomach cramp or a strained muscle, massaged him in an effort to make him more comfortable.

After the final Saturday show, he told his wife what had happened in the dressing room. By then it was too late to get a doctor. An assistant wired the show's advance man in Detroit, asking him to have a physician ready to give Houdini a thorough examination. The train arrived late. The magician went directly to the Garrick Theatre rather than to the Statler Hotel where Dr. Leo Dretzka was pacing in the lobby. When the doctor finally got to the theatre, he found Houdini busy helping his assistants set up the props for the performance. There was no cot in the dressing room; the magician stretched out on the floor. Bess did not see the doctor probe the inflamed area or hear him say that Houdini should be taken to the hospital immediately for an emergency appendectomy. "They're here to see me," the magician said when the theatre manager informed him the house was full. "I won't disappoint them."

Thirty minutes past curtain time the show began. The audience had not known of the backstage drama. Houdini stood in the wings while a clock tolled twelve—the signal for his opening music, "Pomp and Circumstance." He limped slightly as he came to the foot-

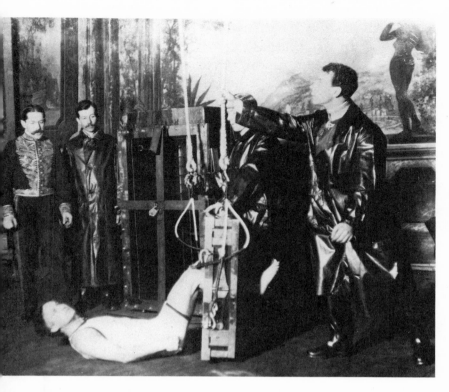

Houdini's ankles being locked in stocks.

One of the last photographs of Houdini. "Spirits" were produced by camera trickery.

He was lowered head-first into the "Water Torture Cell."

lights and said, "We have had a thousand-mile journey, and we are tired." He smiled and the magic began.

Silver coins disappeared from his fingertips and dropped into a crystal box as it swung from ribbons at center stage. The magician lowered a giant cone over a girl; when the cone was lifted, a flower bush had appeared in her place, and she came running down the aisle from the back of the theatre. His fingers were as nimble as ever with card sleights, but after he whirled the first long streamer from a liquid-filled fish bowl, he stepped aside and his chief assistant continued the production. Reaching upward had sent flames of pain through Houdini's stomach.

After the curtains closed for the intermission, Houdini staggered and fell. His assistants helped him to the dressing room. His temperature was 104 degrees. Perspiration rolled down his face, streaking the greasepaint. He reached for a towel, touched up his makeup, and somehow, through sheer willpower, forced himself to return to the stage and complete the performance.

He collapsed again after the final curtain, but he refused to go to a hospital and insisted on being taken to his hotel. Bess knew there was only one way to handle him when he was in a stubborn mood; she had hysterics. Dr. Daniel E. Cohen, the hotel physician, was called. Like Dr. Dretzka, he said Houdini should be in the hospital. Dr. Charles S. Kennedy, a surgeon, who arrived at 3 A.M. agreed, but Houdini would not allow them to call an ambulance until he had conferred by phone with his own doctor in New York.

Within hours the surgeon had removed the magician's ruptured appendix; for three days the poison had been seeping through his system. On Friday streptococcus peritonitis developed, and a second operation was performed. Houdini's condition did not improve. On Sunday afternoon, October 31, 1926, at 1:26 P.M. the great showman died.

Two thousand people jammed into the Elks Lodge ballroom on Forty-third Street, just off Broadway, in New York, to attend his funeral. Even at the end, Houdini drew a standing-room-only audience. He was buried near his mother in the family plot at Machpelach Cemetery in Cypress Hills, Queens (an area that until recent years was a part of Brooklyn).

The date of his death has been set aside as National Magic Day. Every October 31 representatives of the Society of American Magicians gather at Houdini's grave and perform a wand-breaking ceremony in his memory, while conjurers throughout the United States remember him by presenting free shows, as he so often did, in orphanages, homes for the aged, jails, and hospitals.

Almost half a century after his last performance, Houdini's is still the best-known name in magic. Scarcely a day passes without it being mentioned in a newspaper or magazine or on radio or television. Several books have been written about him. A Hollywood film, a London musical, and numerous television programs have dramatized his exploits. There is a Houdini Magical Hall of Fame museum in Niagara Falls, Ontario, Canada, not far from the site of his thrilling rescue scene in *The Man from Beyond*.

Strange that the daredevil who took calculated risks, by dangling hundreds of feet in the air above crowded streets, jumping while manacled from high bridges into rivers, and escaping from submerged boxes, allowed a man he scarcely knew to strike him forcibly. This was not part of Houdini's show, or even an offstage feat to demonstrate his well-developed muscles. Strange, too, that the master mystifier should die on Halloween. Yet, in a way, appropriate: the public had always expected the unusual and the improbable from Houdini.

20

Blackstone Versus Dante

Dante, sent abroad by Thurston with his number-two illusion show in 1927, was still on tour when his sponsor died in 1936. By then, Dante said later, he had purchased the equipment and the full rights to the production, and was making so much money in Europe that he thought it would be foolhardy to return to the United States. Meanwhile Harry Blackstone, long Thurston's principal competitor, became the dominant magician in North America.

Thurston had been dignity personified. Blackstone wore a rakish cowboy hat as he sent a buzz saw through the spine of an assistant, punned as he introduced his vanishing horse, and plugged the firms that supplied automobile tires, bread, and candy for his show.

Thurston, called "the Governor" by his staff, had spoken on "The Business of Magic" at Rotary, Lion, and Kiwanis luncheons, though he seldom performed on these occasions. "Mr. B." delighted in showing even casual acquaintances his skill with cards, corks, matches, and coins. If there was a convention at a hotel where Blackstone was staying, Harry joined the delegates and told outrageous tales about his days as a Cornell undergraduate, his adventures as a brain surgeon in the Congo, and his exploits as a spy in Bulgaria—none of which he had ever been.

With his larger than normal cranium, shock of white hair, and trim moustache, he was recognized wherever he went. He signed autographs freely, drew a quick sketch of his face, and sometimes added

May you live as long as you want
And never want as long as you live
And live ten years longer than I
And I shall never die.

Blackstone was born Henri Bouton in Chicago on September 27, 1885. His surname was often misspelled Boughton; an error, he later said, that dated from his French-Canadian father's enlistment papers in the Civil War. He Anglicized his own given name, first to Henry, then to Harry. The elder Bouton worked at various jobs, including being a florist and baker. A heavy drinker, he went off on long binges, once staying away from his wife and family for three years.

Harry was a newsboy when he saw Kellar perform at McVicker's Theatre. Conjuring became the youth's hobby. He drew his first regular paycheck as a cabinetmaker's assistant. His woodworking skill gave him entry into the world of magic. From August Roterberg, he received an order to construct trick boxes. This inventive German-born conjuring dealer had all but cornered the Midwestern market for equipment. Famous professionals as well as avid amateurs patronized his Chicago shop.

Harry and his brother, Peter, put together a vaudeville act in which they were billed as "Harry Bouton & Co., Straight and Crooked Magic." Harry, dressed in a dinner jacket, was the conjurer; Pete, wearing a bald wig, clown makeup, an oversize coat, and baggy trousers, acted as his comedy assistant.

Harry envied an older performer, Herbert Albini, a headliner on the Sullivan-Considine circuit in the Midwest. There were rumors that Albini had saved the life of Charles Considine, one of the founders of the circuit, and that out of gratitude Considine kept him busy. Albini (Abraham Laski), a Polish magician, had come to the United States from England in 1891, after appropriating the stage name of Lieutenant Albini (Frederick Baxter Ewing) in the British Isles. The second Albini, a man with bulbous eyes and an arrogant manner, mystified large audiences even with the smallest of tricks. The acknowledged master of "The Egg Bag", Albini produced an egg and made it disappear in a small felt bag, though spectators examined the bag and held his wrists. Never using a pack of cards for more than one trick, he hurled the cards in the air after each feat, then reached for another pack in a satchel carried by his assistant. The stage was littered with cards when he took his bows.

By 1911 Albini the Great, with a "$15,000 production" and twelve assistants, owned one of the largest illusion acts in vaudeville. In the dramatic opening scene, a French officer was condemned to die by a military court. Offered a choice of facing a firing squad, being hanged, or being burned alive, he elected to burn. Dragged up a flight of stairs to a platform on a ten-foot-high scaffold, the officer refused to surrender his sword. The commander threatened him with a flag-draped rifle. Still the prisoner shook his head. The commander fired; the flag disappeared and reappeared on the tip of the doomed man's saber. Seized by the other officers who took his sword, the prisoner was cremated.

For a change of pace, Albini produced four girls in four hammocks after the curtains of a large cabinet were closed. Each held a guitar, and played and sang as they came forward. Another girl materialized in a glass-lined trunk, and a "Human Butterfly" burst through the center of a sheet of paper fastened to a metal frame. Appearing in a puff of smoke, Mephisto produced a girl in Oriental costume from an empty sedan chair; then, extending his red cape with his outstretched hands, he turned away from the audience. Then he swung around, and behold! Mephisto was Albini. The girl reclined on a long narrow table. Covered with a silk cloth, she floated upward at Albini's command, then disappeared when he reached up and pulled away the silk. Assistants quickly lowered a trunk, hanging near the balcony, to the stage; the girl was found in the innermost of the two smaller boxes it contained.

Two years after Albini staged this spectacular act, he died at the age of fifty-three in his Chicago hotel room. Harry Bouton bought several pieces of Albini's equipment and branched out as an illusionist. Buying at a cut rate an immense stock of playbills ordered for Fredrik, another Midwestern magician, for a planned, but never carried out, tour, Bouton went on the road as Fredrik the Great.

Harry played as Fredrik until World War I made "German" names poison at theatre box offices. Urged by bookers to take an easier-to-sell stage name, Bouton became Blackstone. Depending on his mood, Harry afterward explained this choice in several ways. Sometimes he claimed Blackstone was the maiden name of his grandmother; more often, he admitted that one day on Michigan Boulevard in Chicago the sign of the famous hotel caught his eye.

By 1917 "Blackstone, the Master Magician" was traveling with ten assistants. Inez Morse, "the Little Banjo Fiend," his first wife, presented a musical specialty; his brother, Pete, worked as principal male assistant, stage carpenter, and as Blackstone's double in quick-change feats. On occasion Blackstone performed in legitimate theatres with his own production, but usually he headlined in vaudeville.

In the Thurston show, assistants had carried out the most strenuous roles; Blackstone reveled in playing these parts himself. Seized by masked, white-robed terrorists, he was tied in a sack and hauled up twelve feet in the air. A Ku Klux Klansman galloped from the wings on horseback and fired a pistol. The sack fell empty to the stage. The rider dismounted and pulled off his hood; he was Blackstone.

Later Harry devised a method to make the horse disappear. He

Harry and his brother, Pete, in the act billed "Straight and Crooked Magic."

Fredrik, whose name Blackstone took after buying a supply of his lithographs.

Later Blackstone performed several of Albini's elaborate illusions.

rode the white steed up a ramp and into an oblong tent as a painted background scene moved on offstage rollers from left to right. Assistants quickly dismantled the tent, taking away the canvas front, back, top, and sides, leaving only the wooden frame; horse and rider were gone. The presentation for this illusion varied. Sometimes only the horse vanished, leaving Harry with the saddle between his legs and a puzzled expression on his face. When the Nobles of the Mystic Shrine in Davenport, Iowa, sold Blackstone a camel at a give-away price, he announced he would make the animal vanish in his striped canvas tent. However, the camel refused to stand still after he disappeared; he poked his head out from behind the false back of the tent frame, which moved like the scene behind it on two rollers concealed in the rear posts.

The balky camel was reduced from star performer to stage extra in *Oriental Nights,* an attraction ballyhooed as "Blackstone's tenfold pageant of the East. A stage spectacle such as rivals the regal splendor of Solomon's court. . . . Corps of bewildering, beautiful nautch [Indian dancing] girls, The Enchanted Camel, the Phantom Stallion." When "The Enchanted Camel" died in Boston, Harry offered the carcass to several institutions. General Robert E. Lee's horse, Traveler, and P. T. Barnum's elephant, Jumbo, had both been preserved; Harry was dismayed to learn that no one wanted the remains of the world's first vanishing camel.

Blackstone followed Houdini's lead in escaping from packing crates and welded boilers. The crate in which he was being lowered from the Minneapolis Steel Arch Bridge into the Mississippi River on October 10, 1922, broke loose from the cables and crashed down into the water, splintering the sides and bottom. Blackstone, bruised and battered, came up from the depths, smiling. Later he had great difficulty releasing himself from another underwater box and vowed he would never smoke again if he survived. He managed to escape and thereafter shunned cigars, pipes, and cigarettes.

In December 1925, while Houdini was playing a full-evening show at the Forty-fourth Street Theatre in New York, an aerial balloon attached to the roof of the nearby Claridge Hotel on Broadway advertised Blackstone's appearance at Werba's Theatre in Brooklyn. Houdini threatened to shoot down the balloon; he was riled because he had not thought of this effective attention-getter himself.

The stable attendant who led Blackstone's white horse to the Brooklyn theatre was late one evening. Harry stalled with small tricks. Then he had a sudden inspiration. He announced that instead of making a horse disappear—this show and this show only—he would conjure away his entire company. Herding his surprised assistants into the tent, he fired a pistol. Bang! When he pulled away the canvas front, they were gone.

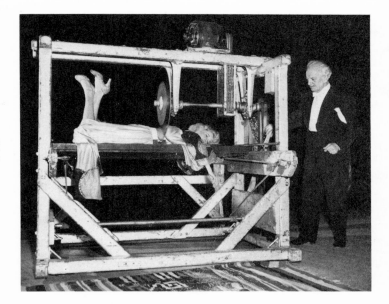

The Blackstone version of Goldin's "Living Miracle."

Blackstone poses for a picture before he is nailed in a crate.

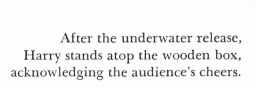

After the underwater release, Harry stands atop the wooden box, acknowledging the audience's cheers.

"Blasted to Bits at the Mouth of a Cannon," a Blackstone feature in 1930, reached its dramatic high point with Harry, in false beard and Indian robes, being lashed to the barrel end of the fieldpiece. An assistant lighted a fuse. The charge exploded, and Blackstone disintegrated in a cloud of smoke. A moment later, he came from the wings without so much as a powder burn.

Following a divorce from his first wife, Blackstone married Billie Mathews (Mildred Phinney), one of his assistants. Harry Bouton Blackstone, Jr., was born on June 20, 1933, in a Three Rivers, Michigan, hospital, not far from Blackstone Island, where the magician and his staff built new illusions and raised ducks and rabbits for the show during the summer.

Soon after Horace Goldin introduced "The Living Miracle" abroad, a buzz-saw illusion went into the Blackstone program. One of his best deceptions began when a blonde climbed into a row of automobile tires, standing on end, side by side, in a rack. Blackstone reached in to tug the girl back, but succeeded only in pulling off her costume. Assistants rolled the tires one by one across the stage where they were stacked on a platform to form a tower. A line was let down into the center, and the missing girl—in another costume—was lifted out.

Blackstone offered his own version of "The Indian Rope Trick," and added eye appeal to the forcing-spikes-through-a-girl illusion by using long glowing neon tubes for the penetration.

In the depression years when Blackstone and Thurston were presenting hour-long segments of their full shows in movie houses, *Variety* reported that Thurston was getting a $7,500 weekly guarantee and Blackstone $2,500, but their share of the gross receipts was not specified. After Thurston died in 1936, Blackstone moved up to fill his competitor's bookings.

Thoroughly at ease on stage, Blackstone was never ruffled. His coolness in what could have been a disaster in Decatur, Illinois, on September 2, 1942, undoubtedly saved many lives. In the middle of his performance at the Lincoln Theatre, an assistant whispered to him that the adjacent buildings were on fire. Harry glanced toward the wings and saw an excited fire chief gesturing for him to stop the show. Realizing that the audience might panic if an abrupt announcement was made, Harry walked to the footlights and said his next feat was too big to be shown on a stage; the spectators would have to go out into the street to see it. He gave precise instructions. Those in the first six rows should leave first, then those in the next six rows, and so on. "When you're on the pavement," he added, "look up in the air." After the orderly exodus, he joined the crowd to watch firemen bring the blaze under control.

Under the sponsorship of the USO, Blackstone took his illusion

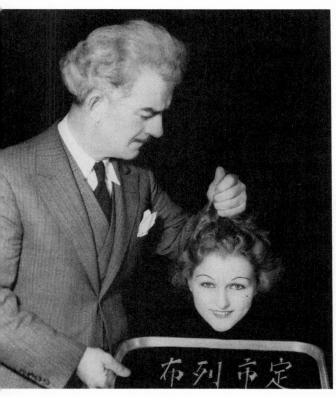

Blackstone displays an assistant's head on a tray. Not a part of his stage routine, this was arranged for a publicity picture.

Blackstone and his pets. There were also ducks, a horse, and a camel in his stage spectacles.

Harry Blackstone, Jr., performs many of his father's tricks and illusions.

show to 165 military posts in the United States during World War II. Then he returned to his usual theatre bookings. He had had occasional respiratory trouble before, but nothing like the severe asthma attack he suffered while performing in Atlanta in March 1945. Physicians at the Crawford Long Hospital advised him to take a holiday and to live less strenuously in the future. Rather than slacken his pace, he accelerated it by setting off on a 1946–47 coast-to-coast tour that lasted nine months. In addition to giving full-evening shows, which required him to be onstage from start to finish, he became the star of a Blackstone radio series. Coincidentally his imaginary adventures were depicted in *Super Magician* and *Blackstone Master Magician* comic books.

He had been divorced from his second wife for many years before he met Elizabeth Ross of Biloxi, Mississippi, while they were patients at a Southern spa. She became the third Mrs. Blackstone in Chicago in November 1950.

Blackstone made birdcages and human beings disappear; he produced giant bottles of liquor from an empty chest, and a burro from a bundle of silk. Lighted electric bulbs and female assistants floated at his command, and he himself was transported mysteriously from one place to another, but his masterpiece was "The Spirit Dancing Handkerchief." The handkerchief, borrowed from a member of the audience, was knotted at one corner to resemble a ghostly head. The handkerchief squirmed realistically in his hand. When he tickled it, it quivered. When he threw it to the floor and clamped down with his foot, the handkerchief struggled to get away. Then he balanced it onstage, so that it stood on end, and the handkerchief danced up and down in time with the music. It continued to cavort until Blackstone picked it up, untied the knot, and returned the handkerchief to its owner. When the owner touched it, the animation ceased; once more it was just a commonplace square of white cloth.

Charles MacDonald, a movie-theatre owner from York, Pennsylvania, took over the management and operation of the Blackstone show in the years after World War II. Harry soon stored the heaviest illusions, such as "The Indian Rope Trick," "The Bachelor's Dream," and a Kellar levitation. The weightiest prop retained was the buzz saw with its massive frame. In the second part of the program Blackstone filled in with twenty or thirty spectators standing around him onstage as he baffled them with a quick release of his tied hands, pocketpicking, and intimate card tricks.

In the mid-1950's Blackstone appeared on CBS-TV's "It's Magic" and NBC-TV's "Tonight" shows; then Edward R. Murrow made a visit to the famed illusionist's apartment at the Royalton Hotel in New York for a "Person to Person" telecast. I suggested to Jackie Gleason in 1957 that Blackstone and his illusions would be effective on Gleason's popular CBS-TV comedy show, and they were.

Eye-catching displays filled the facade of Dante's theatres.

Dante's equipment being set up prior to his opening in Tokyo.

While Blackstone was living in New York, he appeared at sales meetings for large industrial firms there, and in other cities, dramatizing the selling points of new products. He also went to Detroit to introduce Kalanag, the German illusionist, to Motor City audiences, and he traveled to Washington to produce a magic number for a musical.

The 74-year-old illusionist flew to Hollywood in 1960. As the celebrity guest on Ralph Edwards's "This is Your Life," he was visibly surprised when a capsule version of his career unfolded. The Hollywood climate appealed to the Blackstones; they settled there. Shortly after their arrival, the Academy of Magical Arts and Sciences opened the Magic Castle, a private club, in a hillside mansion. This was only a short walk from the Blackstone apartment. Surrounded by professional and amateur conjurers and visiting television and film stars, Blackstone accepted salaams from his admirers. He was in the front row of the audience when I lectured at the club in 1964. Though he walked with a cane, his fingers were still dexterous. He took me aside to show me a new card sleight he had devised.

Blackstone's health began to fail the following year. He died in his home on North Sycamore Street at the age of eighty of pulmonary edema on November 16, 1965. There is now a Blackstone Room in the Magic Castle, and in Colon, Michigan, where he was buried, the main street has been renamed in his honor.

Harry Blackstone, Jr., worked as an assistant with his father during school and college vacations. He originally planned to become a radio announcer. Instead he, too, became a magician. If you shut your eyes as he talks, you would swear that his father was about to make a cage and canary disappear or cause a lighted electric light bulb to float. Taller and stockier than his predecessor, Blackstone, Jr., has traveled in several countries with industrial shows and appeared on network television. He produced a magic number for the 1966 edition of "Holiday on Ice," and he recently appeared with a spectacular illusion act in Las Vegas.

Though the elder Blackstone had competition from The Great Leon, William Neff, The Great Virgil, John Calvert, and other first-rate illusionists during his long career, he reigned supreme as America's leading magician, until Dante, after thirteen years abroad, opened on Broadway in September 1940.

Dante, born Harry Alvin Jansen in Copenhagen on October 3, 1882, came with his parents to St. Paul, Minnesota, when he was six. He saw Herrmann the Great nine years later, and attended a Kellar performance the following year in Chicago. As a schoolboy young Jansen had astonished his classmates by making a button disappear; in Chicago he practiced sleight of hand and became adept with billiard balls, cards, and coins. By 1902 Jansen had an hour show of magic and illusions. Tall, personable, with an individual style, he progressed rapidly and soon toured as far west as Salt Lake City and as far east as Boston, heading his own variety company. During a summer season at Kennybrook Park in Pittsburgh in 1905, Harry met Edna Herr, a talented musician. She became his principal assistant and his wife.

The birth of Alvin, the first of their five children in 1907 led Jansen, by then a skilled builder as well as presenter of illusions, to open a magic company with Charles Halton in Chicago, and to confine his vaudeville engagements to the Midwest. An offer too good to refuse —a tour of Australia and the Orient—came four years later. The show returned to San Francisco on New Year's Day 1915.

Jansen played with his own illusion act in vaudeville and toured with the Johnny J. Jones Exposition until 1921, when he headed a Horace Goldin "Sawing a Woman in Two" road company. The following year Harry sailed without bookings for Australia, hoping to be the first to present this sensational attraction there. Two other performers—one with a Selbit unit; the other, Percy Abbott, an Australian, who had built his own variation of the feat—beat him to the punch; Jansen returned immediately to the United States.

Howard Thurston gave him the name Dante in 1923, and sent him on tour with a lavish show featuring the principal Thurston illusions. There were just two drawbacks to this arrangement. Dante was limited to cities in which his sponsor did not choose to appear, and the bookings included single night stands and two and three day engagements. After almost four years of rugged travel, Dante convinced Thurston that even more money could be made abroad with the production.

The Dante show opened in San Juan, Puerto Rico, on June 29, 1927. Two months later, en route to South America, the troupe had a harrowing experience at sea. The skipper of the two-masted schooner Dante had chartered for the voyage admitted when they were under sail that he did not have a compass. He steered, he patiently explained, by the shadow of a stick and by messages from above. After four days of aimless drifting, the captain took to drink. Rescued finally by the liner *San Juan,* Dante, his sun-blistered, thirsty company, and his paraphernalia were taken to Venezuela.

A week's booking in Georgetown, British Guiana, was prolonged to three. In Paramaribo, Dutch Guiana, the citizens were so pleased with the show that they presented the magician with a gold medal and a silver-mounted snakewood cane. Fire almost destroyed the stage in Bridgetown, Barbados. Rays from the hot tropical sun intensified by a crystal ball, one of Dante's props, on a window ledge, ignited a costume hanging on the wall of his dressing room. The room was ablaze before quick action by a local fire brigade doused the flames.

Dante used a "soldier" in his
version of "The New Page," an
illusion invented by Devant.

Though strapped inside the box,
the "soldier" turned upside-down
in a matter of seconds.

A small box became a large box at Dante's command; then a girl stepped from it.

Business in Brazil, Uruguay, and Argentina far exceeded Dante's expectations; in Buenos Aires he gave a record-breaking 120 performances at the Casino Theatre.

From South America, the show sailed for Europe. There was snow on the ground when Dante opened on the night of December 14, 1928, at the Music Hall in Moscow. The official who introduced him, Dante later said in a souvenir book, "made it clear that there was nothing supernatural about me, that all my work was brought about by a modern technique; also that the costumes worn in the show if elegant were simply those of artists playing a part and he told the audience not to envy us." Despite this cool introduction, the packed house gave Dante an ovation. On New Year's Eve, he was the guest of honor at a seven-course champagne dinner attended by three hundred performers and managers. In Leningrad the Red Army took over the theatre for a week, and Dante played to soldier audiences. Closing night the theatre manager told the magician his money would be waiting for him in Moscow. In Moscow, Dante was informed that a bank draft had been sent to Berlin. Dante's equipment was not loaded on the express train that took the magician and his company to Germany; it followed later on a slow freight. Three weeks passed before he received the money he had earned in Russia. Dante was furious; he had lost a month's work. The Moscow authorities wrote praising his performances and tried to book him for a return engagement. Fed up by the ineptitude of bumbling bureaucrats, he vowed he would never cross the Russian frontier again.

Dante played Berlin, Paris, Copenhagen, Stockholm, Madrid, Barcelona, Rome, Naples, and Nice before returning to Argentina, Brazil, and Uruguay in March 1932. Then he toured South Africa en route to India. As the theatres in Calcutta and Bombay had been booked by other shows, he continued on to Australia, New Zealand, Singapore, Japan, and China before beginning another tour of Europe.

Dante had two major unfulfilled ambitions: to perform in London and on Broadway. British agents who saw him on the Continent reported that he spoke no English. Dante had to go to London himself to prove this was untrue. And this was only half the battle as Britain was then surfeited with outstanding illusionists. Among them, Horace Goldin, Jasper Maskelyne, The Great Carmo, Chris Charlton, Murray, and The Great Levante.

Goldin was an established variety favorite. Jasper Maskelyne, the grandson of John Nevil Maskelyne, had the advantage of a famous name. Charlton, who had performed in the United States and Europe, was noted for pouring drinks from an empty kettle, causing a bathing beauty to disappear from a suspended bathhouse, and his vanishing automobile.

Murray (Murray Walters), an Australian, had arrived in England ten years before, with bulging scrapbooks containing stories of his worldwide exploits. In Australia he freed himself after being manacled, locked in a mailbag, and tossed in the sea. George Bernard Shaw who had seen Murray in South Africa when he escaped on a challenge from a crate, admitted he had not the slightest idea how this was done. The reviews of Murray's shows were ignored by London agents. They said they could not book him until they had seen him work. An upside-down straitjacket escape, made while dangling from the roof of Swan and Edgar's store in Piccadilly, produced so much newspaper space, that they changed their minds.

Murray was heading variety bills with "Shooting Through a Woman," two Selbit illusions ("The Human Pin Cushion" and "The Man Without a Middle") and various escape feats.

Levante (born Leslie George Cole in Sydney on March 5, 1892) left Australia for his first world tour in 1927. Traveling to England by way of the Phillipines, Malaya, Borneo, India, Russia, China, and Japan, he produced girls from empty cabinets, swallowed razor blades and brought them up threaded, made ducks disappear, presented an effective "Spirit Cabinet," and escaped in a "Thousand Pound Challenge," after being tied in a sack and locked in a metal trunk.

Carmo was featuring a remarkable levitation. A mummy floated up from a sarcophagus, turning in the air as it soared. One of his sleight-of-hand feats was as baffling as any of his big-scale mysteries; he produced live canaries from thin air, as other conjurers would cards or coins. Assistants put the birds into cages, and gave them to spectators as souvenirs.

None of these performers, however, was giving a full-evening magic show; they were supported by other variety acts.

Dante's *Sim Sala Bim* (nonsense words from an old Danish song) opened on August 10, 1936, at the Alhambra Theatre in London. In addition to the expected classics, many new illusions added novelty to the show. There was a funny transformation scene in a barber-shop setting. Dante, as the barber, and an assistant, as his customer, wore grotesque heads. After the barber finished giving his customer a slap-dash shave, they removed their artificial heads. The customer was in the barber's uniform while Dante was found in the chair.

"Backstage with a Magician" began with Dante and his assistants facing a curtain at the rear of the stage. A girl bent down to hide behind one of two boxes to the right. Dante straightened his tie; the orchestra played introductory music, and the rear curtain opened to reveal a sea of faces—a painted audience. After one box was shown to be empty, it was placed beside the other, behind which the girl was hiding. She darted across to be concealed by that box while the second one was being shown. When the two boxes were nested, the girl entered them through a secret panel. The real audience was sure they

382

Blackstone Versus Dante

Dante presenting hurston's vanishing horse and rider illusion.

A marked bullet, attached to a long ribbon penetrated an assistant's body.

Stream of water shot high in the air for the finale of *Sim Sala Bim.*

Dante, his wife, sons, and daughter pose for a family portrait in Europe.

The last photograph of Dante, taken by the author at Northridge.

"Out of a Hat" was featured in both the Dante and Thurston shows.

knew exactly how the trick was being done. But, instead of the expected girl, a man emerged from the boxes. Dante bowed to the painted audience, and real hands came through openings in the backdrop to applaud.

Three assistants climbed up into the passenger basket suspended under a giant balloon for "Mystery of the Stratosphere." There was a flash of light and a puff of smoke. The empty basket clattered to the stage. Moments later the assistants ran down the aisles and up behind the footlights to take a bow.

For the finale Dante and the entire company, attired in Chinese costumes, assembled before an Oriental curtain. Water spurted up wherever the magician touched his wand—from fingers, shoes, heads, and shoulders. More than a dozen fountains were playing simultaneously as the curtains closed.

Dante made a tremendous hit. He so captivated the critics and his audiences that his most terrible puns were bearable. He even looked the part he played, with a new goatee to go with the moustache he had worn for years.

After a hundred and fifty weeks in the British Isles, *Sim Sala Bim* moved on to Belgium, then to Germany for a two-month run at the Scala Theatre in Berlin. Dante was there in August 1939 when rumors spread that Hitler was invading Poland; Dante had six hours to cross the border before it was closed. Almost forty pieces of personal luggage were left behind, but he and his company made it to Sweden with the show intact.

Murray, the Australian illusionist, was less fortunate. He, too, had been performing in Germany. Murray and his assistants fled to Denmark at the last moment, leaving his equipment in Berlin.

Dante disbanded his troupe in Sweden; they had joined the show in various parts of the world. With his family and Moi-Yo Miller, his principal assistant—she was an Australian beauty-contest winner—he sailed for the United States. The ship arrived October 15, five days late. It had zigzagged across the Atlantic to elude German submarines.

Dante proceeded to California, where he bought a ranch at Northridge, in the San Fernando Valley. Within a year, however, he was back in New York. *Sim Sala Bim* opened at the Morosco Theatre on September 9, 1940. The critics loved it. *The New York Times* said Dante was a blend of Mephistopheles and Monte Woolley, "an echo of the Palace when the world was young and kind. Marvelous, in short, marvelous."

The *Daily News* reported "Kellar or Herrmann would, and did, spend a good quarter hour shooting a lady from the stage into a chest that has been suspended from the ceiling of the theatre all eve-

385

*Blackstone
Versus Dante*

ning. Dante does it better and, I'll wager, in less than three minutes flat."

After "15 Surprises in 15 Seconds," Dante had welcomed the audience, first in Danish, then in English. He said he was too old to run back and forth from the wings for bows. If there was applause, he would raise his hands over his head to express a hundred thanks. If the applause continued, he would lower them halfway—a thousand thanks. If there was still more, he would bring them all the way down—a million thanks. He raised his hands again, lowered them as he said "Sim Sala Bim," and went on with the show.

"Not bad for an old bird of seventy," he joked as he produced beer from an empty paper-capped barrel; he was then a month short of being fifty-eight.

For the next five years Dante performed in North America, in Canada and Mexico as well as in the United States. Then, after a postwar tour of Britain, Scandinavia, and Holland, he returned to California in 1949. He appeared with Laurel and Hardy in *A-Haunting We Will Go,* played a leading role in the film *Racketbusters,* and was a frequent guest on television's "You Asked for It." He also staged a TV magic act designed to highlight the antics of comedian Alan Young, who played an illusionist's assistant, and occasionally Dante took his show on the road.

Dante's last public appearance came when he delivered a brief speech, to rousing applause, at the combined convention of the Society of American Magicians and the Pacific Coast Association of Magicians in Santa Barbara, California. A few nights later I visited his ranch in Northridge. Dante took me past the swimming pool to his miniature theatre to show me the most recent device he had constructed; the instant production of chinaware, glass, silver, and enough food for a banquet on a long, narrow, bare, except for a cloth, table. Then he went to a storage room and came back lugging a bundle. The seventy-one-year-old illusionist squatted on the floor to open the package. Inside was an enormous American flag. He said he would erect a pole by the entrance to his property for the Fourth of July. "The Rancho Dante," he said proudly, "will fly the biggest Stars and Stripes in the state of California." Four days later, on June 16, 1955, he died. His widow learned of his plan for the holiday in the obituary I wrote for *Variety.* The gigantic flag fluttered in the breeze that Fourth, just as he had said it would.

Dante always thought big. I mentioned in London that Fu Manchu, in Argentina, carried sixty Chinese costumes with his illusion show. "Impossible," Dante stated, "I only have fifty."

During the time Dante played in competition with Blackstone, there was never a rivalry of the sort that once had proven so costly to Herrmann the Great and Kellar. Blackstone had limited his tours to the United States and Canada, with the single exception of an engagement in Bermuda; Dante performed on all five continents. He was willing to accept Blackstone as the leading magician in North America, for Dante, with justification, believed himself to be Number One in the world.

*Blackstone
Versus Dante*

21

Dunninger—

Master Mentalist

I N the fall of 1943, Joseph Dunninger, a mentalist who had headlined in vaudeville, performed his most astonishing feat. The fifty-one-year-old showman convinced millions of Americans that he could read minds—and he did it on his network radio show.

Nine years earlier Dr. Joseph Banks Rhine, a Duke University parapsychologist, had been overwhelmed when some of his subjects made high scores guessing face down symbol cards. He stated unequivocally in his first book that extrasensory perception was "an actual and demonstrable occurrence." The new NBC radio sensation far surpassed Rhine's highest scorers. Calling off all the cards in a shuffled pack was just a warm-up stunt for the broad-shouldered, six-foot performer; Dunninger told studio spectators (people he had never met) their names, addresses, and social security numbers. For a quarter of a century "The World's Greatest Mentalist" maintained his advertised position with provocative programs on radio, on the three American television networks, and with personal appearances across the nation.

The son of poor German immigrants—his father, Nicholas, had learned tailoring in Bavaria; his mother, Lena Gottschalk, came from Cologne—Dunninger was born on April 28, 1892, on the Lower East Side of Manhattan. When he was seven, his father took him to see Harry Kellar at the Academy of Music on Fourteenth Street. Though the boy later attended performances given by the Herrmanns,

Thurston, and Houdini, Kellar continued to be the magician the young-ster most admired. He saved his money, bought apparatus and books at Martinka's magic shop, and met Burling Hull and Paul Carlton, two youths who shared his interest. Hull became a prolific writer of pamphlets on conjuring; Carlton, who earned his living as a marine artist, is best remembered today as the man who supplied the secrets for the Camel cigarette "It's Fun to be Fooled—It's More Fun to Know" advertisements that provoked so much criticism from con-jurers forty years ago.

At sixteen, "J. Dunninger" presented a sleight-of-hand act at a Lenax Club show and dance. Two years later "Mysterious Dunninger" offered card manipulations, "spiritualistic mystifications and a number of Oriental mysteries" on the bill of a smoker at the Masonic Temple in Brooklyn. During the day he worked at John Wanamaker's de-partment store, first as a messenger, then as a stock-room clerk and comparison shopper. Dunninger remained on the Wanamaker payroll coincident with the longest run he was ever to play as a magician—fifty-seven (his later press releases said sixty-five) weeks at the old Eden Musee, a wax museum on West Twenty-third Street, where Buatier de Kolta, Frederick Eugene Powell, and other noted con-jurers had appeared. The hall was torn down shortly after Dunninger closed in 1915. A notable trick introduced by the twenty-five-year-old magician during this engagement was the production of a glass of water from an empty cloth bag, while two spectators held his wrists.

Dunninger wanted people to recognize him in the street, as well as on the stage. And they soon did. He grew a leonine crop of dark hair; he knotted his wide silk tie artist's style, and he wore a diamond stickpin, fancy vests, a wide-brimmed black felt hat, and spats. In Hartford, Connecticut, where he played three shows a night at Bond's restaurant in the fall of 1917, Dunninger presented sleight of hand with cards, coins, and balls, as well as a straitjacket escape.

Dunninger publicized his Hartford opening with a sensational blindfold automobile drive through the city streets on his way to find an object hidden by a committee of townspeople. This space-getting stunt had been introduced in the United States by Washington Irving Bishop, the nineteenth-century mind reader Dunninger later singled out as the greatest of his predecessors.

The term *mind reading* was used in the 1870's to describe a technique known today as muscle-reading. The mind reader holds the wrist of a person who knows where an object is hidden and tells the volunteer to give him mental instructions, such as "Go this way," "Stop," or "Reach higher." With practice a sensitive performer can fol-low his subject's unspoken cues. There is a slight restraining pulsation if the mind reader starts in the wrong direction; no resistance at all when he heads the right way. These tactile signals are not given con-

389

Dunninger—
Master
Mentalist

sciously; as the subject concentrates intently, his muscular reflexes guide the performer. John Randall Brown, a Chicago newspaperman turned showman, was the first to feature this type of mind reading. Bishop, a New Yorker who toured the British Isles, Europe, Cuba, and the United States, was the most successful performer. He died on the morning of May 13, 1889, at the age of forty-three, following a cataleptic attack which immobilized him as he entertained for friends at the Lambs Club in New York. Bishop used horses and a carriage for his publicity drives, and, to be on the safe side, he also employed a trick blindfold, through which he could see. Dunninger updated the feat by traveling in an automobile.

The year after his Hartford engagement, Dunninger staged a blindfold drive in the Bronx to raise funds for the New York Liberty Bond Committee. Keenly aware that mentalism was giving him more press coverage than magic, he began to study methods for secretly obtaining access to his audience's thoughts.

Alexander the Paphlagonian, a second-century charlatan, had read concealed messages by carefully removing the wax seals on scrolls and replacing them. Later mediums, who claimed the spirits aided them, worked out various ways to learn the contents of envelopes without opening them. Pure alcohol rubbed on the outside, for instance, made the paper transparent enough for the words written on slips inside to become visible. A concealed strong light served a similar purpose.

More ingenious was the pad system devised by Samri S. Baldwin, who was born in Cincinnati, Ohio, on January 21, 1850. "The White Mahatma's" routine was copied by Anna Eva Fay and other professed psychics. Spectators were given pads and pencils. Each person wrote a question, tore off the sheet of paper, folded it, and put it in a pocket or purse. Baldwin's assistants collected the pads, took them backstage, and "developed" them. Each second sheet was coated on the underside with pure paraffin. The pencils passed out had hard lead. The pressure of the points made wax impressions of the words on the third sheets. The assistants rubbed plumbago or lampblack over these surfaces. The black powder adhered to the wax when the sheets were tilted, or the soot was blown away. The questions were copied on small cards, and the information was conveyed to the medium. Eventually, carbon paper replaced the wax procedure.

Baldwin also used a data-bank system. When people wrote to the theatres where he was playing for tickets, he filed the letters with assigned seat locations under the dates on which the writers would attend. Each day he went through this file to gather information from the proper folder. Letterheads often supplied additional facts—such as the names of firms and their products. With this material, Kittie Bald-

Joseph Dunninger—
the master mentalist.

The Dunninger illusion
show in 1913.

win (Kate Russell), the "Mahatma's" second wife and his medium, astonished audiences around the world.

Anna Eva Fay (Heathman), however, was the greatest female stage psychic. In the 1870's she appeared in halls and concert rooms with séances; she retired as a vaudeville headliner in 1924. She was bold enough to feature tricks and illusions as well as a "Spirit Cabinet" sequence and question-answering routine. A "Spirit Dancing Handkerchief," a "Rapping Hand," and a "Levitation" were included on her programs for several years in the early 1900's. The magic was almost incidental. Her patrons came primarily to have her solve their problems. David H. Pingree, her second husband, went to great lengths to insure the accuracy of her revelations.

One evening in Brooklyn a man asked where his stolen car could be found. Anna Eva Fay, a small, thin woman with hair the color of honey, gazed into space and gave an address. The car was there, the papers reported the next day. The lines at the box office, always long, became longer, but an inquisitive reporter discovered that the psychic's husband had paid two men to steal the automobile from the owner's garage and park it on a vacant lot near his house.

Dunninger was familiar with Anna Eva Fay's secrets and those of Eva Fay (Anna Norman), a girl from St. Louis who had married John Fay, the medium's only son in 1898. Eva worked with John as "The Fays" until he committed suicide ten years later in San Francisco. With another lecturer to introduce her and supervise the collection of the questions, "The High Priestess of Mystery" equaled her mother-in-law as a moneymaker in Britain and in America.

Spoken codes, employed by The Zancigs, The Powers, The Svengalis, and other vaudeville second-sight acts didn't interest Dunninger; he planned to present his mental magic without an assistant. Perfecting a new approach in 1919, he played the role of a researcher who had made a tremendously important discovery. Performing for the Press Club in Boston in 1920, he introduced himself as the president of the American Psychical Society (a name patterned after the long-established American Society for Psychical Research).

Newton Newkirk, a *Boston Post* columnist, wrote a precise account of the demonstration. The "luxuriantly-haired gentleman" stated that mind reading was a science. In the future, when more people became proficient at it, telepathy would be a boon for mankind. Law-enforcement officers would know the plans of criminals the moment they were made. Prospective buyers of goods would be able to tell immediately if a profiteer had marked up his goods 500 per cent, or only 200 percent. Streetcar passengers on their way to work would share one another's thoughts without speaking.

Dunninger distributed squares of paper, inviting his spectators to write names, dates, or words on them, and then to fold the slips and put them in their pockets. He then instructed a volunteer to gather five of the folded papers. According to Newkirk, the professor, as he called Dunninger, next

> produced an empty envelope and asked the collector to put these five scraps into it, which the collector did with the assistance of the professor, who tucked them deeply into the envelope, which he then threw carelessly on the floor (flap side up) and asked the collector to put his foot on it and keep it there.

> The professor then walked perhaps thirty feet back from the audience and sat down behind a table which concealed from us all there was of him below his elbows. He explained he could read human minds more readily when our mentalities were on the same level as his own.

> To the complete flabbergastation of all present, he easily read exactly what each of the five had written on their scraps of papers. This all the five admitted, and loud applause followed each demonstration.

Soon after stories of this Press Club triumph appeared came accounts of even more dramatic feats. Dunninger astonished the staff of the *Evening Record* by spelling out the words in a headline chosen by editors from the files; he found a hidden key secreted by officials of the Houghton and Dutton department store; he singled out the one person in a crowd of three thousand assembled at the Parkman bandstand on the Boston Common, whose description had been written and retained by a committee.

"Deluged by letters from interested Bostonians anxious to witness the results he is able to obtain through his theory of the 'unconscious consciousness,'" *The Boston Traveler* reported, "Joseph Dunninger, the mental expert, has been prevailed upon to give a series of demonstrations in mind reading at Steinert Hall."

Despite the August heat, the concert room was filled for the opening. *The Boston American* said "the brilliant young investigator" gave the uncanniest performance ever seen in the city; his mental marvels would have convinced any skeptic that Dunninger was supernaturally endowed, but he admitted that "the phenomena is based upon a simple scientific fact."

There is an old axiom among conjurers that intelligent spectators are the easiest to deceive. Dunninger, "The Scientific Sensation of the Hour" confirmed this truism anew. The twenty-eight-year-old "psychological expert" told reporters he had been asked to prepare a telepathy course for Columbia University, and said he was writing a scholarly text explaining his theory of the mind. This was based on Freud, but far greater in scope, since it enabled him to read subconscious thoughts as well as conscious ones.

Charles Ponzi, a dapper diminutive "financial wizard" who promised investors fabulous profits if they backed his schemes, was awed when Dunninger called off the words on a slip in Ponzi's pocket during a demonstration at a Kiwanis Club luncheon in Boston on August 10, 1920. As it happened, the wire services reported the next day that a police fingerprint expert in Montreal had identified Ponzi as an ex-convict who had served a three-year term for forgery in Canada; the resulting front-page stories carried in passing Ponzi's endorsement of the mentalist: "You are no damn fake, you are all right, Signor. You shall have a signed picture of mine, autographed, because I believe you are on the level, as we say in America." Later, Ponzi was tried and convicted for swindling, while Dunninger went on to greater fame as a mind reader in New York City.

Billed as "The Man That Read the Mind of Mayor Hylan," he topped a benefit show at the New York Hippodrome in 1921. In smaller type, the advertisement said Babe Ruth and Jack Dempsey (then the most widely known athletes in the United States) would be his subjects. Most of Dunninger's performances during the next few years were given at high fees for private affairs attended by the Astors, Tiffanys, Wanamakers, Goulds, and Vanderbilts.

Socialites were charmed by his bewildering mental deceptions, but his fellow conjurers were furious when Dunninger started supplying the material for a monthly page of magic in *Science and Invention* in 1923. Several months after the long-running series began, the National Conjurers' Association—the only club of his craft that Dunninger ever joined—expelled him for exposing magic secrets.

Dunninger's biggest press coup came the next year when the Prince of Wales visited New York. The heir apparent to the British throne wrote something on a piece of paper during the party Rodman Wanamaker II gave for him at Oyster Bay, Long Island. The towering mentalist found royal thoughts as easy to read as those he had earlier deciphered from the brains of former President Theodore Roosevelt and President Warren G. Harding.

"I get the impression of a name—Johnny." "Amazing," said the prince, and he asked Dunninger to teach him a few tricks so he could entertain his friends at palace parties.

Houdini's announcement that he was leaving vaudeville to tour with his own full-evening magic show in 1925 was followed by a press release from Dunninger, saying he, too, would front a theatre mystery attraction. He considered himself a far better magician than the escapologist and set about to try and prove it. "The Master Mind of Mystery" opened with his "Bewildering and Astounding Effects and Spiritual Creations which have never before been offered to the American Public" at the Opera House in Philadelphia in June 1925, but the proposed tour was postponed until later in the year. Magicians

Mercedes' wife played, while blindfolded, pieces whispered to him as he walked through the audience.

Karl Germain, famous for artistically presented conjuring, offered mentalism as a part of his magic show.

Frimini and his wife were among the many vaudeville acts that seemed to communicate telepathically.

Chandra (James S. Harto) worked as a crystal gazer in dime museums, circuses, and variety halls.

were eager to see an illusion Dunninger said he had devised six years before—the instant transformation of a horse and carriage into a Ford automobile, but it was not on the program.

Guy Jarrett, illusion-builder for Thurston and several Broadway shows, was Dunninger's stage manager in Philadelphia. Later, Fritz Bucha, who had worked with Kellar, took over this post. Among the illusions in the Dunninger show were Kellar's miniature spirit cabinet—"Cassadaga Propaganda"; "Taka, the Dagger Torture Chest from the Temples of the Hindu"; "Flyto," the invisible passage of an assistant from one suspended, slatted cabinet to another; and "A Chinese box trick, 'Where, Oh Where Do the Girls Come From?'" However, part two of the program, "Mind Reading Extraordinary," completely overshadowed the magic.

Dunninger folded his big show early in 1926 and signed a contract to headline in Keith vaudeville with his mentalism. After proving he could attract and baffle audiences in Boston, Baltimore, Washington, and at the Palace Theatre on Broadway in New York, he went on to head Orpheum bills in the West.

Early in July 1927 the thirty-five-year-old mentalist was charged with parking his car overtime on West Forty-seventh Street near Broadway in New York. Traffic Court Magistrate Andrew Macrery asked Dunninger "Can you tell what is in my mind now?" "Yes, your Honor, you are thinking 'don't park your car near theatres during the rush hour.'" "Right," the magistrate admitted. "Perhaps you can tell me the sentence I am about to give you?" "Yes, it is five dollars or two days in jail." "Right again," Macrery replied. The mind reader paid the fine.

Later that month Dunninger went to the Alexander Avenue police station in the Bronx to report that his automobile had been stolen. A detective asked if the mentalist knew where they could find the car. Dunninger shut his eyes, began to concentrate, then announced, "The car is somewhere in Yorkville—just where I cannot say." After less than fifteen minutes of cruising in Yorkville, officers found the car smashed against a pillar of the elevated railway at Second Avenue and Seventy-second Street. They arrested an eighteen-year-old boy who jumped from the front seat and started to run.

By then, sellers of magic secrets were offering an explanation of how Dunninger performed his baffling act in Keith theatres. The mentalist took note of this in the November 1927 issue of *Science and Invention*. Drawings at the top of his magic page showed a performer palming slips of paper as he helped spectators put them in envelopes, then later opening the slips under cover of a pad. Dunninger flatly denied this was his technique and undoubtedly many readers believed him. Magicians marveled at his audacity.

Meanwhile, as chairman of the *Science and Invention* Committee for Psychical Research, Dunninger was, as *The New York Times* put it, carrying on "Houdini's work of exposing fake mediums." In April 1928, a week after Nino Pecoraro had tried unsuccessfully for a ten thousand dollar award for genuine psychic phenomena, Dunninger, tied and strapped as the Italian-born medium had been, produced a luminous form, lines written in Houdini's handwriting, and impressions in wax of a ghostly hand. Pecoraro's manager, who was present, insisted that Dunninger himself was a medium, which the magician-mentalist denied. Three years later Pecoraro appeared at a press conference called by Dunninger; he signed a confession admitting the manifestations he had used to fool Sir Arthur Conan Doyle and others were fraudulent, and he demonstrated how his tricks were done.

Dunninger ventured into radio, in July 1929, with a series of "Ghost Hours" originating from WJZ in New York; though extensively publicized, the series did not attract a large audience. He continued, however, to earn high fees with his in-person shows and he kept his name in the papers by revealing the methods of mediums. In March 1943 he made another try at radio on KYW, Philadelphia, with a new format. This was a smash hit. That fall, he began a regular 6:30 P.M. Sunday show on the National Broadcasting Company's Blue Network.

Using the same techniques that had been so successful at private affairs and in theatres, he became a sensation. Slips and envelopes were passed out before the program went on the air. Listeners heard him ask the WJZ studio audience to concentrate. He called out the first letters of names. When someone said he was thinking of those initials, Dunninger, letter by letter, spelled out the names. A special test made use of the editor of the New York *Daily Mirror*. Bob Dunn, a King Features artist, who was in the studio, put in a phone call to the newspaper and asked the editor to think of a headline that would appear in Monday's paper. As the editor visualized the words, Dunninger scrawled a message which the studio audience could not see. "How the U.S. Fifth Landed with Its Guns Blazing" was the headline, and those were the words the mentalist displayed to his spectators.

The program was switched to a better time—9 P.M. on Wednesdays, in competition with comedian Eddie Cantor and singer Frank Sinatra. *Life* magazine devoted eight pages of text and photographs to the new phenomenon of the air lanes on March 13, 1944. Not since Houdini had a mystifier so intrigued the American public.

As a national celebrity, the mentalist was taunted incessantly by Richard Himber, a professional bandleader and amateur conjurer. Himber interrupted Dunninger's shows with shouted challenges for the mentalist to read his (Himber's) mind. Dunninger snapped back he would give the heckler a thousand dollars if he could prove he had a mind.

While praising him as a showman, other magicians criticized

Kreskin "tunes in" on the
thoughts of his audience.

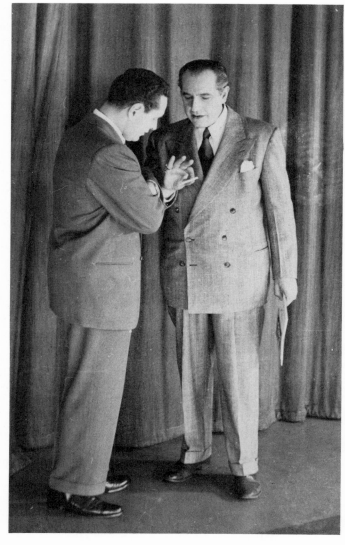

Dunninger and announcer
Danny Seymour on stage.

Dunninger for claiming to have telepathic powers. Dunninger once told me that he would like to hire Madison Square Garden for one evening, advertise "The Floating Elephant" and invite every magician in America to be his guest; Richard Himber would have a special box seat. Once his critics were assembled, Dunninger said, he would blow up the place.

The mentalist progressed from radio to television in 1948; he is one of the few stars to have had series on all three major TV networks—NBC, CBS, and ABC. John Crosby, who covered the broadcasting field for the *New York Herald Tribune* in 1949, said the mentalist had "the personality and many of the mannerisms of Pecksniff, and he addresses the audience like a dancing master talking to a group of idiot children," but Crosby admitted the feats were "awe-inspiring and more than a little disquieting." Crosby promised to stay away from the RCA Building when Dunninger performed in the studio. "My own mind is untidy and frequently libelous, and I don't want anyone messing around up there."

On television, as on radio, Dunninger featured "Brain Busters." He probed secret thoughts as remote cameras showed an officer on a submarine pondering or a man and a woman concentrating as they parachuted down to earth from a tower at Coney Island. When not appearing before the cameras, Dunninger was working for live audiences or gathering material for newspaper and magazine articles and books. There was no hint in his *What's on Your Mind?*, which Walter B. Gibson, who had been a ghost-writer for Thurston and Houdini, prepared for him, that Dunninger was not a legitimate telepathist. Experiments for those who wished to develop their ESP abilities were described in detail. Anyone who tried these tests must have marveled even more as they watched the master mentalist on their home screens.

For years Dunninger had told reporters that if magicians knew how his act was done, it was strange they were not duplicating it. When one did, and began appearing on network interview shows in the mid-1960's, Dunninger was furious.

Kreskin (George Kresge, Jr.) had been fascinated by the comic-strip adventures of "Mandrake the Magician" when he was five. At fifteen, the lanky young man from West Caldwell, New Jersey, who wore horn-rimmed glasses and had a friendly manner, was giving professional shows. He performed mental feats à la Dunninger and hypnotism and muscle reading in the style of Franz Polgar, who was popular on town hall and lecture circuits.

Eventually Kreskin decided there was no such thing as a true hypnotic trance—that "hypnotism" was just a matter of suggestion. Telling audiences this did not interfere with this part of his entertainment; volunteers still carried out the same hilarious antics as before.

Kreskin made frequent appearances with Mike Douglas, Joey

Bishop, and other TV hosts. He moved into night clubs, theatres, and concert halls, and marketed a best-selling game based upon the old "sex indicator" pendulums, which swing either in circles or back and forth in response to unconscious muscular action. He billed himself as "The Amazing Kreskin."

His model, whose ABC-TV series in 1956 had been titled "The Amazing Dunninger," noted with mounting ire that Kreskin was not only using his techniques, but often his exact words. Dunninger began taping his final TV series at WPIX in New York in the fall of 1967. Illness forced the master mentalist's retirement a few years later.

When, in January 1972, Viacom Enterprises syndicated "The Amazing World of Kreskin," television programs that had been taped in Canada by the thirty-five-year-old magician, the seventy-nine-year-old Dunninger was even more distressed. True, Kreskin's guest subjects were minor celebrities whereas Dunninger had worked with such superstars as Gary Cooper, Jack Benny, and Lucille Ball, but Kreskin also sat in a chair doodling in a pad, just as Dunninger had done while he "tuned in on spectators' thoughts," and Kreskin, too, explained that he wore his glasses because he couldn't see the jottings he made without them.

Kreskin has developed a light, bantering style; he delivers his comedy lines effectively. It is unfortunate that both he and Dunninger, a showman second only to Houdini, chose to tell audiences and reporters that they were presenting genuine feats of ESP, when they might have adopted a similar approach to that of Sydney and Lesley Piddington, a husband-and-wife team of mentalists from Australia. In 1949, the Piddingtons went to London and created an absolute sensation on British radio and television. Lesley seemed to read her husband's thoughts, though she was blindfolded, and he was in another studio. Many people thought ESP was the answer; others were sure the Piddingtons used trickery. This clash of opinions heightened interest. The Piddingtons themselves told audiences, "Judge for yourselves."

22

Big Shows and Small Screens

Tʜʀᴇᴇ hundred or more magicians entertained Allied and Axis troops on the Continent during World War II. Some flew to rest areas with civilian shows; others served with the Armed Forces. Conjurers in uniform, carrying lightweight props along with their weapons, performed in the field for infantry, artillery, and armored companies. Working with cards, coins, cigarettes, and ropes, they exhibited on such improvised stages as the tailgates of ammunition trucks and the tops of tanks.

When peace came, more elaborate productions were presented for the occupation armies and entertainment-starved Europeans. The first illusionist to emerge in the postwar period was Kalanag, a plump, balding, bespectacled, fifty-four-year-old former executive of a German film corporation. His spectacular magic revue made a hit with the British Occupation Army in 1947; within four years, he was the dominant magician in Great Britain, as well as in Western Europe.

Kalanag—Kala Nag (Black Snake), the name of an elephant in Rudyard Kipling's *Jungle Books*—was born Helmut Ewald Schreiber in Stuttgart on January 23, 1893. Though interested in magic since childhood, he entered the motion-picture industry after receiving a degree in philosophy from the University of Munich. During his twenty-five years with Tobis-Films in Berlin and the Bavarian Film Corporation in Munich, Schreiber produced more than 180 movies. Before Germany invaded Austria and other neighboring countries, he was president of the German Magic Circle and editor of its magazine. As the war spread, he became the virtual czar of conjuring in the Third Reich.

An edict, sponsored by Schreiber, banned the publication of conjuring secrets in newspapers and popular magazines; his organization set the standards for magic clubs in the countries under German control. He flew with Reichminister Speer to entertain at the *Luftwaffe* base in Lapland and made periodic trips to the front to perform for the Blitzkreig divisions. A Schreiber show became an annual Christmas treat for Field Marshal Hermann Göring and his family at Karin Hall.

Hitler's favorite magician even played an occasional prank on Der Führer. Schreiber, a German paper reported, asked "How much money do you have in your wallet?" Hitler replied that he never carried a wallet. The magician laughed and told Der Führer he had 150 marks in the left-coat pocket of his uniform. Hitler reached in dubiously, took out a billfold he had never seen before, and found that precise amount inside it.

During the bombing of Berlin, Schreiber returned to Munich. After the American Third Army captured the city, he arranged a performance for General George S. Patton with the help of an officer who had read about the German magician in *The Linking Ring,* the monthly journal of the International Brotherhood of Magicians. The occupation troops which replaced Patton's men were less hospitable to the entertainer. Learning that he was to be arrested by the Counter-Intelligence Corps, Schreiber masqueraded as an American officer and fled to the British zone, where he convinced a Hamburg court that he had never been a member of the Nazi party.

Several military officials, who were intrigued by his tricks, aided him in assembling the equipment, costumes, scenery, and assistants for his debut as a professional illusionist. An audience of British soldiers saw his opening performance at the Garrison Theatre in Hamburg on October 17, 1947. The show was called *Sim Sala Bim,* a title pirated from Dante, the Danish-American magician whose 1939 run at the Scala Theatre in Berlin ended abruptly when the German Army marched on Poland.

Kalanag, which was to be his name thereafter, was given an enthusiastic reception. His second wife, Gloria de Vos, a blonde beauty-contest winner, was hailed as "the most beautiful woman in magic," and his clever staging, the *Hamburger Echo* critic reported, had the audience's hair on end. After seventy days in Hamburg, the show went to Bremen, Düsseldorf, and other German cities. In 1949, "Europe's Master of Magic" flew to Spain with fifteen assistants and tons of baggage. By then, the Kalanag production eclipsed the shows of Alois Kassner and Cortini (Paul Korth), the leading prewar German illusionists.

The Kalanag illusion production entertained troops in postwar Europe before it went on tour.

Kalanag's levitation was staged in an Oriental set; the girl floated high over his head as she soared.

Kalanag had been a German film executive previous to World War II.

Booked to open at the Stoll Theatre in London in January 1951, Kalanag was concerned about how the English would receive the first postwar theatrical importation from the country that had tried to bomb them out of existence. He cautiously arranged a Continental tour to follow his first London engagement. His worries were unfounded; the German attraction drew big audiences, and he returned to Britain in the fall as the first illusionist to play the major provincial houses with his own show since Dante.

The London *Stage* summed up Kalanag's appeal when he made another British tour three years later: He "rules the proceedings like a benevolent uncle and, with his portly figure and quaint, albeit slightly ghoulish, sense of humor, does not really look like a magician. But once the show gets under way, it becomes plain that he is one of the world's greatest exponents of large-scale illusions, and, in fact, of the smaller ones as well."

Kalanag's masterpiece began as a suspension and ended as an incredible levitation. Gloria rested vertically in space after he removed the two chairs holding a board that supported her. Then he took away the board, passed a hoop over her body, and she slowly rose twenty feet in the air. A multi-armed gigantic statue of Buddha in the background added to the dramatic impact of this presentation.

Wearing a surgeon's cap and gown, Kalanag gleefully sliced through Gloria as she reclined on an operating table. A motor car disappeared in a puff of smoke at his command. He covered a lighted lamp and caused it to vanish near the footlights; girls dressed in costumes resembling large lamp shades surrounded him and made the small feat look big. Luminous skeletons danced on the darkened stage, and a girl who was hauled aloft in a cargo net disappeared. His staging of "The Indian Rope Trick" was superior to that of Hertz, Le Roy, Goldin, or Thurston.

In subsequent years Kalanag played in Africa, Canada, Brazil, and several American cities. He made his first appearance in New York in 1960 when he brought his company across the Atlantic for a single performance on the Ed Sullivan television program. On December 24, 1963, sixteen years after his first appearance as a postwar illusionist, Kalanag died of a stroke at the age of seventy in his home near Munich.

The magician who was to become Kalanag's principal rival had visited the German illusionist in his Hamburg dressing room in 1950. Protul Chandra Sorcar (Sarcar), a thirty-seven-year-old Bengali, praised the show and said he was sure the ingeniously staged illusions and colorful settings would delight Indian audiences. The next day the German newspapers reported that "The World's Greatest Magician, P. C. Sorcar," then on a trip around the world, had visited

"Europe's Master of Magic." The press had picked up the story from Sorcar's publicity releases and letters.

At the combined convention of the Society of American Magicians and the International Brotherhood of Magicians in Chicago that same year, Sorcar created quite a stir. Wearing a princely costume with a plumed turban and pointed-toed, gold slippers, the Indian illusionist talked with the best-known American performers, passed out leaflets describing his show, and added to his repertoire. At the request of the gracious Indian with the trim black moustache, Harry Blackstone sketched the equipment he used to sever a woman with a buzz saw. Jack Gwynne, who had met Sorcar in India while playing for American troops, showed his friend the book of secrets containing descriptions and drawings of the illusionary devices developed for the Gwynne show.

Ideas garnered during this swing around the globe were incorporated in Sorcar's program on his return to Calcutta. The buzz saw became his feature. He built a vanishing motor car similar to Kalanag's. Sorcar adapted settings from Kalanag's and other big magic shows and rehearsed and perfected routines picked up in Japan and America.

Five years later, Sorcar, by then the most successful magician in the East, invaded the West. He hoped to present a vanishing elephant rather than an automobile when he opened at the Théâtre de l'Etoile in Paris in November 1955, but the wary elephant tested the planking with one foot at a rehearsal and refused to walk out on the stage. Kalanag's friends reported that Sorcar gave an abysmal performance; almost half of his illusions, they said, had been stolen from the German production, and the "self-conceited, self-admiring Oriental" presented them poorly. Yet the attraction played eight weeks—a record run for a magician in modern Paris.

After engagements in other French cities and in Belgium, Sorcar crossed the channel to England. His first London appearance created a sensation. Performing on BBC-TV's "Panorama" on April 9, 1956, the night before his opening at the Duke of York's Theatre, Sorcar ran a power-driven circular saw through the prone body of his "hypnotised" seventeen-year-old assistant, Dipty Dey. To prove the cut was not an optical illusion, he thrust a wide metal cleaver down through the incision. Then he pulled away the blade, rubbed the girl's hands, and told her to wake up. She remained stiff and motionless. As the program was running overtime, host Richard Dimbleby broke in to say good night. Then the telephones began to ring. For more than an hour the switchboard at the Lime Grove studios was jammed. Protesting viewers thought the girl had been murdered. "She's all right," the operators repeated. "She's all right."

Big Shows and
Small Screens

Pageantry added to the excitement of Sorcar's *In-Dra-Jal*.

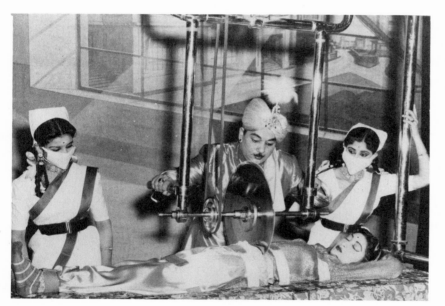

Sorcar made the front pages when his severed girl was not reunited during a TV show in London.

The Indian magician's name appeared on posters in Moscow as Copkap during his tour of Russia.

Sorcar's gallows illusion before it was redesigned for American television; the railing for the steps was removed.

Sorcar, Jr.'s posters emphasize the appeal of the strange and the mysterious.

Igor Kio's "Cremation" at Madison Square Garden in New York. Only ashes remain after the spectacular incineration.

Dozens of doves are produced from an empty box by the adroit Russian illusionist.

Front-page stories the following day reported: "TRICK ALARMS VIEWERS"; "SAWING SORCAR ALARMS VIEWERS"; "GIRL CUT IN HALF—SHOCK ON TV"; "SAWN-UP WOMAN—TV PANIC"; "THE GIRL SAWN IN HALF IS ALL RIGHT, VIEWERS." The girl had not been injured, readers learned. Dipty Dey had been restored to one piece off camera. She was smiling as she signed autographs for the studio audience.

No magic show in British history ever received such fantastic publicity. A political cartoon in the *Daily Mirror* showed the heads of four nations standing behind a divided girl representing the Eastern and Western sectors of Germany. The caption was a quote from Sorcar's post-television statement: "There is no cause for alarm! *Of course,* we know how to do it—we've been doing it for years and years. . . ." A cartoon in the *Daily Express* pictured a man with a telephone in his hand and his TV set sliced through the middle. "Hello, BBC? The girl sawn in half may be all right, but what about my TV set?"

The *Evening News* critic, who covered Sorcar's first night, said "This man is one of the best (if not the very best) magician we have seen. . . . [he] does the most amazing things with chalk on a blackboard while he is blindfolded; he materializes birds from empty air and catches them in a net; he hooks fish on to the end of a line, again from the air." The most unusual feat was the slicing off of the tip of an assistant's tongue, then replacing it as a dozen men came to the stage to observe. "Big gasp of the evening, though, is the trick which kept the BBC telephone lines buzzing, of Sawing a Woman with an Electric Saw."

Sorcar traveled from Calcutta to New York with his staff to present the buzz-saw illusion on NBC-TV's "Festival of Magic" the following year. Then he broke box-office records during a tour of Australia and New Zealand. Two of his sixteen assistants were kept busy mailing newspaper reviews, theatre programs, photographs, and reports on his grosses to conjuring magazines and leading magicians throughout the world. He was determined to make Sorcar the best-known name in magic.

His illusions, settings, and costumes were produced in his own workshop. Sorcar's shows at Calcutta's New Empire Theatre were even more lavish than those he presented abroad. Scenic and lighting devices he had copied from the Folies-Bergère in Paris and the Radio City Music Hall in New York enhanced his productions. With the exception of the tongue cutting, which he dropped after it lost its publicity impact, and "Water of India" (the repeated pouring of liquid from a Hindu lota bowl, inspired by Kalanag's presentation), Sorcar's tricks and illusions were Western in origin. He avoided typical Indian specialities, such as "The Basket Trick," "The Indian Rope Trick," and "The Mango Tree."

Moments after the curtains hide the girl, she appears in another cabinet.

The lady who changed into a lion, at Igor Kio's command, was his mother.

Sorcar toured Japan, Thailand, Singapore, Burma, Lebanon, Iran, Egypt, Kenya, and Zanzibar before he and his company went to the Soviet Union in August 1962 on a cultural-exchange program; the Bolshoi Ballet was sent to India. He arrived in Moscow by Aerflot jet to find that a labor dispute at the Calcutta docks had caused his baggage to be delayed. Soviet authorities, however, solved the problem by forwarding the props from Odessa to Moscow by plane. Billed as Copkap—the Russian transliteration of his name—he worked in English as usual while an interpreter translated his patter. *Izvestia* on September 2 devoted a full page to an illustrated interview with the Indian showman, and *Pravda* and *Veccherniaya* gave him considerable space.

Though Sorcar was scheduled to open at the Palace of Culture in Leningrad on September 9, his Moscow run was extended another ten days. Sorcar noticed that Russian stage technicians were measuring the dimensions of his boxes and cabinets; this did not upset him since his own assistants were busy getting the specifications of Russian lighting units and theatrical equipment. In Leningrad, he was delighted when a critic, who had seen several illusionists, including Dante and Kio, the most famous Soviet illusionist, wrote that "Sorcar is best."

Accolades from abroad were used to publicize his tours in India. He seldom missed a promotional trick. Early in his career, he had joined the Rotary Club. He spoke at meetings in the countries he visited to advertise his appearances, and he brought back foreign club pennants to decorate the Calcutta meeting room.

Sorcar's name was emblazoned in large letters at the top of his five-story apartment building in the Ballyganj district of Calcutta. The lower floor, a storage area, contained tons of crated paraphernalia, costumes, and scenery. Above the ground floor were offices for himself and his staff and a dark room equipped with enlargers, cameras, and chemicals. One office housed his publicity material; another, his stacks of scrapbooks. His own office fronted on a cement area at the rear of the building. He could look out the window and watch his carpenters, artists, metal workers, and designers working in the open air, building new illusions and painting stage flats and backdrops. A spur of a railway track ended a short distance away. When the Sorcar company traveled, it was a simple matter to load his equipment onto baggage cars there.

Upper floors of the building served as living quarters for the magician, his wife, three sons, and two daughters. On the roof stood a private temple with the exotic images and symbols of his Hindu faith.

Though Sorcar's press releases claimed he came from a family of conjurers, this was fiction. He was, however, determined that the magic business he had established would be carried on after his death. He gave each of his sons names that began with his own initials, P. C., and he felt certain that one of them would choose to go on the stage. The two eldest traveled with the show when they were not studying at the University of Calcutta, their father's alma mater. Eventually he selected his second son as his sucessor and trained him as a publicist as well as a performer.

Meanwhile, Sorcar wrote magic books, and articles for the Indian newspapers and magazines, thus keeping his name in print even while he toured abroad. The President of India awarded Sorcar the title *Padmasri* in 1964 and praised him for elevating magic to the level of a fine art. Other Indian conjurers copied his costumes, illusions, stage decorations, and promotional campaigns. They trimmed their moustaches like his and wore pearls in the lobes of their ears as he did on the stage.

Aside from India, where Sorcar worked from Calcutta to New Delhi, his most profitable engagements were in Japan. He performed there first in 1937 with two suitcases of equipment; he returned in 1954 with fifteen assistants and an illusion show. Ten years later his *Ind-Dra-Jal* production was even larger. He built new equipment for each visit. The 1966 tour lasted five months; in 1967–68 he shattered box-office records in sixty-one cities.

Late in 1970, Sorcar flew to Japan for his sixth tour. His fans, as usual, turned out in large numbers, but the bitter cold weather was a strain on the fifty-seven-year-old magician, who was accustomed to the warmer temperatures of India. Fatigue and hypertension brought on a fatal heart attack in Shibetsu, Hokkaido. He died there on January 6, 1971. Four days later, his show reopened with his second son, billed as Sorcar, Jr., in the starring role. P. C.'s eldest son flew from Seattle, Washington, where he was studying for a master's degree in engineering, to take his father's body to Calcutta.

A front-page story on January 11 in the *Hindustan Standard* reported the streets had been crowded with mourners when the funeral procession carried the great magician's body to the riverside where it was burned: "trams were withdrawn and buses diverted as the cortege proceeded." Heaped high on the casket were wreaths from both parties of the Indian Congress, the city of Calcutta, the West Bengal government, the Ashaikawa Rotary Club, and the All-India Magic Circle, of which Sorcar had been the long-term president. Messages of condolence came from the governments of Japan and the United States. Prime Minister Indira Gandhi said the death of Sorcar had ended a glorious chapter in Indian magic.

Sorcar, Jr., returned to India after completing the Japanese itinerary and winning praise for his artistry. In the summer of 1972 he was booked for a repeat season in Japan. The son was making good, just as his father had firmly expected. The assistants had been with the show for years; their stage movements and backstage activities were

Chefalo, the great
Italian magician,
performed on five
continents.

A troupe of
midgets and a
giant were among
his many
assistants.

perfectly timed. More important, the son fully shared the father's fascination with magic and was thoroughly prepared for the smooth transition, which the elder Sorcar had known from the example of the Kios to be possible.

When the Moscow Circus arrived in Japan in March 1966, Sorcar had been distressed to learn that his friend Emil Kio (Renard), the Russian illusionist, had unexpectedly died in Kiev at the age of sixty-five on December 18, 1965. The star of the circus was still Kio, but now Emil's twenty-one-year-old son Igor filled the role. With the help of his father's excellent assistants, Igor gave a magnificent performance.

Emil Kio was the most innovative circus illusionist in history. Since Philip Astley, the founder of the modern circus, mixed feats of conjuring with horsemanship at his London amphitheatre in the eighteenth century, many magicians had performed in sawdust rings, but none equalled Kio's sensational staging.

His most brilliant illusion was a cremation-in-the-round. A girl stood on top of a small white table while a circular cloth canopy was lowered to cover her. Assistants rushed into the ring with lighted torches and set fire to the cloth. Forty-foot-high flames leapt up. Spectators in the arena could feel the intensity of the heat. Soon only a heap of ashes remained. Later the girl emerged unharmed from inside a suspended box.

Another of Kio's presentations centered attention on a large empty cage, raised from the ground on four sturdy, metal legs. A woman sprinted up a flight of stairs and into the cage; the door was locked behind her. Assistants pulled a canopy forward and lowered it to cover the cage on all sides, except the bottom. Quickly the canopy was hauled up and away. The woman was gone; a live lion paced behind the bars where she had been a moment before.

Kio's solid-through-solid penetration, in which a girl crawled through a framed sheet of transparent glass after a small area at the center had been covered with paper, was copied by Sorcar. He would have done the cremation illusion, too, but fire regulations for theatres prohibit open flames on theatre stages.

Igor Kio, who made his circus debut at five, had been well groomed to take his father's place. Emil Kio wore glasses and was somewhat professorial in manner; Igor, though stockier, has a more relaxed style. His thirty—yes, thirty—assistants work as efficiently and as swiftly for him as they did for the first Kio. And the woman he changed into a lion was his mother! Meanwhile his brother Emil, older by five years, was an illusionist with another unit of the Moscow Circus.

Igor Kio headlined when the Moscow Circus came to the United States for the first time. The show opened at Madison Square Garden in New York in October 1967 and toured from coast to coast. Earlier his father had appeared with the troupe in London and other world capitals, as well as in Russia where he held the coveted title—People's Artist.

Another star circus illusionist was Raffael Chefalo. Born in Italy in 1885, he learned his first tricks as a teen-age boy in America. He and his wife topped vaudeville bills throughout the world, first as Capretta and Chefalo, then as Palermo and Chefalo, and eventually as The Great Chefalo.

At the suggestion of his friend, Houdini, Chefalo changed his style in 1907 from rapid talk to mostly pantomime. He framed an act, "The Wizards in White," in which his wife, Magda Palermo, performed the principal tricks while he presented the lesser feats. They were booked abroad for the first time with their "Garden of Magic" in England in 1910. He produced Magda from a folding screen. Singing "I Don't Care," in the manner of the popular star, Eva Tanguay, she languidly pulled flowers from nowhere. For the finish, she capped an empty drum with paper; Chefalo, dressed as John Bull, broke through the drumhead, and her costume changed to a red, white, and blue gown.

Following a tour of South America, Chefalo returned to England and played on the Continent. Performing in the Canary Islands when World War I broke out, he sailed at once for South America. After the war the Italian illusionist performed in South Africa, Australia and the Far East, with a greatly expanded repertoire and himself in the key role. Then he toured India with a full-evening show until 1922 when he circled the globe, filling dates in Egypt, Europe, North America, and Australia before crossing to India again and continuing on to Russia.

Booked for four weeks in Moscow in 1929, Chefalo was so popular that his engagement was prolonged for six months. In the Soviet Union he added a troupe of midgets and a giant to the show. They acted as his assistants in the British Isles, Australia, and Europe.

Magda died in Frankfurt am Main, Germany, on February 12, 1939. His second wife, Magdalena, later replaced her as his chief assistant. As an Italian citizen, Chefalo had to leave England when Britain entered World War II. He spent those years performing first in Italy, then in Czechoslovakia. When the American army arrived, he gave a gala show for the troops. Then after two years of entertaining for the occupation forces in Europe, he returned to the remnants of vaudeville with a sixty-minute act. Equally skillful with sleight of hand and illusions, he featured P. T. Selbit's "Million Dollar Mystery," the production of large objects, including crates containing assistants, from a small empty box.

When it was no longer possible to play the year around in

European variety theatres, he worked with circuses. Chefalo was still a star, touring with a circus in Korea, when he died in 1963 at the age of seventy-seven.

Magicians who traveled with their own circuses—The Great Carmo, an Australian, and Chang, a Panamanian, for example—lost fortunes. Exceptions were the self-styled "Lord" George Sanger, a nineteenth-century British showman, and Tihanyi, a twentieth-century Hungarian. Sanger billed himself as "the Wizard of the West" when he opened a fair booth in 1848 at the age of twenty-seven. Soon he began supplementing his conjuring feats with a "Learned Pig." He purchased Astley's London amphitheatre, staged winter equestrian productions there, then for many years toured with the most popular show under canvas in the British Isles.

Tihanyi, who was born Franz Czeiler in Ketegyhaza, a small town in Hungary, on June 29, 1916, took conjuring lessons from a German magician, Alfred Uferini (Ufer), as a boy. By watching Dr. Giovanni, a dexterous Italian variety performer, who combined magic with pickpocketing, the young Hungarian learned how to take objects from those who came up to assist him during his show without their being aware of it. As Fakir Sanda Ruh, Czeiler performed mental magic and feats of fakirism. Then at the age of twenty he adopted a new approach and the new name of Tihanyi. (In Spanish-speaking countries he drops the final *i*.)

Tihanyi went to Brazil in July 1953 as an act in the Circo Romano. Soon he had his own show, the Circo Magico Tihanyi. For almost twenty years this has been the most successful under-canvas attraction in Latin America. The specially designed tent seats 4,000; the lighting and sound equipment matches that of the world's finest theatres.

The curtains open on fourteen girls in sparkling costumes. Above their heads hangs a gold-framed picture of the magician. The picture is lowered and Tihanyi steps out. For ten minutes he works rapidly, producing bowls of fire, flowers, and birds. A flock of ducks emerges from a tub filled with water. One moment a small upright cage is empty, the next a gyrating dancer appears inside it; suddenly she changes into a clown. Another assistant reclines on her side in a topless box. Assistants close the front, then lower a heavy cage with a "gorilla" behind the bars into the box, apparently crushing the girl. The cage is raised, the front of the box is opened; the girl is relaxing inside, as before.

Tihanyi speaks for the first time to welcome the audience and to introduce a feat of magical marksmanship. A girl is put into a box and the box is hoisted up. Another suspended box is across the stage.

Fu Manchu stepped from the pages of a giant book to make his first appearance in one of his shows.

In Mexico City Fu Manchu wrote and starred in six films. Tricks and illusions enlivened the plots.

Dance numbers in the Fu Manchu show were staged with "black light" and other special visual effects.

Tihanyi fires a cannon. The first box is empty, the girl jumps out of the second one.

Two girls in costumes of contrasting colors stretch out in two boxes with their heads, hands, and feet extending from holes in the ends. Tihanyi saws through the center of each box, then swings around the feet sections until they are side by side with the heads. Assistants roll the severed parts back into position. But somehow a mistake is made; the wrong halves are united! Each girl is in one piece, but each is wearing the lower half of the other's costume.

Variety acts, including one with five elephants, a trapeze artist who swings out over the heads of the audience, and "Dancing Waters" —fountains that shoot up and spray to symphonic music—are interspersed between the magic numbers. Before the program ends, Tihanyi performs the pickpocket routine which brought him his first show business success in Europe.

Like Kio and Sorcar, Tihanyi intends for his show to be carried on. His son, Tihanyi, Jr., has learned his routines and alternates with him as the star of the production.

Three generations of Maskelynes in England, four generations of Uferinis in Germany, and six generations of the Dutch Bamberg family were magicians. David Bamberg, who as Fu Manchu presented the finest illusion show in South America, still devises new mysteries in Buenos Aires.

David's great, great, great grandfather, Eliaser Bamberg (1760–1833), lost his left leg in a shipboard explosion. The wooden leg which replaced it had a secret compartment. With this he could make small objects appear and disappear in a most unbelievable way. "The devil on one leg" performed with cups and balls on the streets of his native Leyden, and in taverns and the homes of his wealthier patrons.

David Leendart Bamberg (1786–1869) assisted his father, then became Court Conjurer to King William II of Holland in 1843. Tobias Bamberg (1812–1870) also appeared for William II and his son, David Tobias Bamberg (1843–1914), received a royal appointment as William III's magician. Theodore Bamberg (1875–1963) appeared with his father at the palace before he took the name Okito and performed in the principal variety theatres of the world as a Chinese magician.

The second David Tobias Bamberg, Theodore's son, was born in Derby, England on February 19, 1904. Brought as a child by his parents to New York, David showed his first trick at a meeting of the Society of American Magicians. One of the two men who volunteered to assist the boy as he made a production from a box was the president of the society, Harry Houdini. Young Bamberg in turn came up from the audience to help Howard Thurston when his father toured with the Thurston show.

At thirteen David worked with Julius Zancig, a noted Danish mentalist, in Manhattan. Later he was employed as an assistant to Professor Seward, a boardwalk astrologer, in Atlantic City. In the 1920's Bamberg traveled with a P. T. Selbit "Divided Woman" company in vaudeville, and for several months he worked as a film extra in Hollywood.

Dressed as an explorer, David sawed through an African in the Congo Room floor show of the New York Alamac Hotel in 1924. Two years later while playing in Bulgaria, billed as Syko, with a sleight-of-hand and shadowgraph act, he received an offer from The Great Raymond to join his company in Portugal before it sailed for a tour of South America. Shadowgraphs—shadows cast on a large screen as the performer uses his hands to form animals, birds and humans—are an effective novelty in a magic show.

Bamberg was performing on his own in Argentina in 1928 when Dante, with the largest and most entertaining illusion show ever seen in Buenos Aires, filled the Casino theatre for 120 performances. Firmly convinced that the handsome, dark-haired descendant of five generations of Dutch magicians could make a fortune in Latin America with a similar production, Walter Gaulke, an executive with a film-distributing company, put up the money required to build one.

At the age of twenty-four, David took a new name—Fu Manchu—and designed sets and apparatus in Chinese decor. His Fu Manchu, unlike the villain in Sax Rohmer's mystery stories, sought only to entertain. A success from the start in Argentina, the show traveled to other South American countries and to Central America, the West Indies, Spanish Morocco, Portugal, and Spain. To avoid lawsuits over the Fu Manchu name, the attraction was billed as *The Mysteries of Fu Chan* when he played the Cervantes, a Spanish theatre in New York, in March 1937. After this run the magician chose to return to Latin America rather than play four shows a day in presentation houses in the United States.

While performing in Mexico City in the early 1940's, he became interested in film making; during the next few years Fu Manchu wrote and starred in six feature movies, most of which capitalized on his skill as a magician.

In February 1947, Fu Manchu opened at the Teatro Nacional in Buenos Aires with a new show, *Crazimagicana*. Staging his tricks and illusions in quick-moving skits and blackouts, similar to those in Olsen and Johnson's Broadway revue, *Hellz-a-poppin,* he won greater acclaim than ever before.

I saw Fu Manchu the following year at the Carlos Gomez

theatre in Rio de Janeiro. Periodically Micalet, a comedian with a black moustache and baggy pants, attempted to top the magician's tricks. After Fu Manchu's silk production, Micalet strode toward a table. Before he reached it, a girl whisked it offstage. Wheeling around, he approached another table; this, too, was carried away. When the last table eluded his grasp, he shrugged and walked to the wings. Only once during this running byplay did the comedian triumph. As Micalet played a flute, a spoon danced in a bottle. Fu Manchu passed his hand over and around the bottle; still the spoon continued to jig. Even when Fu clamped a hand over the mouth of the bottle, the spoon bobbed up and down in time to the music. The magician stepped back with a puzzled expression. A showgirl strolled out, stopped to look at the bottle, and executed a burlesque "bump" with her midsection. The spoon flew out!

Halfway through the show a woman stood up in the audience and demanded that the illusionist fulfill his promise to marry her. Fu invited her to the stage. To prove his good intentions, he showed her a model of the bungalow he would build for her. She was delighted until a girl in a negligee popped up through the roof of what had appeared to be an empty house.

In a black-light production number, luminous skeletons emerged from a coffin and danced while their heads, arms, and legs became detached, floated in space, and finally reunited. For his sawing illusion, Fu used a sharp-edged pendulum that swung back and forth in a slow descent until it sliced through an assistant.

An imaginative presentation for a solid-through-solid feat began when the magician left the stage and stood behind a table to the right of the orchestra. Asking the audience to keep their eyes on a sheet of glass in a wooden frame on the table, he threaded a ribbon through holes in the glass and the frame. It was obviously impossible for him to lift out the glass without releasing one end of the ribon. Just then a man and a woman began quarreling in the upper stage box on the left. The audience cringed as the man lifted the woman and hurled her down to the stage. Only then did the spectators realize the "woman" was a dummy. When they turned their attention to the trick, it was over! Smiling broadly, Fu Manchu held the glass dangling from the ribbon above the frame.

For many years this beautifully costumed, handsomely mounted magic revue played the major cities in South and Central America. Eventually the illusionist restructured the production. He wrote a mystery play, *The Devil's Daughter,* and wove his most popular tricks and illusions into the plot. Despite political upheavals and the loss of his savings after the Peron government was overthrown in Argentina, Fu Manchu kept the best magic show in South America running until March 19, 1966, when he gave his last full-evening program in Buenos

Klingsor, the Belgian illusionist, now owns Kalanag's equipment.

John Calvert starred in several films, as well as his magic show.

Tihanyi's elaborate illusion show made its debut in Brazil.

Blood spurts out as Richiardi, Jr. saws through a girl.

Aires at the age of sixty-one. Since then, the most famous member of the great Bamberg family of magicians—who ranks with Thurston and Dante as a stage personality and master illusionist—has been busy in his Buenos Aires magic shop constructing ingenious equipment for other conjurers.

One of Fu Manchu's competitors in Peru, Richiardi (Ricardo Izquierdo), left his native country to perform in Europe, Africa, Asia, and elsewhere in South America before he opened at the Compoamor Theatre, a Spanish playhouse, in New York in July 1936. A month later at the Bronx Theatre, The Great Richiardi presented a forty-five–minute act featuring "The Guillotine" (the chopped-off head actually fell into a basket) and a chilling version of the buzz-saw illusion. After the whirling blade cut into his subject's body, assistants dressed as nurses daubed the incision with an antiseptic solution, and spectators were invited up for a closer view. While on tour the following year with the Ruby and Cherry Exposition, a tent show, Richiardi died in Atlanta, Georgia, at the age of fifty-two.

His widow went to New York with the illusions and with their son, Aldo, who had been born in Lima on November 24, 1923. Aldo adopted Richiardi, Jr., as his stage name and attempted to front his father's show. The boy had been an assistant previously, but the new venture was not a success. He returned to Lima, entered military school for two years, then tried show business again. The short, slender, dark-haired youth became an accomplished singer and dancer. Using these talents to present the elder Richiardi's magic in a new form, he starred in a revue at the Smart Theatre in Buenos Aires in 1943.

After three months in Argentina, Richiardi, Jr., toured for two years with his own show in Brazil and played in Mexico and at a Spanish theatre in San Antonio, Texas, before opening in February 1949 at the 2,400-seat Puerto Rico playhouse in the Bronx, New York. Robert Sylvester, a *Daily News* columnist, said Richiardi, Jr., had a "first-rate routine," including a feature trick that the theatre patrons loved, but which more squeamish New Yorkers might find appalling. As the magician ran a motor-driven circular saw through the middle of a blonde assistant, blood spurted out and drenched the stage. Fascinated spectators filed down the aisle and across the stage to view "as ghastly a mess of entrails as can be found in any butcher shop." *Time* magazine reported that, while this macabre magician caused women to shriek and faint, the show grossed forty thousand dollars a week—more than all but two of the productions on Broadway.

Richiardi, Jr., toured Europe, the British Isles, and the Orient; whenever he returned to the United States to play Radio City Music Hall and leading hotels and night clubs, he omitted the gory version of the buzz saw. American television viewers saw him suspend a girl with her arm resting on an upright broom, levitate a miniature automobile and its driver, and conjure a shrouded girl out of a chair and into a trunk on the Ed Sullivan show.

Headlining the *World Festival of Magic and Occult* at the Felt Forum in Madison Square Garden in New York in December 1971, Richiardi Jr. followed his artistically presented feats with the buzz saw. Times had changed. No one fainted when the stream of red liquid shot fifteen feet forward. Spectators, like those at the Puerto Rico theatre twenty-two years earlier, left their seats to line up in the aisle and wait their turn to walk past the results of his conjuring carnage on the stage. For three weeks the Felt Forum was packed, and Richiardi, Jr., was signed to star in another magic show there in December 1973.

Blood had been spilled, but to a lesser degree, years earlier when John Calvert severed a head in American vaudeville; Calvert offered his slicing as a burlesque of a horror film, not as serious surgery. Born in Trenton, Indiana, on August 5, 1911, Calvert also gave his first shows as a youngster. At twenty he played variety theatres in the Southern states with six assistants and an act comprised of sleight of hand, illusions, and pseudo-hypnotism. Tall, with reddish-brown hair, a moustache, and an easy manner, he looked and spoke like a film star long before he made his first picture. After a tour of the Hawaiian Islands in 1937, he returned to America. Wearing a double-breasted blue jacket and gray trousers, rather than the formal attire favored by other conjurers, Calvert topped bills in the major film-and-stage-show houses.

His act at the Hippodrome Theatre in Baltimore in November 1945 began with a fast pantomimic sequence, set to the music of "Running Wild." Assisted by several girls in very short spangled dresses and long blue capes, he produced a bowl of water, caught doves in a net, whirled silk streamers from empty boxes, materialized a rabbit, made it disappear, covered another liquid-filled bowl with a cloth, and a moment later, shook out the cloth to prove it empty. The shadowy form of a girl showed on a white shade as she disrobed inside a cabinet, but when the shade flew up, no girl was there; a comedian ran out of the cabinet instead. "We had to end it that way," Calvert explained, "or else they'd close down the theatre."

Briefly the magician told the story of Lady Godiva, finishing with, "Now that the fairy tale is over, close your eyes and go to sleep." The house lights dimmed; a Godiva with long blonde hair, sitting on an illuminated imitation horse, floated out over the heads of the audience, then back to the stage.

Watches and rings, borrowed from spectators by Calvert's

Julius Sundman, Finland's leading conjurer, produces silk from an empty cone.

Marvyn Roy's wife, Carol, appears inside a gigantic electric light bulb in Paris.

Mark Wilson presents Robert Harbin's "Zig Zag" mystery on the syndicated "Magic Circus" TV show.

Cantu, the Mexican magician, first to win fame with doves.

"world's best gold-diggers," were locked in a chest. The magician fired a pistol. The jewelry vanished, then reappeared in the smallest of six nested boxes, tied by a ribbon to the neck of a rabbit. From a suspended cylinder, capped back and front with paper drumheads, came a stream of silk banners, which his assistants stretched down the aisles almost to the back of the theatre. Then a girl jumped out of the cylinder.

Following "hypnotic" experiments with volunteer soldiers and sailors, Calvert donned a surgical gown, gulped down "mummy juice," and bent over as the spotlight turned to green; he stood up as a mad doctor with tousled hair and two fangs protruding from his lips. A boy, his head covered with a black hood, was decapitated by a buzz saw. Calvert picked up the severed head and ran screaming down the aisle. The eerie music changed abruptly to a football tune. He threw the head to an assistant on stage, rushed back, reunited the head with the body, whipped off his disguise and surgical gown, and came forward to bow as the curtains closed behind him.

On January 1, 1947, Calvert flew his full-evening show from Richmond, Virginia, to Nashville, Tennessee, in his own DC-3. Mistaking the lights of a moving train for the airport, he crashed into a snow-covered field. The plane skidded into the side of a farmhouse. A woman in the house and five of Calvert's assistants were injured. His leg was broken, but the magician told a reporter he would open at the Nashville theatre the next day even if he had to work on crutches. Calvert kept his word; though he hobbled about, the show ran smoothly.

The fracture had healed by the time production started on *Devil's Cargo*, the first of the feature films in which Calvert starred as "The Falcon," a magician-detective. Between movies he continued to work on the road with his live magic show. In 1954 the illusionist-actor chose Africa as the locale for his own film production, *Dark Venture*; this time he was a hunter in search of an elephant graveyard.

After playing the British Isles and Australia, the Calvert troupe boarded his yacht, *Thespian,* for the Orient. The ninety-five–ton, two-masted vessel was reported lost in the China Sea, en route from Formosa to Japan in June 1958. When the ship arrived safely in port, newspaper stories hinted this was a publicity stunt. A few years later, another of his yachts did wreck on an island off the north coast of Australia.

Calvert toured South Africa in 1964–65, carrying his own "Magic Circus" tent for areas where there were no large theatres. The magician traveled to the Orient again and was performing in what became a war zone when Indian troops invaded Pakistan in 1971. Officials confiscated his Lincoln Continental and arrested him as an American spy, after finding binoculars, movie cameras, and a darkroom on his yacht. Cleared of these charges, Calvert went to the Middle East. He wrote from Eilat, Israel in March 1973 that every seat for his seven performances had been sold before his opening. The sixty-two-year-old illusionist has lived a life far more exciting than that of any of the characters he portrayed on the screen.

Not every magician has the temperament or the executive ability to succeed with a show such as Calvert's. Illusionists who keep a major production on the road must be sound businessmen and adroit promoters, as well as outstanding showmen. They compete, not with other conjurers, but with all of show business. There are fewer first-class theatres throughout the world than there were before World War II, and television, already the dominant entertainment medium in the United States, Great Britain, and Western Europe, is fast gaining ground elsewhere.

Regular daily television programing started in London in 1936. Fred Culpitt, a magician, appeared on the initial BBC experimental show. "There's a lot of twisting in this business of mine," he said; at that moment his portly body elongated, and his assistant's head disappeared from the screen. This was not a part of Culpitt's routine; the water system used to cool the transmitting equipment had broken down.

Three years later the Radio Corporation of America exhibit at the New York World's Fair featured a television studio. World War II shortages of material delayed the development of "the communications medium of the future." There were fewer than eight thousand receivers in the United States at the end of the war. Production stepped up immediately. By 1948 nearly nine hundred thousand American homes were equipped with video sets.

Magicians working in night clubs, hotels, and the dwindling number of theatres differed as to how television would affect their careers. Some feared that once small-screen viewers saw their acts, few people would pay to watch them in the flesh. Others believed television appearances would enhance their box-office appeal.

A. J. Cantu, a Mexican conjurer, was booked for John Reed King's "Party Line," one of the earliest sponsored programs, on WCBS-TV in New York, in February 1947. Cantu, who performed wearing a broad-rimmed sombrero and fiesta regalia, had introduced a sleight-of-hand specialty that became as popular as card and cigarette manipulations. After each trick the orchestra played "La Paloma," and a white bird materialized at his fingertips. He visited the studio in advance. The lights illuminating the set were almost unbearably hot. He didn't mind the discomfort himself, but he was afraid his doves might suffocate. Cantu canceled the date. As his replacement I made

Big Shows and
Small Screens

my first appearance on American television. There was little time for rehearsal. At one point the camera came in for a close-up of my right hand while my left produced an egg that the home audience never saw. Before a second "Party Line" booking, I wrote a script for the director suggesting how the tricks could be shown with maximum effect and within camera range.

Television grew phenomenally during the next few years. Sets in use in America zoomed from four million in 1950 to thirty-one million in 1955. Conjurers made frequent appearances with Milton Berle, Ed Sullivan, and other variety show hosts. Russell Swann, an American night-club star, who had appeared for BBC-TV in London, played a flute and coaxed an imitation cobra to find a selected card; Gali Gali, an Egyptian, produced live chicks from empty cups—and the trouser legs of volunteer assistants; Randi, a Canadian, escaped from a locked safe; Dominique, a French sleight-of-hand specialist, picked pockets; William Neff, an American illusionist, performed "The Indian Basket" mystery; Kuda Bux, from Kashmir, duplicated—though heavily blindfolded—words written on a blackboard by spectators.

"Masters of Magic" on CBS-TV spotlighted several mystifiers each week; "It's Magic," a later program on the same network, employed a similar format. Dell O'Dell, "The Queen of Magic," presented her own weekly half hour on ABC-TV stations and "Super Circus," also on ABC-TV, booked Jack Gwynne, an outstanding vaudeville and night-club illusionist, for twenty-five weeks, with as many big-scale deceptions. Magicians with a single routine were at a disadvantage; there was a constant demand for new material.

Early in 1957 I arranged the first ninety-minute international television magic spectacular for "Producers Showcase" on NBC-TV. This series had offered the Sadler's Wells Ballet of London and the video debut of Alfred Lunt and Lynn Fontanne in their Broadway play, *The Great Sebastians*.

There were problems. Sorcar, the Indian illusionist, and his company could fly from Calcutta, but his heavy equipment had to be shipped a month in advance by sea. A special permit was required to get French magician René Septembre's birds through American customs; gaining entry for the trained mice and pet rat of Ireland's June Merlin was even more difficult.

Transmitted live, in black and white and in color, on May 27, 1957, "The Festival of Magic" began with a close-up of a letter from Harry Kellar pleading with Houdini not to try the death-defying bullet-catching trick. After reading the warning, the voiceover announcer told viewers the dangerous feat would be attempted on nationwide television for the first time.

Li King Si presented Chinese magic in pantomime. June Mer-

Milbourne Christopher's elephant disappeared on CBS-TV's "The World's Greatest Magicians."

He caught a bullet between his teeth on NBC-TV's "Festival of Magic."

lin, garbed as a fairytale princess in a castle setting, produced six white mice, changed one of them into a rat, then converted imitation rabbits into a rabbit fur cape, and this, in turn, into a long ermine robe.

Robert Harbin, who was born in South Africa, appeared in a jungle scene, dressed as a hunter. He tied a girl in a box, cut through her neck with a blade, moved her head two feet away, then restored head to body and revived the girl. He suspended another assistant in space; then he himself escaped from a straitjacket while hanging upside down thirty feet above the stage. Cardini, the world's finest sleight-of-hand performer, dressed in top hat, cape, and evening clothes, conjured in the lounge of a British club with cards, balls, lighted cigarettes, cigars, and pipes.

Sorcar, in Maharaja costume and an exotic Indian setting, broke through a paper-covered frame to produce silk streamers. A girl sat inside a miniature "Temple of Benares." Sorcar closed the doors and thrust swords through the temple in all directions; he opened the front to display the empty interior. She reappeared after the magician swiftly pulled out the blades and tossed them to his alert assistants. Sorcar's motor-driven buzz saw cut through the girl's middle. He pulled the saw back and inserted a steel plate to separate the two sections of her body. The illusionist had planned for his assistants to take the severed halves, one to each wing, but upon being told that sensitive American viewers would prefer a happy ending, he quickly restored her.

With a French café in the background, René Septembre produced bowls of water and goldfish from scarves, changed a flaming strip of paper into a large white cat, then converted the cat, several squares of silk, and some dice into a rooster. The rooster became a duck, and the duck, when enclosed in a small house, vanished. From the empty house, Septembre rapidly pulled dozens of doves. They circled in the air and landed on top of a large parasol being twirled around and around by his assistant.

Closing the first act, I faced a marksman selected by "Producers Showcase." The camera came in for a close-up as he loaded a twenty-two caliber bullet into the chamber of his rifle. The camera pulled back for a view over the marksman's shoulder. He aimed at my mouth, eighteen feet away, and fired. The camera moved in for another close-up as my head snapped back. I leaned forward, dropped the bullet from between my teeth into a plate held by an assistant.

Between the acts Ernie Kovacs, the comedian, disposed of actors playing the parts of NBC vice-presidents. The funniest episode came when Kovacs forced one of these officials into an upright box, closed the door, and penetrated it with a long sword. The extending handle slowly moved upward as Kovacs stepped back. He peeped into the box, grimaced, and proceeded with the show.

Big Shows and Small Screens

More than thirty-three million people saw "The Festival of Magic" in the United States; additional millions watched the show on kinescope throughout Europe. Then I produced an hour of magic for "The Jackie Gleason Show." Film and stage stars Zero Mostel and Julie Harris were my guests for "Magic! Magic! Magic!" Sorcar flew to New York again to appear on "The World's Greatest Magicians" special, hosted on CBS-TV by Garry Moore, on January 1, 1967. The Great Virgil, an American illusionist who had toured Australia, the Orient, and Great Britain, came from the West Coast to present his "Spirit Cabinet." Roy Benson, a master billiard-ball manipulator and adept comedian, added humor. Marvyn Roy, long a feature at the Lido night club in Paris, swallowed small light bulbs and a long piece of wire. His wife, Carol, took the end of the wire from between his lips and stretched a string of lighted bulbs across the stage. Roy called attention to a large glowing bulb on a stand; in an instant the filament disappeared and Carol appeared, curled up inside the bulb.

A trainer led a full-grown elephant on stage for my feature illusion. Assistants closed barred gates in front of the cage. I fired a pistol. There was a puff of smoke; elephant and trainer disappeared.

Television has continued to be an important outlet for magic. Mark Wilson's "Magic Land of Allakazam," a weekly show designed for children, ran two years on CBS-TV and three on ABC-TV. His "Magic Circus," a more elaborate program for family audiences, was syndicated. Fred Kaps, the Dutch magician, frequently performs on European telecasts. David Nixon, the most popular conjurer in Britain, presents an annual "It's Magic" series.

There is no shortage of new acts. The Wychwoods conjure with poodles in England; Pierre Brahma performs with jewels in France. The Keeners travel in the United States and abroad with dove and balloon deceptions. Johnny Hart, winner of the London Magic Circle's "Young Magician of the Year" award, produces parakeets and a parrot in clubs and hotels on the Continent and in North America.

Haruo Shimada, a skillful, young Japanese magician, patterned his style after Channing Pollock, suavest of the American card and dove manipulators. Shimada toured Australia, married there, and with his wife, Deanna, performed for twenty weeks on television in Mexico before coming to the United States to appear in Las Vegas. He has since perfected a traditional Japanese routine, conjuring with fire and parasols.

Often there are five conjurers working in five different Las Vegas hotels. It is not unusual for a magician to be booked for a year; Siegfried and Roy played three years in the "Lido de Paris" revue at the Stardust Hotel, with a routine that won them the Las Vegas "Best Show Act of the Year" award in 1971. The climax of their turn comes when Roy Horn enters a cage, supported on four high metal legs. Under the cage is a locked trunk. Siegfried Fischbacker covers the cage with a canopy, then pulls the drape away. A live Bengal tiger appears behind the bars. Screams from the trunk prompt the German illusionist to pull it forward, open the lock, and throw up the lid. Out leaps another jungle beast, a cheetah—followed by the smiling Roy.

Around the world conjurers are busier today than they have been since the demise of vaudeville. Leading manufacturers employ magicians to devise illusions and to put across the selling points of new products at trade exhibitions and industrial shows. Close-up performers work at parties. Sleight-of-hand specialists and illusionists play cabarets, casinos, and hotels. Crowds line up at box offices for the big-scale shows of Sorcar Jr., Tihanyi, the Kios, Richiardi Jr., and Calvert.

Dexterous young performers compete for originality and showmanship awards at the annual conventions of the Society of American Magicians and The International Brotherhood of Magicians in the United States, at conclaves of The British Ring and The Magic Circle in England and of the Federation Internationale des Sociétés Magiques in Europe. Public shows staged by these and similar organizations play to standing-room-only crowds. There is ample evidence that the new generation of mystifiers will intrigue future audiences as their predecessors have for five thousand years past.

Sources and Acknowledgments

In the author's collection are thousands of letters written by famous magicians, among them: Signor Blitz, Robert-Houdin, Robert Heller, Harry Kellar, the Herrmanns, the Maskelynes, the Bambergs, Howard Thurston, and Harry Houdini; thousands of programs, woodcuts, engravings, posters, and photographs; files of conjuring periodicals in many languages; more than seven thousand books on magic, and the personal scrapbooks of Horace Goldin, Servais Le Roy, Thurston, Houdini, Hardeen, Jean Hugard, P. C. Sorcar, and Fu Manchu. Especially useful were Houdini's notes for a projected biography of Kellar, an unpublished account of Buatier de Kolta's career and inventions by one of his assistants, and H. J. Moulton's unpublished *Magic in Boston 1792–1918*.

Fellow collectors who gave the writer access to their materials in the United States include the late John Mulholland, the late John J. Crimmins, Jr., the late Dr. Henry Ridgely Evans, the late Ernest B. Marx, the late Henry N. Fetsch, the late John J. McManus, the late Leo Rullman, and H. Adrian Smith, George Pfisterer, Sidney Hollis Radner, Dr. Morris N. Young, Tad Ware, Philip T. Thomas, George Goebel, Carroll Bish, Fred Rickard, John Booth, Dr. Joseph H. Fries, the Rev. William C. Rauscher, Manuel Weltman, William W. Larsen, Jr., Kirk Kirkham, John Daniel, Stanley Palm, Jay Marshall, Robert Lund, Edgar Heyl, Stuart Cramer, Al Guenther, Neil See, W. J. Gydesen, Larry Weeks, Cedric Clute, Arthur Leroy, Bob Rossi, and Charles Reynolds.

Photographs of Kuma, Sundman, Kio, and the author were taken by Irving Desfor.

Equally helpful were the late Dr. Kurt Volkmann in Düsseldorf; Dr. Javier de Areny-Plandolit in Madrid; the late Agosta-Meynier, the late Dr. Jules Dhotel, André Mayette, Georges Gaillard, and Michel Seldow in Paris; Jean Chavigny and Paul Robert-Houdin in Blois; Robelly in Orléans (Loire); the late Monarque, Klingsor, and Louis Tummers in Brussels; Peter and Jorgen Borsch and Leo Leslie Clemmensen in Copenhagen; Topper Martyn in Stockholm; Metin And in Ankara; Zati Sungar in Istanbul; the late Peter Kwok in Hong Kong; Fu Manchu in Buenos Aires; Roberto Rivas Ossa in Santiago; the late P. C. Sorcar in Calcutta; Araki in Tokyo; the late Chris Charlton, Stanley Thomas, Horace King, Bert Pratt, Arthur Ivey, and John Salisse in London; the late Roland Winder in Leeds; Dr. E. J. Dingwall in Crowhurst and J. B. Findlay in Shanklin, Isle of Wight.

Librarians in the cities mentioned were most cooperative, as were those in Cairo, Tel Aviv, Beirut, Athens, Singapore, Rome, Nice, Lisbon, Berlin,

Amsterdam, Glasgow, Dublin, Liverpool, Lisbon, Bangkok, Teheran, New Delhi, Honolulu, Port-of-Spain (Trinidad), Hamilton (Bermuda), Rio de Janeiro, Montevideo, Lima, San Francisco, Los Angeles, Chicago, Detroit, Boston, Philadelphia, New York, Baltimore, Washington, Montreal, and Mexico City.

Of special interest to students of conjuring are the Houdini and McManus-Young Magic Collections in the Library of Congress and at the University of Texas in Austin, the John Mulholland Magic Collection of the Walter Hampden Memorial Library at The Players club in New York, the Society of American Magicians Collection in the New York Public Library Theatre Collection at Lincoln Center; the collection of the Academy of Magical Arts and Sciences in Hollywood; The Magic Circle Collection in London, and the Harry Price Collection at the University of London.

Important sources of historical data are the magazines of magic: *Mahatma, The Sphinx, Magic, The Wizard, The Magic Wand, The Magic World, The Magical World, The Magic Circular, The Budget, The Linking Ring, M-U-M, Hugard's Magic Monthly, Tops, Abracadabra, Conjurers' Monthly Magazine, Genii, L'Escamoteur, L'Illusionniste, Le Magicien, Magia Moderna, Magie, Die Zauberwelt,* and *Der Zauberspiegel,* to mention a few; and the collectors' quarterlies: *The Magic Cauldron* and *Magicol.*

Bibliography

There are many bibliographies of conjuring: Sidney W. Clarke and Adolphe Blind's *The Bibliography of Conjuring and Kindred Deceptions*, London, George Johnson, 1920; the *Short-Title Catalogue* of the Harry Price Collection. Proceedings of the National Laboratory of Psychical Research, Volume I, Part II, London, National Laboratory of Psychical Research, April 1929; *Short-Title Catalogue of the Research Library: From 1472 A.D. to the Present Day*, compiled by Harry Price, London, University of London Council for Psychical Investigation, 1935; Trevor H. Hall's *A Bibliography of Books on Conjuring in English from 1580 to 1850*, Minneapolis, Carl Waring Jones, 1957; *A Contribution to Conjuring Bibliography English Language 1550 to 1850* by Edgar Heyl, published in Baltimore by the author in 1936; a bibliography of Scottish conjuring books by J. B. Findlay, published in Shanklin, Isle of Wight, by the author in 1951; R. Toole-Stott's *Circus and Allied Arts: A World Bibliography*, four volumes published in Derby, England, by Harpur & Sons (Derby) Ltd. in 1958, 1960, 1962, and 1971 (a section on "Hocus Pocus Books" is in volume III, and many listings of conjuring books may be found throughout the work); Victor Farelli's *Magical Bibliographies: A Guide,* with an appendix by James B. Findlay, was published in Shanklin, Isle of Wight, by Findlay in 1953.

Among those in other languages are Théodore Ruegg's *Bibliographie de la prestidigitation française ancienne et moderne*, published in Dijon by the author in 1931; Javier de Areny-Plandolit's *Bibliografía Española de la Prestidigitación*, Barcelona, Casa "Magicus," 1950; Kurt Volkmann and Louis Tummers' *Bibliographie de la Prestidigitation* (German and Austrian books), published in Brussels by the Cercle Belge d' Illusionnisme in 1952; Jonnie Ackerlind-Casino's *Svensk Bibliografi För Trollkarlar,* published in Stockholm by the Svensk Magisk Cirkels Förlag in 1963; and Jan Brabec and Julius Markcshiess-van Trix's *Artistik Auswahl-Bibliographie,* published in East Berlin by the Deutsch Staatsbibliothek in 1968.

Adrion, Alexander, *Zauberei Zauberei*. Olten und Freiburg, Walter-Verlag, 1968.
And, Metin, *Kirk Gün, Kirk Gece*. Istanbul, Taç Yayinlari, 1959.
———, *A History of Theatre and Popular Entertainment in Turkey*. Forum Yayinlari, 1963–64.
Anderson, John Henry, *Twenty-five Cents' Worth of Magic and Mystery*. New York, 1860, published by author.

————, *The Fashionable Science of Parlor Magic*. Various undated editions published by author in Great Britain, some with a biography.

————, *The Fashionable Science of Parlour Magic*. Various undated editions published by author in the United States.

Anonymous, *The Davenport Brothers, the World-Renowned Spiritual Mediums*. Boston, William White and Company, 1869.

————, *Reflexões sobre as Habilidades do Cavalheiro Pinetti, sobre os Cavallinhos, e sobre os Automatos que Escreven e Desenhão*. Lisbon, Simão Thaddeo Ferreira, 1791.

————, *Ultimas Habilidades, despedida e Grande Automato do Cavalheiro Pinetti*. Lisbon, Simão Thaddeo Ferreira, 1791.

Bamberg, Theodore, with Robert Parrish, *Okito on Magic Reminiscences and Selected Tricks*. Chicago, Edward O. Drane and Company, 1952.

Bertram, Charles, *Isn't It Wonderful?* London, Swan Sonnenschein & Co., Ltd., 1896.

————, *A Magician in Many Lands*. London, George Routledge & Sons, Limited, 1911.

Blackstone, Harry, *Blackstone's Secrets of Magic*. New York, George Sully and Company, Inc., 1929.

Blitz, Signor, *Fifty Years in the Magic Circle*. Hartford, Conn., Belknap & Bliss, 1871.

Boston, George L., with Robert Parrish, *Inside Magic*. New York, Beechhurst Press, 1947.

Bureau of Ethnology, *Fourteenth Annual Report 1892–93*, Part 1. Washington D.C., Government Printing Office, 1896.

Burlingame, H. J., *Leaves from Conjurers' Scrap Books*. Chicago, Donohue, Henneberry & Co., 1891.

————, *History of Magic and Magicians*. Chicago, Chas. L. Burlingame & Co., 1895.

————, *Around the World with a Magician and a Juggler*. Chicago, Clyde Publishing Co., 1891.

————, *Herrmann the Magician: His Life, His Secrets*. Chicago, Laird & Lee, 1897.

Chavigny, Jean, *Robert-Houdin Rénovateur de la Magie Blanche*. Blois, published by author, 1969.

Christopher, Milbourne, *Panorama of Prestidigitators*. New York, The Christopher Collection, 1956.

————, *Panorama of Magic*. New York, Dover Publications, Inc., 1962.

————, *Houdini: The Untold Story*. New York, Thomas Y. Crowell Company, 1969.

————, *ESP, Seers and Psychics*. New York, Thomas Y. Crowell Company, 1970.

Clarke, Sidney W., *The Annals of Conjuring*. London, George Johnson, 1929; also published serially in *The Magic Wand*, 1924–1928.

Decremps, Henri, *La Magie Blanche Dévoilée ou Explication*. Paris, published by author, 1784.

————, *Supplément à La Magie Blanche Dévoilée*. Paris, published by author, 1785.

Denton, Thomas, *The Conjuror Unmasked*. London, published by author, 1785.

————, *O Pelotiqueiro Desmascarado*. Lisbon, Antonio Rodrigues Galhardo, 1791.

Devant, David, *My Magic Life*. London, Hutchinson & Co., Ltd., 1931.

————, *Secrets of My Magic*. London, Hutchinson & Co., Ltd., 1936.

Dexter, Will, *The Riddle of Chung Ling Soo*. London, Arco Publication Ltd., 1955.

———, *This is Magic*. London, Arco Publications, Ltd., 1958.

Downs, T. Nelson, *Modern Coin Manipulation*. London, T. Nelson Downs Magical Co., 1900.

———, *The Art of Magic*. Edited by John Northern Hilliard. Buffalo, Downs-Edwards Company, 1909.

Dunninger, Joseph, *What's on Your Mind?* Introduction by Walter B. Gibson. Cleveland and New York, World Publishing Company, 1944.

Evans, Henry Ridgely, *Magic and Its Professors*. New York, George Routledge & Sons, Limited, 1902.

———, *The Old and the New Magic*. Chicago, Open Court Publishing Company, 1906; 2nd ed., revised and enlarged, 1909.

———, *Adventures in Magic*. New York, Leo Rullman, 1921.

———, *History of Conjuring and Magic*. Kenton, Ohio, International Brotherhood of Magicians, 1928; new and rev. ed., Kenton, Ohio, William W. Durbin, 1930.

———, *A Master of Modern Magic: The Life and Adventures of Robert-Houdin*. New York, Macoy Publishing Company, 1932.

———, *Edgar Allan Poe and Baron von Kempelen's Chess-Playing Automaton*. Kenton, Ohio, International Brotherhood of Magicians, 1939.

———, *Some Rare Old Books on Conjuring and Magic of the Sixteenth, the Seventeenth and the Eighteenth Century*. Kenton, Ohio, International Brotherhood of Magicians, 1943.

Findlay, J. B., *Anderson and His Theatre*. Shanklin, Isle of Wight, published by author, 1967.

Frost, Thomas, *The Old Showmen, and the London Fairs*. London, Tinsley Brothers, 1874.

———, *Circus Life and Circus Celebrities*. London, Tinsley Brothers, 1876.

———, *The Lives of the Conjurers*. London, Tinsley Brothers, 1876.

Gaddis, Vincent H., *The Wide World of Magic*. New York, Criterion Books, 1967.

Gibson, Walter B., and Morris N. Young, *Houdini's Fabulous Magic*. Philadelphia and New York, Chilton Company, 1961.

———, *The Master Magicians*. Garden City, N. Y., Doubleday & Company, Inc., 1966.

Goldin, Horace, *It's Fun To be Fooled*. London, Stanley Paul & Co., Ltd., 1937.

Goldston, Will, *Sensational Tales of Mystery Men*. London, Will Goldston, Ltd., 1929.

———, A Magician's Swan Song. London, John Long, Ltd., n.d.

Gresham, William Lindsay. *Houdini, the Man Who Walked Through Walls*. New York, Henry Holt & Company, Inc., 1959.

Hallowell, A. Irving, *The Role of Conjuring in Saulteau Society*. Philadelphia, University of Pennsylvania Press, 1942.

Heyl, Edgar, *Cues for Collectors*. Chicago, Ireland Magic Company, 1964.

Hertz, Carl, *A Modern Mystery Merchant*. London, Hutchinson & Co., Ltd., 1924.

Hiraiwa Hakufu, *Stage Magic Highlights*. Text in Japanese. Tokyo, Araki, 1961.

Houdini, Harry, *The Unmasking of Robert-Houdin*. New York, Publishers Printing Co., 1908.

———, *Mein Training und meine Tricks*. Leipzig, Berlin, München, Paris, Grethlein & Co., 1909.

———, *Handcuff Secrets*. London, George Routledge & Sons, Ltd., 1910.

————, *Miracle Mongers and Their Methods*. New York, E. P. Dutton & Co., 1920.

————, *Magical Rope Ties and Escapes*. London, Will Goldston, Ltd., 1921.

————, *A Magician Among the Spirits*. New York, Harper & Brothers, 1924.

Hunt, Kari and Douglas, *The Art of Magic*. New York, Atheneum, 1967.

Jenness, George A., *Maskelyne and Cooke. Egyptian Hall, London 1873–1904*. Enfield, Middlesex, published by author, 1967.

Kalanag, *Simsalabim wirbelt und die Welt*. Karlsruhe in Baden, Schwerdtseger-Verlag, 1948.

————, *Der Magier Erzählt Sein Leben*. Hamburg, Blüchert Verlag, 1962.

Kellar, Harry, *A Magician's Tour Up Down and Round About the Earth*. Chicago, R. R. Donnelly & Sons, 1896.

Kellock, Harold, *Houdini, His Life-Story. By Harold Kellock from the Recollections and Documents of Beatrice Houdini*, New York, Harcourt, Brace & Company, 1928.

Laureau, Marcel, *The Robert-Houdin Theatre 1879–1914*, translated by D. W. Findlay. Shanklin, Isle of Wight, J. B. Findlay, 1968.

Lynn, H. S., *The Adventures of a Strange Man, Dr. H. S. Lynn*. London, published by author, 1873.

————, *Travels and Adventures of Dr. Lynn*. London, published by author, 1882.

Maskelyne, John Nevil, *Modern Spiritualism*. London, Frederick Warne & Co., 1876.

Maskelyne, Jasper, *White Magic: The Story of the Maskelynes*. London, Stanley Paul & Co., Ltd., 1936.

————, *Magic—Top Secret*. London, Stanley Paul & Co., Ltd., 1949.

Mulholland, John, *Quicker Than the Eye*. Indianapolis, Bobbs-Merrill Company, 1932.

————, *The Story of Magic*. New York, Loring & Mussey, 1935.

————, *Beware Familiar Spirits*. New York, Charles Scribner's Sons, 1938.

Pinetti, Giovanni Giuseppe, *Amusemens Physiques, et Différentes Expériences Divertissantes*. Paris, Chez Hardouin, 1784. 3rd augmented edition, Paris, Chez Gattey, 1791.

————, *Physical Amusements and Diverting Experiments*. London, 1784, published by author.

Robelly, *Le Livre d'Or de Ceux qui ont eu un Nom dans la Magie*. Tours, 1949, published by author.

Robert-Houdin, Jean Eugène, *Confidences d'un Prestidigitateur*. Blois, Lecesne, 1858.

————, *Memoirs of Robert-Houdin*. New introduction and notes by Milbourne Christopher. New York, Dover Publications, Inc., 1964.

————, *The Secrets of Conjuring and Magic*. Translated and edited with notes by Professor Hoffmann. London, George Routledge and Sons, Limited, 1877.

————, *The Secrets of Stage Conjuring*. Translated and edited, with notes by Professor Hoffman. London, George Routledge and Sons, 1881.

Scot, Reginald, *The discoverie of witchcraft*. London, William Brome, 1584. Recent edition: Carbondale, Illinois, Southern Illinois University Press, 1964.

Selbit, P. T., *The Magician's Handbook*, London, Marshall & Brookes, Dawbarn & Ward, Ltd., 1901.

————, *The Magical Entertainer*. London, Ornum's, 1906.

————, *The Magic Art of Entertaining*. London, Dawbarn & Ward, Ltd., 1907.

Seldow, Michel, *Les Illusionnistes et Leurs Secrets*. Paris, Librairie Arthème Fayard, 1959.

———, *Vie et Secrets de Robert-Houdin*. Paris, Librairie Arthème Fayard, 1971.

Severn, Bill, *Magic and Magicians*. New York, David McKay Company, Inc., 1958.

Sorcar, P. T., *Sorcar on Magic Reminiscences and Selected Tricks*. Calcutta, Indrajal Publications, 1960.

———, *TW'sGM* [*The World's Greatest Magician*] *The Great Sorcar*. With a prologue by Milbourne Christopher. Calcutta, All India Magic Circle, 1966.

———, *History of Magic*, Calcutta, Indrajal Publications, 1970.

Stodare, Colonel, *A New Handy-Book of Magic*. London, published by author, 1865.

———, *The Art of Magic*. London, published by author, 1865.

Thurston, Howard, *My Life of Magic*, Philadelphia, Dorrance & Company, Inc., 1929.

Von Klinckowstroem, Carl Graf, *Die Zauberkunst*. Munich. Ernst Heimeran Verlag, 1954.

Wilsmann, Aloys Christof, *Die Zersägte Jungfrau*. Berlin, Verlag Scherl, 1938.

Zmeck, Jochen, *Wunderwelt Magie*. Berlin, Hensehelverlag, 1967.

Index

DATE DUE